IV Advances in System Performance Methodologies   261

Introduction to Advances in System Performance Evaluation

Edited by Erol Gelenbe

Software and hardware systems, computer architectures and networks have become pervasive in all fields of human activity. Their performance and reliability is now crucial to the proper functioning of all areas of industry, commerce, the arts and entertainment. Thus, Performance Evaluation of Software, Computer Architectures and Computer Communication Networks is, even more than in the past, a key issue in computer science and information technology. Many of the well known challenges of system performance are being constantly revisited while new problems and concerns are coming to the forefront of this area.

As examples of classical performance problems that we are now re-discovering, we see that the virtual memory and input-output performance problems of the 70's are now replaced at the end of the millennium by the performance issues of memory caches, of transaction processing systems and of redundant arrays of independent disks. The performance issues of packet switching are still with us in the Internet of the end of the late 90's even as we address very fast networks and new networking services. Performance issues of electronic telephony of the 70's are now replaced by performance evaluation of ATM. Performance issue of databases of the 70's have shifted to the performance of Web based systems at the end of this decade.

This volume of papers brings together work by some of the leading international experts in the field. It addresses both methodological advances, and new perspectives in the various application areas. Many of the top academic and industrial experts of system performance evaluation and its applications bring together their deep understanding to review the key problems we are facing in this area. In a series of structured and focused chapters, advances in key performance methodologies and in major application areas are presented. Itopics which are covered include performance evaluation methodologies for large scale software systems both in general, and in the context of critical applications such as nuclear reactor control and air transportation systems. Special emphasis is placed on network performance both in the Internet and in novel

ATM (asynchronous transfer mode) networking. Novel areas such as electronic commerce are also discussed in some of the papers.

Specifically, three chapters devoted to "Advances in Internet Network Performance" discuss the characteristics of internet traffic and the manner in which network performance is impacted by it, as well as techniques for regulating this traffic to provide better performance, and the means to design new Internet-like protocols to take advantage of local area networks from which many networks are accessed. In the chapters which address "Advances in ATM Networks," various aspects of ATM network performance are covered. They include routing of traffic, sharing of capacity to include different types of quality of service requirements, novel delay based access control methods, and different analytical and simulation techniques to evaluate ATM network performance.

Several chapters on "Traffic Based System and Network Design" consider both analysis and design issues in networks. One problem is to determine the trade-off between traffic buffering, which is needed to protect against temporal irregularities in traffic, and smoothing which can reduce the need for buffering. Analytical techniques for multiplexing are considered both in a conventional and a wireless framework. Specific issues related to traffic generated by the World Wide Web are also considered, as are questions that arise in many-to-many communications known as "multicast." Methods for analysis and design of large networks, including approximation and algorithmic techniques are also discussed.

Other chapters dealing with "Advances in System Performance Methodologies" consider a variety of methods for hardware and software systems which take into account specific requirements such as real-time, as well as specific architectural characteristics such as multiprocessors and memory hierarchies. Several other chapters address issues which combine "System Performance and Reliability" both for hardware-software systems and to support software design and validation. The integration of performance in the system development cycle, specific approaches to validation of systems with stringent performability constraints, and the role of work-load in the novel web based environment, are considered in some final papers.

We are convinced that the wealth and variety of information available in this volume will be useful both to the computer system practitioner, and to researchers who would like to explore novel and exciting directions for their investigations.

About the Editor

Erol Gelenbe is a Professor of Computer Science, Associate Dean of Engineering and Computer Science, and Director of the School of Electrical Engineering and Computer Science at the University of Central Florida in Orlando. Previously he was the Nello L. Teer Jr. Professor and Chair of Electrical and Computer Engineering at Duke University, where he held secondary appointments as a professor of Computer Science and Psychology-Experimental. His technical interests span performance analysis of computer systems and communication networks, neural networks, and discrete stochastic processes. He has authored four books, and published over one hundred journals articles. He has supervised more than 50 Ph.D. dissertations. His former students are active in industry, academia, and research. A fellow of IEEE since 1986, his honors include the Grand Prix France Telecom (1996) of the French Academy of Science for his work on stochastic networks and system performance, the Honorary Doctorate from the University of Rome (1996), the Science Award of the Parlar Foundation of Turkey (1995), the "Chevalier de l'Ordre du Mérite" award (1992) from the French Government, and the IFIP Silver Core Award (1980).

Part I

Advances in Internet Network Performance

Chapter 1

Rate Adapters with Bursty Arrivals and Rational Rate Reduction: Queuing Analysis

Veronique Inghelbrecht, Bart Steyaert, Herwig Bruneel and Sabine Wittevrongel[1]

SMACS Research Group[2]

Abstract   In ATM-based communication networks, the transmission links that interconnect the network nodes do not necessarily operate at the same transmission speeds. If the speed of the incoming link in a node exceeds the speed of the outgoing link, a rate adaptation buffer must be provided in order to avoid frequent cell loss. This paper presents an analytical queuing analysis of a rate adaptation buffer in the case where the cell arrival stream on the incoming link is modeled as an interrupted Bernoulli process and the ratio of the arrival rate versus the transmission rate can take any rational value. Based on a generating-functions approach, an expression for the probability generating function of the buffer contents is derived. From this result, closed-form formulae for several performance measures are obtained. The results are illustrated by some numerical examples.

---

[1]The fourth author is postdoctoral fellow of the Fund for Scientific Research-Flanders (Belgium)(F.W.O.).
[2]SMACS: Stochastic Modeling and Analysis of Communication Systems.

1.1   Introduction

In ATM (asynchronous transfer mode) based communication networks information is transmitted under the form of fixed-length packets, referred to as ATM cells [1]. The cells generated by a source are typically sent over the network to their destination via several network nodes and interconnecting links, which do not necessarily operate at the same transmission speeds [2]. Consequently, if at some point in the network, the speed of the incoming link exceeds the speed of the outgoing link, it may happen that more cells arrive in a given time interval than can be transmitted. In this case, if excessive cell loss is to be avoided, a so-called rate adaptation buffer must be provided for the temporary storage of incoming cells.

In the past years, a number of papers have dealt with the dimensioning of a rate adaptation buffer, see [2]–[6]. For a Bernoulli arrival process and any values of the input rate/output rate ratio, an approximate closed-form expression for the cell loss ratio (CLR) was derived in [2], whereas [3] presents approximate results for the CLR which are accurate as long as the difference between the input and output rate remains sufficiently small (less than 2%). In [4], also for a Bernoulli arrival stream and any input rate/output rate ratio, exact closed-form expressions were obtained for the mean values, the variances and the tail distributions of the buffer contents and the cell delay in case of an infinite-capacity rate adaptation buffer, as well as an expression for the CLR in case of a finite storage capacity. Considering a time-correlated arrival process on the incoming link, an approximate analysis for the case where the input rate/output rate ratio is equal to $k/(k-1)$ for some integer $k \geq 2$ is given in [5], whereas the analysis presented in [6] assumes that the rate ratio takes an integer value.

Although many papers on various types of buffer systems with correlated arrivals have appeared in the literature (see e.g., [7]–[10] and the references therein), to the best of the authors' knowledge, a full queuing analysis of a rate adaptation buffer has never been reported in the case of a correlated cell arrival process and an arbitrary rational value for the input rate/output rate ratio. The purpose of this paper is exactly to provide such an analysis. Specifically, the arrival process on the input link is modeled in this paper as an interrupted Bernoulli process (IBP) (see [11],[12]).

The outline of the paper is as follows. In Section 1.2, we describe the system under study and the source model. In Section 1.3, we define a set of state variables and we obtain a functional equation for the probability generating function (pgf) of the system state vector. Section 1.4 concentrates on the derivation of the pgf of the buffer contents from the functional equation. This pgf is then used in Section 1.5 to derive closed-form expressions for several performance measures, namely the CLR and the means and the tail distributions of the buffer contents and the cell delay. A number of numerical results are presented and discussed in Section 1.6. The paper is concluded in Section 1.7.

1.2 System and Source Model

In this paper, it is assumed that the rate adaptation buffer has an infinite storage capacity for cells. The transmission speed of the incoming link is assumed to be r times higher than the transmission speed of the outgoing link for some rational value r greater than one. This means that we have the following relationship between the input rate and the output rate:

$$I = n \cdot O + m , \tag{1.1}$$

where I and O are, respectively, the input rate and the output rate, both expressed as an integer number of cells per fixed time period, n is an integer greater than one and m is an integer between 0 and $O - 1$. As in most ATM-related discrete-time models, time is slotted and one slot is the fixed-length time interval which suffices for the transmission of exactly one fixed-length cell. However, because of the rate difference between the input and output, a slot on the output link of the rate adaptation buffer is r times longer than a slot on the input link. Stated otherwise, during the time period required for the transmission of O cells on the output link, a maximum of I cells could arrive on the input link. A time interval composed of I input slots or O output slots will be called a "frame" in the sequel (see Fig. 1.1). In this way a frame at the input of the buffer has the same length as a frame at the output. We furthermore assume that input frames and output frames occur synchronously, i.e., have exactly the same sequence of starting points.

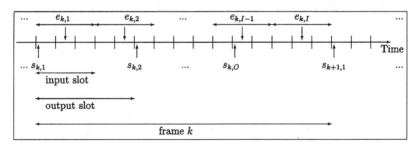

FIGURE 1.1

Illustration of the definitions of the random variables $s_{k,j}$ and $e_{k,i}$.

The cell arrival process on the input link of the rate adapter stochastically alternates between so-called "passive" and "active" periods, being defined as a number of consecutive input slots during which there is either one or no cell arrival with probability p or $1 - p$, respectively. It is assumed that the lengths of the active and passive periods (expressed as a number of input slots) are two independent sets of independent geometrically distributed random variables with parameters α and β, i.e.,

$$\text{Prob[active period} = i \text{ input slots]} = (1 - \alpha)\alpha^{i-1}, \qquad i \geq 1; \quad (1.2)$$

$$\text{Prob[passive period} = i \text{ input slots]} = (1 - \beta)\beta^{i-1}, \qquad i \geq 1. \quad (1.3)$$

Note that this assumption implies a first-order Markovian correlation in the cell arrival process. The case of an uncorrelated arrival process from slot to slot corresponds to $\alpha + \beta = 1$. The mean activity σ on the input link is defined as the fraction of time the input is active, i.e.,

$$\sigma = \frac{E[\text{active period}]}{E[\text{active period}] + E[\text{passive period}]} = \frac{1 - \beta}{2 - \alpha - \beta}, \qquad (1.4)$$

where $E[.]$ denotes the expected value of the argument between the square brackets. The mean number of cell arrivals during an input slot is then given by σp.

1.3   Functional Equation

As can be observed from Fig. 1.1, it is possible that an input slot (and hence, a cell arrival on the input link) crosses an output slot boundary. The analysis presented in this paper considers a cell to be in the buffer only when the cell has arrived completely, i.e., when its input slot of arrival has ended. Now let input slot j^* of a frame denote the last input slot that ends during the jth output slot of this frame. Input slot j^* is given by

$$\text{input slot } j^* = \text{input slot } \left\lfloor \frac{I}{O} j \right\rfloor, \qquad 1 \leq j \leq O, \qquad (1.5)$$

where $\lfloor x \rfloor$ denotes the integer part of the real number x. Also, let m_j denote the number of input slot boundaries that fall within the duration of the jth output slot of a frame. With (1.5), we have that m_j is given by

$$m_j = j^* - (j - 1)^* = \lfloor \frac{I}{O} j \rfloor - \lfloor \frac{I}{O}(j - 1) \rfloor, \qquad 1 \leq j \leq O, \qquad (1.6)$$

where $0^* \triangleq 0$. Note that, in view of the above, m_j corresponds to the maximum number of cells that can enter the buffer during the jth output slot of a frame.

Let us now define the random variable $s_{k,j}$ as the system contents (i.e., the total number of cells in the buffer, including the cell currently under transmission, if any) at the beginning of the jth output slot of the kth frame (see Fig. 1.1). We denote by $e_{k,i}$ the number of cell arrivals during the ith input slot of the kth frame. In order to characterize the state of the arrival process on the input link during the ith input slot of frame k, we introduce the random variable $\chi_{k,i}$, which takes the value 0 or 1, depending on whether input slot i of frame k belongs to a passive period or to an active period.

With the previous definitions and assumptions, the following system equations can then be established:

$$s_{k,j+1} = \left(s_{k,j} - 1\right)^+ + \sum_{i=(j-1)*+1}^{j*} e_{k,i}, \qquad 1 \le j \le O - 1; \quad (1.7)$$

$$s_{k+1,1} = \left(s_{k,O} - 1\right)^+ + \sum_{i=(O-1)*+1}^{I} e_{k,i}, \qquad (1.8)$$

where the notation $(...)^+ = \max(0, ...)$. From the system equations (1.7) and (1.8) and the description of the cell arrival process in the previous section, it is not difficult to see that the vector $\left(s_{k,j}, \chi_{k,(j-1)*}\right)$ constitutes a Markovian state description of the buffer system at the start of the jth output slot of frame k.

In order to analyze the queuing behavior of the rate adaptation buffer, we now define the functions

$$P_{k,j+1}(z, \overline{x}) \stackrel{\triangle}{=} E\left[z^{s_{k,j+1}} x_0^{1-\chi_{k,j*}} x_1^{\chi_{k,j*}}\right], \qquad 1 \le j \le O - 1; \quad (1.9)$$

$$P_{k+1,1}(z, \overline{x}) \stackrel{\triangle}{=} E\left[z^{s_{k+1,1}} x_0^{1-\chi_{k,I}} x_1^{\chi_{k,I}}\right], \qquad (1.10)$$

where

$$\overline{x} = \begin{pmatrix} x_0 \\ x_1 \end{pmatrix}.$$

Then, using the definition (1.9) and the system equation (1.7), we can express the function $P_{k,j+1}(z, \overline{x})$, $1 \le j \le O - 1$, subsequently as

$$P_{k,j+1}(z, \overline{x}) = E\left[z^{\left(s_{k,j}-1\right)^+} z^{\sum_{i=(j-1)*+1}^{j*} e_{k,i}} x_0^{1-\chi_{k,j*}} x_1^{\chi_{k,j*}}\right]$$

$$= \text{Prob}\left[s_{k,j} = 0\right] E\left[z^{\sum_{i=(j-1)*+1}^{j*} e_{k,i}} x_0^{1-\chi_{k,j*}} x_1^{\chi_{k,j*}} \,\middle|\, s_{k,j} = 0\right] \qquad (1.11)$$

$$+ \sum_{n=1}^{\infty} \text{Prob}\left[s_{k,j} = n\right] z^{n-1} E\left[z^{\sum_{i=(j-1)*+1}^{j*} e_{k,i}} x_0^{1-\chi_{k,j*}} x_1^{\chi_{k,j*}} \,\middle|\, s_{k,j} = n\right].$$

Next, if we define the function $\gamma_{k,j,n}(z, \overline{x})$ as

$$\gamma_{k,j,n}(z, \overline{x}) \triangleq E\left[z^{\sum\limits_{i=(j-1)^*+1}^{j^*} e_{k,i}} x_0^{1-\chi_{k,j^*}} x_1^{\chi_{k,j^*}} \middle| s_{k,j} = n \right],$$

$$1 \leq j \leq O, \qquad (1.12)$$

Equation (1.11) can be further transformed into

$$P_{k,j+1}(z, \overline{x}) = z^{-1} \sum_{n=0}^{\infty} \text{Prob}\left[s_{k,j} = n \right] z^n \gamma_{k,j,n}(z, \overline{x}) \qquad (1.13)$$

$$+ \left(1 - z^{-1} \right) \text{Prob}\left[s_{k,j} = 0 \right] \gamma_{k,j,0}(z, \overline{x}),$$

$$1 \leq j \leq O - 1.$$

In the appendix it is shown that $\gamma_{k,j,n}(z, \overline{x})$ is equal to

$$\gamma_{k,j,n}(z, \overline{x}) = E\left[\beta_{0,j}(z, \overline{x})^{1-\chi_{k,(j-1)^*}} \beta_{1,j}(z, \overline{x})^{\chi_{k,(j-1)^*}} \middle| s_{k,j} = n \right],$$

$$2 \leq j \leq O; \qquad (1.14)$$

$$\gamma_{k,1,n}(z, \overline{x}) = E\left[\beta_{0,1}(z, \overline{x})^{1-\chi_{k-1,I}} \beta_{1,1}(z, \overline{x})^{\chi_{k-1,I}} \middle| s_{k,1} = n \right], \qquad (1.15)$$

where

$$\begin{pmatrix} \beta_{0,j}(z, \overline{x}) \\ \beta_{1,j}(z, \overline{x}) \end{pmatrix} \triangleq Q(z)^{m_j} \begin{pmatrix} x_0 \\ x_1 \end{pmatrix}, \qquad 1 \leq j \leq O, \qquad (1.16)$$

and

$$Q(z) \triangleq \begin{pmatrix} \beta & (1-\beta)E(z) \\ 1-\alpha & \alpha E(z) \end{pmatrix}, \qquad (1.17)$$

with $E(z) = 1 - p + pz$ the pgf of the number of cell arrivals during an input slot of an active period. Using the result (1.14) in (1.13), we then get the following equation for $P_{k,j+1}(z, \overline{x})$, valid for $2 \leq j \leq O - 1$:

$$P_{k,j+1}(z, \overline{x}) = z^{-1} \sum_{n=0}^{\infty} \sum_{l=0}^{1} \text{Prob}\left[s_{k,j} = n, \chi_{k,(j-1)^*} = l \right]$$

$$z^n \beta_{0,j}(z, \overline{x})^{1-l} \beta_{1,j}(z, \overline{x})^l$$

$$+ \left(1 - z^{-1} \right) \sum_{l=0}^{1} \text{Prob}\left[s_{k,j} = 0, \chi_{k,(j-1)^*} = l \right]$$

$$\beta_{0,j}(z, \overline{x})^{1-l} \beta_{1,j}(z, \overline{x})^l,$$

which, in view of the definition (1.9), can be rewritten as

$$P_{k,j+1}(z, \overline{x}) = z^{-1} P_{k,j}\left(z, Q(z)^{m_j} \overline{x} \right) + \left(1 - z^{-1} \right) R_{k,j}\left(Q(z)^{m_j} \overline{x} \right),$$

$$2 \leq j \leq O - 1, \qquad (1.18)$$

with

$$R_{k,j}(\overline{x}) \triangleq \sum_{l=0}^{1} \text{Prob}\left[s_{k,j} = 0, \chi_{k,(j-1)^*} = l\right] x_0^{1-l} x_1^l ,$$

$$2 \leq j \leq O - 1. \tag{1.19}$$

In a similar manner, the combination of (1.13), for $j = 1$, (1.15) and the definition (1.10) leads to

$$P_{k,2}(z, \overline{x}) = z^{-1} P_{k,1}\left(z, Q(z)^{m_1} \overline{x}\right) + \left(1 - z^{-1}\right) R_{k,1}\left(Q(z)^{m_1} \overline{x}\right), \tag{1.20}$$

where

$$R_{k,1}(\overline{x}) \triangleq \sum_{l=0}^{1} \text{Prob}\left[s_{k,1} = 0, \chi_{k-1,l} = l\right] x_0^{1-l} x_1^l . \tag{1.21}$$

From the system equation (1.8), if we define the function $R_{k,O}(\overline{x})$ as in (1.19), we get the equation

$$P_{k+1,1}(z, \overline{x}) = z^{-1} P_{k,O}\left(z, Q(z)^{m_O} \overline{x}\right)$$

$$+ \left(1 - z^{-1}\right) R_{k,O}\left(Q(z)^{m_O} \overline{x}\right). \tag{1.22}$$

In the steady state, as $k \to \infty$, both the functions $P_{k,j}(z, \overline{x})$ and $P_{k+1,j}(z, \overline{x})$ will converge to a common limiting function

$$P_j(z, \overline{x}) \triangleq \lim_{k \to \infty} P_{k,j}(z, \overline{x}) .$$

Note that the buffer system will reach a steady state only if the equilibrium condition is satisfied, which means that the output load $\rho = \frac{1}{O} \sigma p$ must be strictly less than one. In this case, we can suppress the k-dependence of the pgf's in (1.18), (1.20) and (1.22), which gives

$$P_{j+1}(z, \overline{x}) = z^{-1} P_j\left(z, Q(z)^{m_j} \overline{x}\right) + \left(1 - z^{-1}\right) R_j\left(Q(z)^{m_j} \overline{x}\right),$$

$$1 \leq j \leq O - 1; \tag{1.23}$$

$$P_1(z, \overline{x}) = z^{-1} P_O\left(z, Q(z)^{m_O} \overline{x}\right)$$

$$+ \left(1 - z^{-1}\right) R_O\left(Q(z)^{m_O} \overline{x}\right), \tag{1.24}$$

where

$$R_j(\overline{x}) \triangleq \lim_{k \to \infty} R_{k,j}(\overline{x}) = p_{j,0} x_0 + p_{j,1} x_1 ;$$

$$p_{j,l} \triangleq \lim_{k \to \infty} \text{Prob}\left[s_{k,j} = 0, \chi_{k,(j-1)^*} = l\right], \qquad 2 \leq j \leq O ;$$

$$p_{1,l} \triangleq \lim_{k \to \infty} \text{Prob}\left[s_{k,1} = 0, \chi_{k-1,l} = l\right] . \tag{1.25}$$

Finally, by repeated use of the Equations (1.23) and (1.24), we find the following functional equation for $P_j(z, \overline{x})$:

$$P_j(z, \overline{x}) = z^{-O} P_j\left(z, Q(z)^I \overline{x}\right)$$

$$+ \left(1 - z^{-1}\right) \left(\sum_{n=1}^{j-1} z^{-j+1+n} R_n\left(Q(z)^{\sum_{l=n}^{j-1} m_l} \overline{x}\right)\right.$$

$$\left. + \sum_{n=j}^{O} z^{n-O-j+1} R_n\left(Q(z)^{I - \sum_{l=j}^{n-1} m_l} \overline{x}\right)\right),$$

$$1 \le j \le O. \tag{1.26}$$

1.4 Generating Function of the System Contents

From the functional equation (1.26), it is possible to derive an expression for the pgf $S(z)$ of the system contents s at the beginning of an arbitrary slot in the steady state. For this purpose, for each value of z, we denote by $\lambda_i(z)$, $1 \le i \le 2$, the two eigenvalues of the matrix $Q(z)$, by $w(z) = [w_{ij}(z)]$ a 2×2 matrix for which the ith row $w_i(z)$ is a left row eigenvector of $Q(z)$ with eigenvalue $\lambda_i(z)$, and by $u(z) = [u_{ij}(z)]$ the inverse matrix of $w(z)$, which is a 2×2 matrix for which the jth column is a right column eigenvector of $Q(z)$ with eigenvalue $\lambda_j(z)$. The eigenvalues $\lambda_1(z)$ and $\lambda_2(z)$ are given by

$$\lambda_1(z) = \frac{\beta}{2} + \frac{\alpha E(z)}{2} + \frac{\left((\beta + \alpha E(z))^2 - 4(\alpha + \beta - 1)E(z)\right)^{\frac{1}{2}}}{2} ;$$

$$\lambda_2(z) = \frac{\beta}{2} + \frac{\alpha E(z)}{2} - \frac{\left((\beta + \alpha E(z))^2 - 4(\alpha + \beta - 1)E(z)\right)^{\frac{1}{2}}}{2} ,$$

with the agreement that $\left(\epsilon e^{\iota\theta}\right)^{\frac{1}{2}} = \sqrt{\epsilon} e^{\frac{\iota\theta}{2}}$ for all ($\epsilon > 0$, $0 \le \theta < 2\pi$), where ι is the imaginary unit. In the following, it will become clear that it is preferable to define the left row eigenvectors of $Q(z)$ such that

$$w_{i1}(z) + w_{i2}(z) = 1, \qquad i = 1, 2,$$

which also implies that

$$u_{i1}(z) + u_{i2}(z) = 1, \qquad i = 1, 2.$$

The 2×2 matrix $u(z)$ is hereby uniquely determined as follows:

$$u(z) = \begin{pmatrix} u_{11}(z) & u_{12}(z) \\ u_{21}(z) & u_{22}(z) \end{pmatrix} = \begin{pmatrix} \frac{(1-\alpha-\beta+\lambda_1(z))(1-\beta)E(z)}{(\lambda_2(z)-\alpha E(z))(\lambda_2(z)-\lambda_1(z))} & \frac{(1-\alpha-\beta+\lambda_2(z))(1-\beta)E(z)}{(\lambda_1(z)-\alpha E(z))(\lambda_1(z)-\lambda_2(z))} \\ \frac{1-\alpha-\beta+\lambda_1(z)}{\lambda_1(z)-\lambda_2(z)} & \frac{1-\alpha-\beta+\lambda_2(z)}{\lambda_2(z)-\lambda_1(z)} \end{pmatrix}.$$

Let us now return to the functional equation (1.26), from which we obtain the following relationship:

$$z^{-O(i-1)} P_j\left(z, Q(z)^{I(i-1)}\overline{x}\right) = z^{-Oi} P_j\left(z, Q(z)^{Ii}\overline{x}\right) + z^{-O(i-1)}\left(1 - z^{-1}\right)$$
$$\cdot \left(\sum_{n=1}^{j-1} z^{-j+1+n} R_n\left(Q(z)^{\sum_{l=n}^{j-1} m_l} Q(z)^{I(i-1)}\overline{x}\right)\right.$$
$$\left. + \sum_{n=j}^{O} z^{n-O-j+1} R_n\left(Q(z)^{I-\sum_{l=j}^{n-1} m_l} Q(z)^{I(i-1)}\overline{x}\right)\right), \quad 1 \le j \le O,$$

for all $i \ge 1$. Summing the above equation for consecutive values of i, with (1.9), (1.10), (1.19) and (1.21), we then get

$$P_j(z, \overline{x}) = P_j\left(z, \frac{Q(z)^{Iv}\overline{x}}{z^{Oi}}\right)$$
$$+ \sum_{i=1}^{v}\left(\sum_{n=1}^{j-1} R_n\left(\frac{Q(z)^{\sum_{l=n}^{j-1} m_l} Q(z)^{I(i-1)}\overline{x}(z-1)}{z^{j-n+O(i-1)}}\right)\right. \tag{1.27}$$
$$\left. + \sum_{n=j}^{O} R_n\left(\frac{Q(z)^{I-\sum_{l=j}^{n-1} m_l} Q(z)^{I(i-1)}\overline{x}(z-1)}{z^{-n+Oi+j}}\right)\right), \quad 1 \le j \le O,$$

for any value of $v \ge 1$.

We now consider values of z for which $|\lambda_a(z)| < z \le 1$, $a = 1, 2$. Such values of z exist; in reference [14], this inequality is proved to hold for all $\{z : |z| = 1 \text{ and } z \ne 1\}$. Then, in view of the expression

$$\left[Q(z)^{Iv}\overline{x}\right]_i = \sum_{a=1}^{2} u_{ia}(z)\lambda_a(z)^{Iv} w_a(z)\overline{x}$$

for the ith row element of the column vector $Q(z)^{Iv}\overline{x}$, which readily follows from the definitions introduced above, if we let v approach to infinity, the sum for i in the right-hand side of Equation (1.27) converges, and we obtain

$$P_j(z, \overline{x}) = \sum_{i=1}^{\infty} \left(\sum_{n=1}^{j-1} R_n \left(\frac{Q(z)^{\sum\limits_{l=n}^{j-1} m_l} Q(z)^{I(i-1)} \overline{x}(z-1)}{z^{j-n+O(i-1)}} \right) \right.$$

$$\left. + \sum_{n=j}^{O} R_n \left(\frac{Q(z)^{I - \sum\limits_{l=j}^{n-1} m_l} Q(z)^{I(i-1)} \overline{x}(z-1)}{z^{-n+Oi+j}} \right) \right), \quad 1 \le j \le O,$$

where we have also used the property that $P_j(z, 0, 0) = 0$. Working out the sum for i in the above formula, we finally find the following expression for the function $P_j(z, \overline{x})$:

$$P_j(z, \overline{x}) = (z-1)$$

$$\sum_{n=1}^{j-1} \left(\sum_{a=1}^{2} \frac{z^{O+n-j} \lambda_a(z)^{\sum\limits_{l=n}^{j-1} m_l}}{z^O - \lambda_a(z)^I} w_a(z) \overline{x} \left(u_{1a}(z) p_{n,0} + u_{2a}(z) p_{n,1} \right) \right)$$

$$+ \sum_{n=j}^{O} \left(\sum_{a=1}^{2} \frac{z^{n-j} \lambda_a(z)^{I - \sum\limits_{l=j}^{n-1} m_l}}{z^O - \lambda_a(z)^I} w_a(z) \overline{x} \left(u_{1a}(z) p_{n,0} + u_{2a}(z) p_{n,1} \right) \right),$$

$$1 \le j \le O. \tag{1.28}$$

From (1.28), the pgf $S_j(z)$ of the random variable s_j, the system contents at the beginning of the jth output slot of an arbitrary frame in the steady state, can be obtained by setting $x_0 = x_1 = 1$. The pgf $S(z)$ of the system contents s at the beginning of an arbitrary output slot is then given by the arithmetic mean of the $S_j(z)$:

$$S(z) = \frac{1}{O} \sum_{j=1}^{O} S_j(z) = (z-1) \frac{1}{O} \sum_{a=1}^{2} \frac{1}{z^O - \lambda_a(z)^I} \sum_{j=1}^{O} H_{ja}(z), \tag{1.29}$$

where $H_{ja}(z)$ is defined as

$$H_{ja}(z) \triangleq \sum_{n=1}^{j-1} z^{O+n-j} \lambda_a(z)^{\sum\limits_{l=n}^{j-1} m_l} \left(u_{1a}(z) p_{n,0} + u_{2a}(z) p_{n,1} \right)$$

$$+ \sum_{n=j}^{O} z^{n-j} \lambda_a(z)^{I - \sum\limits_{l=j}^{n-1} m_l} \left(u_{1a}(z) p_{n,0} + u_{2a}(z) p_{n,1} \right), \tag{1.30}$$

$$1 \leq j \leq O \, .$$

Equation (1.29) gives $S(z)$ in terms of known quantities on the one hand, and the $2 \cdot O$ unknown constants $p_{n,l}$ (with $1 \leq n \leq O$ and $l = 0, 1$) on the other hand. These unknowns can be determined based on the analyticity property of the pgf $S(z)$ inside the unit disk of the complex z-plane and Rouché's theorem which gives $2 \cdot O - 1$ linear equations, and the normalization condition $S(1) = 1$, which gives one equation.

1.5 Derivation of Performance Measures

In this section, the expression (1.29) for the pgf $S(z)$ is used to derive closed-form formulae for several performance measures related to the system contents and the cell delay.

1.5.1 Mean System Contents

We can obtain the mean system contents by taking the first-order derivative of Equation (1.29) for $S(z)$ with respect to z in the point $z = 1$. After some calculations, we then find

$$E[s] = S'(1) = \frac{\frac{1}{O} \sum_{j=1}^{O} H'_{j1}(1)}{O - I\sigma p} + \frac{I\lambda''_1(1) + I(I-1)\sigma^2 p^2 - O(O-1)}{2(O - I\sigma p)} \, , \qquad (1.31)$$

with

$$\begin{aligned}
H'_{j1}(1) &= \sum_{n=1}^{j-1} \left(O + n - j + \sum_{l=n}^{j-1} m_l \right) (p_{n,0} + p_{n,1}) \\
&+ \sum_{n=j}^{O} \left(n - j + I - \sum_{l=j}^{n-1} m_l \right) (p_{n,0} + p_{n,1}) \qquad (1.32) \\
&+ \frac{p}{2 - \alpha - \beta} \sum_{n=1}^{O} \left((1 - \beta - \sigma) p_{n,0} + (\alpha - \sigma) p_{n,1} \right) , \\
& \qquad 1 \leq j \leq O \, ,
\end{aligned}$$

and

$$\lambda_1''(1) = -\frac{((\alpha + \beta)(\alpha p) + 2(1 - \alpha - \beta)p)^2}{2(2 - \alpha - \beta)^3} + \frac{(\alpha p)^2}{2(2 - \alpha - \beta)}. \quad (1.33)$$

1.5.2   Tail Distribution of the System Contents

As indicated in e.g., [13] and [15], for sufficiently large values of S, the tail distribution of the system contents can be accurately approximated by the following geometric form:

$$\text{Prob}\,[s > S] \cong -b_0 \frac{z_0^{-S-1}}{z_0 - 1}. \quad (1.34)$$

In the above expression, z_0 is the pole of $S(z)$ with the smallest modulus. The pole z_0 must be a real and positive quantity to ensure that the tail distribution is always nonnegative and it has been observed that it is the solution of the equation

$$z^O - \lambda_1(z)^I = 0 \quad (1.35)$$

outside the unit disk with the smallest modulus. The constant b_0 in (1.34) is the residue of $S(z)$ in the point $z = z_0$ and can be calculated from the expression (1.29) for $S(z)$, with de l'Hospital's rule, as

$$b_0 = \frac{z_0 - 1}{O} \frac{1}{Oz_0^{O-1} - I\lambda_1(z_0)^{I-1}\lambda_1'(z_0)} \sum_{j=1}^{O} H_{j1}(z_0), \quad (1.36)$$

where $\lambda_1'(z_0)$ is given by

$$\lambda_1'(z_0) = \frac{\alpha p}{2} + \frac{(\beta + \alpha E(z_0))\alpha p - 2(\alpha + \beta - 1)p}{2\left((\beta + \alpha E(z_0))^2 - 4(\alpha + \beta - 1)E(z_0)\right)^{\frac{1}{2}}}. \quad (1.37)$$

A closed-form expression for the tail distribution of the system contents (in terms of z_0) can be obtained from (1.34), (1.36) and (1.37). The resulting expression is easy to evaluate from a computational point of view, since it only requires the numerical calculation of z_0. This can easily be done from (1.35) by means of e.g., the Newton-Raphson iteration method.

1.5.3   Cell Loss Ratio

In the analysis throughout the previous sections, we have assumed an infinite buffer size for the rate adapter. In practice, however, buffers always have a finite storage capacity and a fraction of the arriving cells will be lost upon arrival because of buffer overflow. In [4], for the case of an uncorrelated Bernoulli arrival process, the following exact relationship has been shown between the cell loss ratio (CLR) in a finite rate adaptation buffer of size L and the probability Prob $[s > L]$ of having a system contents larger than L in the corresponding infinite-capacity buffer with the same arrival process and input rate/output rate ratio:

$$\text{CLR} = \frac{(1 - \rho) \, \text{Prob} \, [s > L]}{\rho \, (1 - \text{Prob} \, [s > L])} . \tag{1.38}$$

The exactness of the above relationship was a consequence of the uncorrelated nature of the cell arrival process on the input link. For the correlated arrival process considered in the present paper, however, formula (1.38) still constitutes an accurate approximation for the CLR, as will be confirmed by some numerical examples in Section 1.6.

1.5.4 Cell Delay Characteristics

In this subsection, it is assumed that the rate adaptation buffer operates according to an FCFS (first-come-first-served) queuing discipline. The delay d of a cell is defined as the number of output slots between the end of the output slot during which the cell has arrived in the buffer and the departure instant of this cell, i.e., the end of the output slot during which the cell is transmitted from the buffer. In reference [16], the following relationship was established between the pgf $D(z)$ of d and the pgf $S(z)$ of s:

$$D(z) = \frac{S(z) - S(0)}{1 - S(0)} , \tag{1.39}$$

which is valid for any discrete-time G-D-1 queuing system with an FCFS queuing discipline, irrespective of the nature of the cell arrival process. From (1.39), all the characteristics of the cell delay can be expressed in terms of characteristics of the system contents. In particular, the mean value and the tail distribution of the cell delay are obtained as

$$E\,[d] = \frac{E[s]}{\rho} ; \tag{1.40}$$

$$\text{Prob}\,[d > D] = \frac{\text{Prob}[s > S]}{\rho} , \qquad D \geq 1 . \tag{1.41}$$

1.6 Results and Discussion

As a measure for the degree of correlation or burstiness in the cell arrival process we introduce a parameter K defined by

$$\frac{1}{1 - \alpha} = \frac{K}{1 - \sigma} \quad \text{and} \quad \frac{1}{1 - \beta} = \frac{K}{\sigma} , \tag{1.42}$$

where $\frac{1}{1-\alpha}$ and $\frac{1}{1-\beta}$ are the mean lengths of the active and passive periods on the input link. For a given value of the mean activity σ, i.e., a given ratio of the mean active and passive periods, high values of K indicate long absolute lengths of the active and passive periods, and hence a more bursty cell arrival stream. In the following discussion the parameter K will be referred to as the correlation factor. Note that the value $K = 1$ corresponds to the case of an (uncorrelated) Bernoulli arrival process.

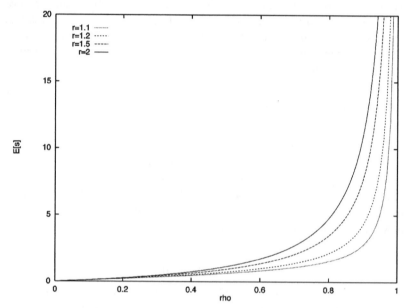

FIGURE 1.2

Mean system contents $E[s]$ vs. the output load ρ, for $p = 0.9$, $K = 3$ and $r = 1.2, 1.5, 2, 2.8, 8.$

In Fig. 1.2, the mean system contents $E[s]$ is plotted as a function of the output load ρ, for $p = 0.9$, $K = 3$ and various values of the input rate/output rate ratio r. Figure 1.3 shows the mean system contents in terms of the correlation factor K, for $p = 0.9$, $\rho = 0.8$ and various values of r. Very similar curves can be obtained for the mean cell delay $E[d]$ [from Eq. (1.40)]. The figures clearly indicate that the mean system contents is higher if ρ, K and/or r are higher. Especially, we observe that the curves in Fig. 1.3 are straight lines, which means that the mean system contents is a *linearly* increasing function of the correlation factor K.

In order to illustrate the accuracy of the proposed approximation (1.38) for the cell loss ratio, we have plotted in Fig. 1.4 the exact CLR (dashed line) together with the approximation obtained from (1.38) (full line) in terms of the buffer size L, for $p = 1$, $\rho = 0.8$, $K = 3$ and various values of r. The exact

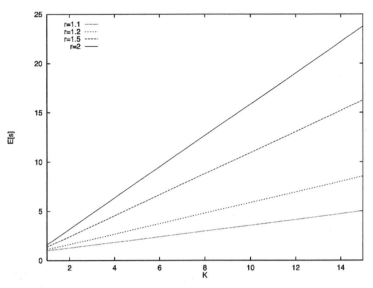

FIGURE 1.3
Mean system contents $E[s]$ vs. the correlation factor K, for $p = 0.9, \rho = 0.8$ and $r = 1.2, 1.5, 2, 2.8, 8$.

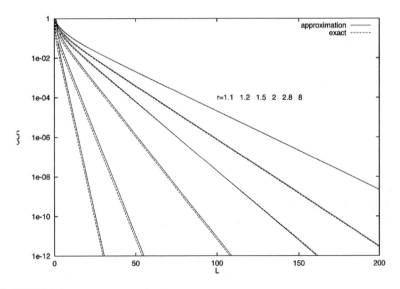

FIGURE 1.4
Cell loss ratio vs. the buffer size L, for $p = 1$, $\rho = 0.8$, $K = 3$ and $r = 1.1, 1.2, 1.5, 2, 2.8, 8$.

values were obtained by solving one set of balance equations for each value of L. The curves show that the approximate results constitute a very tight upper bound for the exact results, especially for higher values of r, and, therefore, can be used for buffer dimensioning.

Equation (1.38) for the CLR is very useful in practice since it is closed-form and can easily be inverted to give the minimum buffer size $L(X)$ in the rate adapter, which is required to have a cell loss ratio below a specified value X. Specifically, from (1.34) and (1.38), it follows that $L(X)$ is given by

$$L(X) \cong \left\lceil \frac{\ln\left(\frac{-b_0}{z_0(z_0-1)}\left(1 + \frac{1-\rho}{\rho X}\right)\right)}{\ln(z_0)} \right\rceil, \tag{1.43}$$

where $\lceil x \rceil$ denotes the smallest integer number which is larger than or equal to x.

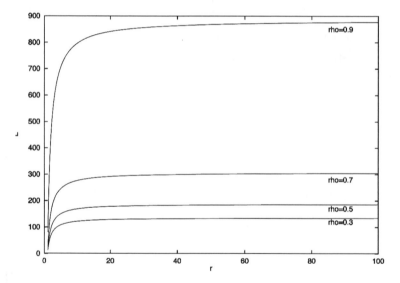

FIGURE 1.5
Required buffer size $L(X)$ to have a CLR $\leq X$ vs. the input rate/output rate ratio r, for $X = 10^{-12}$, $p = 1$, $K = 4$ and $\rho = 0.3, 0.5, 0.7, 0.9$.

In Figs. 1.5 and 1.6, the necessary buffer size $L(X)$ to guarantee a cell loss ratio less than $X = 10^{-12}$ is shown as a function of the input rate/output rate ratio r, for $p = 1$ and various values of ρ and K. Several conclusions can be drawn from these figures. First, we see that for a given value of r, the buffer requirements increase as the output load ρ increases and/or as the arrival stream becomes more bursty (i.e., as K becomes higher). Second, it is clear that for

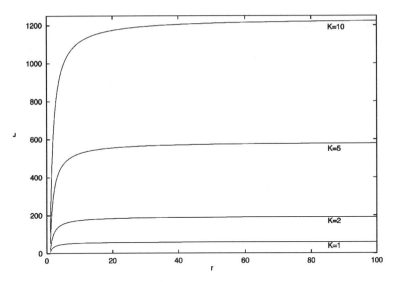

FIGURE 1.6

Required buffer size $L(X)$ to have a CLR $\leq X$ vs. the input rate/output rate ratio r, for $X = 10^{-12}$, $p = 1$, $\rho = 0.8$ and $K = 1, 2, 5, 10$.

given values of ρ and K, the required buffer space is an increasing function of r and approaches to some limiting value for high values of r. Furthermore, we notice that even for relatively small mismatches between input and output rates, a quite substantial amount of buffer space may be required in the rate adapter in order to keep the CLR below a given value.

1.7 Conclusions

In this paper, we have analyzed the queuing behavior of a rate adaptation buffer. Based on a generating-functions approach, we have derived exact expressions for the means and the tail distributions of the buffer contents and the cell delay, as well as an accurate approximation for the CLR. The obtained expressions are easy to evaluate numerically. From the numerical results, we may conclude that the buffer requirements of the rate adapter increase as the input rate/output rate ratio and/or the degree of correlation in the arrival stream increase.

Appendix: Proof of the Result for $\gamma_{k,j,n}(z,\overline{x})$

From the definition (1.12) for $\gamma_{k,j,n}(z,\overline{x})$, we have, for $2 \leq j \leq O$:

$$\gamma_{k,j,n}(z,\overline{x}) = E\left[z^{\sum_{i=(j-1)^*+1}^{j^*} e_{k,i}} x_0^{1-\chi_{k,j^*}} x_1^{\chi_{k,j^*}} \,\Big|\, s_{k,j} = n\right]$$

$$= \sum_{l_0=0}^{1}\sum_{l_1=0}^{1}\cdots\sum_{l_{m_j}=0}^{1} \mathrm{Prob}\left[\chi_{k,(j-1)^*} = l_0, \chi_{k,j^*-m_j+1} = l_1, \ldots,\right.$$

$$\chi_{k,j^*} = l_{m_j}\,\Big|\, s_{k,j} = n\right]$$

$$\cdot E\left[z^{\sum_{i=(j-1)^*+1}^{j^*} e_{k,i}} x_0^{1-\chi_{k,j^*}} x_1^{\chi_{k,j^*}} \,\Big|\, \chi_{k,(j-1)^*} = l_0, \chi_{k,j^*-m_j+1} = l_1,\right.$$

$$\ldots, \chi_{k,j^*} = l_{m_j}, s_{k,j} = n\right]$$

$$= \sum_{l_0=0}^{1} \mathrm{Prob}\left[\chi_{k,(j-1)^*} = l_0 \,\Big|\, s_{k,j} = n\right] \cdot \left\{\sum_{l_1=0}^{1}\cdots\sum_{l_{m_j}=0}^{1}\right.\qquad\text{(A.1)}$$

$$\mathrm{Prob}\left[\chi_{k,j^*-m_j+1} = l_1 \,\Big|\, \chi_{k,(j-1)^*} = l_0\right]$$

$$\cdot\mathrm{Prob}\left[\chi_{k,j^*-m_j+2} = l_2 \,\Big|\, \chi_{k,j^*-m_j+1} = l_1\right]\cdots$$

$$\left.\cdot\mathrm{Prob}\left[\chi_{k,j^*} = l_{m_j} \,\Big|\, \chi_{k,j^*-1} = l_{m_j-1}\right] E(z)^{l_1+\ldots+l_{m_j}} x_0^{1-l_{m_j}} x_1^{l_{m_j}}\right\}.$$

If we now define

$$\begin{pmatrix} \beta_{0,j}(z,\overline{x}) \\ \beta_{1,j}(z,\overline{x}) \end{pmatrix} \triangleq Q(z)^{m_j} \begin{pmatrix} x_0 \\ x_1 \end{pmatrix},\qquad\text{(A.2)}$$

where

$$Q(z) \triangleq \begin{pmatrix} \beta & (1-\beta)E(z) \\ 1-\alpha & \alpha E(z) \end{pmatrix},\qquad\text{(A.3)}$$

it can be shown by induction that the expression (A.1) for $\gamma_{k,j,n}(z,\overline{x})$ equals

$$\gamma_{k,j,n}(z,\overline{x}) = \sum_{l_0=0}^{1} \mathrm{Prob}\left[\chi_{k,(j-1)^*} = l_0 | s_{k,j} = n\right] \beta_{0,j}(z,\overline{x})^{1-l_0} \beta_{1,j}(z,\overline{x})^{l_0}$$

$$= E\left[\beta_{0,j}(z,\overline{x})^{1-\chi_{k,(j-1)^*}} \beta_{1,j}(z,\overline{x})^{\chi_{k,(j-1)^*}} \,\Big|\, s_{k,j} = n\right],$$

$$2 \leq j \leq O,\qquad\text{(A.4)}$$

which ends our proof. The result (1.15) for $\gamma_{k,1,n}(z,\overline{x})$ can be proved in a similar manner.

References

[1] M. De Prycker, *Asynchronous Transfer Mode: Solution for Broadband ISDN*, Ellis Horwood Limited, New York, 1991.

[2] K. Rothermel, Traffic studies of transmission bit rate conversion in ATM networks, *Proceedings of ITC 13* (Copenhagen, June 1991), volume *Queuing, Performance and Control in ATM*, pp. 65–69.

[3] H. Michiel, Dimensioning of a rate adapter, research report ATG_029/HM_901019, 1990.

[4] H. Bruneel, V. Inghelbrecht and B. Steyaert, Buffering for transmission rate reduction by a rational factor, *Electronics Letters,* vol. 33, no. 7, 1997, pp. 550–551.

[5] B. Steyaert and H. Bruneel, Buffer dimensioning for rate adaptation modules, *Proceedings of the International IFIP-IEEE Conference on Broadband Communications, BROADBAND COMMUNICATIONS '96,* (Montreal, April 1996), pp. 489–500.

[6] V. Inghelbrecht, B. Steyaert, H. Bruneel and S. Wittevrongel, Buffer behavior of a rate adapter with correlated arrivals, *Proceedings of the Sixth IFIP Workshop on Performance Modelling and Evaluation of ATM Networks* (Ilkley, July 1998), *Research Papers,* pp. 64/1–64/10.

[7] C. Blondia and O. Casals, Statistical multiplexing of VBR sources: a matrix-analytic approach, *Performance Evaluation,* vol. 16, no. 1–3, 1992, pp. 5–20.

[8] S.-Q. Li, A general solution technique for discrete queuing analysis of multimedia traffic on ATM, *IEEE Transactions on Communications,* vol. 39, no. 7, pp. 1115–1132, 1991.

[9] K. Sohraby, On the theory of general ON-OFF sources with applications in high-speed networks, *Proceedings of INFOCOM '93,* (San Francisco, March-April 1993), pp. 401–410.

[10] T. Takine, T. Suda and T. Hasegawa, Cell loss and output process analyses of a finite-buffer discrete-time ATM queuing system with correlated arrivals, *IEEE Transactions on Communications,* vol. 43, no. 2/3/4, pp. 1022–1037, 1995.

[11] A.-L. Beylot, I. Kohlenberg and M. Becker, How important is the burstiness of the input traffic on the performance of an ATM Clos switch under

symmetric bursty traffic? *Proceedings of the Second Workshop on Performance Modelling and Evaluation of ATM Networks,* (Bradford, July 1994), pp. 4/1–4/12.

[12] M. E. Woodward, Burstiness of interrupted Bernoulli process, *Electronics Letters,* vol. 30, no. 18, pp. 1466–1467, 1994.

[13] C. M. Woodside and E. D. S. Ho, Engineering calculation of overflow probabilities in buffers with Markov-interrupted service, *IEEE Transactions on Communications,* vol. 35, no. 12, pp. 1272–1277, 1987.

[14] B. Steyaert and H. Bruneel, Analysis of ATM Switching Modules with Channel Grouping in a Bursty-Source Environment, *Proceedings of the IFIP TC6/ICCC International Conference on Integrated Broadband Communication Networks and Services,* (Copenhagen, April 1993), pp. 383–394.

[15] H. Bruneel, B. Steyaert, E. Desmet and G. H. Petit, Analytic derivation of tail probabilities for queue lengths and waiting times in ATM multiserver queues, *European Journal of Operational Research,* vol. 76, pp. 563–572, 1994.

[16] H. Bruneel and B.G. Kim, *Discrete-Time Models for Communication Systems Including ATM,* Kluwer Academic Publishers, Boston, 1993.

Chapter 2

Internet Traffic: Periodicity, Tail Behavior, and Performance Implications

Mark S. Squillante

IBM Thomas J. Watson Research Center

David D. Yao[1]

SEEM Department, The Chinese University of Hong Kong

Li Zhang

IBM Thomas J. Watson Research Center

Abstract   We present a study of the traffic patterns for a dynamic and heavily-accessed Web server environment, and the impact of such traffic patterns on Web server performance. Using the data from the official Web site during the 1998 Winter Olympic Games in Nagano, Japan, we develop traffic models to represent the process of user requests that are the input to the geographically-distributed Web server systems. Our analysis of the traffic data illustrates traffic patterns that exhibit both light-tailed and heavy-tailed behaviors. We then feed these traffic processes into one of the Web server systems modeled as a general single-server queue and analyze the waiting-time process, which models the latency encountered by user requests, a key measure of quality of service (QoS).

Keywords: traffic modeling, queuing analysis, heavy-tail distributions, World Wide Web.

[1]Research undertaken while an academic visitor at the IBM Thomas J. Watson Research Center, and while on leave from Columbia University; supported in part by NSF Grant ECS-9705392.

2.1 Introduction

While a significant amount of research (e.g., see [8, 10] and the references cited therein) has examined the network traffic for different Web server environments and developed models to characterize these network traffic patterns, there has been very little research attempting to understand and model the request traffic of recent heavily-accessed and dynamic Web server environments. These system environments are becoming increasingly common as the Web is used more and more often as a means to access news, financial data and other information, and to support a wide range of Internet applications from email to E-commerce, and from education to entertainment. Recent representative examples include the Web sites for popular sporting events such as the 1998 Olympic Games and the 1998 Championships at Wimbledon, and the Web sites for popular news and financial services such as CNN and Schwab. Furthermore, many aspects of these Web server environments are very different from those that have been previously considered in the literature. For example, the Web site for the 1998 Olympic Games served 56.8 million requests on the peak day, and recorded a maximum of 110,414 hits per minute. Similarly, the Web site for the 1998 Championships at Wimbledon recorded a maximum of 145,478 hits per minute.

The purpose of this paper is to understand the key characteristics of the Web request traffic patterns in these heavily-accessed and dynamic Web server environments, and to understand the impact of such request patterns on Web server performance. To enhance or to optimize the performance of Web servers in these environments, the starting point is to study the traffic patterns, or more specifically, to develop a model for the process of user requests that are the input to such servers. This is fundamental to gaining key insights and a better understanding of the impact of these traffic patterns on server performance, in terms of quality of service (QoS), availability, reliability, scalability, and other performance measures. Since our focus in this paper is on Web server requests, we restrict our use of the term *traffic* to such access patterns.

In Section 2.2 we describe the IBM Web site for the Nagano Olympic Games and illustrate two types of traffic patterns from this environment. In Section 2.3, we present the traffic models, including the light-tailed and heavy-tailed marginals, and the autoregressive dependence model. These traffic processes are inputs to a single-server $G/G/1$ queue model in Section 2.4, where we characterize the tail behavior of the delay distribution.

2.2 Web Environment

We consider a Web server system based on the official IBM Web site for the 1998 Olympic Games in Nagano, Japan, which is representative of the class of dynamic and heavily-accessed Web server environments motivating our study. The system consisted of multiple SP2 machine frames at four different locations (Schaumburg, Illinois; Columbus, Ohio; Bethesda, Maryland; and Tokyo, Japan), where each SP2 frame was composed of 10 uniprocessor nodes that serve Web requests, and 1 multiprocessor node that handles all updates of the underlying data. Incoming requests for the various Olympic Web pages from around the globe are routed by a set of Network Dispatcher routers (NDs) to specific nodes of a certain SP2 machine. A requested Web page is then sent directly to the user from the SP2 node serving the request without going back through the ND. Each ND follows a weighted round-robin policy, where the weight for a node is a function of its current load. By sending more traffic to less heavily loaded nodes, this scalable approach balances the load of the server across the set of SP2 machines and their nodes. In this regard, each ND has the effect of smoothing out and equalizing (in a statistical sense) the request arrival process among the SP2 nodes. The goal in designing this system architecture was to guarantee a certain level of high-performance for access from the Web to Olympic results and data that were constantly changing, and to provide 100% availability throughout the duration of the Nagano Games. The machines in Schaumburg and Columbus served requests originating from the Americas, the SP2 frames in Bethesda served requests from Europe, and the frames in Tokyo served requests originating from Asia. The interested reader is referred to [5] for additional details.

The Web requests fall into two categories: those that access pages which are created dynamically, and those that access static files such as GIF and JPG images. When a request for static data arrives, the server simply returns the content of the corresponding file. In contrast, dynamic requests are for HTML pages, which require the server to execute a program in order to generate the dynamic pages. Dynamic data generally change more frequently than static data, since a dynamic page may, for instance, contain certain information that is maintained in an evolving database such as the current score of a game.

A high percentage of the pages at the Web site was created dynamically, since the contents of these pages were constantly changing, a phenomenon that is essential to this kind of environment. Embedded image files, on the other hand, comprised the majority of the static data requests. The time to serve a dynamic page request is often significantly longer than the time required to satisfy a static request. In particular, the average processing time to satisfy requests for static files is on the order of a few milliseconds, whereas the average processing time to serve a dynamic page request is longer by several orders of magnitude. Since the serving of dynamic pages dominates performance in the Web server environment under consideration, it is very important to understand the request patterns for dynamic pages in this class of Web environments and to understand the impact of these traffic patterns on various aspects of Web server performance.

Therefore, we focus on the requests for dynamic pages recorded by the servers at two locations, namely Bethesda and Tokyo, noting that the traffic patterns for the Bethesda site are similar in characteristics to those found at the Schaumburg and Columbus locations. We examined the number of requests for dynamic pages at different time scales. As a representative example, the graphs in Fig. 2.1 show the aggregate number of requests received every 300 seconds (5 minutes) at the Bethesda and Tokyo locations.

We observe that the traffic from Asia contains huge bursts and strong periodic behavior, whereas the traffic from Europe is much less bursty. The large traffic bursts from Asia are primarily due to a strong public interest in Japan for events related to ski jumping. Most of the traffic from Asia originated from Japan, and this traffic was concentrated around the time when these popular ski jumping events were taking place. In contrast, likely due to the time differences and the more diverse interests in Europe, the Bethesda traffic data are more scattered and they do not contain huge spikes like those found in the Tokyo data. Another possible cause for the smoother traffic from Europe is the limited bandwidth for the trans-Atlantic traffic, which acts as a "filter" that smooths out the burstiness.

To better understand these traffic patterns, we plot in Fig. 2.2 the tail distributions of the "batch size," i.e., the number of requests within each time unit. The leftmost graph in Fig. 2.2 plots $-\log(P[\text{Batch} > x])$ as a function of x, for the Bethesda data. The quadratic curve suggests that the distribution is light-tailed, i.e., $P[\text{Batch} > x] \sim e^{-\alpha x^2}$, as we alluded to earlier in Section 2.1. In the rightmost graph of Fig. 2.2, we plot $-\log(P[\text{Batch} > x])$ against $\log x$ for the Tokyo data. The result is also a quadratic curve (but in terms of $\log x$). This suggests a heavy-tailed distribution; i.e., $P[\text{Batch} > x] \sim e^{-\beta(\log x)^2}$ (refer to Section 2.3).

Whereas the light-tailed and heavy-tailed distributions only characterize the marginals of the input traffic in terms of the batch size per time unit, we have also studied the dependence structure and periodicity of the batch sizes over time. In particular, we find the autoregressive models recently developed in [5] quite suitable. Although the models in [5] are for traffic processes with light-tailed marginals, they are readily adapted to handle heavy-tailed marginals as well, which we consider in the next section.

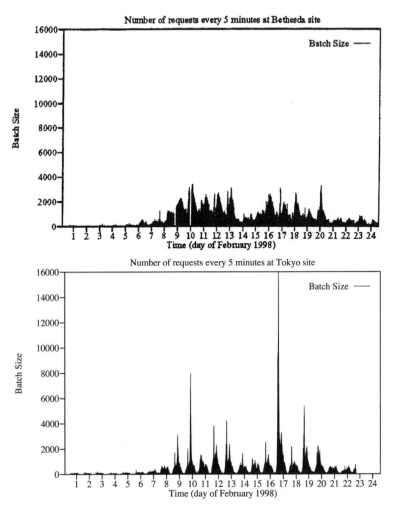

FIGURE 2.1
Traffic patterns from Europe and Asia at a time scale of 300 seconds.

2.3 Traffic Models

We start with some preliminaries. A distribution function $F(x)$ is called *light-tailed* if the tail of the distribution $\bar{F}(x) := 1 - F(x)$ decays at least exponentially fast. If the tail decays in a sub-exponential fashion, then $F(x)$ is called a *heavy-tailed distribution*. (More precisely, this belongs to the *sub-exponential class* of distributions; refer to [7].) For example, when $F(x)$ is

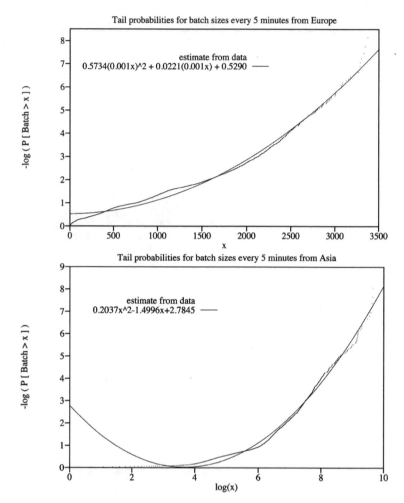

FIGURE 2.2

Tail distribution of the request batch size at 300-second intervals.

a Pareto distribution, we have the log-tail distribution function being linear in $\log x$ instead of in x. When the log-tail is a quadratic function of $\log x$ (instead of a linear function as in the case of Pareto distributions), a good model to capture this type of burstiness is the log-normal distribution.

A stationary time series $\{Z_t\}$ is said to satisfy an order (p, q) *autoregressive moving average* model, denoted by ARMA(p, q), if it can be represented as

$$Z_t - \phi_1 Z_{t-1} - \ldots - \phi_p Z_{t-p} = \epsilon_t - \theta_1 \epsilon_{t-1} - \ldots - \theta_q \epsilon_{t-q},$$

where p and q are, respectively, the orders of the AR and MA processes. A time series is an ARIMA(p, d, q) process if $(1 - B)^d Z_t$ is an ARMA(p, q) process, where $BZ_t = Z_{t-1}$ defines the backwards shift operator. Periodic, or seasonal, patterns can be additionally captured by extending this class of statistical models to the so-called *seasonal ARIMA* models, denoted by ARIMA$(p, d, q) \times (P, D, Q)_s$, where P defines the order of the seasonal autoregressive process, D defines the degree of seasonal differencing, Q defines the order of the seasonal moving average process, and s defines the span of the seasonality.

Let $\{X_n\}$ denote the input process to a Web server, with X_n denoting the number of requests that arrive in the nth time period, a pre-specified time unit. We suppose $\{X_n\}$ is a stationary sequence, and denote by $X \overset{d}{=} X_n$ the generic r.v. that follows the (common) marginal distribution $F(\cdot)$.

For the type of less bursty traffic represented by the Bethesda data, X follows a standard, light-tailed distribution. Specifically, we shall model X as a normal variate:

$$X = \mu + \sigma Z \, ,$$

where μ and σ are positive real values, and Z denotes the standard normal variate (i.e., with zero mean and unit variance). Notice that

$$- \log \mathsf{P}(X > t) \sim \frac{(t - \mu)^2}{2\sigma^2} \, .$$

This is consistent with our observations of the quadratic curves fitting the Bethesda data in Fig. 2.2.

To model the bursty traffic as observed from the Tokyo data, we let X follow a lognormal distribution:

$$X = e^{\mu + \sigma Z} \, . \tag{2.1}$$

The nth moment of X is:

$$\mathsf{E}(X^n) = e^{n\mu} \mathsf{E}\left(e^{n\sigma Z}\right) = e^{n\mu + n^2 \sigma^2 / 2} \, ;$$

in particular,

$$\mathsf{E}(X) = e^{\mu + \sigma^2 / 2}, \qquad \mathsf{Var}(X) = \mathsf{E}(X)\left(e^{\sigma^2} - 1\right) \, .$$

Let $\Phi(x)$ and $\phi(x)$ denote, respectively, the distribution function and the density function of Z; let $\bar{\Phi}(x) := 1 - \Phi(x)$. We then have

$$\bar{F}(x) = \mathsf{P}(X \geq x) = \mathsf{P}(\mu + \sigma Z \geq \log x) = \bar{\Phi}(z_x) \, , \tag{2.2}$$

where

$$z_x := (\log x - \mu)/\sigma \, .$$

It is easy to verify that $\bar{\Phi}(z) \sim \phi(z)/z$ when $z \to \infty$. Hence, when $x \to \infty$, we have $z_x \to \infty$ and

$$- \log \bar{F}(x) \sim \frac{1}{2\sigma^2}(\log x - \mu)^2 + \log(\log x - \mu). \tag{2.3}$$

That is, the log-tail distribution behaves as a quadratic function of $\log x$, and in this sense, X follows a heavy-tailed distribution.

We next consider the dependence structure of the sequence $\{X_n\}$, first for the case of a light-tailed marginal distribution. To start with, consider the following simple model. For each n, let

$$X_n = \mu + Y_n, \tag{2.4}$$

with $\{Y_n\}$ being an autoregressive process of order 1 (AR(1)):

$$Y_n = \epsilon_n + \phi_1 Y_{n-1}, \tag{2.5}$$

where ϕ_1 is a real parameter, and $\{\epsilon_1, \epsilon_2, \ldots\}$ is a sequence of i.i.d. normal r.v.s with mean 0 and variance σ_ϵ^2. Since $\{X_n\}$ is assumed to be a stationary sequence, $\{Y_n\}$ must also be a stationary sequence. Hence, for all n, Y_n is also a normal r.v. with a zero mean and a variance σ_y^2 that must satisfy

$$\sigma_y^2 = \sigma_\epsilon^2 + \phi_1^2 \sigma_y^2,$$

or, equivalently,

$$\sigma_y^2 = \frac{\sigma_\epsilon^2}{1 - \phi_1^2}. \tag{2.6}$$

From the recursion in (2.5), we have

$$Y_n = \epsilon_n + \phi_1 \epsilon_{n-1} + \phi_1^2 \epsilon_{n-2} + \cdots.$$

The autocorrelation function at lag k is:

$$\rho_k := \mathsf{Cov}(Y_n, Y_{n+k})/\mathsf{Var}(Y_n) = \phi_1^k.$$

Hence, $\{X_n\}$ has a short-range dependent structure, and so does $\{Y_n\}$. In practice, the parameters of the model are obtained by fitting the real data using standard time-series analysis. It is possible that the real data possesses more complicated dependency structures which require a higher order ARMA model for the fitting.

For the case of heavy-tailed marginals, replace (2.4) by

$$\log X_n = \mu + Y_n. \tag{2.7}$$

As before, the stationarity of $\{X_n\}$ requires that $\{Y_n\}$ be a stationary process as well. Hence, the relation in (2.6) still applies, and

$$X_n = e^{(\mu + \epsilon_n + \phi_1 \epsilon_{n-1} + \phi_1^2 \epsilon_{n-2} + \cdots)}.$$

The kth moment of X_n is

$$\mathsf{E}[X_n^k] = \mathsf{E}[e^{k\mu + kY_n}] = e^{k\mu + k^2\sigma_y^2/2} .$$

The autocorrelation function for $\{X_n\}$ can then be derived as:

$$\rho_k \sim \frac{1}{e^{\sigma_y^2} - 1} \sigma_y^2 \phi_1^k \quad \text{as } k \to \infty .$$

Therefore, $\{X_n\}$ continues to be a process with short-range dependence. In practice, we can take the log of the data and then apply the time-series analysis to obtain the parameters for the model. The real data may exhibit more complicated dependent structures, in which case a higher order ARMA process may be needed for a good fit of the data.

We followed the above approach for the request traffic at the Tokyo site (see Fig. 2.1). Since the traffic patterns before February 7, when the Olympic games started, is quite different from the traffic patterns afterwards, we only analyze the traffic after that date. We first perform the log transformation of the original times series data. The shape of the autocorrelation function for the transformed time series very closely resembles the autocorrelation function of a seasonal AR(1) model, ARIMA$(1, 0, 0) \times (1, 0, 0)_{288}$. Therefore, we performed another transformation, $Z_n = Y_n - 0.9Y_{n-288}$, to remove the seasonality. The number 288 is the period which represents the daily cycle, and the coefficient 0.9 is estimated from the data. The transformed series Z_n is plotted in the leftmost graph of Fig. 2.3.

It follows from our time-series analysis that the following ARMA(2,1) model is a good fit for Z_n:

$$Z_n = \mu + H_n, \quad H_n = \epsilon_n + \phi_1 H_{n-1} + \phi_2 H_{n-2} + \theta_1 \epsilon_{n-1} ,$$

where $\mu = 0.62091$, $\phi_1 = 1.23131$, $\phi_2 = -0.24350$, $\theta_1 = 0.59744$, and $\{\epsilon_n\}$ is a sequence of i.i.d. normal r.v.s with mean 0 and variance 0.04427. In addition, a simpler AR(1) model as follows is also found to provide a reasonably good fit for Z_n:

$$Z_n = \mu + H_n, \quad H_n = \epsilon_n + \phi_1 H_{n-1} ,$$

where $\mu = 0.62313$, $\phi_1 = 0.88332$, and ϵ_n has mean 0 and variance 0.12545. We generated a sample trace from the seasonal model by first generating a sample of the ARMA series $\{H_n\}$, and then calculating $Z_n = \mu + H_n$. From this we then obtain Y_n as

$$Y_n = Z_n + 0.9Y_{n-288} ;$$

and set $X_n = e^{Y_n} - 3$, which we call an *eARIMA*, or *logARIMA*, process. The resulting traffic is plotted in the rightmost graph of Fig. 2.3. Observe that the generated traffic looks very similar to the traffic from the Tokyo site in Fig. 2.1.

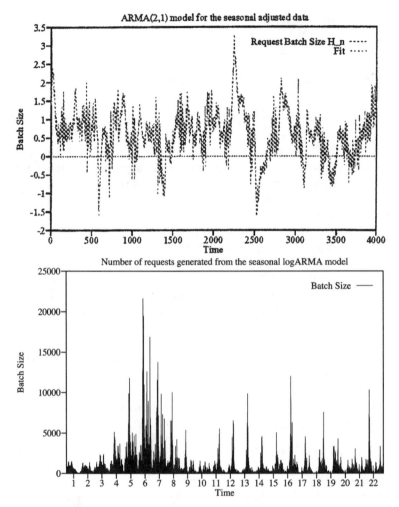

FIGURE 2.3
Time-series analysis of the transformed traffic from Tokyo and the gener-ated seasonal logARMA process.

2.4   Web Server Performance

Here we model the Web server of interest as a $G/G/1$ queue that takes as input the sequence $\{X_n\}$, which follows the traffic models developed in Section 2.3. When considering the waiting-time process, we focus on an individual SP2 node as a G/G/1 queue based on our statistical analysis showing that the set of

ND routers has the effect of smoothing and equalizing the statistical properties of the arrival processes for each individual node. With respect to the workload process, however, the G/G/1 queue equally models the entire Web server system.

Suppose every period the server depletes c units of requests, where c is a deterministic constant. For the queue to be stable, we assume $c > \mathsf{E}(X)$. Let W_n denote the amount of work (i.e., the number of requests) in the system at time n (i.e., in the nth period). Then, W_n follows the well-known Lindley recursion:

$$W_n = [W_{n-1} + X_n - c]^+ . \tag{2.8}$$

Since $c > \mathsf{E}(X)$, we know that, as $n \to \infty$, W_n will converge (weakly) to a finite r.v., denoted by W_∞.

Consider first light-tailed input. Iterating on the Lindley recursion in (2.8) and making use of the stationarity of $\{X_n\}$, we know that W_n is equal in distribution to the following:

$$\max \{0,\, X_1 - c,\, X_1 + X_2 - 2c,\, \ldots,\, X_1 + X_2 + \cdots + X_n - nc\} .$$

Making use of the traffic model in the previous section, we have

$$S_n := \sum_{i=1}^{n} (X_i - c) = n(\mu - c) + \frac{1}{1 - \phi_1}[(1 - \phi_1)\epsilon_n + (1 - \phi_1^2)\epsilon_{n-1}$$

$$+ \cdots + \phi_1(1 - \phi_1^n)\epsilon_0 + \phi_1^2(1 - \phi_1^n)\epsilon_{-1} + \cdots] .$$

Hence, S_n is a normal r.v. with mean $m_n = n(\mu - c)$ and variance (with algebra)

$$\sigma_n^2 = \frac{1 + \phi_1}{1 - \phi_1}\sigma_y^2 \left\{ n - \frac{2\phi_1(1 - \phi_1^n)}{1 - \phi_1^2} \right\} .$$

Following the large deviation theory for the steady-state tail probabilities in a single-server queue [4], we know that as $W_n \to W_\infty$ w.p.1, we have

$$x^{-1} \log \mathsf{P}(W_\infty > x) \longrightarrow -\theta^* \tag{2.9}$$

as $x \to \infty$, with

$$\theta^* = \frac{2(c - \mu)(1 - \phi_1)}{\sigma_y^2(1 + \phi_1)} . \tag{2.10}$$

That is, the tail probability of the workload process decreases (as x increases) exponentially fast with rate θ^*. Note that ϕ_1 is the autocorrelation of lag 1 for the input process. Hence, the higher the correlation of the input process, the slower the decay rate of the tail probability of the workload process. This is very much in line with our intuition.

Next, we consider heavy-tailed input. In this case, the generating function for X does not exist. Hence, the large deviations result above no longer applies.

To start with, we consider the case of a renewal input, with the same (heavy-tailed) marginals. Specifically, let $\{X'_n\}$ denote an i.i.d. sequence, with the same marginal distribution as $\{X_n\}$, i.e.,

$$X'_n \overset{d}{=} X_n \overset{d}{=} X = e^{\mu + \sigma Z} ,$$

for all n. Let W'_n and W'_∞, respectively, denote the corresponding workloads (i.e., via the Lindley recursion) at time n and in the limit (steady state). Then, from standard queuing theory [1, 3, 6], we have the following tail distribution for W'_∞:

$$P(W'_\infty \geq x) = [c - E(X)]^{-1} \int_x^\infty \bar{F}(y + c) dy .$$

Note that $\bar{F}(y + c) = P(X_n - c \geq x)$ is the tail distribution of the displacement, $X_n - c$, in the random walk associated with $\{W_n\}$. With a change of variable, $y \leftarrow y + c$, we can rewrite the above tail distribution as

$$P(W'_\infty \geq x - c) = \frac{E(X)}{c - E(X)} \bar{F}_0(x) , \tag{2.11}$$

where

$$\bar{F}_0(x) := \frac{\int_x^\infty \bar{F}(y) dy}{E(X)}$$

is a familiar object in renewal theory: the stationary excess-life distribution associated with $F(x)$. In the literature on heavy-tailed distributions (e.g., [7]), it also has a prominent status, and its numerator $\int_x^\infty \bar{F}(y) dy$ is usually referred to as the "integrated tail." For instance, the result in (2.11) simply says that the tail behavior of the delay in a single-server queue with *renewal* input is essentially the same (up to a multiplicative constant) as the *integrated* tail behavior of the input distribution.

Making use of the properties of the log-normal distribution, in particular (2.2), we can derive

$$\bar{F}_0(x) = \frac{\sigma \phi(z_x - \sigma)}{z_x(z_x - \sigma)} . \tag{2.12}$$

Substituting the above into (2.11), we obtain

$$P(W'_\infty \geq x - c) \sim \frac{\rho}{1 - \rho} \cdot \frac{\sigma \phi(z_x - \sigma)}{z_x(z_x - \sigma)} , \tag{2.13}$$

where $\rho := E(X)/c$ is the traffic intensity. Furthermore,

$$-\log P(W'_\infty \geq x - c) \sim (z_x - \sigma)^2/2 + \log z_x + \log(z_x - \sigma) . \tag{2.14}$$

Comparing the above with (2.3), we obtain

$$\frac{-\log P(W'_\infty \geq x - c)}{-\log P(X' \geq x)} \sim O(1) . \tag{2.15}$$

On the other hand, from (2.8), we have

$$P(W_n \geq x - c) \geq P(X_n \geq x) \, ;$$

and hence,

$$P(W_\infty \geq x - c) \geq P(X \geq x) = \bar{F}(x) \, , \qquad (2.16)$$

or, equivalently,

$$- \log P(W_\infty \geq x - c) \leq - \log \bar{F}(x) \, . \qquad (2.17)$$

In a special case considered in [2], where the input process is a Markov modulated Poisson process, it is shown that the relation in (2.13) also holds for W. Specifically,

$$P(W_\infty \geq x - c) \sim C \cdot \bar{F}_0(x) \, , \qquad (2.18)$$

where the constant multiplier C, which depends on the Markov chain that modulates the arrival rate, will of course be different in value from the constant in (2.13), $\rho/(1 - \rho)$. In other words, when the marginals are heavy-tailed, the dependence structure of the input process does not have much impact on the tail distribution of the delay; the tail behavior is essentially the same, up to a multiplicative constant, as the tail behavior in the case of renewal inputs.

Therefore, in view of the above analysis, it appears that in our case, we can reasonably expect the relation in (2.18) to hold as well.

In summary, we have established that for both light-tailed and heavy-tailed input traffic, the tail behavior of the delay distribution is qualitatively the same as the tail behavior of the input. The parameters involved are, of course, different. For light-tailed input, the delay distribution has an exponential tail, with the decay rate following (2.10). For heavy-tailed input, with the batch size marginals following a lognormal distribution, it appears that there is enough evidence for us to expect the tail of the delay distribution to also follow a lognormal distribution, which is essentially the integrated tail of the input distribution; refer to (2.13), (2.14), and (2.18).

To further support this result, we simulated the above G/G/1 queue under the heavy-tailed input process from Section 2.3 and obtained the tail of the delay distribution. Our results are shown in Fig. 2.4, where we plot the negative log of the tail of the delay distribution as a function of $\log x$. We first observe that the shapes of the tails of the delay distributions in Fig. 2.4 are indeed quadratic, i.e., they follow lognormal distributions and thus are qualitatively the same as the tail behavior of the input processes, which is consistent with the corresponding result established above by our analysis.

We also observe from the results in Fig. 2.4 that the delay distribution is always worse when the arrival patterns are positively correlated (i.e., $0 < \phi_1 < 1$) than when the arrival patterns contain no correlations (i.e., $\phi_1 = 0$). In fact, we see in Fig. 2.4 that the delay improves as the positive correlation decreases from $\phi_1 = 0.9$ toward $\phi_1 = 0$. Interestingly, we further observe that this

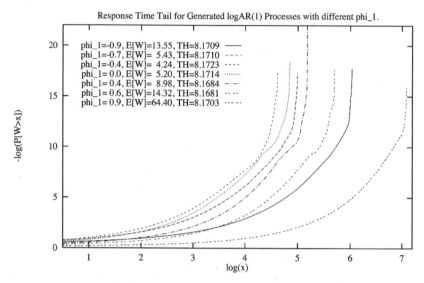

FIGURE 2.4
Tail distribution of the response time for the logARMA input.

improvement in the delay distribution continues as ϕ_1 decreases from 0 to -0.4 beyond which the delay distribution continues to worsen as ϕ_1 decreases from -0.4 to -0.9. This is due to the convexity of the exponential function in the logARIMA process.

References

[1] Asmussen, S., Rare Events in the Presence of Heavy Tails. *Stochastic Networks: Stability and Rare Events,* P. Glasserman, K. Sigman, and D.D. Yao (eds.), Springer-Verlag, New York, 197–214, 1996.

[2] Asmussen, S., Henriksen, L.F., and Klüppelberg, C., Large Claims Approximations for Risk Processes in a Markovian Environment. *Stoch. Proc. Appl.,* **54**, 29–43, 1994.

[3] Embrechts, P. and Veraverbeke, N., Estimates for the Probability of Ruin with Special Emphasis on the Possibility of Large Claims, *Insurance: Mathematics and Economics,* **1**, 55–72, 1982.

[4] Glynn, P.W. and Whitt, W., Logarithmic Asymptotics for Steady-State Tail Probabilities in A Single-Server Queue. *Studies in Applied Probability,* J. Galambos and J. Gani (eds.), *J. Appl. Prob.,* **31A**, 131–156, 1994.

[5] Iyengar, A.K., Squillante, M.S., and Zhang, L., Analysis and Characterization of Large-Scale Web Server Access Patterns and Performance. To appear, *World Wide Web,* Baltzer, 1999.

[6] Jelenković, P. and Lazar, A.A., A Network Multiplexer with Multiple Time Scale and Subexponential Arrivals. *Stochastic Networks: Stability and Rare Events,* P. Glasserman, K. Sigman, and D.D. Yao (eds.), Springer-Verlag, New York, 215–235, 1996.

[7] Klüppelberg, C., Subexponential Distributions and Integrated Tails. *J. Appl. Prob.,* **25**, 132–141, 1988.

[8] Leland, W.E., Taqqu, M.S., Willinger, W., and Wilson, D.V., On the Self-Similar Nature of Ethernet Traffic (Extended Version). *IEEE/ACM Trans. on Networking,* **2(1)**, 1–15, 1994.

[9] Shaked, M. and Shanthikumar, J.G., *Stochastic Orders and Their Applications.* Academic Press, New York, 1994.

[10] Willinger, W., Taqqu, M.S., Sherman, R., and Wilson, D.V., Self-Similarity through Hight-Variability: Statistical Analysis of Ethernet LAN Traffic at the Source Level. *IEEE/ACM Trans. on Networking,* **5(1)**, 71–86, 1997.

Chapter 3

A Generalization of a TCP Model: Multiple Source-Destination Case with Arbitrary LAN as the Access Network

Oleg Gusak and Tuğrul Dayar

Bilkent University

Abstract   This paper introduces an analytical model of an access scheme for Wide Area Network resources. The model is based on the TCP-modified Engset model of Heyman, Lakshman, and Neidhardt. The proposed model employs a LAN with arbitrary topology as the access network and is able to take into consideration files of arbitrary size. Through simulations, we show that our model is applicable for the multiple source case where each source corresponds to a different Web server at a possibly different location on the Internet. The average reception time of a file computed analytically is acceptably close to the simulation results.

Keywords: TCP-Reno, TCP-modified Engset model, LAN-WAN access scheme.

3.1   Introduction

Nowadays the Transmission Control Protocol (TCP) is omnipresent. TCP indeed is Internet itself and it makes the network transparent for any application using this protocol as a transport service. A complete TCP utilization requires appropriate models that can describe the behavior of TCP under certain conditions and network patterns. Various studies have been done in this

direction. The new research direction in this area relates to new TCP modifications [4, 8, 9, 10] such as TCP Reno and TCP Sack that perform dynamic flow
control.

The majority of previous studies consider the TCP model for a single source-
destination pair, where the source is a particular server or a station like a router,
which accumulates traffic from different sources. Detailed studies of TCP
under the single source-destination assumption have allowed researchers to
develop more complex and realistic models of networks. Our work is based on
one such model proposed in [6] by Heyman, Lakshman, and Neidhardt. That
model considers an access network to Internet resources, such as Web servers,
for users working from terminals through Integrated Services Digital Network
(ISDN) lines. The model gives an analytical description for the process of Web
page retrieval from a remote server residing on a Wide Area Network (WAN)
and connected to local terminals by a backbone link. Each terminal is described
by average idle (thinking) time and average file size requested from the remote
Web server. Such a process in which each station alternates between working
and thinking states is called an alternating renewal process. The steady-state
probability of finding a station in working state depends only on the average
idle time and the average file size requested by that station [6, p.26]. Hence,
it is possible to use a memoryless distribution for both idle time and busy time
which in turn allows modeling of terminal behavior as an ordinary birth-death
process.

The contribution of our paper is the following. First, we extend the TCP-
Modified Engset model [6, pp. 30–31] to the general case of an access network,
which is a Local Area Network (LAN) with arbitrary topology. The performance measure of interest is the average reception time of a file for a station
residing on the LAN. Second, we introduce the description of a slow start phase
in the TCP-Modified Engset model, which allows us to take into consideration
small file sizes. As recent studies show [2, 3], the average file size of Web
traffic tends to be small. However, the model in [6] considers the average file
size requested by a station to be sufficiently large so that the effect of the slow
start phase of the TCP protocol can be neglected. In this connection, the simulations in [6] use an average file size of 200 Kbytes. In our model, we do not
have any constraints on file size. Finally, through simulations we show that the
improved model can be applied to the multiple source (i.e., Web servers) case
which implies variable Internet delay for packets sharing the same backbone
link.

The paper is organized as follows. In Section 3.2, we discuss a general model
describing TCP behavior over a bottleneck channel. In Section 3.3, we present
an improved model for the LAN-WAN access scheme and the particular case
where the access network is Ethernet. We verify the analytical model through
simulations in Section 3.4 and conclude in Section 3.5.

3.2 TCP Behavior: Contest for the Pipe

We consider a model for TCP Reno, which is currently one of the most popular protocols on Internet. From this point on, we refer to TCP Reno as TCP. There are two operating phases of TCP called slow start and congestion avoidance (see [12, pp. 285–286, 310–312] for details). When the sender starts transmitting at the beginning of a connection, it is in the slow start phase, and current window size, W_c, is equal to 1. Upon receiving each successful ACK, the sender increments W_c by 1. When W_c becomes large enough to create congestion, packet losses occur. When the sender detects packet losses by duplicate ACKs, it halves W_c, records the value in W_t, and enters the congestion avoidance phase. When losses are detected by timeouts, TCP halves W_c, records the value in W_t, sets W_c to 1, and enters the slow start phase (if it is already not in it). During the congestion avoidance phase, W_c is incremented by 1 each time W_c packets are successfully acknowledged. When TCP is in the slow start phase and W_c reaches W_t, it enters the congestion avoidance phase.

Let us consider the behavior of TCP for an arbitrary source and destination pair connected by a link where the source is persistent. The link is characterized by the transmission speed S, the round trip delay D (which includes channel transmission and propagation delays for a packet and an acknowledgement), and the transmitter buffer capacity B. There are two communication patterns that are possible under the given assumptions. The first one takes place when the transmission speed of the source is less than or equal to the link bandwidth. In this case, congestion in the buffer cannot occur, and data is transferred at a rate equal to the source transmission speed. This is the trivial case and it is not interesting for modeling purposes. The second one happens when the link bandwidth is less than the transmission speed of the source and the link is the bottleneck. In this case, the TCP algorithm increments W_c, which after some time causes congestion in the buffer (i.e., some packets will be dropped). The value of W_c at the point of congestion is called the congestion window size and is denoted by $W_{highest}$. Hence, for the case of always dropping a single packet upon congestion, W_c oscillates between $W_{highest}$ and $W_{highest}/2$. When packets are lost and consequently W_c is reduced, the transmission proceeds with a rate less than the link bandwidth. The goal is to estimate this reduction in transmission rate.

A detailed description of the TCP model construction can be found in [4, 6]. Therein, the discussion is based on estimating the channel capacity, which is the number of packets that can reside in the channel between source and destination. Right before congestion occurs, the channel contains $D/P_t + B$ packets [6, p. 28], where $P_t = P_{tcp}/S$ is the time required to transmit one TCP packet of size P_{tcp} by the bottleneck link since the buffer is full before congestion.

Assuming that loss detection happens only through duplicate ACKs, after

TCP discovers a packet loss, it halves W_c and enters the congestion avoidance phase. During this phase, W_c increases by 1 starting from $W_{highest}/2$ up to $W_{highest}$ each D time units. We remark that in the last part of this growing phase when the population of packets in the channel has reached its maximum value, packets start accumulating in the buffer, and W_c will be increasing by 1 in larger time intervals than D due to the queuing of packets in the buffer. When buffer size is small, we can neglect the nonlinearity of the growth during this last phase and assume that W_c grows linearly. When the channel is full, the source transmits with a rate equal to the link bandwidth. Due to the linear growth assumption of W_c, we can estimate the TCP degradation factor using the normalized lowest and largest window sizes of the connection. Normalization has to be done with respect to the link capacity excluding the buffer size, since packets accumulated in the buffer do not contribute to a service rate increase. In other words, packets are served with maximum possible speed equal to S when the channel is full, and the situation does not improve with additional packets in the buffer. The maximum number of packets that can fit to the channel is therefore $W_{highest} = D/P_t + B$. The lowest packet population size of the connection is the highest packet population size divided by 2 for each packet discarded due to buffer overflow. In other words, $W_{lowest} = 2^{-l} \cdot (D/P_t + B)$, where l is the number of packets lost in a congestion. In [6], various cases for different queuing service disciplines and lower layer protocols such as ATM are considered. There it is shown that when each TCP packet is divided into more than one lower layer cell depending on the service policy of the router, it is possible to lose up to 3 TCP packets in a congestion [6, p. 29]. For the sake of simplicity, in our model we consider the case in which TCP packets are not segmented, that is, each TCP packet can fit into one cell of the lower layer protocol. Under this assumption, only one packet is lost per congestion at the router's buffer.

As stated before, normalization has to be done with respect to channel capacity excluding buffer size, i.e., D/P_t. Hence, the corresponding normalized values of $W_{highest}$ and W_{lowest} can be written as [6, p. 29] $w_{highest} = W_{highest}/(D/P_t) = 1 + b$, $w_{lowest} = W_{lowest}/(D/P_t) = 2^{-l} \cdot (1 + b)$, where $b = B/(D/P_t)$ is the normalized buffer size.

The TCP degradation factor, ρ, is the average of the normalized packet population over the increase of W_c from $W_{highest}$ to W_{lowest} [6, p. 30]:

$$\rho = 1 - \frac{((1 - w_{lowest})^+)^2}{2 \cdot (w_{highest} - w_{lowest})}. \tag{3.1}$$

Note that when $w_{highest}$ exceeds 1, ρ remains equal to 1. The positive operator enables handling the case where W_c is always greater or equal to D/P_t (i.e., channel is always full).

3.3 Multiple Source-Destination Model

Let us consider a typical model of access for local users to Internet resources. Local users are sharing a common LAN (e.g., campus network) and this network is connected by a dedicated link to the Internet. Usually the bandwidth of the dedicated link is smaller than the transmission rate of the LAN as well as the throughput of the Internet server. In this case, the Internet link can be considered as a bottleneck along the way from a local user to an Internet resource. The communication pattern for such access scheme is the following. Local users request files from servers residing on the Internet, which may have different network distances to the Internet router (router through which the link is connected to the Internet) and hence different Internet delays. We assume that this delay is a random variable with mean D_I. We also assume that the number of bytes (e.g., Web page size) requested by each station has the same distribution with mean f_s for all stations. Let t_f denote the average reception time of a file for a station. Upon retrieval of a file, a station enters the idle phase (i.e., thinking state) which has mean t. Such a process in which local stations oscillate between idle and working states is called an alternating renewal process [11, p. 66]. Previous studies of such a process show that the long run probability of a station being in the working state does not depend on the distribution functions of these on and off periods but it depends only on their means: $P(\text{station is active}) = t_f/(t_f+t)$ [11, p. 67]. This fact allows us to use exponential distribution for the on and off periods. Hence, one can model the access network behavior as an ordinary birth-death process with, respectively, the following birth and death rates:

$$\begin{aligned}
\beta_j &= (n - j) \cdot \lambda, \ j = 0, 1, \ldots, n - 1, \\
\delta_j &= j \cdot \mu, \qquad\quad j = 1, 2, \ldots, n \, ,
\end{aligned} \tag{3.2}$$

where $\lambda = 1/t$ is the rate of exit from the idle state, n is the number of stations on the LAN, and $\mu = 1/t_f$ is the rate of file retrieval from the server.

Under the given assumptions, when the Internet link is the bottleneck, each station competes to acquire the resource, which in turn leads to congestion. So, the situation in the channel will be the same as that of the single source communication scheme we considered before. That is, channel efficiency will be reduced by the factor ρ. We remark that for the multiple station case, $W_{highest}$ and W_{lowest} are, respectively, the highest and lowest total number of packets that can reside on the channel for all sessions. Let us also note that in order to be able to determine the measure ρ for the multiple source-destination model, the round trip delay of section 2 has to be extended by the delays packets experience in the LAN (D_L) and the Internet (D_I). In this case, the file transfer (i.e., death) rate can be expressed as $\delta_j = \rho \cdot S/f_s, \ j = 1, 2, \ldots, n$. Such a system has the trivial product-form solution [7, p. 92]

$$P_j = P_0 \cdot \frac{\beta_0 \cdot \beta_1 \cdot \ldots \cdot \beta_{j-1}}{\delta_1 \cdot \delta_2 \cdot \ldots \cdot \delta_j}, \quad j = 1, 2, \ldots, n, \tag{3.3}$$

where P_j is the probability of having j active stations and P_0 is the normalization coefficient. Now, let $r_j = \rho \cdot S/(f_s \cdot j)$ denote the file transmission rate of each active station when there are j active stations. Then the average file transmission rate can be expressed as $r = \sum_{j=1}^{n} P_j \cdot r_j$.

In the next subsection we extend our model to the case of small file size, and in the second subsection we consider the particular case of Ethernet as the access network.

3.3.1   Adaptation to Small File Size

In the previous discussion, we did not take into consideration the slow start phase of TCP. We assumed that W_c always oscillates between W_{lowest} and $W_{highest}$. When $W_{highest}$ is large enough, a connection has to spend a relatively significant amount of time to reach this threshold. Moreover, if we consider small file sizes, the time spent to reach $W_{highest}$ will be significant compared to the total time required for file transmission.

For the case of small files, we make the following observation. The file size can be so small that W_c does not exceed $W_{highest}$. That is, TCP does not enter the congestion avoidance phase and the results obtained in Section 3.2 and earlier in this section are not applicable. Before we start discussing this extreme case, let us first consider the process of window growth in the slow start phase.

By definition (see TCP description in Section 3.2), W_c of a single connection starts growing from 1. After D time units (recall that D for the multiple source-destination case is extended by delays D_I and D_L), the sender is acknowledged upon the successful transmission of the first packet. In response to this event, the sender increments W_c by 1 and emits two new packets. The first new packet is transmitted because the very first packet has already been acknowledged. The second new packet is transmitted because $W_c = 2$ and there is only one unacknowledged packet. So, it is easy to see that each D time units, the number of packets in the channel is doubled. Based on this observation, we can determine the duration of the slow start phase for the multiple station case as follows. By using the total population of packets residing in the channel and the number of active stations, we can find the largest window size for each active connection. Then the duration of the slow start phase is given by

$$D_{sl\_st} = D \cdot \left(\log_2 \left(W^j_{highest} \right) + 1 \right), \tag{3.4}$$

where $W^j_{highest} = W_{highest}/j$ is the largest window size per active connection when there are j active stations.

To determine the average retrieval time of a file taking into account the slow start phase, we have to divide the total number of packets required to transmit a file of average size f_s into two groups: packets transmitted during the slow start phase,

$$N_s = 2 \cdot W_{highest}^j - 1 , \qquad (3.5)$$

and packets transmitted during the following congestion avoidance phase(s),

$$N_{ca} = f_s / P_{tcp} - N_s . \qquad (3.6)$$

Thus, the total average retrieval time of a file for an active connection when j stations are active can be expressed as $t_f^j = N_{ca} \cdot P_{tcp} / (\rho \cdot S / j) + D_{sl\_st}$.

Thereafter, the modified death rates for the system are given by the following:

$$\begin{aligned}
1/\delta_j &= t_f^j / j \\
&= \left[\frac{(f_s / P_{tcp} - N_s) \cdot P_{tcp}}{\rho \cdot S / j} + D \cdot \log_2(W_{highest}/j + 1) \right] / j . \quad (3.7)
\end{aligned}$$

Let us now return to the extreme case in which the file size is smaller than the number of packets transmitted during the slow start phase. In this case, since $N_s = f_s / P_{tcp}$, the largest window size is obtained from Eq. (3.6) as $W_{sfs} = (f_s / P_{tcp} + 1)/2$. Hence, the average retrieval time of a file using Eq. (3.4) is given by $t_{sfs}^j = D \cdot (\log_2(W_{sfs}) + 1)$.

Finally, the death rates for the system in general can be written as

$$\delta_j = \begin{cases} j/t_{sfs}^j, & [2 \cdot (W_{highest}/j) - 1] \cdot P_{tcp} \geq f_s \\ j/t_f^j, & \text{otherwise} \end{cases} . \qquad (3.8)$$

3.3.2 A Case Study: Ethernet as the LAN

We consider an application of our model where the access network is Ethernet. The communication scenario remains the same. We assume that the LAN stations do not communicate with each other except for the communication between each station and the router, which is also a station on the LAN. Stations request files of average size f_s from a remote server on the Internet. Between successive requests, each station spends an arbitrary amount of time with mean t in the idle state. In order to adapt our model to this communication scheme, we have to estimate the round trip delay experienced by a packet of a connection. The LAN delay D_L is equal to $D_{Ethernet}$, which is the average delay packets experience on the Ethernet. For $D_{Ethernet}$, we use the result derived in [5, p. 230, Eq. (8.30)].

All input parameters for $D_{Ethernet}$ (such as Ethernet transmission speed, propagation delay, etc.) are well defined. The only parameter we have to determine is the input rate imposed on the LAN. According to our model, D is calculated for the case when packet population reaches it highest value, $W_{highest}$. In this case, the channel is full and packets are transmitted with the maximum possible speed (i.e., the channel rate S). Based on this observation and the fact that each packet is acknowledged by the receiver, the total input rate to the LAN in packets per unit time can be expressed as $\gamma = 2 \cdot S/P_{tcp}$.

In the following section, we present simulation and analytical results for the multiple source-destination LAN-WAN access scheme with Ethernet as the LAN.

3.4   Simulations and Analytical Results

In our simulations, we consider Ethernet (10 Mbps, 300 m cable segment) as the LAN. Internet link transmission speed is 512 Kbps, and end-to-end propagation delay is 0.1 sec. Internet delay with mean D_I modeled as Gamma distribution (see [1, p. 290] for a justification) with shape parameter b taking the values 1, 2, or 4, and D_I taking the values 0.1 or 0.2 sec. Note that when $b = 1$ we have the exponential distribution. We also run simulations for the single source case, i.e., when Internet delay is constant. Capacity of the Internet link router buffer is 20 packets. TCP packets have a fixed size of 512 bytes. For a particular simulation, 1,000 events (i.e., file retrievals) per station are generated. Confidence intervals of 90% with 9 degrees of freedom are computed for the average retrieval time of a file in seconds. Analytical and simulation results with confidence intervals for the model in Section 3 are presented in Tables 3.1 and 3.2 for 20 stations, and in Table 3.3 for 30 stations on the LAN.

According to the analytical and simulation results, the average retrieval time of a file increases almost linearly with average file size. Analytical results for $D_I = 0.1$ sec are within 5% and for $D_I = 0.2$ sec are within 8% of simulation results. The difference between analytical and simulations results is also relatively larger for small average file sizes. Our explanation is the following. When the average file size is small, we are more likely to have a smaller average number of active stations, and a larger average number of files can be transmitted within the slow start phase. In this case, connections cannot fill the channel to create congestion; that is, there are no collisions and TCP never leaves the slow start phase. However, traffic is bursty since upon receiving each ACK, the sender increments the current window size by one and therefore emits two packets, doubling the number of packets in the channel each round trip delay. Therefore, packets are not distributed uniformly across the channel. See each table for increasing average file size. For instance, in Table 3.1 the const column for average file size of 20 kB has a value which is within 10% of the analytical result.

Table 3.1 $D_I = 0.1$, 20 Stations

f_s	analytical	const	$b=1$	$b=2$	$b=4$
20	4.718	4.267±0.025	4.307±0.013	4.290±0.025	4.277±0.026
60	17.628	16.721±0.075	16.706±0.067	16.756±0.077	16.761±0.088
100	30.671	29.144±0.163	29.322±0.120	29.347±0.119	29.424±0.149
140	43.724	41.633±0.116	41.956±0.116	41.949±0.164	41.887±0.190
180	56.781	54.095±0.166	54.837±0.252	54.733±0.091	54.428±0.193

Table 3.2 D_I=0.2, 20 Stations

f_s	analytical	const	$b=1$	$b=2$	$b=4$
20	5.157	4.378±0.024	4.480±0.014	4.456±0.022	4.442±0.020
60	18.386	16.727±0.075	16.801±0.069	16.807±0.109	16.822±0.100
100	31.81	29.151±0.164	29.518±0.126	29.500±0.127	29.547±0.151
140	45.253	41.635±0.115	42.328±0.125	42.290±0.174	42.162±0.115
180	58.701	54.099±0.167	55.374±0.251	55.142±0.232	54.777±0.380

Table 3.3 D_I=0.1, 30 stations

f_s	analytical	const	$b=1$	$b=2$	$b=4$
20	7.737	7.262±0.024	7.254±0.025	7.244±0.037	7.240±0.030
60	27.29	25.950±0.126	25.951±0.088	26.003±0.081	26.054±0.097
100	46.876	44.617±0.123	44.814±0.134	44.756±0.097	44.658±0.104
140	66.465	63.642±0.136	63.571±0.209	63.482±0.146	63.297±0.235
180	86.055	82.311±0.131	82.448±0.241	82.214±0.405	82.366±0.144

3.5 Conclusion

In this paper, we have extended the TCP-Modified Engset model to the general case of an access network for local users that are on a LAN with arbitrary topology and delay function. We have also introduced modifications that enable us to consider files of arbitrary size. We have shown through simulations that our model can be applied to the multiple source case. The simulation results show that the analytical model provides a good estimation for the average retrieval time of a file in this LAN-WAN access scheme. The error in the analytical model is within 8% of the simulation results for the chosen parameters.

References

[1] J.-C. Bolot, End-to-End Packet Delay and Loss Behavior in the Internet, *Proc. of SIGCOMM '93,* San Francisco, pp. 289–298, August 1993.

[2] H.-W. Braun, K.C. Claffy, Web Traffic Characterization: An Assessment of the Impact of Caching Documents from NCSA's Web Server, *Computer Networks and ISDN Systems,* Vol. 28, pp. 37–51, 1995.

[3] M.E. Crovella, A. Bestravos, Self-Similarity in World Wide Web Traffic: Evidence and Possible Causes, *IEEE/ACM Trans. on Networking,* Vol. 5, pp. 835–846, 1997.

[4] J.-L. Dorel, M. Gerla, Performance Analysis of TCP-Reno and TCP-Sack: The Single Source Case, Computer Science Department, University of California, Technical Report 97003, 1997.

[5] J.F. Hayes, *Modeling and Analysis of Computer Communication Networks,* Plenum, New York, 1984.

[6] D.P. Heyman, T.V. Lakshman, A.L. Neidhardt, A New Method for Analysing Feedback-Based Protocols with Applications to Engineering Web Traffic Over the Internet, *Performance Evaluation Review,* pp. 24–38, 1997.

[7] L. Kleinrock, *Queuing Systems,* Vol. 1, The Theory, Wiley, New York, 1975.

[8] T.V. Lakshman, U. Madhow, The Performance of TCP/IP for Networks with High Bandwidth-Delay Products and Random Loss, *IFIP Trans. C-26, High Performance Networking V,* North-Holland, pp. 135–150, 1994.

[9] T.J. Ott, J.H. Kemperman, M. Mathis, *The Stationary Behavior of Ideal TCP Congestion Avoidance,* ftp://ftp.bellcore.com/pub/tjo/TCPwindow.ps, 1996.

[10] J. Padhye, V. Firoiu, D. Towsley, J. Kurose, Modeling TCP Throughput: A Simple Model and Its Empirical Validation, Department of Computer Science, University of Massachusetts, CMPSCI Technical Report TR 98-008, 1998.

[11] S.M. Ross, *Stochastic Processes,* Wiley, New York, 1983.

[12] W.R. Stevens, *TCP/IP Illustrated,* Vol. 1. The Protocols, Addison Wesley, 1994.

Vitae

Oleg Gusak received his B.S. degree in computer engineering and his M.S. degree in computer science from Kharkov State Technical University of Radio Electronics, Kharkov, Ukraine, in 1994 and 1995, respectively.

In 1995–1997 he was working as a software engineer of Scientific-Research Institute of Automated Control Systems of Gas Pipelines (Concern UkrGasProm).

Since September 1997, he has been a Ph.D. student at the Department of Computer Engineering and Information Science of Bilkent University, Ankara, Turkey. His present research interests include performance modeling and analysis, mathematical models of Markov chains, and computer and communication networks.

Tugrul Dayar received his B.S. degree in computer engineering from Middle East Technical University, Ankara, Turkey, in 1989, and his M.S. and Ph.D. degrees in computer science from North Carolina State University, Raleigh, NC, USA, in 1991 and 1994, respectively.

Since 1995, he has been an Assistant Professor in the Department of Computer Engineering and Information Science of Bilkent University, Ankara, Turkey. His research interests are in the areas of performance modeling and analysis, numerical linear algebra for stochastic matrices, scientific computing, and computer networks.

Dr. Dayar is a member of Upsilon Pi Epsilon, IEEE Computer Society, ACM Special Interest Group on Measurement and Evaluation, SIAM Activity Group on Linear Algebra, and AMS.

Part II

Advances in ATM Networks

Chapter 4

A Virtual Path Routing Algorithm for ATM Networks Based on the Equivalent Bandwidth Concept [1]

Kaan Bür and Cem Ersoy

Boǧaziçi University

Abstract

The coexistence of a wide range of services with different quality of service (QoS) requirements in today's networks makes the efficient use of resources a major issue. It is desirable to improve network efficiency by adaptively assigning resources to services that have different bandwidth demands. Implementing Broadband Integrated Services Digital Networks (B-ISDN) therefore requires a network control scheme that can absorb unexpected traffic fluctuations. Asynchronous Transfer Mode (ATM) technology provides this flexibility by virtualizing network resources through the use of the virtual path (VP) concept. The traffic demand of new services in a B-ISDN environment may be highly bursty and difficult to predict. The implementation of the equivalent bandwidth concept provides an efficient method to estimate capacity requirements. In this study, a method for designing a VP-based ATM network is proposed. The developed heuristic design algorithm uses the equivalent bandwidth concept to compute the capacity needs of the connection requests and guarantee the QoS requirements. The observations on the algorithm performance show that the developed method is able to facilitate an efficient use of network resources through the introduction of VPs.

Keywords: asynchronous transfer mode (ATM), equivalent bandwidth, link utilization, virtual circuit (VC), virtual path (VP).

---

[1]This work is partially funded by State Planning Organization (DPT) under the grant number 96K120490.

4.1 Introduction

A substantial amount of research effort in communication network engineering has been spent on service integration during recent years. Various new information services with different quality of service (QoS) requirements have to be handled in the most efficient and economical way possible while traditional ones are kept maintained [1]. Broadband Integrated Services Digital Networks (B-ISDN) support a wide range of applications with different QoS requirements in a flexible and cost-effective manner. The goal of B-ISDN is to define a user interface and network that meets varied requirements of these applications. The transfer mode chosen as the basis of B-ISDN is called the Asynchronous Transfer Mode (ATM). ATM is a high-bandwidth, low-delay, packet-like switching and multiplexing technique, which provides the required flexibility for supporting heterogeneous services in a B-ISDN environment [2].

Simplification of network architecture and node processing is the key to developing a cost-effective, flexible network. This will be possible by implementing the virtual path (VP) concept. The fundamental advantage of this concept is that it allows the grouping of individual connections, also known as virtual circuits (VC), sharing common paths through the network to be handled and switched together as a single unit. Network management actions can then be applied to a small number of groups of connections instead of a large number of individual connections, resulting in smaller total processing requirements, faster processing per VC, and in general, a significantly better use of network resources [3]. Transit nodes are free from the routing and bandwidth allocation procedures of call setup. Routing is done by selecting the most appropriate VP between the end nodes. Bandwidth allocation is carried out by comparing the bandwidth of the requested call to the unused bandwidth of the VP at the beginning node. VPs have guaranteed bandwidth along their paths.

The purpose of this study is to develop a method of VP routing and bandwidth allocation in ATM networks. The proposed method applies dynamic capacity control in order to meet QoS requirements such as limited delay and bounded cell loss probability. It also distributes the network traffic in such a way that: (a) the effect of link failures is kept as small as possible; (b) link saturations are rare; (c) the network robustness is increased. As a result, the method can facilitate an efficient use of the network resources. This study is organized as follows: Section 4.2 introduces the network model and the formulation of the problem. In Section 4.3, the VP routing algorithm is described. Section 4.4 presents computational experiments and comments on the algorithm performance. Finally, a summary, conclusions and subjects for further work are given in Section 4.5.

4.2 Problem Statement

The existence of VPs improves the network performance in terms of call setup, cell processing time, adaptability and administration. However, if the VP routing and capacity assignment issues are not handled effectively to optimize the network performance, these advantages are lost against the negative effects of VPs on capacity sharing, call blocking, processing load and throughput. Therefore, an efficient method has to be developed so that an optimal VP network design can be achieved. This study proposes a general design model for VP routing to exploit the benefits of the VP concept as much as possible without letting its disadvantages prohibit the network performance. The algorithm tries to find the optimal VP layout according to the selected cost function and QoS requirements.

The network topology is modeled by a directed graph $G = (V, E)$, where V is the set of nodes and E is the set of links. A VP is defined by a starting node and an ending node, a directed route between these nodes and a capacity assigned to this connection. Given the network topology, and the demand for VP capacity between specified pairs of nodes (VP terminators), one can choose VP routes connecting the terminators, such that the maximum link utilization is minimized. The load, or congestion, of a link is defined as the summed capacity of VPs traversing the link. The system of VPs is optimal if the maximum link utilization is the smallest possible. The motivation behind this objective is ATM realization in bandwidth restricted systems. A viable VP system depends on the value of the maximum link utilization that can be achieved, making the chosen objective a primary design consideration [1, 3, 4]. The homogeneous distribution of the link utilizations and dynamic VP bandwidth control absorb the effects of traffic imbalances in the network. This effectively improves throughput, flexibility and the robustness of the network against unexpected traffic conditions [5]. With increasing user access speeds, such as 45 or 155 Mbps, it does not take too many connections to saturate a link that works in the gigabit range. Even in the hypothetical case of practically unlimited bandwidth, it is important to distribute traffic in a way that reduces the maximum link utilization in order to increase network robustness. Clearly, the higher the maximum load on any specific link in the network, the more catastrophic may be the effect of the failure of a link carrying a potentially very large number of connections [3].

The proposed design model should provide the set of VPs with their routes, i.e., start, intermediate, and end nodes with allocated capacities. It is also the task of the model to determine the combination of VPs to be assigned in order to route the VCs. To prevent bandwidth fragmentation, more than one VP with the same endpoints is not allowed. VPs are assumed to have deterministic bandwidths that are not subject to statistical multiplexing with cells from different VPs. Statistical multiplexing between VCs within the same VP is allowed.

The cell loss probability is one of the requirements to be satisfied in the design of the VP layout. Conservation of the cell loss rate is one of the basic requirements for a good VP accommodation design [6]. In order to keep the cell loss probability below a given value, the equivalent capacity concept is applied. The cell loss probability is a critical QoS constraint. It is easily converted to capacity requirements and, under certain assumptions, provides a basis for satisfying call blocking constraints with a classical Erlang-B formula [7, 8].

For the delay time requirement, the number of VPs traversed by a VC is used as a constraint in the optimization problem. The rationale behind this limitation is that the VP hop count is related to the number of VP switching nodes on the route of a connection and represents the connection setup times (processing delay) for all VCs. To reduce complexity, VP topologies are composed entirely of direct VPs between node pairs or routes with the allowed maximum number of hops $h \leq 2$ [7, 8, 9, 10, 11].

Because of the statistical multiplexing of connections in the network, capacity reservation is based on some aggregate statistical measures matching the overall traffic demand rather than on physically dedicated bandwidth per connection. The equivalent bandwidth of a set of VCs multiplexed on a VP is defined as the amount of bandwidth required to achieve a desired QoS. In order to characterize the equivalent bandwidth or effective bit rate of VCs in terms of known parameters, the statistical characteristics of the VPs at cell level are used as an appropriate model [7, 8].

In order to characterize the effective bit rate of a connection, a two-state fluid-flow model is adopted. Based on this two-state fluid-flow model, idle and burst periods are defined to be the times during which the source is transmitting at zero bit rate or at its peak rate, respectively [12]. The peak rate of a connection $R_{peak,k}$ and distributions of idle and burst periods completely identify the traffic statistics of a connection. Assuming the parameters of a connection are stationary, its peak rate $R_{peak,k}$ and utilization ρ_k, i.e., fraction of time the source is active, completely identify other quantities of interest such as mean m_k and variance σ_k^2 of the bit rate. For exponentially distributed burst and idle periods, the source is furthermore completely characterized by only three parameters, namely $R_{peak,k}$, ρ_k and b_k, where b_k is the mean of the burst period. The equivalent capacity associated with a single connection in isolation is approximated to [13]:

$$c_k' = \frac{\alpha b_k(1-\rho_k)R_{peak,k}-x+\sqrt{(\alpha b_k(1-\rho_k)R_{peak,k}-x)^2+(4\alpha b_k\rho_k(1-\rho_k)R_{peak,k})}}{2\alpha b_k(1-\rho_k)} \;, \quad (4.1)$$

where $\alpha = \ln(1/\varepsilon)$ and ε is the maximum cell loss probability. Note that in the case of a continuous bit stream connection, $\rho_k = 1$ and $b_k = \infty$, and taking limits in Eq. 4.1 yields the expected result $c_k' = R_{peak,k}$. In the case of multiple superposed sources, the value of the equivalent capacity $C'(F)$ given by the flow approximation for n multiplexed connections is defined by [13]:

$$C'(F) = \sum_{k=1}^{n} c'_k , \tag{4.2}$$

where c'_k values are determined from Eq. 4.1.

The simplifying assumption in Eq. 4.1 amounts to ignoring the effects of statistical multiplexing. In particular, unless the equivalent capacities of individual connections are themselves close to their mean bit rates, their sum is typically an overestimate of their equivalent capacity. Another approximation is, therefore, needed to accurately determine the required bandwidth allocation for cases in which statistical multiplexing is significant. It is then reasonable to allocate enough bandwidth to make the probability of an overload condition equal to the desired buffer overflow probability. The value of $C'(S)$ can then be obtained from approximations for the inverse of the Gaussian distribution, which is given by [13]:

$$C'(S) \cong m + \alpha'\sigma , \tag{4.3}$$

with

$$\alpha' = \sqrt{-2\ln(\varepsilon) - \ln(2\pi)} , m = \sum_{k=1}^{n} m_k , \text{ and } \sigma^2 = \sum_{k=1}^{n} \sigma_k^2 , \tag{4.4}$$

where m is the mean aggregate bit rate, and σ is the standard deviation of the aggregate bit rate.

As both approximations overestimate the actual value of the equivalent capacity and are inaccurate for different ranges of connections characteristics, the equivalent capacity C' is taken to be the minimum of $C'(F)$ and $C'(S)$ [12, 13].

In summary, the problem can be formulated as follows.

Given:	G, the physical network topology with nodes, links and link capacities;
	C, the set of all VCs defined by R_{peak}, the traffic demand;
Minimize:	Maximum value of u_{ij}, the link utilization on any link l_{ij};
Subject to:	Cell loss probability $\leq \varepsilon$;
	Number of VPs traversed by a VC $\leq h$;
Design Variables:	P, the set of all VPs defined by their routes and allocated capacities;
	Route of each VC in terms of VPs.

4.3   Heuristic Design Algorithm

In order to solve the complex optimization problem described above in a reasonable amount of time, the design algorithm is based on heuristics. It is a search algorithm looking for the optimum solution in the domain of valid VP assignments. The algorithm consists of initialization and optimization phases. In the former, a starting point is found which is a feasible solution, i.e., a valid VP network that satisfies the constraints. In the latter, incremental changes are made in the VP network that achieve a lower value for the objective function and satisfy the constraints, until no more improvement can be found. The pseudo-code for the algorithm is given in Fig. 4.1. The design algorithm should be able to find a high quality solution, i.e., a VP network design that balances link sharing, blocking probabilities and processing cost in the best possible way.

Phase 1: Initialization
Compute equivalent bandwidths of all VCs;
Create VPs for node pairs connected by direct links;
Try to route all VCs over these VPs;
Phase 2: Optimization
Repeat
        Sort remaining VCs in descending order of bandwidth;
        For every VC in the list try to find the most idle alternate route;
        Sort the physical links in descending order of utilization;
        For every physical link in the list
            Make a list of VPs on that link;
            Repeat for every VP in the list
                Try to find a better alternate route;
            Until a VP is rerouted successfully or end of VP list;
            If no VPs are rerouted then make a list of VCs on the same link;
            Repeat for every VC in the list
                Try to find a better alternate route;
            Until a VC is rerouted successfully or end of VC list;
Until no improvement can be achieved on any link;

FIGURE 4.1

Pseudo-code for the Heuristic Design Algorithm (HDA).

In the initialization phase, a set of VPs, P, is initialized by creating a VP p_{ij} on every physical link l_{ij} of the network if there is sufficient physical link capacity to accommodate the traffic demand between the nodes i and j. Every p_{ij} is assigned automatically to the VC c_{ij} carrying the traffic t_{ij}, which requires a bandwidth c'_k determined by means of the equivalent bandwidth method for a single connection. The selection order of the VPs is irrelevant since there is no multiplexing of VCs on VPs or physical links yet. This initial VP layout where every physical link has a VP makes use of direct physical routes.

After this first step, the remaining VCs, i.e., the ones representing connection requests between nodes without a direct physical link from the source to the destination, are handled. For this purpose, the best combination of existing and new VPs, i.e., the idlest one in terms of link utilization, is sought after. At the end of the initialization phase, a feasible solution, i.e., a VP routing scheme in which all VCs are assigned to some combination of VPs without violating any of the constraints, should appear. If, however, some of the VCs are left unassigned, the algorithm proceeds with the optimization phase because these VCs might still get a chance to be assigned as a result of reallocations.

Once an initial VP layout is designed which serves all the VCs and satisfies the QoS requirements, it is time to start with the optimization phase, where the main concern is to reduce the link utilization on the most heavily loaded link of the network by applying VP and VC movement activities. The algorithm also tries to reduce the congestion of other links, even if no improvement can be made on the worst loaded link at some point. These reallocations may lead to free bandwidth that can be used for reallocating VPs or VCs on the worst loaded link in later turns.

In the optimization phase, the possibility of moving a VP from P_{ij}, the set of the VPs using l_{ij}, to other links is checked for every physical link l_{ij}. The aim of changing the physical route of a VP is the reduction of the link utilization u_{ij} of l_{ij}. The VP to be rerouted first is the one with the largest capacity. When the VP with the larger bandwidth is first moved to other links, the remaining capacities on these links become small. However, even in that case, there still remains a possibility that the VP with smaller bandwidth can be fit into those links. If the suitable alternate path cannot be found for that VP, the next VP with the largest capacity of the same link is checked. This procedure is repeated until all VPs from P_{ij} are checked. If the VP movement activity on the link l_{ij} yields no result, then the VC movement activity begins on that link. The procedure has the same motivation as the VP movement activity, this time concerning VCs instead of VPs. In this procedure, one of the VCs using link l_{ij}, i.e., a VC from the set C_{ij}, is separated to be rerouted over an alternate VP combination. The alternate VPs should have a less heavily loaded physical route and enough free bandwidth to accommodate the newly coming VC. This procedure is repeated this way until all VCs from C_{ij} are checked.

The VP movement activity is prior to the VC movement activity because the statistical multiplexing gain implies that the total required bandwidth is increased when a single VP is separated into several VCs. On the other hand, the statistical multiplexing gain is not lost when a whole VP is rerouted. Separation of one or more VCs from a VP also requires equivalent bandwidth recalculations on the old and new routes, whereas there is no such need for VP movements. In the case where more than one of the alternate routes offers the same amount of improvement, use of existing VPs is always encouraged since it increases capacity sharing and decreases call blocking probabilities. The optimization activities are restarted whenever there is some improvement in any of the links utilization u_{ij}. If there are remaining VCs from the previous phase, the algorithm tries to route them first. Then the whole process is repeated.

The optimization phase is terminated when iteration is completed without an improvement for any link.

4.4 Computational Experiments

The heuristic design algorithm proposed in this study uses the equivalent bandwidth concept to guarantee a desired QoS, limits the maximum allowed number of VP hops to meet processing delay constraints and tries to optimize the network performance by minimizing the maximum link utilization under these conditions. There are no computational results or numerical examples achieved by using exactly the same formulation in the literature to compare the quality of the proposed algorithm directly. A lower bound for the objective function is also hard to find since the link utilization is not an absolute value but the ratio of the used capacity over the total capacity of the link. Moreover, a network large enough to yield a non-trivial VP system is too large for an exhaustive search unless the number of VCs to be routed is limited, which is not a realistic approach since a traffic matrix is normally not sparse. Therefore, competitor algorithms are developed in order to evaluate the quality of the heuristic design algorithm results. The first competitor, which is called "Idlest Path Routing," is a variation of the proposed heuristic design algorithm itself, where the initialization phase and the sorting of waiting VCs in the original algorithm are omitted. The solutions found by the heuristic design algorithm are also evaluated using statistical quality measures implemented as two additional competitors. These random search algorithms route arbitrarily chosen VCs in on randomly selected combinations of physical links, disregarding all constraints concerning QoS like cell loss probability and delay. The idea is to see the distribution of the quality of the results in the solution space and have a statistical notion about the goodness of the heuristic solutions.

The heuristic design algorithm is tested regarding four important criteria in the evaluation of a network design methodology. These are network size, network density, traffic type and traffic load. Varying the size and the density of a network gives an idea about the behavior of the algorithm in different physical network topologies. The network size and density are represented by the number of nodes and links in the network, respectively. Changing the type and the load of the network traffic shows the quality of the heuristic design algorithm under different traffic conditions. To simulate different traffic types, or patterns, and traffic loads on the network, several distributions and peak rate ranges of connection requests are used in the traffic demand matrices.

To demonstrate a typical run of the heuristic design algorithm with the input, output and design variables, a network model with 8 nodes and 31 directed links is designed. STS-3 (155.520 Mbps) and STS-12 (622.080 Mbps) are used to simulate network connections. The offered traffic load in the network is obtained by scaling the results of a metropolitan area network simulation [5, 7, 8] such that the capacity limitations do not become a bottleneck for the demonstration. The heuristic design algorithm is run on the designed network topology with the offered traffic load and additional network parameters such as $x = 5$ Mbps, $\varepsilon = 10^{-5}$, $h = 2$, $\rho_i = 0.5$ and $b_i = 100$ ms. The algorithm creates a total of 43 VPs and routes all 56 VCs over them. The average VP hop count for the VCs is 1.357, and 86% of the assignments is to the VPs created in the initialization phase. This shows that the algorithm tends to use VPs with short physical routes in order to decrease the maximum link utilization, which is logical since short VP routes mean low resource usage, as mentioned above.

Comparisons are made with the competitors to show the quality of the results. Table 4.1 displays the results of the random solutions and the idlest path routing solution in comparison with the result of the heuristic design algorithm. The "Best Result" row shows that the heuristic design algorithm finds a lower value than its competitors for the maximum link utilization. The best result of the idlest path routing algorithm is 12% worse than the one found by the heuristic design algorithm. The difference of the performances is even bigger when the heuristic design algorithm is compared to the random solution generators. Besides, it takes the heuristic design algorithm a few iterations to find the result, while its competitors have to make 10.000 consecutive trials to find a good solution.

Table 4.1 Comparison of the Solutions for the Demonstrative Example

	Heuristic Design Algorithm	Idlest Path Routing (10.000 Runs)	10.000 Feasible Random Solutions	10.000 Random Solutions
Best Result	0.493	0.553	0.644	0.968
Average Result	0.493	0.741	0.918	1.991
Worst Result	0.493	1.000	1.000	4.192

The quality of the results improves as intelligence replaces randomness. Figure 4.2 shows the distributions of the competitor solutions and how the results are shifted from smaller utilization values achieved by Idlest Path Routing towards larger values found by the random solutions. In other words, Idlest Path Routing solutions are distributed among smaller utilization values than the solutions of the statistical quality measures. Therefore, in the next section, only those results are presented which compare the heuristic design algorithm with its closest competitor, Idlest Path Routing.

In the experiments, four different sizes of networks with 8, 16, 32 and 64 nodes and three different types of traffic are used. The first traffic type is

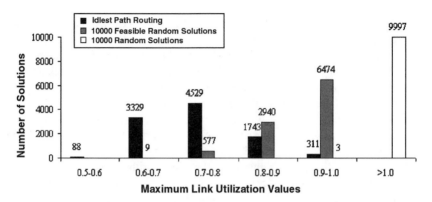

FIGURE 4.2
Distributions of the competitor solutions.

uniform, where the demand between nodes is uniformly distributed. The second type is called centralized traffic, where the demand to and from certain nodes (centers, or servers) is defined to be higher than the demand between others. Finally, the third type builds communities of interest, where there are user groups in the network. The traffic between members within the same group is defined to be higher compared to the traffic between members from different groups. Two major factors, network size and traffic type, greatly effect the performance of the proposed algorithm. In Figs. 4.3 and 4.4, the heuristic design algorithm is compared to the idlest path routing algorithm, which proves to be the best of the competitors in the tests, to show their behaviors when these network evaluation criteria are changed.

The relation between the performances of the algorithms and the network size is shown in Fig. 4.3, which is obtained by computing the average ratio of the difference between the results of both algorithms over the result of the heuristic design algorithm. In other words, Fig. 4.3 shows the factor by which the result of the heuristic design algorithm is better than the best result of the idlest path routing algorithm. The idlest path routing algorithm has a better performance in small networks consisting of 8 nodes. This is because the solution space is not very large and a random design algorithm still has a chance to search it thoroughly and find a better solution than an algorithm with certain engineering rules. However, as the network size gets larger, the solution space grows and a heuristic algorithm that tries to design a VP network systematically has a greater chance of finding a better solution than a random one.

The relation between the algorithm performance and the traffic types can be explained by the distribution principles associated with these traffic patterns. Figure 4.4 is obtained in a way similar to Fig. 4.3 and shows again the factor by which the heuristic design algorithm is better than its closest competitor. In fact, the trend of improved performance is observed by all traffic types as

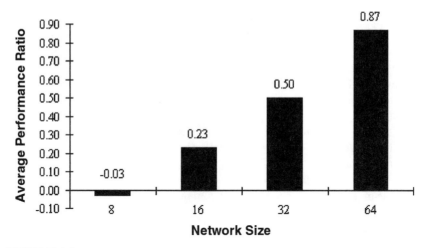

FIGURE 4.3
Quality of HDA solutions as the network size changes.

the number of the nodes in the network increases. Besides, the average of the results for these three kinds of traffic (10% for centralized traffic, 43% for groups of interest and 64% for uniform traffic) show that the solutions of the heuristic design algorithm are acceptable in all cases. However, these average values also show that the traffic type by itself has an effect on the algorithm performance.

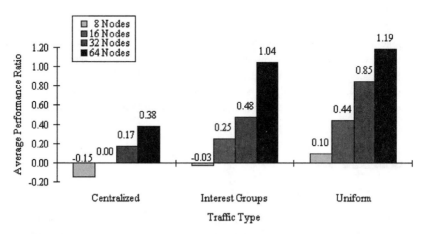

FIGURE 4.4
Quality of HDA solutions as the traffic type changes.

The heuristic design algorithm sorts the connection requests in decreasing order according to their peak rates, which means that, under centralized traffic conditions, the traffic to and from the center is routed first over the least utilized path. Then the remaining requests are handled. However, because of the nature of the traffic at the center, several links become congested before the optimization phase. Rerouting is also not as easy as with uniformly distributed traffic since the peak rate of the traffic from and to the center is too high to find an alternative route that has enough unallocated capacity. The idlest path routing algorithm, on the other hand, selects the connection requests to be routed at random. This way, it has a chance to find a better combination of assignments since the physical links are not overloaded at the very beginning of the routing process. In the case of communities of interest, the performance difference is much better since the distribution of the traffic load is uniform in each of the four blocks in the traffic matrix. This results in a somewhat more balanced utilization of links than the centralized traffic type, at least between the members of the same group. Finally, under uniform traffic conditions, the performance difference is the highest because of the homogeneous nature of the traffic demand. This way, the possibility of rerouting of the VPs from highly utilized paths to less utilized ones is high enough to find a good traffic distribution since no links are overloaded too early, even before the optimization.

In general, the quality of the results given by the heuristic design algorithm on medium to large size networks is better than its competitors for communities of interest or uniform traffic, whereas it is acceptable for centralized traffic. For small size networks, the solutions are not as good as the competitors, but they are still acceptable and can be applied much quicker since the algorithm finishes within a few iterations whereas its competitors need 10.000 runs for better solutions. A slight decrease in the average number of VCs per VP is to be observed as the network size grows. However, the equivalent bandwidth concept still holds since it covers such cases, where a VP is assigned to only a few VCs, by its fluid-flow approximation. In the worst case, where a VP is assigned to just one VC, the equivalent bandwidth of the VP is very close to the peak rate of the VC. In fact, the stationary approximation can only be advantageous as a result of statistical multiplexing gain if several VCs share a VP.

4.5   Conclusion

In this study, a method for designing the VP layout of an ATM network, which makes possible the efficient use of the network resources under QoS constraints, is proposed. The developed heuristic algorithm applies the equivalent bandwidth approach to compute the capacity requirements of the connection requests such that a desired QoS defined by the cell loss probability is guaranteed. The algorithm tries to minimize the maximum link utilization by applying VP and VC routing techniques under processing delay constraints. The quality of the solutions achieved by the heuristic design algorithm is compared to several competitors under varying network topologies and traffic conditions. The observations on the algorithm performance show that the developed method is able to facilitate an efficient use of network resources through the introduction of VPs.

An important implementation issue involves the handling of the case where new nodes or links are added to the backbone ATM network. An extension to the algorithm is needed to make incremental changes in the VP routing scheme, concerning especially the new nodes, to offer a temporary solution to be applied until the heuristic design algorithm redesigns the VP layout. The initialization phase of the proposed algorithm can find a temporary solution by creating VPs on the links of these new nodes. Similarly, the failure of a node or link is a case where immediate action has to be taken. To handle the case of link failures, the heuristic design algorithm can be modified such that it applies the VP and VC movement techniques on the failed link to reroute its traffic. Since the time complexity of the algorithm comes from the process of looking for a link to improve its utilization and not from the search for an alternate route, a quick solution for the failed link can be achieved. Besides, the alternate routes do not have to be optimal to recover from link failures. In the case where a node fails, this procedure has to be repeated for every link connecting the failed node to the other nodes.

The equivalent bandwidth is an effective way to practically implement advanced network control functions because it provides a unified connection metric for network management. To further improve its accuracy, investigation of better approximations is necessary. The approach can also be used for satisfying call level QoS constraints like call blocking probability with assumptions of certain traffic conditions. Other issues concerning further work are reliability and recovery from failures. Secondary VPs can be created to backup every primary VP between two end nodes such that primary and secondary VPs are passed on completely disjoint physical paths to assure the network survivability. Since the heuristic design algorithm developed in this study does not guarantee an optimal solution, the degree of its optimality is a subject to investigate as another further research topic.

References

[1] Plotkin, S., Competitive Routing of Virtual Circuits in ATM Networks, *IEEE J. Selected Areas in Communications,* Vol. 13, No. 6, pp. 1128–1136, August 1995.

[2] Minzer, S.E., Broadband ISDN and ATM, *IEEE Communications Magazine,* Vol. 27, No. 9, pp. 17–24, September 1989.

[3] Chlamtac, I., A. Farago and T. Zhang, Optimizing the System of Virtual Paths, *IEEE/ACM Trans. Networking,* Vol. 2, No. 6, pp. 581–587, December 1994.

[4] Chlamtac, I., A. Farago and T. Zhang, How to Establish and Utilize Virtual Paths in ATM Networks, *Proc. Globecom'93,* pp. 1368–1372, December 1993.

[5] Shioda, S. and H. Uose, VP Bandwidth Control Method for ATM Networks: Successive Modification Method, *IEICE Trans. Communications,* Vol. E74-b, No. 12, pp. 4061–4068, December 1991.

[6] Aoyama, T., I. Tokizawa and K. Sato, Introduction Strategy and Technologies for ATM VP-Based Broadband Networks, *IEEE J. Selected Areas in Communications,* Vol. 10, No. 9, pp. 1434–1447, December 1992.

[7] Ryu, B. H., H. Ohsaki, M. Murata and H. Miyahara, Design Algorithm for Virtual Path Based ATM Networks, *IEICE Trans. Communications,* Vol. E79-b, No. 2, pp. 97–107, February 1996.

[8] Ryu, B. H., H. Ohsaki, M. Murata and H. Miyahara, Design Method for Virtual Path Based ATM Networks with Multiple Traffic Classes, *Proc. ICCC'95,* pp. 336–341, August 1995.

[9] Lin, F. Y. S. and K. T. Cheng, Virtual Path Assignment and Virtual Circuit Routing in ATM Networks, *Proc. Globecom'93,* pp. 436–441, December 1993.

[10] Aneroussis, N. G. and A. A. Lazar, Virtual Path Control for ATM Networks with Call Level Quality of Service Guarantees, *Proc. Infocom'96,* pp. 312–319, 1996.

[11] Shioda, S., H. Saito and H. Yokoi, Sizing and Provisioning for Physical and Virtual Path Networks Using Self-Sizing Capability, *IEICE Trans. Communications,* Vol. E80-b, No. 2, pp. 252–262, February 1997.

[12] Onvural, R. O., Asynchronous Transfer Mode Networks: Performance Issues, Artech House Inc., Norwood, 1995.

[13] Guerin, R., H. Ahmadi and M. Naghshineh, Equivalent Capacity and its Application to Bandwidth Allocation in High-Speed Networks, *IEEE J. Selected Areas in Communications,* Vol. 9, No. 7, pp. 968–981, September 1991.

Vitae

Kaan Bür received his B.S. degree in control and computer engineering from Istanbul Technical University in 1995 and his M.S. degree in computer engineering from Boòaziçi University in 1998. Currently, he is a Ph.D. candidate in the Computer Engineering Department of Boòaziçi University. His research interests include high-speed networking, ATM networks, wireless and multimedia communications.

Cem Ersoy received his B.S. and M.S. degrees in electrical engineering from Boòaziçi University in 1984 and 1986, respectively. He received his Ph.D. in electrical engineering from Polytechnic University in 1992. Currently, he is an associate professor in the Computer Engineering Department of Boòaziçi University. His research interests include performance evaluation and topological design of communication networks, wireless and multimedia communications.

Chapter 5

Link Capacity Sharing Between Guaranteed and Best Effort Services

Sándor Rácz and Miklós Telek

Technical University of Budapest

Gábor Fodor

Ericsson Radio Systems

Abstract   While link allocation policies in multi-rate circuit switched loss models have drawn much attention in recent years, it is still an open question how to share the link capacity between service classes in a fair manner. In particular, when an ATM link is offered calls from service classes with/without strict QoS guarantees one is interested in link capacity sharing policies that maximize throughput and keep the per-class blocking probabilities under some GoS constraints. In this extended abstract we propose a model and associated computational technique for an ATM transmission link to which CBR/VBR and ABR classes offer calls. We also propose a simple link allocation rule which takes into account blocking probability constraints for the CBR/VBR calls and a throughput constraint for the ABR class and attempts to minimize the ABR class blocking probability.

Numerical examples demonstrating the effectiveness of the policy and of the applied computational technique are provided in the full paper version.

Keywords: multi-rate loss models, link capacity sharing, blocking probabilities, ATM service categories, Markov reward model.

[1]S. Rácz thanks the support of HSNLab. M. Telek was partially supported by OTKA F-23971. G. Fodor gratefully acknowledges the support from the Technical University of Denmark in Lyngby. The authors wish to thank Gergely Mátéfi for his help in the implementation of the proposed method.

5.1   Introduction

In recent years the various aspects of the coexistence of different service classes in ATM gained much attention and significant advances in the management of ATM traffic have been achieved. Most of the ATM traffic management efforts both within the major standardization bodies and the industry have been focusing on the *cell level* aspects of ATM, such as devising efficient congestion control- and policing mechanisms, and also call admission control (CAC), buffer allocation- and cell scheduling rules. Although *call level* issues in the multi-rate environment, like the computation of the blocking probabilities and establishing link capacity sharing policies, have also been addressed by many papers, very few paper deals with the problem of blocking probability calculations and link allocation policies when service classes with/without congestion control and with/without cell level QoS guarantees are present in a system simultaneously. The investigation of the call level aspects is important, since the blocking probability constraints are the primary inputs to the network dimensioning process. The hardship of this type of problem lies in the fact that the classical method of the *equivalent bandwidth* connecting the cell- and call level aspects is not directly applicable to an ATM link supporting CBR/VBR and ABR service classes simultaneously. This is because while it has been possible to associate a bandwidth-like quantity even with the VBR class, it is difficult to do the same for the ABR service class, because

- ABR does not provide the same level of QoS as the CBR/VBR classes

- there is very limited or no resource allocation prior to the information transfer phase

- the bandwidth available for the ABR calls fluctuate in time in accordance with the load on the link [1].

Since we have to dispose of the direct application of the equivalent bandwidth based approach when devising and analyzing link capacity sharing policies, we seek alternative methods to do this. This problem has been raised by, for instance, in [2] without providing an analytical approach or a modeling framework. While many interesting contributions have proposed link allocation- and associated performance analysis methods for complete sharing, complete partitioning, partial overlap, trunk reservation, class limitation [3] and Markov decision [4], very few proposes efficient computational technique for ATM with CBR^2 and ABR classes, especially when the state space becomes large, say in

---

[2]Because we model the system on the call level, in the rest of this paper we use the CBR service class as one which represents strict QoS guarantees, with the understanding that by adopting the notion of equivalent bandwidth, this class could as well be the VBR class.

the order of $10^4 - 10^6$. Thus, our goal is to 1) extend the widely used multi-rate models such that they allow the ABR bandwidth to fluctuate between the minimal and the peak bandwidth during the call's holding time, 2) propose a simple and yet efficient method for link capacity sharing between calls coming from different ATM service classes and 3) devise an efficient computational technique for the calculation of the throughput and blocking probabilities, applicable for large systems.

5.2 The Multi-Service Model of an ATM Link

In this section we formulate the Markovian model of a single ATM transmission link receiving CBR and ABR traffic. In the presentation we restrict ourselves to two CBR classes and a single ABR class, but the model is extendible to more general cases. More traffic classes increase both the complexity and the size of the state space, and the numerical results become more difficult to interpret, and, therefore, we believe that it is reasonable to start with these restrictions. It should be pointed out, however, that both the basic idea of the model extension to include ABR traffic and the results are applicable to more general cases as well.

The system under consideration consists of an ATM link with capacity C, which is supposed to be an integer number in some suitable bandwidth unit, say $Mbps$. Calls arriving at the link belong to one of the following three traffic classes:

- Narrow-band CBR calls are characterized by their peak bandwidth requirement b_1, call arrival rate λ_1 and departure rate μ_1;

- Wide-band CBR calls are characterized by their peak bandwidth requirement b_2, call arrival rate λ_2 and departure rate μ_2;

- ABR calls characterized by their peak bandwidth requirement b_3, call arrival rate λ_3, minimal bandwidth requirement b_3^{min}, and their *ideal* departure rate μ_3. By ideal we mean that the peak bandwidth is available during the entire duration of the call.

One may think of an ABR class call as one that upon arrival has an associated amount of data to transmit (W) sampled from an exponentially distributed service requirement, with distribution $G(x) = 1 - e^{-\frac{b_3}{\mu_3}x}$, which in the case when the peak bandwidth b_3 is available during the entire duration of the call gives rise to an exponentially distributed service time with mean $1/\mu_3$. Since the free capacity of the link fluctuates in time in accordance with the instantaneous number of CBR and ABR calls in service, the bandwidth given to the ABR calls may drop below the peak bandwidth requirement, in which case the actual holding time of the call increases. All three types of calls arrive according to independent Poisson processes, and the holding times for CBR calls are exponentially distributed. As we will see, the moments of the holding time of the ABR calls can be determined using the theory of Markov reward processes. Three underlying assumptions of the above model are noteworthy. First, we assume that the ABR calls are greedy, in the sense that they always occupy the maximum possible bandwidth on the link, which is the smaller of their peak bandwidth requirement b_3 and the equal share of the bandwidth left for ABR calls by the CBR calls (which will depend on the link allocation policy). Second, we assume that all ABR calls in progress share equally the available bandwidth among themselves, i.e., the newly arrived ABR call and the in-progress ABR calls will be squeezed to the same bandwidth unless each of them gets their peak bandwidths. Note that if a newly arriving call decreased the ABR bandwidth below b_3^{min}, that call is not admitted into the system, but it is blocked and lost. Also note that arriving CBR as well as ABR calls are allowed to "compress" the in-service ABR calls, as long as the minimal bandwidth constraint is kept. Third, the model assumes that the rate control of the ABR calls in progress is ideal, in the sense that an infinitesimal amount of time after any system state change (i.e., call arrival and departure) the ABR sources readjust their current bandwidth on the link.

It is intuitively clear that the residency time of the ABR calls in this system not only depends on the amount of data they want to transmit, but also on the bandwidth they receive during their holding times. In order to specify this relationship we define the following quantities:

- $\theta(t)$ defines the instantaneous *throughput* of the ABR calls at time t (e.g., if there are n_1, n_2, n_3 narrow-band CBR, wide-band CBR and ABR calls in the system at time t, respectively, the instantaneous throughput is $min(b_3, (C - n_1 b_1 - n_2 b_2)/n_3))$. Note that $\theta(t)$ is a discrete r.v. for any $t \geq 0$.

- $T_x = \inf\{t \mid \int_0^t \theta(\tau)d\tau \geq x\}$ (r.v.) gives the time it takes for the system to transmit x amount of data through an ABR call,

- $\theta_x = x/T_x$ defines the *throughput* of the ABR call during the transmission of x data unit. Note that θ_x is a continuous r.v.

- $\theta = \int_0^\infty \theta_x \, dG(x)$ (r.v.) defines the *throughput* of the ABR call.

In addition, we associate the maximal accepted blocking probabilities with both CBR classes, i.e., B_1^{max} and B_2^{max}, respectively, and the minimal accepted throughput θ^{min} with the ABR class. We refer to the set of the arrival

$(\lambda_1, \lambda_2, \lambda_3)$ and departure rates $(\mu_1, \mu_2, \mu_3)^3$, the bandwidths (b_1, b_2, b_3) and minimal ABR bandwidth (b_3^{min}), the blocking probability (B_1^{max}, B_2^{max}) and ABR throughput constraints (θ^{min}) as the *input parameters* of the system.

The system under investigation (with the above assumptions on the arrival processes and holding times/transmission requirements) is a Continuous Time Markov Chain (CTMC) whose state is uniquely characterized by the triple $i = (n_1, n_2, n_3)$, where n_1 and n_2 are the number of narrow-band and wide-band CBR calls in the system, respectively, and n_3 is the number of ABR calls in the system. The structure of the CTMC's generator matrix $\mathbf{Q}$ reflects the applied link allocation policy and, therefore, we first need to define it.

We would like to define the link allocation policy such that it is able to minimize the call blocking probability for the ABR calls while it is able to take into account the GoS (blocking probability) constraints for the CBR calls and the minimal throughput constraint for the ABR calls. Because of its flexibility (in that it is able to take into account the above constraints) and simplicity (in that the performance measures of interest can be determined even for large systems) we adopt the *partial overlap, POL* link allocation policy from the multi-rate circuit switched modeling paradigm [5].

According to the POL policy the link capacity C is divided into two parts, the C_{COM} common part and the C_{ABR} part, which is reserved for the ABR calls only, such that $C = C_{COM} + C_{ABR}$. Under the considered POL policy the number of calls in progress on the link is subject to the following constraints:

$$n_1 \cdot b_1 + n_2 \cdot b_2 \leq C_{COM} \tag{5.1}$$

$$N_{ABR} \cdot b_3^{min} \leq C_{ABR} \tag{5.2}$$

$$n_3 \leq N_{ABR}, \tag{5.3}$$

where N_{ABR} stands for the maximum number of ABR calls in the system and will be determined later. Note that this policy has two free parameters (C_{COM} and N_{ABR}), which allows for the easy dimensioning of a system with blocking and throughput constraints. Furthermore, we find it relatively easy to analyze systems with large state space as well.

The set of such triples which satisfy these constraints constitutes the set of *feasible states* of the system which we denote by S. Cardinality of the state space can be determined with (5.4):

$$\#S = (N_{ABR} + 1) \cdot \sum_{i=0}^{\lfloor C_{COM}/b_1 \rfloor} \left\lfloor \frac{C_{COM} - i \cdot b_1}{b_2} + 1 \right\rfloor. \tag{5.4}$$

In (5.1) the ABR connections are protected from CBR calls. In (5.2) and (5.3) the maximum number of ABR connections is limited by two constraints. (5.2)

$^3\mu_3$ is the maximum departure rate of the ABR class assuming that the bandwidth of the ABR connection is equal to b_3.

protects the CBR calls from ABR connections while (5.3) protects the ABR connections from the new ABR calls, because if too many ABR connections were admitted into the system then θ could decrease below θ^{min}. Clearly, θ can be modified by changing the value of N_{ABR}.

It is easy to realize that the **Q** generator matrix possesses a nice structure, because only transitions between "neighboring states" are allowed in the following sense. Let $q_{i,j}$ denote the transition rate from state i to state j. Then, taking into account the above constraints associated with the proposed POL policy, the non-zero transition rates between the states are

$$q_{i,i_{k+}} = \lambda_k , \qquad k = 1, 2, 3 \tag{5.5}$$

$$q_{i,i_{k-}} = n_k \cdot \mu_k , \qquad k = 1, 2 \tag{5.6}$$

$$q_{i,i_{3-}} = r_i \cdot \mu_3 , \tag{5.7}$$

where $i_{1+} = (n_1 + 1, n_2, n_3)$ when $i = (n_1, n_2, n_3)$; i_{k+} and i_{k-} ($k = 1, 2, 3$) are defined similarly; and

$$r_i = \min \left(n_3 , \frac{C - (b_1 \cdot n_1 + b_2 \cdot n_2)}{b_3} \right) . \tag{5.8}$$

(5.5) represents the state transitions due to a call arrival, while (5.6) and (5.7) represent the transitions due to call departures. The $r_i b_3$ quantity as defined by (5.8) denotes the total bandwidth of the ABR connections when the system is in state i. The **Q** generator matrix of the CTMC is constructed based on the transition rates defined in (5.5), (5.6) and (5.7). Note that the POL policy as described above is fully determined by specifying its two parameters: the C_{COM} common part and the N_{ABR} maximal number of ABR calls. We refer to the C_{COM} and the N_{ABR} parameters of the POL policy as the *output parameters* of the system.

Now, we consider a small system for illustration purposes. Figure 5.1 depicts the state space of a system with capacity $C = 4$ and with a CBR and an ABR class (i.e., for ease of presentation $n_2 = 0$ is kept fixed). We let $C_{COM} = 2$, $b_1 = 1$ and $b_3 = 2$. The ABR class is further characterized by its *minimal* accepted bandwidth, which we here let $b_3^{min} = 2/3$. This setting gives rise to 12 feasible states, out of which there are 5 (gray) states where the ABR bandwidth is compressed below the peak bandwidth specified by b_3. In, for instance, state $(1, 0, 3)$ each of the 3 ABR calls receive 1/2 bandwidth, which gives rise to an aggregated ABR death rate $1.5\mu_3$.

It can be seen that the system in Fig. 5.1, as well as the considered system in general, is not reversible, since the local balance equations do not hold due to the possible compression of ABR bandwidth. Hence, the steady state distribution does not obey a product form solution. However, the generator matrix, as we will see next, possesses a nice birth-death structure allowing for efficient numerical solution approaches.

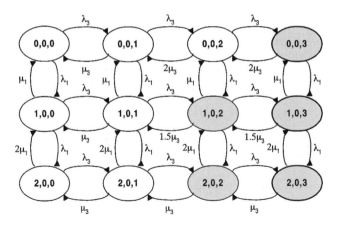

FIGURE 5.1

The state space of the small example when $b_2 = 0$.

As we will see, the POL policy is easy to dimension, and it has two free parameters, with which the performance of the system can be tuned. It guarantees call level GoS for CBR calls and throughput for ABR services. The GoS of CBR calls is guaranteed by the proper setting of C_{COM}. In case of a change in the ABR load (i.e., the call arrival intensity (λ_3) or the parameter of required data to transmit (b_3/μ_3)), the N_{ABR} parameter has to be adjusted to keep the required throughput. We divide the problem of determining the output parameters of the POL policy into two steps. In the first step we determine the minimum required capacity for CBR calls, which guarantees the required blocking probability:

$$\min\left\{C_{COM} \ : \ B_1 \leq B_1^{max} \ , \ B_2 \leq B_2^{max}\right\}, \tag{5.9}$$

where B_1 (B_2) is the blocking probability of the narrow-band (wide-band) CBR class. In the second step we determine the maximum number of ABR calls simultaneously present in the system. In fact, we minimize the blocking probability of the ABR calls (by determining the maximum number of admissible ABR calls) applying constraints on the throughput of the ABR connections. The following two constraints are considered:

- *the average throughput constraint* :

$$\max\left\{N_{ABR} \ : \ E(\theta) \geq \theta^{min}, \ N_{ABR} \leq \frac{C - C_{COM}}{b_3^{min}}\right\}, \tag{5.10}$$

i.e., the average throughput of ABR connections can not be less than θ^{min}.

To make a plausible interpretation of this constraint let us assume that the distribution of θ is fairly symmetric around $E(\theta)$, i.e., the median of θ is close to $E(\theta)$. In this case the probability that an ABR call obtain less bandwidth than θ^{min} is around 0.5. Users (even with ABR traffic) often prefers more informative throughput constraints like the next one.

- *the throughput threshold constraint*:

$$\mathbf{max}\left\{N_{ABR} \; : \; Pr(\theta_x \leq \theta^{min}) \leq \varepsilon, \; \forall x, \; N_{ABR} \leq \frac{C - C_{COM}}{b_3^{min}}\right\}$$
(5.11)

This throughput threshold constraint requires that the throughput of ABR connections is greater than θ^{min} with a predefined probability $(1 - \varepsilon)$ independent of the associated service requirements (x). Hence, if the (input) parameter θ^{min} is much less than $E(\theta)$ then this second constraint is much more informative for the user about the expectable minimal level of the ABR throughput.

The call blocking probabilities of the CBR and ABR calls are calculated from the steady state distribution $(\underline{P} = [p_i])$ of the CTMC specified by its generator matrix $\mathbf{Q}$.

5.3 Analysis of ABR Throughput Measures

Once the steady state distribution of the CTMC has been found, we can determine the required throughput measures, the *average throughput* and the *throughput threshold* defined by Eqs. (5.10) and (5.11), respectively.

The calculation of the average throughput of the ABR calls is straightforward, since

$$E(\theta) = \frac{\displaystyle\sum_{(n_1,n_2,n_3)\in S} b_3 \, p_{(n_1,n_2,n_3)} \, r_{(n_1,n_2,n_3)}}{\displaystyle\sum_{(n_1,n_2,n_3)\in S} n_3 \, p_{(n_1,n_2,n_3)}}.$$
(5.12)

Unfortunately, it is much harder to check the throughput threshold constraint in (5.11), since neither the distribution nor the higher moments of θ_x can be analyzed based on the steady state distribution of the above studied Markov chain. Hence, in this section, a different approach is applied to analyze the system with the throughput threshold constraint.

The constraint in (5.11) can be analyzed based on the distribution of T_x applying

$$Pr\left(\theta_x \leq \theta^{min}\right) = Pr\left(\frac{x}{T_x} \leq \theta^{min}\right) = Pr\left(T_x \geq \frac{x}{\theta^{min}}\right).$$
(5.13)

It is hard to evaluate the distribution of T_x directly, but there are effective numerical methods to obtain its moments through the Markov Reward Model [6] that describes the system behaviour during the sojourn of the tagged ABR call [6]. We check the throughput threshold constraint in (5.11) based on the moments of T_x applying the Markov inequality, which gives the following relations:

- if applied for $T_x^n \geq \frac{x^n}{b_3^n}$:

$$Pr\left(T_x \geq \frac{x}{\theta^{min}}\right) \leq \frac{\dfrac{E(T_x^n)}{x^n} - \dfrac{1}{b_3^n}}{\dfrac{1}{\theta^{min^n}} - \dfrac{1}{b_3^n}} \tag{5.14}$$

- if applied for $(T_x - E(T_x))^{2n} \geq 0$:

$$Pr\left(T_x \geq \frac{x}{\theta^{min}}\right) \leq \left(\frac{x}{\theta^{min}} - E(T_x)\right)^{2n} \leq \frac{M^{(2n)}(T_x)}{\left(\dfrac{x}{\theta^{min}} - E(T_x)\right)^{2n}}, \tag{5.15}$$

where $n \in \mathbb{N}$ and $M^{(2n)}(T_x) = E\big([T_x - E(T_x)]^{2n}\big)$ denotes the $2n$-th central moment of T_x. The inequalities (5.14)–(5.15) applied for different n provide different upper bounds for $Pr\left(T_x \geq \frac{x}{\theta^{min}}\right)$. If at least one of the upper bounds of $Pr\left(T_x \geq \frac{x}{\theta^{min}}\right)$ is less than ε for the considered x then the throughput threshold constraint is fulfilled.

The complete link allocation procedure is summarized in Fig. 5.2.

5.4 Conclusion

An ATM call level model is proposed, which is an extension of the classical multi-rate loss model in that it allows one to model service classes whose bandwidth fluctuates in time in accordance with the instantaneous load on the link. This is achieved by allowing such service classes to specify their minimal accepted bandwidth in addition to their peak bandwidth requirement. Furthermore, these types of calls specify their ideal mean call holding time, which corresponds to the total amount of required service, rather than specifying the mean call holding time.

We have used this model to investigate the performance of the adoption of the Partial Overlap link allocation policy for an ATM transmission link which is

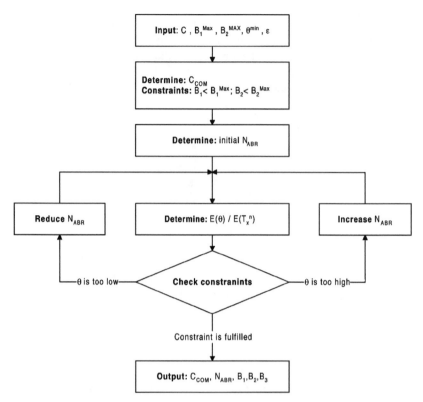

FIGURE 5.2
The block diagram of the link allocation procedure.

offered CBR and ABR calls. By employing efficient numerical methods to find
the steady state of the system and the reward measures of a modified system,
we have found that the POL policy is relatively easy to dimension and is able
to take into account GoS and throughput constraints and to minimize the ABR
class blocking probability.

References

[1] T. M. Chen, S. L. Liu, V. K. Samalam, The Available Bit Rate Service for
     Data in ATM Networks, *IEEE Communications Magazine,* pp. 56–71,
     May 1996.

[2] J. W. Roberts, Realizing Quality of Service Guarantees in Multi-service Networks, *Performance Management of Complex Communication Networks,* T. Hasegawa, H. Takagi, Y. Takahashi, Eds., IFIP., Chapman & Hall, pp. 277–293, 1998.

[3] J. W. Roberts (Ed.), Methods for the Performance Evaluation and Design of Broadband Multiservice Networks, *Published by the Commission of the European Communities, Information Technologies and Sciences, COST 242 Final Report,* 1996.

[4] K. W. Ross, D. K. H. Tsang, Optimal Circuit Access Policies in an ISDN Environment: A Markov Decision Approach, *IEEE Transactions on Communications,* Vol. 37, No. 9, pp. 934–939, September, 1989.

[5] E. D. Sykas, K. M. Vlakos, I. S. Venieris, E. N. Protonotarios, Simulative Analysis of Optimal Resource Allocation and Routing in IBCN's, *IEEE J-SAC,* Vol. 9, No. 3, 1991.

[6] M. Telek, S. Rácz, Numerical Analysis of Large Markov Reward Models, *Performance Evaluation,* to appear, 1999.

Chapter 6

QoS Management with Delays and Cell Drops[1]

Erol Gelenbe, Jun Wang and Juan-Manuel Barrionuevo

University of Central Florida

Abstract   We consider maximum allowable delays through a switch to control of Quality of Service for different classes of real-time traffic. We model the switch by a single server queue with different arrival streams and identical deterministic service times. Each incoming cell belongs to a class of traffic which is characterized by constraints on maximum allowable delay as it traverses the switch. The admission control procedure may accept an incoming cell, or decide to drop it at the input to avoid needless congestion when it appears that the cell's delay constraints will not be respected. The performance metric is the total cell loss rate, plus the rate of non-respect of desired maximum cell delay. We first present an approximate analytical method to evaluate the effective average delay experienced by each class of real-time traffic without drops, based on a stochastic decoupling of the interdependent queues by modeling their interaction via equivalent random variables. The distribution of this service time is computed based on characteristics of each of the classes of traffic, and on their interaction, which is determined by the scheduler. This leads to a non-linear iterative solution technique. Numerical computations are carried out for a system with two and with three maximum delay classes, and compared with simulation results for varying arrival rates of Poisson traffic. Then we summarize simulation results for the following variants of the basic technique: (1) all cells are admitted and then served with a Time-Stamp based priority queuing discipline (TSQD), or (2) a cell can be dropped according to its maximum allowable delay (Time Stamp Queue Discipline with Drops or TSQDwD).

---

[1]Partial support for this research was provided by Allied Telesyn Inc.

Keywords: ATM, QoS, deadline-based scheduling, time stamps, bursty traffic.

6.1   Introduction

Currently, the Internet offers a "best effort" service typified by First-In-First-Out (FIFO) scheduling at each hop in the network. For real-time traffic such as voice and video, the current Internet Protocol has performed well only across unloaded networks. An obvious drawback of the FIFO discipline is that it makes it difficult to fulfill the delay requirements of each class of traffic since all cells arriving at the system receive the same treatment independently of their priority. When a system is overloaded, not all the cells having real-time requirements can be served by their deadlines. Thus, new classes of services and protocols are being introduced in the Internet in order to provide guaranteed quality to real-time traffic, and signaling for such services may be carried out using the Resource ReSerVation Protocol (RSVP) [1, 2, 3, 11, 18].

In this work we consider time-stamp based queuing disciplines as a means of controlling QoS for connections based on user requirements in ATM switches, which may be used in the Internet or at the tabletop. In real-time oriented applications, each cell has an associated deadline derived from the maximum delay it can incur through a switch, and then through the network. In such circumstances, the Time Stamp Queuing Discipline (TSQD), with or without cell drops at the input and from the queue, can be used effectively. TSQD schedules the cells arriving at the queue depending on the maximum delay permitted, which will be different for each class of traffic.

One of the first algorithms to consider the problem of scheduling jobs with deadlines was the Earliest-Deadline-First (EDF) algorithm proposed by Jackson [12]. In this algorithm, each customer has a deadline assigned when entering the queue and the one with the earliest deadline is selected first to be serviced. There have been several studies about meeting end-to-end deadlines in ATM networks, and some have concentrated on the design and analysis of scheduling policies [4, 5, 6, 7, 13, 15, 16, 17]. Several queue managers adopt the Earliest-Due-Date (EDD) algorithm for cell scheduling [10] which time stamps each arriving cell. This value is equal to the sum of the maximum allowable queuing delay and the arrival time of the arriving cell. The cell with the smallest time stamp is served first. This is equivalent to the EDF policy when due dates and deadlines are the same, and to the TSQD where we serve the arriving cells to the queue depending on their time stamp. Recently we have proposed the Time Stamp Queuing Discipline with Drops (TSQDwD) [19] as a means to deal with real-time requirements in overloaded networks. Here, service in the queue is ordered according to time stamps, and an arriving cell is dropped at the input if we know that its deadline is not going to be fulfilled. This idea may be extended to allow dropping a cell whenever the switch has sufficient information indicating that the cell cannot be served before its deadline.

6.2 Time-Stamp Based Algorithms

Let us assume that we have an unbounded queue with a single server. Let a_n be the arrival instant of the nth cell to the queue, and let D_n be the maximum delay that is allowed for that cell to be out of the server after the time it enters the queue. The *time stamp* is the latest time at which the cell should leave the queue in order to assure the QoS required; denote it with t_n. Clearly, $t_n = a_n + D_n$. Let us denote the actual instant the cell exits the server by d_n (the departure time). Let W_n be the waiting time in the queue, and S_n be the service time. Here the time spent in the queue includes the service time. In ATM we can take $S_n = 1$. It follows that $d_n = a_n + W_n + S_n$, and since $S_n = 1$, $d_n = a_n + W_n + 1$. We are interested in $P[d_n > a_n + D_n]$, i.e., the probability that the cell will fail its QoS requirement. We call this the *probability of failure*. In the sequel we will evaluate two algorithms which are designed to decrease this probability: the Time Stamp Queue Discipline with Drops algorithm (TSQDwD) and the TSQD. The TSQD scheduler orders arrivals in the queue as follows. If $Q(a_n, t_n)$ is the position of a cell which arrived at time a_n, then $Q(a_i, t_i) < Q(a_j, t_j)$ implies that $t_i < t_j$. Note that the smaller position number implies that the cell is closer to the head of the queue.

TSQDwD is similar to the TSQD algorithm with an important difference in the admission criterion of cells. TSQD accepts every new arrival. Clearly, this is not very efficient since we know in advance that some cells' QoS will fail, and admitting them increases buffer requirements and will also create greater delays for other cells, causing some later arriving cells to fail. In TSQDwD, the admission criterion is based on the cell's position in the queue. If the position the cell will have in the TSQD queue is greater than its maximum allowable delay D_n, then we know that the cell's QoS requirement will not be satisfied since $S_n = 1$. If this is the case, then the TSQDwD algorithm rejects the cell at the input to the switch; we call this a *cell drop*. Clearly, when there are only a finite (say K) number of possible values of D_n, we may model the system in terms of K queues, where cells inside any given queue are served in FIFO order.

6.3   An Approximate Analytical Model

In recent work [20] we have considered a related but simpler queuing problem arising from another network scheduling policy. In that policy, cells queue up in different buffers depending on the class of traffic to which they belong, and the switch services for transmission one of the queues based on the amount of time the cell has waited *at the head of the queue*, rather than in the queue as a whole, as is the case with the TQSD and the TSQDwD. In this section, we propose an approximate technique to analyze the performance of the TQSD, or the TQSwD, using an approach to handling couples queues similar to that of [20].

We will concentrate on the TSQD, since the approach for the TSQDwD is very similar. In the approach we propose, we consider multiple queues which share a single server, and where cells in each queue are ordered in Time-Stamp order. Cells arriving to the system can only have a finite number of values of D_n. Each queue receives a separate flow of cells, and each cell in the same queue has the same value of D_n. At the end of any service epoch, the server is allocated to the queue in which the cell at the *head of the queue* has the shortest deadline. After each service, the server's allocation can again be changed; however, service is non-preemptive so that once the server is allocated the service is completed. To the best of our knowledge, there is no available exact analysis of this type of service despite the fact that it concerns a well known service discipline. The analysis we present is for the case where arrivals are Poisson. However, the key of the approximate analysis refers to the derivation of distributions for equivalent service times as perceived by each queue. Thus, it can be applied to any circumstance where the arrival process would allow an analytical treatment.

For the sake of clarity, the following analysis is presented for just two classes of service (i.e., only two possible values of D_n), although it may be extended to any number of classes. Numerical results and simulations will be presented both for two and three classes. Finally, in this paper we will present only results for mean queue length with Poisson arrivals, although one can also derive the approximate stationary queue length distribution using standard methods, which would in turn yield the probability that the cells' deadline is not respected (the probability of failure).

Consider now a system of two queues where queue 1 receives cells whose values of maximum allowable delay is D_1, while queue 2 receives cells with maximum allowable delay D_2. Let the arrival rates to the queues be λ_1 and λ_2. The first step of the approximation consists in considering that the server turns to one queue or the other at random, whenever both queues are busy, while (of course) it serves the busy queue if there is just one busy queue. Denote by p_i the probability that the server serves queue i given that both of the queues are busy

($p_1 + p_2 = 1$). The second step of the approximation consists in considering that an equivalent service time for queue i is composed of a random number $K_i - 1$ of services for the other queue, followed by one real service time for queue i, where K_i is determined by the scheduling discipline and the fact that the other queue may or may not be busy. Thus, if ρ_i, $i = 1, 2$, is the probability that queue i is busy, then:

$$Pr[K_1 = k] = (\rho_2 p_2)^{k-1}(1 - \rho_2 p_2),\qquad(6.1)$$
$$Pr[K_2 = k] = (\rho_1 p_1)^{k-1}(1 - \rho_1 p_1).$$

If S_1 and S_2 denote the random variables representing the equivalent service times perceived by each class of traffic, we will have $\rho_1 = \lambda_1 E[S_1]$ and $\rho_2 = \lambda_2 E[S_2]$, and we can easily compute:

$$E[S_1] = \sum_{k=1}^{\infty} k(\rho_2 p_2)^{k-1}(1 - \rho_2 p_2) = \frac{1}{1 - \rho_2 p_2},\qquad(6.2)$$

$$E[S_2] = \sum_{k=1}^{\infty} k(\rho_1 p_1)^{k-1}(1 - \rho_1 p_1) = \frac{1}{1 - \rho_1 p_1},\qquad(6.3)$$

$$E[S_1^2] = \sum_{k=1}^{\infty} k^2(\rho_2 p_2)^{k-1}(1 - \rho_2 p_2) = \frac{1 + \rho_2 p_2}{(1 - \rho_2 p_2)^2},\qquad(6.4)$$

$$E[S_2^2] = \sum_{k=1}^{\infty} k^2(\rho_1 p_1)^{k-1}(1 - \rho_1 p_1) = \frac{1 + \rho_1 p_1}{(1 - \rho_1 p_1)^2}.\qquad(6.5)$$

By representing each individual queue as an M/G/1 system, we obtain the average waiting times W_i and the average response times R_i to be:

$$W_i = \frac{\lambda_i E[S_i^2]}{2(1 - \lambda_i E[S_i])}\qquad R_i = W_i + E[S_i].\qquad(6.6)$$

Now, the only remaining unknown variables are p_1 and p_2. To compute these quantities, consider the Delay-Based Scheduling server in steady state. It checks the head of each of the two queues (if they are both busy). By an abuse of notation let a_i and D_i denote the arrival instant and the maximum allowable delay for the cell which is at the head of queue i. When the service of the currently served cell ends at some time t, the server serves the queue whose cell at the head of the queue has the smallest $a_i + d_i$. Note that if W_1^* and W_2^* denote the respective waiting times at the two queues in steady state, then we may approximately write $a_i = t - W_i^*$ so that $a_1 + d_1 < a_2 + d_2$ implies $(t - W_1^*) + D_1 < (t - W_2^*) + D_2$. Thus, $a_1 + d_1 < a_2 + d_2$ implies $W_2^* < W_1^* + D_l - D_2$. Hence:

$$p_1 = P[W_2^* < W_1^* + D_l - D_2].\qquad(6.7)$$

At this point, we can use several heuristics to compute (6.7). We could use the tail probabilities of the "approximate" M/G/1 queue we have described previously, or diffusion approximations, or some other technique for computing the tail probabilities. Here we will select a fast and simple approach to deal with this issue, and expect to examine it in greater detail in later work.

6.3.1   Iterative Solution

Based on the binomial approximation for service times, we will assume that the W_i^* are mutually independent and exponentially distributed with parameters $a = \frac{1}{W_1}$ and $b = \frac{1}{W_2}$. Then $P[W_1^* > x_1] = e^{-ax_1}$ and $P[W_2^* > x_2] = e^{-bx_2}$. Then,

$$p_1 = \int_0^\infty ae^{-ax_1}dx_1 \int_0^{x_1+D_l-D_2} be^{-bx_2}dx_2 = 1 - \frac{a}{a+b}e^{-b(D_l-D_h)} . \quad (6.8)$$

To obtain the numerical solution of the model, we first choose an initial value of the unknown probabilities $p_1 = p_2 = \frac{1}{2}$. Using these initial values and the known arrival rates $\lambda_1, \lambda2$, we obtain W_i, for $i = 1, 2$ using (6.6), and then a and b.

Using (6.8) the new values of the probabilities p_i are obtained. We continue the iteration until a stopping condition is attained. Here we have used the stopping condition which is a predefined very small difference between the old and the new value of p_1. We have observed that the interactions converge rapidly.

In Fig. 6.1, we present a comparison of the approximate analytical results for two classes of traffic with a simulation model. The average response time for each of the two classes of Poisson traffic with $D_1 = 10$ and $D_2 = 100$ are presented. The approximate analytical results are derived in two different ways, yielding the curves shown on the left and on the right of the figure. The analytical results plotted on the left-hand side use the fact that the system as a whole acts as an M/D/1 system with known average waiting time $E[W]$, so that:

$$E[W] = \frac{\lambda_1}{\lambda_1 + \lambda_2}E[W_1] + \frac{\lambda_2}{\lambda_1 + \lambda_2}E[W_2] . \quad (6.9)$$

Thus, if $E[W_1]$ is computed approximately, then $E[W_2]$ can be obtained directly from $E[W]$, and vice-versa. The results plotted on the figure on the right-hand side of Fig. 6.1 do not use $E[W]$ at all, and compute by iteration as described above both $E[W_1]$ and $E[W_2]$.

In the numerical and simulation results shown in Fig. 6.1, we take $\lambda_1 = \lambda_2$, with $D_1 = 10$ and $D_2 = 100$, and plot the average response time against the total arrival rate of cells $\lambda = \lambda_1 + \lambda_2$. We observe a good agreement between the analytical model and the simulations for the class having larger maximum delay, for which the average response time will be higher. We also observe

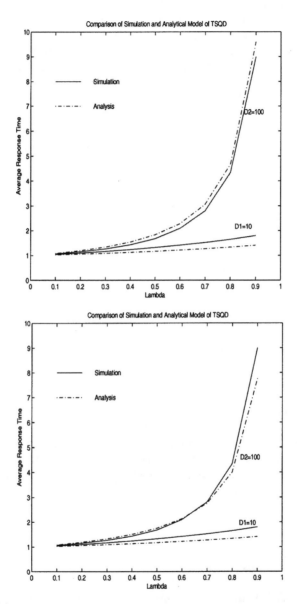

FIGURE 6.1

Comparison of the approximate analytical model predictions with the simulation model when we use (left), and do not use (right), the known behavior of the two queues together as an M/D/1 queue.

that the analytical model provides a *worst case* estimate of average response time, which is a desirable feature of the model. We extend this approach to three classes of traffic. In Fig. 6.2 we present numerical results for three classes of traffic with for $D_1 = 10$, $D_2 = 100$ and $D_3 = 300$, and compare them with simulation results. We have used the analysis of the global behavior as an M/D/1 queue (left). We observe that the approximate technique is more accurate for the traffic classes which have lower priority, and that it provides a *worst case* estimate of response time.

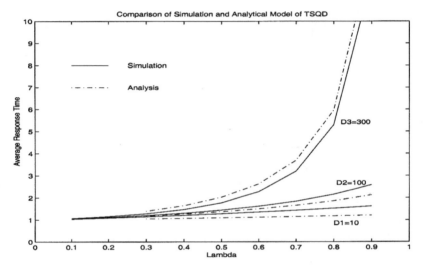

FIGURE 6.2

Comparison of the approximate analytical method with simulation results for three classes of traffic using the analysis of the global behavior of the system as an M/D/1 queue. The average response time of each class of traffic is shown as a function of total arrival rate of cells, for $D_1 = 10$, $D_2 = 100$, $D_3 = 300$ and $\lambda_1 = \lambda_2 = \lambda_3$.

6.4   Simulation Results for the Probability of Failure with and without Cell Drops

In this section we present results based purely on simulation. We use the IPP (Interrupted Poisson Process) model which is commonly used to represent bursty traffic. We group arriving cells into three classes according to their values of D_n, and take $D_n = 10$, 100, 300. The purpose is to distinguish between highly "real-time" traffic ($D_n = 10$), and traffic which is more tolerant to delay. We also provide simulation results for IPP traffic with the TSQDwD algorithm for different activity rates in Figs. 6.3, 6.4 and 6.5. These plots show the probability of failure vs. the load of the system for different activity rates. In Fig. 6.6 the probability of failure is plotted against activity for fixed arrival rates of cells, in order to evaluate the behavior of the TSQDwD algorithm under highly bursty traffic.

The "gain" of TSQDwD against TSQD for Poisson traffic is shown in Fig. 6.4. This graph was obtained by dividing the Probability of Failure for TSQD by the Probability of Failure for TSQDwD. From Fig. 6.4 we see that for λ's up to 0.995, the higher priority classes have less gain. For λ greater than 0.995, the class with $D_n = 100$ has a higher gain than with $D_n = 300$.

Bursty traffic can be characterized by a bit rate which changes randomly between different values according to the activation and deactivation of different services or behavior sequences. The simplest such representation is an On-Off source which is alternatively active and inactive. Let a be the activity rate of the source given by:

$$a = \frac{\theta}{\beta + \theta} \, , \tag{6.10}$$

where θ^{-1} is the average length of the "Off" period and β^{-1} is the average length of the "On" period. Therefore, as a decreases, the burstiness of the arrival traffic increases. Figs. 6.3, 6.4, and 6.5 show that the TSQDwD scheduling algorithm keeps its good performance under bursty traffic. In Fig. 6.6, we see that QoS with the TSQDwD algorithm degrades gracefully under highly bursty traffic compared to other algorithms. Thus, the drop mechanism in TSQDwD adjusts to overload during traffic bursts. The overall probability of failure shows a peak between $a = 0.2$ and $a = 0.3$, and decreases at lower and higher values of a.

6.5 Conclusions

In this paper we have analyzed and simulated two admission controls for deadline driven traffic. This admission policy is based on trying to satisfy the delay constraints for each class of traffic as it traverses a switch. We consider the Time Stamp Queue Discipline (TSQD), and a modified version of this algorithm with cell drops at the input (TSQDwD). We present a novel approximate analytical model of TSQD which allows us to compute the response time obtained for each class of traffic. We also present simulation results for these algorithms using Poisson and On-Off traffic which show that both TSQDwD and TSQD greatly reduce the probability that a cell will not be served by the switch before its deadline, compared to the FIFO schedule. Additionally, the

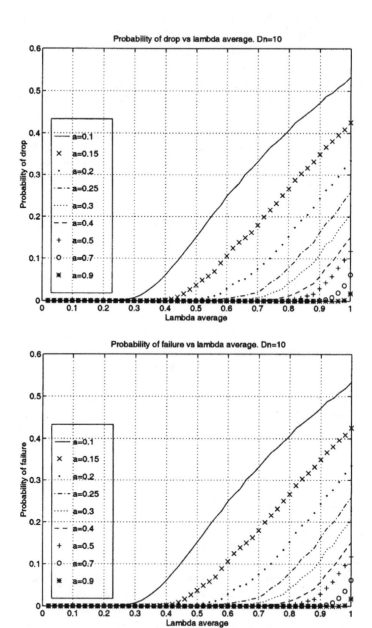

FIGURE 6.3

Probability of drop and probability of failure vs. arrival rate for the TSQDwD algorithm with $D_n = 10$.

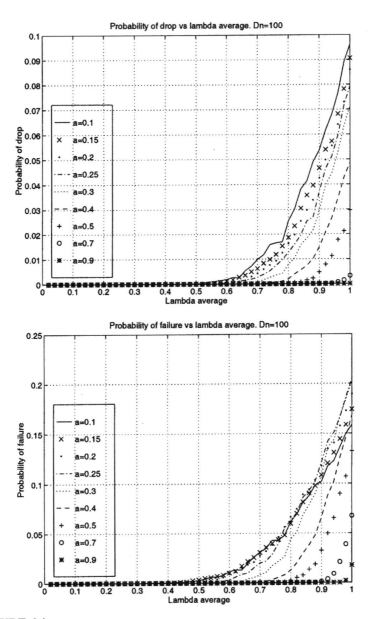

FIGURE 6.4
Probability of drop and probability of failure vs. arrival rate λ for deadline $D_n = 100$. **TSQDwD algorithm.**

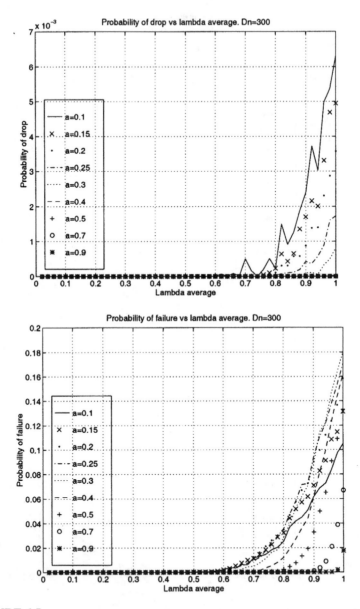

FIGURE 6.5
Probability of drop and probability of failure vs. arrival rate λ for deadline $D_n = 300$. **TSQDwD algorithm.**

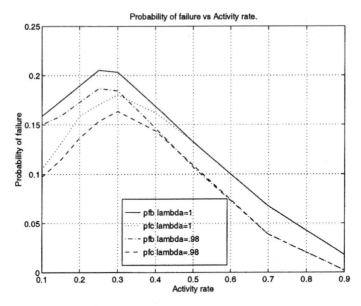

FIGURE 6.6
Probability of failure vs. activity rate a **for deadlines** $D_n = 100$**(pfb) and**
$D_n = 300$ **(pfc) and** $\lambda = .98$ **and** $\lambda = 1$**. TSQDwD algorithm.**

buffer size requirement of TSQDwD is much smaller than that of FIFO and
TSQD, and is bounded, since the queue length for TSQwD cannot exceed
$D_{n_1} + D_{n_2} + D_{n_3} + \cdots + D_{n_m}$, where m is the number of classes of traffic.
Our simulations also indicate that the TSQDwD algorithm protects against total failure of the cells to meet their deadlines under overload conditions when
traffic is very bursty.

References

[1] F. Baker, *RSVP Cryptographic Authentication,* Internet Draft, June 1996.

[2] M. Borden, E. Crawley, J. Krawczyk, F. Baker, S. Berson, *Issues for
RSVP and Integrated Services over ATM,* Internet Draft, February 1996.

[3] R. Braden, L. Zhang, S. Berson, S. Herzog, S. Jamin, *Resource ReSer-
Vation Protocol (RSVP) – Version 1 Functional Specification,* Internet
Draft, February 1996.

[4] H. Chao, H. Cheng., *A new QoS-guaranteed cell discarding strategy: self-calibrating pushout,* 1994 IEEE GLOBECOM. Communications: The Global Bridge, volume 2, pp. 929–934. IEEE, Nov.-Dec. 1994.

[5] D.D. Clark, S. Shenker, L. Zhang, Supporting real-time applications in an integrated services cell network: Architecture and mechanism, *Proc. ACM SIGCOMM'92,* pp. 14–26, Aug. 1992.

[6] A. Demers, S. Keshav, S. Shenker, Analysis and simulation of a fair queuing algorithm, *Proc. ACM SIGCOMM'89,* pp 1–12, Sept. 1989.

[7] D. Ferrari, D.C. Verma, A scheme for real-time channel establishment in wide-area networks, *JASC,* SAC-8(3): 368–379, Apr. 1990.

[8] E. Gelenbe and Mitrani, *Analysis and Synthesis of Computer Systems,* Academic Press, 1980.

[9] E. Gelenbe and Pujolle, *Introduction to Queuing Networks,* 2nd Edition, John Wiley & Sons, Chichester and New York, 1998.

[10] H.M. Goldberg, Analysis of the Earliest Due Date Scheduling Rule in Queuing Systems, *Math. Oper. Res.,* 2(2), 1997.

[11] S. Herzog, *RSVP Extensions for Policy Control,* Internet Draft, June 1996.

[12] J.R. Jackson, *Scheduling a Production Line to Minimize Maximum Tardiness, Technical Report* Research Report 43, Management Science Research Project, UCLA, 1955.

[13] Ting-Li Ling, Ness Shroff, Scheduling real-time traffic in ATM networks, *IEEE INFOCOM,* 1996.

[14] V. Srinivasan, A. Ghanwani, E. Gelenbe, Block loss reduction in ATM networks, *Computer Communications,* 19(13), 1077–1091, Nov. 1996.

[15] L. Trajkovic, S.J. Golestani, Congestion control for multimedia services, *IEEE Network,* 20–26, Sept. 1992.

[16] J.S. Turner, Maintaining high throughput during overload in ATM switches, *IEEE INFOCOM,* 1996.

[17] H. Zhang, Virtual clock: A new traffic control algorithm for packet switching networks, *Proc. ACM SIGCOMM'90,* pp. 19–29, Sept. 1990.

[18] L. Zhang, S. Deering, D. Estrin, S. Scott , D. Zappala, RSVP: A New Resource ReSerVation Protocol, *IEEE Network,* Sept. 1993.

[19] J.M. Barrionuevo, E. Gelenbe, E. Icoz, (Invited Paper) Controlling QOS with delays and cell drops, *37th IEEE Conf. Decision and Control,* Tampa, FL, Dec. 1998.

[20] E. Gelenbe, A. Ghanwani, Approximate analysis of coupled queuing in ATM networks, *IEEE Communications Letters,* 3(2), pp. 31–33, Feb. 1999.

Vitae

Erol Gelenbe is a Professor of Computer Science and the Director of the School of Computer Science at the University of Central Florida. His interests span modeling and simulation with applications in computer systems and networks. His recent work has included neural networks, image processing, discrete stochastic processes, autonomous navigation and generic algorithms. Before joining UCF he was the Nello L. Teer Jr. Professor of Electrical and Computer Engineering and Chair of his Department at Duke University where he also held appointments in Computer Science and Psychology (Experimental). He has authored or co-authored 4 books and monographs. His book with I. Mitrani on computer performance analysis which was published by Academic Press (1980), later appeared in Japanese with the Ohm-Sha Press (1988). His book with G. Pujolle on queuing networks has been published in English translation by John Wiley (1988), after appearing in French (1984); a second edition recently appeared in 1998. He has also authored a monograph on parallel processing performance which appeared with John Wiley in 1989, and co-authored a monograph on distributed data bases which was published by Elsevier (1988). He has edited several other books and conference proceedings. Gelenbe has published over one hundred journal articles in the main journals of Computer Science, Applied Probability, Computer Engineering and Neural Computation. He has supervised over fifty Ph.D. dissertations and his former students are active in academia, research and industry in several countries including France, the USA, Italy, the UK, Greece, Turkey, Venezuela, Canada and Colombia. He is a Fellow of the IEEE since 1986. His honors include the Grand Prix France Telecom (1996) of the French Academy of Science, the Honorary Doctor's degree from the University of Rome (1996) in "Ars Computandi," the Science Award of the Parlar Foundation (Turkey, 1995), the Chevalier de l'Ordre du Merite (1992) from the French Government, the IFIP Silver Core Award (1980) and two service awards from the IEEE.

Jun Wang received his B.S. degree in Electrical Engineering from the Department of Electronics at Peking University, Beijing, P.R. China in 1996. He then held a temporary appointment with the Center for Information Science at Peking University for Advanced Computer Studies. Currently he is a Ph.D. candidate at the School of Computer Science of the University of Central Florida. His research interests include computer communication networks, distributed operating systems and performance evaluation techniques. He works both on ATM technology and on problems related to control and performance of the Internet and new packet switching methods. His areas of interest also cover image, video and speech signal processing and artificial neural networks.

Chapter 7

Fluid Analysis of TCP Connections Over ABR VCs

Jean-Laurent Costeux

France Telecom - CNET - BD/CNET/DSE/ISE

Abstract   This paper reports on an analytical study of the performances of the ATM-ABR transfer capacity in transporting TCP/IP flows over an ATM network. We explore the behavior of TCP connections over ATM-ABR virtual circuits (VCs), in presence of exogenous non-controlled traffic. This fluid analysis of the system allows the study of the interaction between the window-based end-to-end flow control TCP protocol and the rate-based flow control ABR mechanism, which is restricted to the ATM part of the network. The main aim of this study is to give performance evaluation formulae to model the behavior of such a TCP over ABR connection.

Keywords: ATM networks, ABR transfer capacity, TCP protocol, traffic and congestion control, queuing theory.

7.1   Introduction

The ATM Forum has defined in the draft standard [3] the ABR (Available Bit Rate) transfer capacity. The goal of ABR is the support of applications with vague requirements for throughput and delay, for example the support of data traffic. The idea behind the ABR service is to convey feedback information about network congestion status from network elements to end systems, in order to dynamically adapt the cell emission process of the ABR sources to the current load of the network. Details on how the ABR mechanism works can be found in [3]. The problem that we can encounter with ABR could come from interferences with other data transport applications in the Internet World, like with TCP. The goal of this paper is to analyze the performances of the ABR service category in transporting the ATM cells resulting from segmentation of TCP/IP packets.

7.1.1   TCP Protocol and ABR Mechanism

TCP protocol is the most commonly used transport protocol on the Internet. It implements a window-based end-to-end flow control mechanism. We recall here the main principles of TCP.

The congestion window of TCP is called W. It increases by reception of acknowledgments. We note two phases for increasing W:

- the slow start phase (SS): each time TCP source receives one acknowledgment, the congestion window W is increased by one. The period of slow start starts from W=1 until $W = W_{th}$. We call W_{th} the slow start threshold

- the congestion avoidance phase (CA): each time TCP source receives one acknowledgment, W is increased by 1/W. The period of congestion avoidance starts from $W = W_{th}$ until a loss occurs.

This means that W grows much more rapidly in the slow start mode than in the congestion avoidance. We can define a TCP cycle by the time period between two packet losses. There are several ways to detect a packet loss, such as:

- a timer: when the timer is greater than the retransmission time out (RTO), we assume that a packet has been lost. The window size becomes equal to 1, we come back to slow start mode and W_{th} is divided by 2

- duplicate acknowledgments: when a packet has been acknowledged more than 3 times, we assume that the following packet has been lost.

Several versions of TCP have been implemented. TCP-Tahoe and TCP-Reno are the most current versions. For these versions, it is very important to note that, in case of congestion, TCP uses packet losses to control its congestion window, which is directly connected to the TCP incoming rate thp_{in}.

The ABR mechanism is for its part responsible for avoiding a congestion in the ATM part of the network, i.e., between the ABR control unit at the Source End System (SES) and the ABR control unit at the Destination End System (DES). To do so, the ABR control unit adjusts the rate of ATM cells into the network dynamically, according to the congestion status of this network. This rate is called Allowed Cell Rate (ACR): to avoid network congestion, the source is not allowed to send cells faster than ACR. The congestion status of the network is indicated through the specific fields of the resource management cells (RM cells) sent by the source and modified by network elements (switches, routers, destination...). The major schemes for indicating the congestion are:

- relative rate marking (EFCI-based): in case of congestion, the network elements mark the CI (Congestion Indication) bit of the RM cells to indicate to the source that it should reduce its rate; they can also mark the NI (No Increase) bit to indicate that it should keep the ACR at the same rate

- explicit rate marking (ER-based): the network elements can change the ER field of the RM cells to indicate to the source the explicit rate at which it should transmit.

There are several rules, defined in [3], for modifying the ACR according to the received informations. We recall here the major ones:

- ACR should never be greater than PCR (Peak Cell Rate) and never be smaller than MCR (Minimum Cell Rate)

- if CI bit = 0,
$$ACR := \min\{ER, ACR + RIF \cdot PCR\}$$

- if CI bit = 1,
$$ACR := \min\{ER, ACR - RIF \cdot ACR\}.$$

RIF (Rate Increase Factor) and RDF (Rate Decrease Factor) are defined in [3]. These rules will be used in our analytical study.

7.1.2 Problems and Motivation of the Work

On a TCP connection over ATM implementing the ABR service, the problems come from the interactions between both congestion control methods.

First, due to its dynamical window mechanism, TCP is quite simple and indeed appropriate for a wide range of network configurations without any need of explicit tuning. On the contrary, due to the multiplicity of parameters, the ABR service category is much more complicated and hard to configure: the performance strongly depends on the choice of control parameters and on the congestion schemes used by network elements.

Besides, TCP and ABR use two different ways to detect congestion in the network: as TCP uses packet losses to regulate its rate, ABR uses information transported by RM cells to control its ACR. Thus, ABR does not have to wait for a packet loss to reduce its rate.

Finally, the ABR control loop is designed to slow down the SES in case of congestion; however, in case of a TCP connection running over an ATM-ABR VC (Virtual Connection), ABR is unable to signal to the *real* traffic sources the rate at which they should transmit. Although ABR is aware of the congestion, the ABR source cannot communicate with the TCP source and cannot inform

TCP that it should reduce its rate.[1] Thus the TCP source sends packets until loss. This means that congestion may be avoided in the ATM part of the network, but not for the end-to-end TCP traffic flows. In fact, the congestion is only relocated: the cells are not buffered in the network (because ABR reduces its rate so that the network is not saturated) but in the buffer of the ABR control unit, because TCP continues to send packets while ACR is reduced.

The goal of this study is to analyze and quantify in terms of performance the interaction between TCP and the ABR flow control mechanisms. In this paper, we summarize an analytical approach to describe the dynamical evolution of the ACR of the ABR sources and the resulting buffer content in the bottleneck, i.e., the slowest or most congested queue on the path. Besides, we describe the evolution of the window size of TCP protocol and the queue length in the ingress buffer, i.e., the queue in which the ATM cells are buffered before being sent into the ATM network by the ABR control unit. We study the correlation between these quantities and indicate the different states the system is entering during a control cycle. We try to understand how the connections work and point out the phenomena that affect the performance.

7.1.3   Outline

We adapt the fluid analysis of [10] and [2], from which we recall the main results in Section 7.3, to study the impact of a single TCP connection running over an ATM-ABR VC, combined with exogenous traffic, i.e., traffic that is not correlated to the connection, but affects this connection by increasing the incoming flow to the bottleneck. Our model is presented in Section 7.2 and resolved in Section 7.4. Explicit analytical results with accurate formulae are given to estimate the expressions of ACR, the congestion window, and the two queue lengths mentioned above, as functions of the time and of the state of system. In Section 7.5, we show how to modify these results in order to analyze a more realistic system with several synchronized TCP connections over many ATM-ABR Virtual Circuits.

7.2   The Model and Notations

We first model a single TCP connection, running over an ATM-ABR VC, and sharing a bottleneck with exogenous traffic. Our model contains two queues: the ingress buffer of the ABR control unit and the bottleneck. The bottleneck

---

[1] S. Floyd in [7] proposed to use an Explicit Congestion Notification to inform TCP source about a congestion before loosing a packet. This mechanism has not been implemented yet.

is to follow the congestion status of the network and the ingress buffer is to survey the relocation of the congestion, due to the fact that ABR reduces its rate whereas TCP continues to transmit packets. The service rate of the bottleneck is constant, equal to C packets/s. Bottleneck queue is assumed to be FIFO served. All rates are expressed in packets/s to simplify the analysis of the TCP behavior. The service rate of the ingress buffer is then equal to $\frac{ACR}{n_1}$ packets/s, where n_1 represents the number of cells corresponding to one segmented TCP packet. The exogenous traffic is assumed to be constant fluid, equal to E packets/s. It models the other communications sharing the bottleneck, typically the other data transfers on ABR VCs. The studied model is represented in Fig. 7.1.

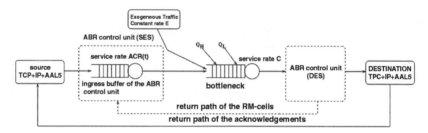

FIGURE 7.1
Model of our TCP over ABR connection.

We consider an infinite TCP connection, which always has a packet to send. We study the performances of one of the most widely used TCP versions, TCP Tahoe. Round trip propagating time and waiting time, excluding the bottleneck node and the effects of bottleneck changes, are assumed to be constant and modeled by a fixed delay τ. $T = \tau + \frac{n_1}{ACR} + \frac{1}{C}$ is the sojourn time of a packet in an empty system; a represents the number of packets acknowledged by reception of one acknowledgment. thp_{in} is the rate of the TCP packets at the output of the TCP controlled source and thp_{out} is the rate of the TCP packets at the output of the bottleneck.

N_{rm}, RIF (Rate Increase Factor) and RDF (Rate Decrease Factor) are parameters of the ABR control units and are defined in [3]. We first consider EFCI-based switches, but our study can easily be adapted to ER-based switches. The congestion detection scheme used by the network elements is a queue-based detection scheme, which implements two thresholds in the bottleneck queue: an upper threshold, Q_H, and a lower threshold, Q_L. When the occupation of the bottleneck is greater than Q_H, a congestion indication is returned to the source by RM cells. The ABR source starts to decrease ACR until the occupation of the bottleneck becomes smaller than Q_L. F_1 is the denomination of the ingress buffer (Q_1 its occupancy) and F_2 the denomination of the bottleneck buffer (Q_2 its occupancy).

7.3   Established Results and Evolutions

We recall here the fluid analysis of [10], on the ABR service without exogenous flow, and [2], on a TCP connection with exogenous flow.

In [10], by modeling the cell flow of the ABR sources as a fluid, the evolution of the ACR and of the bottleneck queue length is described using differential equations. Therefore, a control cycle consisting of a congested period followed by a non-congested period is divided into a number of phases which are considered separately. The phases are differentiated by the current congestion status of the bottleneck and by whether the buffer is empty:

- phase 1: non-empty buffer, non-congested state: the ACR is increased by $RIF \cdot PCR$ at each arrival of an RM cell, as long as the ACR is lower than PCR; in case of a non-empty buffer, these arrivals occur with a constant rate $\frac{C_F}{N_{rm}}$, where C_F is the capacity available for the ABR connection (in cells/s). The increase of the ACR during this phase is thus expressed by the differential equation (linear increase):

$$\frac{dACR(t)}{dt} = \frac{RIF \cdot PCR \cdot C_F}{N_{rm}} \qquad (7.1)$$

The ACR increases linearly.

- phase 2: non-empty buffer, congested state: the ACR is then decreased by $RDF \cdot ACR$ at each arrival of an RM cell, as long as the ACR is greater than MCR; in case of a non-empty buffer, these arrivals occur at the same rate $\frac{C_F}{N_{rm}}$. The decrease of ACR during this phase is thus expressed by the differential equation:

$$\frac{dACR(t)}{dt} = -ACR(t)\frac{RDF \cdot C_F}{N_{rm}} \qquad (7.2)$$

The ACR decreases exponentially.

- phase 3: empty buffer, non-congested state: due to the empty buffer, the return rate of backward RM cells at time t depends on the ACR τ time units before. Thus, we obtain the differential equation:

$$\frac{dACR(t)}{dt} = ACR(t - \tau)\frac{RIF \cdot PCR}{N_{rm}} \qquad (7.3)$$

The ACR increases exponentially.

Papers [2] and [4] for their parts describe the fluid analysis of a single TCP Tahoe connection interacting at a bottleneck with exogenous traffic. Different phases of window evolution in time are observed:

- an exponential increase of the window size while this window size is lower than $\min\{W_{th}, T(C - E)\}$

- a linear increase when it is between
  $\min\{W_{th}, T(C - E)\}$ and $\max\{W_{th}, T(C - E)\}$

- a square root increase once it is greater than $\max\{W_{th}, T(C - E)\}$.

In the present paper we combine the two previous studies and try to adapt them to solve our model: we introduce also a differential equations approach for our fluid analysis and try to indicate the different phases and states our system is entering during a control cycle. But analyzing this type of single TCP over ABR connection is much more complex than the two previous studies. First, the different states of the system are much more numerous, due to the fact that we are considering two queues and analyzing the two congestion control mechanisms together. Secondly, we discover new behaviors on this type of connection due to the interactions between TCP and ABR: in fact the evolution of W depends on the evolution of ACR and vice versa, which is why we observe unusual evolutions of these variables, as well as of the occupancy of the buffers. To observe and analyze these behaviors, different phases of the system are distinguished by the states of the following variables and elements of the network:

- the ingress buffer is empty (symbolized by F_1) or not empty (symbolized by $\bar{F}_1$)

- the bottleneck is empty (F_2) or not empty ($\bar{F}_2$)

- the ingress queue increases ($\bar{F}_1^{\,i}$) or decreases ($\bar{F}_1^{\,d}$)

- when the buffer of the bottleneck is not empty, the ACR increases ($\bar{F}_2^{\,i}$) or decreases ($\bar{F}_2^{\,d}$)

- the TCP source is in the slow start mode (SS) or in the congestion avoidance mode (CA).

These simple states lead to a complex 18-states diagram to model the behavior of this single TCP over ABR connection, after excluding the impossible states. For each state, we have studied the evolution of the state variables ($ACR(t)$, $W(t)$, $Q_1(t)$ and $Q_2(t)$) and defined the transition conditions. We have then discovered new behaviors for these variables, such as parabolic increase for $ACR(t)$, logarithmic increase for $W(t)$ or decrease like *arctanh* for $Q_1(t)$.

7.4   Analysis of a State

To explain how we have studied our model, we give an example of analysis of one state. We choose the state where F_1 is empty and F_2 is not empty, ACR is increasing and the TCP source is in slow start mode: this means we are in state $F_1 \bar{F}_{2_{SS}}^i$, which gives a good idea of the method we use to characterize each state. Analysis of a different state can be found in [5].

First, we note X_0, the initial value of the variable X at the beginning of each phase and $t_{k_p}^{mn}$, the date of the transition in next state: $k \in [0, 3]$ (0 represents the states $F_1 F_2$, 1 the states $\bar{F}_1 F_2$, 2 the states $F_1 \bar{F}_2$ and 3 the states $\bar{F}_1 \bar{F}_2$), $p \in \{SS, CA\}$ indicates that we are in slow start or in congestion avoidance mode, $m \in \{i, d\}$ indicates that the occupancy of the ingress buffer is increasing or decreasing, and $n \in \{i, d\}$ indicates that the ACR is increasing or decreasing. Thus, $t_{k_p}^{mn}$ is the date on which we are coming into the state characterized by $\{k, p, m, n\}$.

Let us solve now the state $F_1 \bar{F}_{2_{SS}}^i$. As ACR(t) is increasing, we have, according to [10] and to the differential equation written in the previous section and adapted to our model:

$$\frac{d ACR(t)}{dt} = n_1 \frac{RIF \cdot PCR \cdot thp_{out}}{N_{rm}} \tag{7.4}$$

According to [2], we have, in slow start mode:

$$thp_{out} = C - \frac{a \cdot E}{1 + a} \tag{7.5}$$

Thus, when ACR is increasing:

$$ACR(t) = \min \left\{ PCR, ACR_0 + \frac{n_1 \cdot RIF \cdot PCR \cdot \left(C - \frac{a \cdot E}{1+a}\right)}{N_{rm}} t \right\} \tag{7.6}$$

Now

$$thp_{in}(t) = \min \left\{ \frac{W(t)}{T}, \left(1 + \frac{dW}{dack}\right) thp_{out}(t) \right\} \tag{7.7}$$

This leads to

$$thp_{in}(t) = \min \left\{ \frac{W(t)}{T}, \left(1 + \frac{1}{a}\right) C - E \right\} \tag{7.8}$$

in slow start mode, because TCP is increased by one for each acknowledgment received by the source, i.e., every "a" packet(s) received by the destination.

As $\frac{dW(t)}{dt} = \frac{thp_{out}}{a}$, we find the following expression of W:

$$W(t) = W_0 + \left(\frac{C}{a} - \frac{E}{1+a} \right) t \tag{7.9}$$

The TCP source will come into congestion avoidance mode when W will reach the slow start threshold W_{th}. This happens at time t_{th} so that:

$$t_{th} = \frac{W_{th} - W_0}{\frac{C}{a} - \frac{E}{1+a}} \tag{7.10}$$

By integrating the incoming rate minus the outgoing rate of the bottleneck queue, we can compute the occupation of the bottleneck (Q_2). We have indeed:

$$Q_2(t) = Q_{2_0} + \int_0^t thp_{in}(u) + E - C du \tag{7.11}$$

Thus, in slow start mode:

$$Q_2(t) = Q_{2_0} + \frac{C \cdot t}{a} \tag{7.12}$$

We now study the possible transitions from state $F_1 \bar{F}_{2_{SS}}^i$. First, we can observe that W, ACR and Q_2 are increasing. As thp_{in} is constant and $thp_{in} < \frac{ACR}{n_1}$ (because the ingress buffer is empty), we deduce that thp_{in} cannot become greater than $\frac{ACR}{n_1}$. The only possible transition comes when the bottleneck queue reaches the upper threshold Q_H. This happens at time $t_{2_{SS}}^d$, when $Q_2(t_{2_{SS}}^d - \tau) = Q_H$; τ quantifies the time it takes for the information to be relayed to the Source End System.

Possible transitions from state $F_1 \bar{F}_{2_{SS}}^i$ are then:

- if $t_{2_{SS}}^d < t_{th}$, the ABR source is informed in slow start mode that the upper threshold of the bottleneck queue has been reached. The ACR starts to decrease. The next state is $F_1 \bar{F}_{2_{SS}}^d$

- if $t_{2_{SS}}^d \geq t_{th}$, the ABR source receives the information (conveyed by RM cells) that it has to decrease ACR in congestion avoidance mode. The next state is $F_1 \bar{F}_{2_{CA}}^d$.

We can also compute the performance of the system during the phase $F_1 \bar{F}_{2_{SS}}^i$, by calculating:

- the duration of this period, T_2, which is equal to the transition date t_2^d

- the number of successfully transmitted packets in this period,

$$N_2 = \int_0^{T_2} thp_{out}(t) dt \tag{7.13}$$

- the mean delay of transmission in this period,

$$R_2 = T + \frac{1}{T_2} \int_0^{T_2} \frac{Q_2(t)}{C} dt \qquad (7.14)$$

These values will be useful to calculate the mean throughput and the mean round trip time at the end of the TCP cycle.

This was an example to show how we analyzed and resolved our model. Forms of $ACR(t)$, $W(t)$, $Q_1(t)$ and $Q_2(t)$ in each of the 18 states of our system can be calculated in the same way. According to these forms, we programed a network analyzer to study the performance of TCP over ABR. Practical case studies realized using this analyzer can be found in [5] and [6].

7.5   Case of Several TCP Connections on Many ATM-ABR VCs

We now consider the possibility that several TCP applications from the same workstation use the same ATM-ABR VC, and that several workstations using different ATM-ABR VCs send data to the same destination. We then have m ABR virtual circuits, representing the m workstations; each workstation has opened n TCP connections. All connections are synchronized; this means that they all have the same characteristics, start at the same time and loose packets at the same time. This kind of configuration is common and can be modeled as shown in Fig. 7.2.

We observe, for each TCP connection and each VC, how the evolutions of $ACR(t)$ and $thp_{out}(t)$ are modified, compared to the case of a single TCP over ABR connection. As we saw in the previous section, we can deduce from ACR and thp_{out} the forms of thp_{in}, W, Q_1 and Q_2.

7.5.1   Both Queues are Empty

When both queues are empty, all TCP windows grow normally, as the acknowledgements are not slowed down. Expressions of W, thp_{in} and thp_{out} are the same for n TCP connections as for one connection. But ACR rate increases n times faster, as there are n times packets more sent into the network. As a consequence, we have :

$$\frac{dACR(t)}{dt} = n_1 \frac{n \cdot W(t - \tau)}{T \cdot N_{rm}} RIF \cdot PCR \qquad (7.15)$$

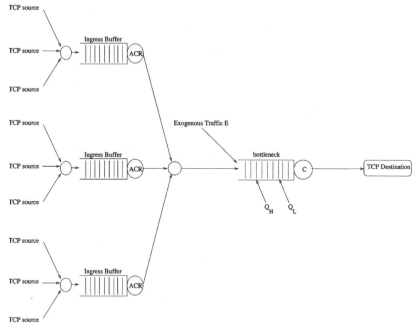

FIGURE 7.2

Model of *n* synchronized TCP connections over *m* ABR virtual circuits, with exogenous flow.

Transition arrives when the link capacity is reached, that is to say when the packet entry rate thp_{in} reaches $\min\{\frac{ACR}{n_1 \cdot n}, \frac{C-E}{n \cdot m}\}$ for each TCP connection. This often comes very rapidly when there are many involved connections.

7.5.2 Ingress Buffers Saturation

As the TCP sources are synchronized, buffers start to fill up at the same time. When ingress buffers are not empty, the acknowledgements are coming back *n* times slower, as the buffers are shared by *n* connections. By calling THP_{OUT} the "global" arrival rate of all packets coming from all TCP connections, the arrival rate of packets coming from connection *i* is equal to :

$$thp_{out_i} = \frac{THP_{OUT}}{n} \tag{7.16}$$

THP_{OUT} is clearly equal to the rate thp_{out} calculated in the previous section for the case of one single TCP connection over ABR. The number of ABR connections has no influence here because the bottleneck is empty and the ingress buffer stands before the entry in the network. On the other hand, the bottleneck will be saturated more rapidly, as we have m ABR VCs sharing the bottleneck. This happens when:

$$\frac{ACR}{n_1} = \frac{C - E}{m} \tag{7.17}$$

7.5.3   Bottleneck Saturation

When the bottleneck is not empty, RM cells are coming back m times slower than in the case of one TCP over ABR connection. ACR rate is thus increasing or decreasing m times slower. As far as the arrival rate per connection is concerned we have now:

$$thp_{out_i} = \frac{THP_{OUT}}{n \cdot m} \tag{7.18}$$

Expressions of ACR, thp_{out_i}, W, thp_{in} and Q_1 are the same whether the ingress buffers are empty or not. But expression of Q_2 is different, because the coming rate to the bottleneck F_2 is different:

- when the ingress buffers are empty, the coming rate to F_2 is equal to $n \cdot m \cdot thp_{in}$

- when the ingress buffers are not empty, the coming rate to F_2 is equal to $m \times ACR$.

We deduce that the bottleneck fills up more rapidly than in the case of a single TCP over ABR connection. But packets flows are diluted between the different TCP connections. Thus, acknowledgements from each connection come back slowly. Consequently, TCP windows increase slowly.

7.6   Conclusion

We have given in this analysis the expressions of $ACR(t)$, $W(t)$, $Q_1(t)$ and $Q_2(t)$ as functions of time and of the parameters of the system. We have first studied the case of a single TCP over ABR connection and have calculated formulae containing all the expressions for each of the 18 states of our system. We have shown how differential equations can be applied to model the dynamical system behavior of TCP over ABR.

This study allows us to predict the behavior of a TCP connection over an ATM-ABR VC, according to the parameters we choose: we can identify the states we will enter and the values the ACR, W, Q_1 and Q_2 will take. We can then adjust these parameters according to what we expect, what kind of traffic and load we would like to achieve, and what kind of quality of service we want to guarantee. The formulae allow indeed an easy comparison of the performance for different parameters and for different schemes of signaling and detecting congestion: according to the network we want to optimize, we can calculate the ideal dimension of the essential parameters of ABR (MCR, PCR, RIF and RDF) and of the bottleneck thresholds Q_L and Q_H. Furthermore, the formulae we obtained give information about the achievable throughput and the buffer size required to avoid cell losses.

This analysis also allows us to understand the behavior we observe in the simulations. First, we have clearly identified that some behaviors of a TCP over ABR connection have never been seen before and are due to the interactions between TCP and ABR. This causes strange and unexplored evolutions of the main variables of the system. Secondly, if we compare the results obtained by this theoretical approach and the results obtained by the simulation approach, we can see that our results are very accurate and that our fluid analysis gives a good approximation of the TCP over ABR behavior; it explains in a significant way what we obtain in the simulations. Thus, dependencies on system parameters, such as the throughput or the round trip time, can be studied without running time-consuming simulations.

We also extended this analysis to a larger number of TCP connections and ATM VCs. We have worked on several ABR circuits transporting a set of synchronized TCP connections. We showed how the evolutions of the state variables can be influenced by the number of connections and VCs. This allows us to predict the behavior of a more realistic system and to see the impact on the dimensioning of Internet links, where TCP connections are numerous.

Finally, we would like to give to the reader a more general conclusion concerning our work on TCP connections over ATM. After several experiences on different network configurations, with different parameters, we discovered that combining TCP with ABR can provide good performances: if we choose correct and robust ABR parameters (the goal of our analysis is to help the operator to choose the right parameters), we can avoid losses inside the network and extend TCP cycles in time, which improves the throughput. Furthermore, we believe that the ABR mechanism is at the moment the best and even the only right way to transport TCP. The main advantage of ABR with respect to GFR, for example, is that it tries to adapt its rate to the network status and thus tries to avoid losses as long as it can. This decrease in packet losses allows us to optimize TCP performances.

We now try to understand with the help of simulations the relative importance of other ABR parameters, like $ADTF$, M_{rm}, T_{rm} and CDF. This will be the subject of a future article. Future work will try to extend this study to new versions of TCP (Reno or Vegas).

References

[1] O. Ait-Hellal, E. Altman, D. Elouadghiri, M. Erramdani, Performance Evaluation of the Rate-Based Flow Control Mechanism for ABR Service, *Second IFIP Workshop on Traffic Management and Synthesis of ATM Networks,* Montreal, September 1997.

[2] E. Altman, F. Boccara, J. Bolot, P. Nain, P. Brown, D. Collange, Analysis of TCP/IP Flow Control Mechanism in High-Speed Wide Area Networks, *IEEE Conf. Decision and Control,* New Orleans, December 1995.

[3] ATM Forum Technical Committee, *Traffic Management Specification,* Version 4.0, April 1996.

[4] J.-L. Costeux, Fluid analysis of a TCP connection in presence of exogenous flow and random loss, *IEEE Conf. Decision and Control,* Tampa, December 1998.

[5] J.-L. Costeux, Fluid analysis of a TCP connection over ABR, *ITC 16,* Edinburgh, June 1999.

[6] J.-L. Costeux, Analysis of a TCP connection over ABR, in presence of exogenous flow, *ICATM'99,* Colmar, June 1999.

[7] S. Floyd, TCP and Explicit Congestion Notification, *ACM Computer Communication Review,* vol. 24, n. 5, pp. 10–23, October 1994.

[8] A. Legout, Etude d'une connexion TCP travers un systme 2 files d'attente, *France Telecom-CNET Technical Report RP/PAA/ATR/ORE/4824,* August 1996.

[9] S. Manthorpe, Implications of the Transport Layer for Network Dimensioning, *Ph.D. Thesis,* EPFL, 1997.

[10] M. Ritter, Network Buffer Requirements of the Rate-Based Control Mechanism for ABR Services, *IEEE Infocom'96,* San Francisco, March 1996.

Vitae

Jean-Laurent Costeux received his M.S. in Electrical Engineering at the Institut National des Télécommunications in 1996. After studying at Eurecom

Institute, he joined the CNET, France Telecom Research Center. He will obtain his Ph.D. in Telecommunications from the Ecole Nationale Superieure des Telecommunications in October 1999. His research interests include performance of data transfer applications over ATM networks.

Chapter 8

On the Exact Performance Analysis of Multicast Switches with Input Buffering

B. Doshi, T. V. Lakshman, W. Matragi and Kazem Sohraby
Lucent Technologies

Khosrow Sohraby
University of Missouri

Abstract   Most of the existing work in the analysis of multicast switches with input buffering concentrate on large switches and uniform loading. In this paper, we consider an $N \times N$ (N finite and usually small) multicast switch. Unless sophisticated scheduling policies are employed, such switches are known to be non-work-conserving. In such switches, in the simplest case, a cell is only removed from an input port if it can be transmitted to all the intended output ports in one time slot. This case is of particular interest since it provides a lower bound on the maximum switch throughput over any scheduling policy used.

In general, we show that the system can be modeled as a Quasi-Birth-and-Death (QBD) Markov chain with *infinite* number of phases. Through numerical experimentation, it is demonstrated that the HOL contention could result in very high percentile of buffer fill. Moreover, a typical exponential tail behavior appears to take place only after very high percentiles even in moderate loading.

Keywords: multicast switch, QBD chains, head-of-line blocking.

8.1   Introduction

It is expected that ATM switching will be used directly or indirectly in most high speed transport networks. For instance, ATM switches combined with optical transmission are used in high-speed backbone networks. Also, these switches can be used to build fast routers or routers with switching capability for high-speed transport of Internet traffic [2]. Although most of the capacity of today's information carrying networks are allocated to the delivery of voice (in circuit, and in few instances packet switched mode), it is expected that data (such as for providing today's Internet-type services) and video teleconferencing and video broadcast will consume most of the capacity in broadband networks. A significant component of traffic in both ATM networks and the Internet is expected to be multicast traffic. This is because of the advent of applications built on the Internet MBONE and ATM LAN emulation, which are inherently multicast in nature. With the inherent high capacities of optical transmission, the bottlenecks are likely to be at the routers and switches. Hence, it is important that ATM switches perform well when carrying multicast traffic.

In principle, there are two ways to deal with multicast issues in a network. In the past, ATM switch architectures with specialized fabrics, have been devised to deal with broadcast and multicast features. Among most recent developments are [3], [4] and [5].

Most of the above literature deals with the multicast/broadcast capability with new fabric architectures. This approach may not be feasible in situations where the network is already planned and/or built. For previously designed fabrics which may be based on input, output, shared memory, or other architectures, and multicast may not be inherent in their fabrics, a new approach is necessary. An architecture that has received considerable attention, due to its simplicity, is the input buffer switch. For example, [6] comparatively shows performance of input vs. output buffer switches.

In that paper it is shown that under certain traffic assumptions, in space-division input buffer switches it is possible to achieve switch throughput of about 58.6% in point-to-point (unicast) for large switches. The throughput limitation is due to the Head-Of-Line (HOL) blocking whereby a packet at the head of the line in an input port may block other packets in the same input buffer destined for output ports that are not blocked by input requests from other input ports. Later, [7] considers a space division switch with input buffering and multicasting.

In this paper, we consider the performance of an $N \times N$ input buffered ATM switch with multicast traffic. We study only input queued switches in this paper. The analysis for output queued switches (particularly when multicast can be split) is similar to that for unicast. However, completely output buffered switches require an N-fold speed-up of the switch fabric. Hence, there is interest in shifting buffers to the input and using some combination of input and output queues with congestion feedback from the output to the inputs. For purely input queued switches, the throughput limit due to head-of-line (cell) blocking [6] has motivated study of scheduling schemes which schedule cells other than the HOL cell and try to maximize throughput.

Hayes et al. [8] consider a random HOL service discipline. They assume slot to slot independence and ignore HOL destination coupling. Hui and Renner [7] assume that each HOL destination is served independently across all inputs and slots with identical probability.

In this paper, we consider the simplest case where only the head-of-line cells in each input queue are eligible for transmission and no call-splitting is allowed. This case is of interest because it provides a lower bound on the maximum throughput over any scheduling policy. Even in this case, the behavior is quite complex and exact analysis for a general $N \times N$ switch is difficult. We model the system as a QBD Markov Chain with an infinite number of phases. We exactly analyze a 2×2 switch which is motivated by the consideration that many large switches are built from typically small switching elements (such as a network of 4×4 or 8×8 switching elements). For a 2×2 switch with non-uniform traffic we derive the system stability condition as a function of buffer size. A numerical algorithm for throughput computation is developed for the infinite (large) buffer case.

8.2 Mathematical Model and Analysis

We assume an $N \times N$ multicast switch with input buffering. In a slot n, the arrivals to port i are denoted by $A_n^{(i)} \in \{0, 1\}$, $1 \leq i \leq N$. This condition is dictated by the physical limitation where a maximum of one cell per slot is transmitted to any input port. A cell from the input port i is sent *simultaneously* (i.e., in one time slot) to a number of output ports. We define a connectivity multicast matrix $\mathbf{C} = \{c_{i,j}\}$ of size $N \times N$ where $c_{i,j} = 1$ denotes that the cell from input port i will be sent to output port j and $c_{i,j} = 0$ denotes otherwise. An output port can only receive a maximum of one cell per slot. In the event of multiple transmissions to an output port j, a randomly chosen input from the set of contending input ports to this output port is selected. A transmission from an input port i is successful (i.e., the cell is removed from the port) only if all the output ports to which the cell is destined choose the input port i.

In what follows, we describe the system evolution more formally. Define $q_i^{(n)}$ as the number of cells in input port i at slot n. Also, define $m_n^{(j)}$ as the number of cells destined to output port j in slot n. We have

$$m_n^{(j)} = \sum_{i=1}^{N} c_{i,j} \, \mathbf{1}_{q_i^{(n)} \neq 0} \,, \tag{8.1}$$

where $\mathbf{1}_E = 1$ if event E is true and zero, otherwise.

Denote the binary random variable $f^{(n)}(i, j)$ as taking a value of one if the output port j chooses the non-empty input port i and zero, otherwise. With the random (uniform) assumption, we have

$$\Pr[f^{(n)}(i, j) = 1] = \frac{1}{m_j^{(n)}}, \quad i \in \{i : c(i, j) = 1, \; q_i^{(n)} \neq 0\}. \quad (8.2)$$

Now we are ready to provide the evolution equations for an input port i. We have

$$q_i^{(n+1)} = \left(q_i^{(n)} - \prod_{j \in \{j : c(i, j) = 1\}} f^{(n)}(i, j) \right)^+ + A_i^{(n+1)}, \quad (8.3)$$

which indicates that a successful transmission of an input port takes place if in one time slot it is picked by the all output ports a cell is being multicast.

For the sake of simplicity, let us assume that the arrival sequence to the input port i is Bernoulli with average r_i. With this assumption, it is easy to see that the vector $(q_1^{(n)}, q_2^{(n)}, \cdots, q_N^{(n)})$ is Markov. However, we have an N dimensional chain where all the dimensions can extend to infinity. In general, there is no systematic methodology for the determination of the stationary solution of such chains.

Under the assumption that the maximum number of cells arriving to any port is one and all the ports have finite capacity, the transition probability matrix of the above N dimensional system has a Quasi-Birth-and-Death (QBD) block structure.

In a finite QBD chains we identify $K + 1$ levels (level 0 to K). The transition probability matrix $\mathbf{P}$ has $K + 1$ rows and it is in the block structure form

$$\mathbf{P} = \begin{bmatrix} B_0 & D_0 & & & & & \\ B_1 & D_1 & A_0 & & & & \\ & & D_2 & A_1 & \ddots & & \\ & & & A_2 & \ddots & A_0 & \\ & & & & \ddots & A_1 & C_0 \\ & & & & & A_2 & C_1 \end{bmatrix}, \quad (8.4)$$

where all the blocks are square matrices of dimension $m \times m$. We first partition the stationary probability vector Π of the Markov chain as $\Pi = \begin{bmatrix} \Pi_0 & \Pi_1 & \cdots & \Pi_K \end{bmatrix}$.

Following the formulation of [1], we have a forward-backward matrix geometric solution

$$\Pi_k = v_1 R_1^{k-1} + v_2 R_2^{K-k}, \quad 1 \leq k \leq K, \quad (8.5)$$

where R_1 and R_2 are the desired solutions to the matrix equations

$$R_1 = A_0 + R_1 A_1 + R^2 A_2, \quad R_2 = A_2 + R_1 A_1 + R^2 A_0. \quad (8.6)$$

The properties of R_1 and R_2 depend on the matrix sequences A_i. Let π denote the stationary distribution of the chain $A = A_0 + A_1 + A_2$. I.e., we have $\pi A = \pi$ and $\pi e = 1$. We recall that $\pi A_2 e > \pi A_0 e$ is the condition of stability of an infinite QBD chain, that is, as $K \to \infty$. The numerical treatment of finite QBD depends on whether $\pi A_2 e > \pi A_0 e$ or $\pi A_2 e < \pi A_0 e$. The latter case is very similar to the former and only needs a small modification (see [1]). In what follows, we assume that the infinite version of the above chain is stable $(\pi A_2 e > \pi A_0 e)$.

The vectors v_1 and v_2 should be found to satisfy the boundary equations. See [1] for details.

Next, we turn our attention to the switch model. In our system, one may take the number of cells in the first queue as the level process and the combination of other finite dimensions as the phase process. Obviously, as the capacity and/or the number of ports increase, number of possible phases grows very quickly. Recognizing this complexity for an exact solution, we only consider the case of $N = 2$. We assume the worst case, namely a full fan out (i.e., each input port is multicasting to all output ports), so $\mathbf{C} = \begin{bmatrix} 1 & 1 \\ 1 & 1 \end{bmatrix}$. In what follows, we concentrate on the model and provide the block structure of the chain. We consider three cases. In the first case, we assume both ports have finite capacity. In the second case, only one port is finite and in the last case both ports have infinite capacity. This case is treated as we consider the limiting behavior of the second case as the buffer size of the second port increases.

Two Input Ports with Finite Capacity. As discussed, with independent Bernoulli arrivals to each port, $(q_1^{(n)}, q_2^{(n)})$ is Markov. We can write down its transition probability matrix $\mathbf{P}$ by using the model discussed. In (8.4), the block matrices summarize the transitions between levels. The details of the phase transitions are summarized within the blocks. For example, the matrix B_0 summarizes all the transitions from level zero to level zero, namely $(q_1^{(n)} = 0, q_2^{(n)} = i)$ to $(q_1^{(n)} = 0, q_2^{(n)} = j)$.

We define the stationary probability vector ($0 \le i \le K_1$),

$$\Pi_i = [\Pr(q_1 = i, q_2 = 0), \Pr(q_1 = i, q_2 = 1), \cdots, \Pr(q_1 = i, q_2 = K_2)]$$
(8.7)

and the vector $\Pi = (\Pi_0, \Pi_1, \cdots, \Pi_{K_1})$, then $\Pi = \Pi P$, where $\mathbf{P}$ is a finite QBD chain of the general form (8.4) with $K = K_2$. All the blocks are of size $(K_2 + 1) \times (K_2 + 1)$ and tridiagonal. We depict them here for $K_2 = 4$:

$$B_0 = \begin{bmatrix} (1-r_1)(1-r_2) & (1-r_1)r_2 & 0 & 0 & 0 \\ (1-r_1)(1-r_2) & (1-r_1)r_2 & 0 & 0 & 0 \\ 0 & (1-r_1)(1-r_2) & (1-r_1)r_2 & 0 & 0 \\ 0 & 0 & (1-r_1)(1-r_2) & (1-r_1)r_2 & 0 \\ 0 & 0 & 0 & (1-r_1)(1-r_2) & (1-r_1)r_2 \end{bmatrix},$$

$$B_1 = \begin{bmatrix} (1-r_1)(1-r_2) & (1-r_1)r_2 & 0 & 0 & 0 \\ 0 & \frac{(1-r_1)(1-r_2)}{4} & \frac{(1-r_1)r_2}{4} & 0 & 0 \\ 0 & 0 & \frac{(1-r_1)(1-r_2)}{4} & \frac{(1-r_1)r_2}{4} & 0 \\ 0 & 0 & 0 & \frac{(1-r_1)(1-r_2)}{4} & \frac{(1-r_1)r_2}{4} \\ 0 & 0 & 0 & 0 & \frac{1-r_1}{4} \end{bmatrix},$$

$$D_0 = \begin{bmatrix} r_1(1-r_2) & r_1 r_2 & 0 & 0 & 0 \\ r_1(1-r_2) & r_1 r_2 & 0 & 0 & 0 \\ 0 & r_1(1-r_2) & r_1 r_2 & 0 & 0 \\ 0 & 0 & r_1(1-r_2) & r_1 r_2 & 0 \\ 0 & 0 & 0 & r_1(1-r_2) & r_1 r_2 \end{bmatrix},$$

$$A_0 = \begin{bmatrix} 0 & 0 & 0 & 0 & 0 \\ \frac{r_1(1-r_2)}{4} & \frac{r_1(2-r_2)}{4} & \frac{r_1 r_2}{2} & 0 & 0 \\ 0 & \frac{r_1(1-r_2)}{4} & \frac{r_1(2-r_2)}{4} & \frac{r_1 r_2}{2} & 0 \\ 0 & 0 & \frac{r_1(1-r_2)}{4} & \frac{r_1(2-r_2)}{4} & \frac{r_1 r_2}{2} \\ 0 & 0 & 0 & \frac{r_1(1-r_2)}{4} & \frac{r_1(2+r_2)}{4} \end{bmatrix},$$

$$D_1 = A_1 = \begin{bmatrix} r_1(1-r_2) & r_1 r_2 & 0 & 0 & 0 \\ \frac{(1-r_1)(1-r_2)}{4} & \frac{2-r_1-r_2}{4} & \frac{(2-r_1)r_2}{4} & 0 & 0 \\ 0 & \frac{(1-r_1)(1-r_2)}{4} & \frac{2-r_1-r_2}{4} & \frac{(2-r_1)r_2}{4} & 0 \\ 0 & 0 & \frac{(1-r_1)(1-r_2)}{4} & \frac{2-r_1-r_2}{4} & \frac{(2-r_1)r_2}{4} \\ 0 & 0 & 0 & \frac{(1-r_1)(1-r_2)}{4} & \frac{2-r_1+r_2-r_1 r_2}{4} \end{bmatrix},$$

and finally

$$D_2 = A_2 = B_1, C_0 = A_0, C_1 = A_0 + A_1 .$$

One Input Port with Infinite Capacity. We assume the first input port has an infinite capacity (i.e., $K_1 = \infty$). In this case, we discuss the stability condition of the system. Given the simple structure of the A_i matrices, it is easy to show that the chain $A_0 + A_1 + A_2$ is a simple Birth-and-Death chain. Substituting π, the stationary distribution of this chain in the condition of stability $\pi A_2 e > \pi A_0 e$, it is not difficult to find the stability condition. We summarize the result in the following theorem.

Theorem: The 2×2 multicast switch with input rates r_1 and r_2 is stable iff r_1 and r_2 satisfy

$$r_1 < \frac{3 - 2w - w^{K_2+1}}{3 + w - 4w^{K_2+1}} , \qquad w \overset{\Delta}{=} \frac{3r_2}{1 - r_2} , \qquad (8.8)$$

where the first port has an infinite capacity and the buffer size of the second port is limited to K_2 cells.

Two Input Ports with Infinite Capacity. We treat this case as the limiting case of K_2 finite. First, we examine the stability condition of the system as $K_2 \to \infty$. Using the condition (8.8), it is not difficult to conclude: 1) For zero r_2, stable system for $r_1 < 1$ (as expected). 2) If $0 \le r_2 < \frac{1}{4}$ (i.e., $w < 1$) system stable in rectangular box $\{0 \le r_1 \le 1 - 3r_2, 0 < r_2 < \frac{1}{4}\}$ as $K_2 \to \infty$. 3) For $r_1 < \frac{1}{4}$, the system is stable for all $r_2 < 1$ and all finite (but arbitrary large) K_2. 4) For symmetric system $r_1 = r_2 = r$, the queuing system is stable for $r < \frac{1}{4}$ as $K_2 \to \infty$.

The maximum throughout of the switch in the symmetric case is limited to 50 percent. This is due to the HOL contention between the two ports. In the asymmetric cases, depending on the values of r_1 and r_2, the throughput $r_1 + r_2$ could increase even to 125 percent (take r_1 and r_2 arbitrary close to $\frac{1}{4}$ and 1, respectively). However, this requires finite (but arbitrary large) K_2.

For the numerical calculation of the stationary distribution of queue for the case of infinite (large) K_2, our approach is numerical. We increase K_2 until the relative change in any metric (say probability of empty queue for either port) does not change more than a pre-defined small ϵ. In a symmetric system (i.e., $r_1 = r_2 = r$) the increase in K_2 could continue until some performance measure of both input ports become arbitrary close to each other.

8.3 Numerical Results, Conclusions and Future Work

First, we present a set of numerical results. These results are obtained assuming that the first port has an infinite buffer. We consider various cases with different utilization and buffer size of second port. The numerical results are obtained using the algorithm in Section 8.2. Due to space limitation, we do not provide numerical results for the case where all the ports are finite.

Table 8.1 assumes $r_1 = r_2 = .2$. The value of the second buffer is assumed to be 5 (small). This results in $E[q_1] = .4838$ and $E[q_2] = .4597$. Since the system utilization is not large, even a small buffer for port 2, gives results which are fairly close to that of port 1. Also, based on the last column in the table, the geometric tail behavior kicks in rather quickly.

In Table 8.2, the same example is repeated for $K_2 = 10$. In this case, the distribution of the two queues are very close to each other. As K_2 increases, the distribution of the two queues approaches to each other in the symmetric case.

In the next example, we concentrate on a high load situation where $r_1 = r_2 = .24$ is assumed (recall that in the symmetric case the maximum throughput for each port is .25). With a buffer size of $K_2 = 70$, the distribution of the two queues were found to be sufficiently close to each other. We can make some

Table 8.1 Queue Size Distribution for
$K_1 = \infty$, $K_2 = 5$. $r_1 = r_2 = .2$

i	$\Pr[q_1 = i]$	$\Pr[q_2 = i]$	$\frac{\Pr[q_1=i]}{\Pr[q_1=i-1]}$
0	0.67766237	0.6784557	-
1	0.23951038	0.2403987	0.3534361
2	0.04466022	0.0454987	0.1864642
3	0.01909845	0.0199427	0.4276391
4	0.00914427	0.0100394	0.4787964
5	0.00464194	0.0056645	0.5076336
6	0.00243423	-	0.5243991
7	0.00130077	-	0.5343687
8	0.00070288	-	0.5403575
9	0.00038234	-	0.5439697
10	0.00020881	-	0.5461485

Table 8.2 Queue Size Distribution for
$K_1 = \infty$, $K_2 = 10$. $r_1 = r_2 = .2$

i	$\Pr[q_1 = i]$	$\Pr[q_2 = i]$	$\frac{\Pr[q_1=i]}{\Pr[q_1=i-1]}$
0	0.6752610	0.6753122	-
1	0.2391321	0.2391860	0.3541329
2	0.0450619	0.0451071	0.1884397
3	0.0195413	0.0195811	0.4336552
4	0.0095611	0.0095975	0.4892796
5	0.0050059	0.0050404	0.5235692
6	0.0027350	0.0027689	0.5463641
7	0.0015384	0.0015731	0.5624954
8	0.0008837	0.0009207	0.5744153
9	0.0005156	0.0005575	0.5834868
10	0.0003044	0.0003550	0.5905245

very interesting observations. Although the probability of empty queue is not small (about .46) and the average queue length is found to be small (about 2.4 cells), the queue length distribution decays quite slowly, especially in the high percentiles. An interesting issue is if both ports are assumed to have an infinite capacity, to what extent (or if) the exponential tail assumption is valid.

In this paper, we provided a mathematical model for an $N \times N$ multicast switch when no splitting is allowed (worst case). It was shown that if all the ports are assumed to be finite, the system can be modeled as a finite QBD chain with modified boundary. A backward-forward matrix geometric solution for a generic chain of this form was provided.

Table 8.3 Queue Size Distribution
for $K_1 = \infty$, $K_2 = 70$. $r_1 = r_2 = .24$

i	$\Pr[q_1 > i]$	$\frac{\Pr[q_1=i+1]}{\Pr[q_1=i]}$
0	0.538594	0.571528
1	0.307821	0.109333
2	0.033655	0.750743
5	0.0157426	0.814603
6	0.012824	0.826331
9	0.0074695	0.849875
10	0.00634815	0.855347
19	0.00180749	0.882686
20	0.00159545	0.884444
100	6.36744×10^{-7}	0.914811
200	1.04633×10^{-10}	0.917158

In the special case of a 2×2 switch, we provided a detailed analysis of the system and its stability condition. It was shown that in the symmetric case with Bernoulli arrivals, the maximum throughput of the switch is 50 percent (25 percent per port). In the asymmetric case, the stability condition has a non-trivial form and was presented in the manuscript.

Through numerical experimentation, we observed that if the input ports have infinite capacity, the exponential tail behavior *may* kick in after very high percentiles if the loading of the switch is high, even though the average number of cells in each port could be relatively small.

Our solution methodology is applicable to any Markovian arrivals. It would be interesting to examine the impact of the burstiness on the switch capacity, especially in the asymmetric case. In this work, we have not utilized the triangular structure of the block matrices in the QBD chain. It would be interesting to examine if a more efficient solution would be possible by careful examination of the blocks.

References

[1] N. Akar and K. Sohraby, Finite and infinite QBD chains: A simple and unifying algorithmic approach, *Proc. of IEEE INFOCOM'97*.

[2] P. Newman, T. Lyon, G. Minshall, Flow Labeled IP: A Connectionless Approach to ATM, *IEEE Infocom 96 Proc.,* pp. 1251–1259.

[3] Jae W. Byun, Tony T. Lee, The Design and Analysis of an ATM Multicast Switch with Adaptive Traffic Controller, *IEEE/ACM Trans. on Networking,* Vol. 2, No. 3, June 1994.

[4] J.S. Turner, Design of a Broadcast Packet Switching Network, *IEEE Trans. Comm.,* Vol. 36, pp. 734–743, June 1988.

[5] W. De Zhong, Y. Onozato, J. Kaniyil, A copy Network with Shared Buffers for Large-Scale Multicast ATM Switching, *IEEE/ACM Trans. Networking,* Vol. 1, pp. 157–165, April 1993.

[6] M.J. Karol, M.G. Hluchyj, S. Morgan, Input versus Output Queuing on a Space-Division Packet Switch, *IEEE Trans. Comm.,* Vol. COM-35, pp. 1587–1597, Dec. 1987.

[7] Joseph Y. Hui, Thomas Renner, Queuing Analysis for Multicast Packet Switching, *IEEE Trans. Comm.,* Vol. 42, No. 2/3/4, February/March/April, 1994.

[8] J.F. Hayes, R. Breault, M. K. Mehmet-Ali, Performance Analysis of a Multicast Switch, *IEEE Trans. Comm.,* Vol. 39, No. 4, April 1994.

Chapter 9

Performance Evaluation of a Scene-Based Model for VBR MPEG Traffic

A. Mashat and M. Kara

ATM-Multimedia Group
The University of Leeds

Abstract

Variable Bit Rate (VBR) MPEG traffic is expected to be one of the major traffic sources for high speed networks. Compressed video traffic (MPEG) exhibits complex patterns which vary from one stream to another. One of the most important reasons for these fluctuations (or patterns) in the overall bit rate are the scene changes within a video stream. The aim of this paper is to propose a novel *scene-based* model considering scene change characteristics. We analyze the scene changes within an MPEG stream in more detail including scene change identification techniques. Compared to Markovian models, we show that the proposed model (*scene-based*) provides a good approximation of the statistical characteristics behavior of the real MPEG stream. We also show that the model is capable of capturing the Long Range Dependency (LRD) feature of such traffic. To examine the appropriateness and limitations of these models, simulation experiments are conducted to study the performance over an ATM multiplexer using the generated (synthetic) sequence based on the presented models and the real traffic.

9.1 Introduction

For efficient traffic management in a high speed network, it is important to know the basic characteristics of multimedia traffic [18]. This information can be used either to study the network utilization or to develop appropriate control schemes for handling multimedia traffic. In order to achieve that, a traffic source model should be developed based on the measurements of the existing multimedia applications. A number of models have been proposed to approximate individual and/or aggregate traffic sources [3, 5, 2].

Nowadays, video becomes an increasingly important component of multimedia communications because of the increasing user demand for video and rapid advances in coding algorithms. The focus of this paper is on a particular coding algorithm which has recently received a great attention, namely the Motion Picture Experts (MPEG) standard. We have focused on MPEG because it is widely available and it has been standardized by CCITT. In addition, MPEG is an example of Variable Bit Rate (VBR) video traffic.

One of the most important reasons for the fluctuations in the overall bit rate are the scene changes within the video stream. In [8] and [12], we showed that the amount of activities within an MPEG stream affects not only the traffic model but also the queuing performance at an ATM multiplexer. Thus, the scene change should be incorporated at the characterization process. Various models have been proposed for VBR MPEG traffic [8, 16, 17, 5] and [3], but a few models incorporate scene changes [9, 10] and [6]. Complex traffic models are useful only when their parameters can be estimated accurately. In some models, it is possible to achieve different classes of traffic characterization by varying the model parameters even when the model is simple (for instance an On/Off source). An overview of these models can be found in [3, 15, 7]. The source model[1] cannot only be used for the traffic characterization, but also to generate a synthetic traffic with a similar behavior of the real traffic. There are many advantages from generating a synthetic video traffic, especially at performance studies. The performance studies cannot be carried out without providing the actual video traces. Furthermore, a stochastic model encompasses many realizations (sample path) which represent 'structurally' similar but not identical streams [9]. Therefore, generated streams are ideal for performance evaluation studies, especially statistical multiplexing studies.

This paper is organized as follows: In the next section, we present a brief overview of MPEG sequences. In addition, we present two methods to identify the scene changes within an MPEG stream. In Section 9.3, we undertake the statistical modeling of an MPEG-Coded stream. Two simple Markovian based models and one scene-based model for VBR MPEG traffic are presented. Then, a validation of the models is performed to assess its suitability to capture the statistical behavior of the empirical sequence. We conclude in Section 9.4.

---

[1]In this paper, the terms "source model" and "traffic model" will be used interchangeably.

9.2 Scene-Based Characterization of MPEG-Coded Sequence

9.2.1 MPEG Encoder

The MPEG coding algorithm was developed initially to store a compressed video on digital-storage media [14]. MPEG is a flexible coding scheme which makes this type of coding widely spread and most frequently used for video encoding [1]. The basic scheme of MPEG coding is to predict motion from frame to frame in the temporal direction, and then to use DCTs (Discrete Cosine Transforms) to organize the redundancy in the spatial directions. Thus, MPEG coding is a combination of interframe and intraframe coding techniques. Considering the output of an MPEG-I encoder, the reduction can be achieved by producing three types of frames: I (Intra-frame), P (Predictive) and B (Bidirectional predictive) frames (see Fig. 9.1). An MPEG encoder repeats these frames periodically. Thus, the output of the encoded stream (the sequence of decoded frames) contains a deterministic periodic sequence of frames such as [IBBPBBPBBPBB], which is called Group Of Pictures (GOP).

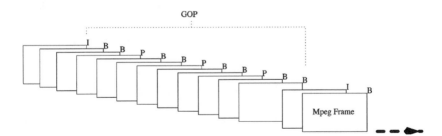

FIGURE 9.1
Encoded MPEG video stream.

MPEG traffic can be characterized using different levels: macroblock, slide, frame, GOP, or even the entire MPEG stream. However, we will be focusing on GOP level in our modeling because a GOP contains most of the picture's details. GOP is also playing the most important role concerning autocorrelation effects of an MPEG sequence because the GOP fixes the periodic picture of the sequence. This could be seen when multiple MPEG streams are multiplexed [12].

It is difficult to characterize a video traffic by using a short sequence of real data (few seconds). For our statistical analysis study, we use a long sequence of real MPEG video (about 30 min) which contains 40.000 frames. Empirical data sets for MPEG video streams have been retrieved from the ftp site [19]. The video streams have been encoded at the Institute of Computer Science,

University of Wurzburg. These sets represent frame size traces from MPEG-I encoded video sequences with encoder input 384X288 pel (Berkeley MPEG-encoder ver. 1.3 has been used). The traced videos were captured in motion-JPEG format from VCR (VHS) with a captured rate between 19 to 25 fps. Our analysis of MPEG-I is applicable to MPEG-II (video sequence) since both MPEG types use the same compression concept.

It has been shown in our previous studies [8, 12, 13] that the amount of activities has to be considered at the modeling process as well as the multiplexing process due to its impact on the traffic behavior. We have also examined the dependencies feature of the MPEG sequence. This information is one of the most important features of an MPEG sequence [7]. The analysis of any video sequence shows dependencies between the frames and between the GOPs within the same video sequence. These dependencies can be measured by using the AutoCorrelation Function (ACF).

9.2.2   Scene Change Identifiers

In the visual sense, a scene can be defined as a portion of the movie without sudden changes in view [9]. In an empirical data set for a traced MPEG traffic, a significant change in the size of two consecutive GOPs is an indication of a scene change. This section presents two methods to detect and measure the amount of the overall bit rate fluctuations. We then use these methods to identify the amount of scene changes within an MPEG stream.

9.2.2.1   Scene Change Identification Using the Outlier Method

The basic idea of MPEG is that when a new scene starts, the size of the frames will be larger than the previous frame sizes. In other words, within the same data set, changes in the size of two consecutive GOPs could be an indicator for a scene change. The amount of change could be measured by using one of the most commonly used measures of data variation (variability), namely: the *variance* or the *standard deviation*. However, these parameters give only the overall measurement of the data variation and cannot be used as a measurement of location relating to the rest of the data set. We will use another statistical parameter, called *outlier*, to describe each element *relative* to the other elements in the same data set [11]. The *outlier* is an element value which seems to be unusual (abnormal) compared with the other elements within the same data set. Within an empirical data set, outliers could be detected by using either a numerical method based on a *z-score* measure or a graphical technique called *Box Plot* [4].

The *z-score* measure can be used to describe the location of a Y_i relative to the mean in units of the standard deviation. Let $\{Y_i\,,\ 0 \leq i \leq N - 2\}$ where $Y_i = X_{i+1} - X_i$, X_i is the number of cells in the ith GOP and N is the number of GOPs. Then, *z-score* can be calculated as follows:

$$z\_score_i = \frac{Y_i - E[Y]}{\sqrt{Var[Y]}} \quad \text{where } E[Y] = \mu \quad \text{and} \quad Var[Y] = \sigma^2 .$$

In the *z-score* definition, negative z-score values indicate that Y_i lies to the left of the mean and positive values indicate that Y_i lies to the right of the mean. Therefore, if Y_i is unusually large relative to the other within $\{Y\}$ in the empirical data set, then Y_i is called *outlier*. We use Rule of Thumb for detecting outliers within an empirical data set [11]. The rule states that if the *z-score* value is greater than a *Threshold* (τ), usually $\tau \leq 3$, then an outlier is identified.

For the sake of brevity, we demonstrate the technique using only one empirical set ('Dino' sequence). However, this technique can be adopted on any empirical data set. We plot z-scores for 'Dino' sequence (see Fig. 9.2). The figure shows many spikes caused by large changes in the GOP sizes (large scene changes). Every spike over the τ value is considered to be an *outlier*. Consequently, each outlier is a significant scene change. It is important to notice that smaller values of τ capture more scene changes and vice versa.

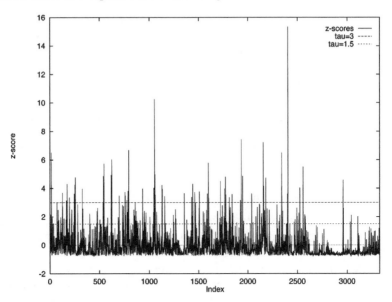

FIGURE 9.2
z-score plots for 'Dino' sequence.

A similar method could be used to detect an outlier by constructing the box plot of the empirical data set (see Fig. 9.3). First, the method constructs two intervals based on a quantity value called the interquartile range (IQR):

$$IQR = Q_u - Q_l ,$$

where Q_u and Q_l are the *upper* and *lower* quartiles, respectively.

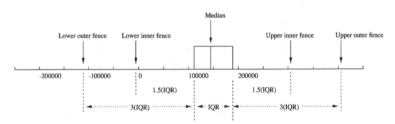

FIGURE 9.3
Box plot for 'Dino' sequence.

Next, we construct two sets of limits out of (IQR) called *Inner* fences (If) and *Outer* fences (Of). *Inner* fence values are located a distance of $1.5IQR$ below Q_l and above Q_u, whereas *Outer* fence values are located a distance of $3IQR$ below the Q_l and above Q_u. Similarly, according to the statistical theory of the Rule of Thumb for detecting outliers, every $\{Y_i, i \geq 0\}$ which falls between the *inner* and *outer* fences is called *suspect outlier*. But, if Y_i is located outside the *outer* fence it is called *a highly suspect outlier.* In other words, every *suspect outlier* could be a moderate scene change while every *highly suspect outlier* could be a significant scene change.

These two methods produce similar results. However, the presence of one or more *outlier* in a data set can inflate the value of the standard deviation (σ) used to calculate the z-score. Consequently, it will be less likely to detect an element value with a high z-score. In contrast, the value of the quartiles used to calculate the fences for a box plot are not affected by the presence of outliers. As a result, both methods can be used to identify the significant scene changes within an MPEG video stream.

9.2.2.2   Scene Change Identifier Using Second Difference Method

The previous method identifies the scene changes based on the differences between only two consecutive GOPs. In order to impose more accuracy on the scene change identification result, it is desirable to compare the GOP with the previous and the next GOPs. Therefore, we will use a method which is based on the *Second Difference* method. It has been used previously to analyze the frame variation in the case of broadcast-video sequence [6]. For VBR MPEG video stream, the method can be used for any MPEG sequence at GOP level to identify the scene changes within the sequence. Similarly, we shall use 'Dino' stream to demonstrate this method. The time series plot of GOP sizes (see Fig. 9.4) shows several spikes (peaks) due to possible scene changes. In order to determine which spike represents a true scene change, we need to analyze its magnitude. This could be achieved by relating each GOP spike with its neighbors (GOPs) according to the amount of movement within the same stream. As described before, a scene change occurs when a GOP size is abnormally larger than its neighbors. Based on this fact, we can quantify the scene change in the following way:

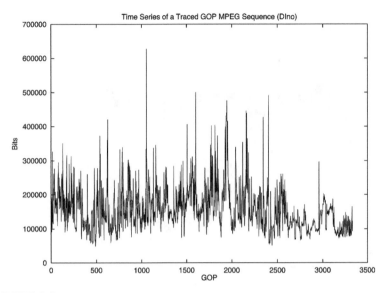

FIGURE 9.4
GOP time series (Dino).

Let us assume that $\{X_i\}$ is the size of a GOP: $\{X_i : i = 1, 2, \ldots, N\}$. At a scene change, the second difference $(Diff_2)$ will be large in magnitude and negative in sign [6]. The *Second Difference* is given by:

$$Diff_2 = ((X_{i+1} - X_i) - (X_i - X_{i-1})) .$$

Figure 9.5 shows the plot of the second difference for 'Dino' stream. Every large negative spike could be an indicator for a scene change. In order to quantify only the significant scene changes, we divide the second difference by the GOP average ($\frac{1}{t} \sum_{j=i-t}^{i} X_j$) of the past few seconds (t). The period of the last few seconds, t, might vary. We have tested various values for t and all of them gave similar results for $\{Y_i\}$:

$$Y_i = \frac{(X_{i+1} - X_i) - (X_i - X_{i-1})}{\frac{1}{t} \sum_{j=i-t}^{i} X_j} , \qquad i = 2, 3, \ldots, N - 1 .$$

A significant scene change can be identified with every negative large spike when we plot the division result Y_i from the above equation. We chose a *threshold* (T) as a critical value, where $0 < |T| < Max_Y$. The number of spikes below the *threshold* indicates the amount of large movements within the

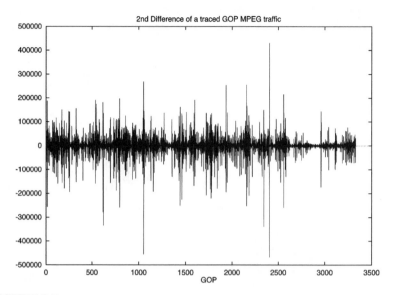

FIGURE 9.5
Second difference.

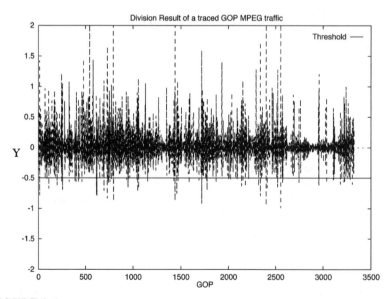

FIGURE 9.6
Scene change identifying.

same MPEG stream (see Fig. 9.6). Lower values of the *threshold*, $|T|$, capture more scene changes. In order to capture only the large scene changes, it is more obvious when T is below the mean value of $\{Y\}$. In fact, Figs. 9.5 and 9.6 can be worked as a filter of scene changes from the time series plot (Fig. 9.4).

In order to justify the criteria, (see Fig. 9.7) we plot $\{X_i\}$ time series and the second difference $Diff_2$. It is clear that there is a good match between the two series. Every large and negative spike in the $Diff_2$ is associated with a large spike in the GOP time series plot.

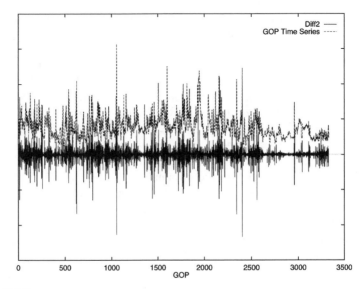

FIGURE 9.7
The time series plot of GOP associated with $Diff_2$.

9.3 Statistical Modeling of MPEG

This section describes the statistical models which are used to characterize an MPEG sequence. The main objective is to find a suitable and simple model to capture the statistical behavior of a VBR MPEG sequence.

9.3.1 Markovian-Based Models

This section presents two Markovian-based models, namely the Histogram model and the Detailed Markov Chain model (DMC). The Markov chain process has been used because its parameters can be found easily and it can be easily analyzed. The Markov chain method can be used to model different layers of an MPEG sequence (scene, GOP, frame or slide). It is very difficult to find a model that covers all three types [16]. Therefore, we have to decide which layer will be used. A higher layer will add more complexity to the model but it will also improve long-range dependencies behavior. The GOP layer can be used for our models without modeling frame-by-frame correlation and the only correlation used is GOP-by-GOP (frame-by-frame correlation will be used at the traffic generation process, see Section 9.3.3). In addition, an experimental result showed that frame-by-frame correlation has no influence on cell loss results [16]. Therefore, in some cases it could be enough to use only one level of correlation.

For the histogram model, a 0-order Markov chain method has been used and 1st-order Markov chain for the DMC. Both models have a finite number of states and will be used to generate a GOP size process. For both models, the range of GOP sizes of the empirical MPEG sequence will be divided into several quantization intervals $\{q_i : i = 0, 1, 2, 3, ..., M - 1\}$, where M is the number of quantization intervals and the number of the intervals depends on the formulated model. Each interval is related to a state of Markov chain. Therefore the number of states is equal to the number of GOP intervals. For each state, there is a *Mean* value (μ_{q_i}) of the GOP interval associated with it. The *Mean* value of interval i, μ_{q_i}, represent the size of the quantization interval q_i. In the Markov chain context, the transition from a state to another is controlled by a transition matrix. With each state transition (entrance from the current state into the next state) a GOP size will be generated according to the *Mean* value of the next state.

9.3.1.1 Histogram Model

The Histogram model can be described by a simple Markov chain with a finite number of states (M) which is equal to the number of the quantization intervals. The number of quantization intervals is based on the selected number of the histogram bins. It is possible to improve the distribution feature of the model by increasing the number of quantization intervals (smaller size of bin interval), but this will lead to an increase in the number of states. We estimate and define the transition matrix of size $1 \times M$ as follows:

$$P_{ij} = \frac{n_i}{N} \quad \text{where} \quad N = \sum_{i=1}^{M-1} n_i \quad \text{and} \quad n_i = \text{number of GOPs in } q_i \;.$$

9.3.1.2 Detailed Markov Chain Model (DMC)

The DMC model differs from the Histogram model in two main ways: the number of quantization intervals (number of states) and the estimation of transition matrix. A careful selection of the number of states should be achieved.

Thus, the number of states (M) can be found as follows:

$$Size_q = \frac{Max_{GOP} - Min_{GOP}}{k},$$

where Max_{GOP} and Min_{GOP} are the maximum and the minimum value of the GOP and k is a selected quantization value. The first quantization interval q_0 starts with the Minimum value of GOP (Min_{GOP}). The transition matrix of size $M \times M$ is defined and estimated as follows:

$$P_{ij} = \frac{n_{ij}}{N_i} \text{ where } N_i = \sum_{i=0}^{M-1} n_{ij} \text{ and } \sum_{j=0}^{M-1} P_{ij} = 1 \text{ for } i = 0, 1, \ldots, M-1.$$

n_{ij} is the number of transitions from state i to state j, N_i is the total number of transitions out from state i.

9.3.2 Scene Change-Based Model

The Markovian Models are not adequate (in most cases) to capture the long range dependency feature. In this section, a new form for scene-based model is introduced based on characterizing MPEG traffic as a collection of scenes. The model is used to capture the lone range dependency feature of MPEG traffic. In order to model VBR MPEG traffic based on the scene change, we need a functional definition of scene duration based on the bit rate variations. From Section 9.2.2, we are able to identify and quantify scene changes within an MPEG sequence. As illustrated in Fig. 9.8, an MPEG stream can be characterized using two processes, namely: scene length $\{Sl_i, i > 0\}$ and the scene fluctuations process $\{Sc_i, i > 0\}$, where S_i is the starting point of scene i. Thus, an MPEG sequence can be seen as a collection of scenes with different sizes.

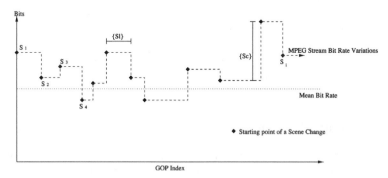

FIGURE 9.8
Scene change model.

The first process $\{Sl_i, i = 1, 2, 3, \ldots, n\}$ can be defined as the scene length duration within the MPEG sequence, where n is the number of scene changes.

In other words, Sl_i is the number of GOPs in the ith scene. The scene length can be easily calculated by summing-up the number of GOPs between the starting points of two consecutive scenes. The statistical characteristics of the scene length were examined. Then, the fitted curve for the histogram of the scene change length process was drawn in Fig. 9.9. The figure shows that the scene length can be modeled by a geometric distribution. The shape of the probability density function (*pdf*) in the figure was also observed on all other analyzed MPEG sequences. In [10], it has also been confirmed that scene length for VBR video traffic can be modeled as a geometric distribution. Therefore, we use the *pdf* with a parameter q for this distribution as the basis for our model. The scene length process can be described as follows:

$$Pr\{Sl_i = n\} = q^{n-1}p \ , \quad p = 1 - q \quad \text{for } n = 1, 2, 3, \ldots$$

$$E[Sl_i] = \frac{1}{p} \ .$$

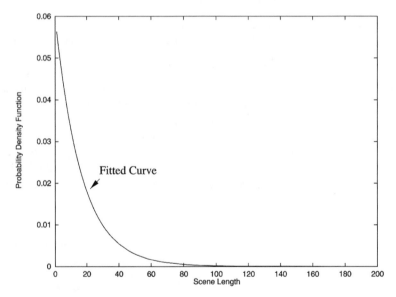

FIGURE 9.9

The fitted curve for scene length distribution.

The average size of the scene changes could be used as another indicator of the stream activities. Table 9.1 presents the number of scenes within MPEG sequence and the mean value of the scene change duration for various MPEG sequence. The average size of the scene changes can be used as indicator of the video activity (a smaller size indicates a more active sequence). For our analyzed trace (Dino), the average of the scene length is about 12 GOPs (6 seconds) while 'Movie' sequence has a smaller average size (means more active sequence). In addition, we calculate the autocorrelation function (ACF) for scene lengths. Figure 9.10 shows that the shape of the ACF for $\{Sl\}$ alternates very closely on either sides around the 0-line. In other words, there is a very weak presence of correlations among scene lengths (we could say it is uncorrelated). Therefore, the main issue is characterizing only the distribution of the scene change. Consequently, the scene lengths constitute a sequence of *i.i.d.* random variables with a geometric distribution.

Table 9.1 Statistical Parameters of Scene Change Durations

Sequence	Number of Scenes	Mean (GOP)
Dino	569	11.27
Race	579	13.41
Movie	670	5.3
Video Conference	65	20.2

The second process $\{Sc_i\}$ is based on the fact that a significant difference between two consecutive GOPs is an indication of a scene change. Hence, we model the GOP variation using $\{Sc_i\}$ and the *mean* value of GOPs for the previous scene ($\widetilde{gop}_k$, $k > 0$). From our observation of the $\{Sc\}$ histogram (not shown here), we have found that the GOP variation could be modeled using a *histogram-based model* (with a transition matrix $[P]$ and M states). Thus, the i-th GOP size (within the kth scene) can be found as follows:

$$X_i = \widetilde{gop}_{k-1} + Sc_i \ , \quad 0 < i < N \ \text{ and } \ k = 1, 2, \ldots, n \ ,$$

where N is the number of GOPs in the sequence and n is the number of scenes within the sequence.

A synthetic GOP sequence has been generated using the scene-based model. The generated sequence was based on the fitting of the original 'Dino' sequence.[2] Firstly, a scene length is determined using a given geometric distribution. Then, GOPs are generated using the scene variation process. The following algorithm describes the method which generates a GOP sequence of size N:

START
N = number of scenes
Scene variation $\{Sc\} \equiv$ Histogram (μ_{q_t}; $1 \leq t \leq M$)
For $i = 1$ To N
   Get Scene$_i$ length $= sl$
   For $k = 1$ To sl

---

[2]The Dino sequence has been selected due to its long range dependency feature.

$$\{Sc\} = \text{Histogram } (\mu_{q_t})$$
$$GOP_{i+k} = \widetilde{gop}_{i-1} + \{Sc\}$$

End Loop k

End Loop i

END

9.3.3   The Overall Model's Comparison

In this section, we present the overall comparison of the three presented MPEG models to examine whether the models are able to approximate the long range dependency behavior of the real MPEG sequences or not. In other words, we consider the strength and the limitations of the model with respect to several statistical properties and the ability to capture ACF of VBR MPEG traffic. In order to validate a model, the statistical analysis result of the model should be compared with empirical data in terms of the statistical distribution and the sequence correlation (ACF).

Table 9.2 shows the comparison of the most important moments of GOP sizes. It is interesting to observe that Scene-based model matches exactly the Real sequence in terms of mean value. However, for network dimensioning purposes it is more convenient to use a model which behaves worse than the real traffic [16]. This is the case for a scene-based model which overestimates the Peak value. Thus, it gives higher value of burstiness parameter. The CoV and STDEV parameters are also used to assess the overall burstiness of the video sequence. The scene-based model is also overestimates these parameters due to the burstiness feature of the model.

Table 9.2   The Simple Statistical Parameters for 'Dino' Sequence and the Models

Data Sets	Mean(μ) Cells	STDEV(σ) Cells	CoV ($\frac{\sigma}{\mu}$)	Max (Peak) Cells	Peak/Mean Burstiness
Real Sequence (Dino)	408	164	0.401	1634	4.00
Histogram Model	410	166	0.404	1270	3.09
DMC Model	402	162	0.402	1634	4.06
Scene-Based Model	408	173	0.420	1845	4.52

The main difference of the models is their capability to approximate the autocorrelation function (dependences feature) of the original MPEG sequence (empirical MPEG data set). Figure 9.11 plots the ACF of the generated sequence using the three proposed models at the GOP level. Comparing the plots of the three models leads to the conclusion that the scene based model with multiple level of modeling shows better agreement with the empirical (real) data sets, whereas the simpler models are unable to model the correlation feature of the data sets over a larger period of time (lags). In other words, the scene-based model captures the LRD feature of the original video sequence (since the LRD feature is an important characteristic of video traffic [7]) while the DMC model exhibits only the SRD feature. The Histogram model does not approximate the dependency feature at all.

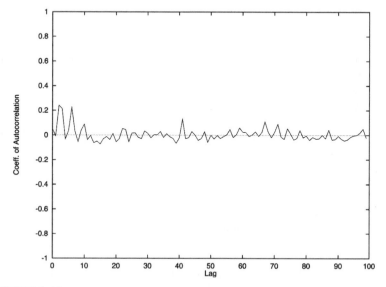

FIGURE 9.10
Autocorrelation function of the scene length.

In order to produce a synthetic sequence of MPEG frame sizes (I, P and B) similar to a real MPEG frame sequence, we could use the following method: the frame sizes could be derived from GOP sizes by scaling the frame sizes of different types with GOP sizes. This process uses a scaling parameter called Scaling Factor (f). The parameter f is calculated by dividing the *mean* value for the frame type by the *mean* value of GOP:

$$f_I = \frac{E[\{I\}]}{E[\{GOP\}]} \quad f_P = \frac{E[\{P\}]}{E[\{GOP\}]} \quad f_B = \frac{E[\{B\}]}{E[\{GOP\}]}.$$

For each generated GOP, a frame of type I, P or B is multiplied by the corresponding f parameter. It has been observed that this method gives a good approximation of deriving the frame sizes (I, P and B) from GOP sizes (see [8] for more details). In order to validate the model at the frame level, a synthetic sequence has been generated emulating real MPEG video sequence based on the method. We have calculated the correlation between the generated sequence and the empirical sequence (actual sequence). Table 9.3 shows a strong correlation for both Markovian models while a stronger one for the scene-based model. On the other hand, we plot the autocorrelation function of IPB frames for both

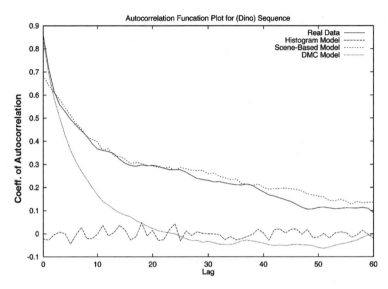

FIGURE 9.11
ACF for real and the three models for Dino stream.

the generated and the actual data. Figure 9.12 shows the ACF curves for actual 'Dino' sequence and the generated sequences using the three presented models. It is clear that 'I' frames cause a large positive peak followed by another smaller positive peak from P frames, while B frames cause the negative and the smallest peaks. The shape of the curve is the result of the periodic coding pattern (the pattern [IBBPBBPBBPBB] is repeated) and the different mean sizes of the frame types. The top points represent I frames, the middle points represent P frames and the bottom points represent B frames. In the case of DMC and scene-based models, there is a good agreement between the ACF curves of the three frame types (IPB) for the generated and the actual sequence. In contrast, a weaker agreement can be shown in the case of the Histogram model.

Table 9.3 Correlation Factor Between the Generated and Actual Sequence

	$f_I = 0.351$	$f_P = 0.092$	$f_B = 0.047$
Model	Corr(Empirical,Generated)		
Scene-based	0.864		
DMC	0.768		
Histogram	0.771		

In order to add more accuracy to the model validation, simulation experiments were conducted to study the performance of an ATM multiplexer using the generated (or synthetic) sequence based on the scene-based model and the original traffic (including the two Markovian models). This will help us to examine the performance of the model in terms of the queuing performance. The simulation results obtained from the performance of the model should then be compared with that obtained from the original sequence. The experiment (simulation) model can be described as an ATM multiplexer, with a finite buffer size that accepts ATM cells from MPEG sources, and then transmits them through a link speed C (i.e., single server). The link speed (output link) was fixed (50 Mbits) to achieve consistent results from the simulation of the different models. The number of stream was selected to adjust the system load at 0.8. First, the MPEG frame sizes are packetized into ATM cells with a payload of 48 bytes. The cell stream is assumed to be suitably spaced during a frame duration. The spacing between the cells within a frame duration in turn should vary based on the frame bit rate. However, the spacing within each frame duration is the same. At the multiplexer, the incoming cells are served based on the FIFO manner. A cell loss occurs when the multiplexer buffer becomes full. Incoming cells which arrive during such a buffer-full condition are discarded.

The simulation results obtained from the performance of each model are shown in Fig. 9.13. This figure depicts the cell loss ratio (CLR) against different buffer sizes. The figure shows only the *mean* values for the several simulations which have been conducted in order to achieve a 95% confidence interval. The cell loss ratio results were obtained from the simulation of the generated IPB sequences which were originally generated based on the three presented models. The CLR curve for the original sequence is also plotted based on 'Dino' stream for the sake of overall comparison. For small buffer sizes, it was observed that all generated sequences show close/good agreement of the losses curve of the original sequence. However, for larger buffer sizes, the CLR curve for the scene-based model is performed more closer to the original sequence than others.

9.4 Conclusions

In this paper, we presented a comprehensive scene change characterization based on the amount of activity within each stream. We also presented two methods and algorithms to identify the scene changes within the MPEG stream. Then, we introduced a novel scene-based model which describes an MPEG sequence as a collection of scenes. We showed that the scene-based model approximates not only the statistical behavior but also captures the dependencies feature of the original sequence, including the long range dependency feature. We also conducted simulation experiments to study the performance of an ATM

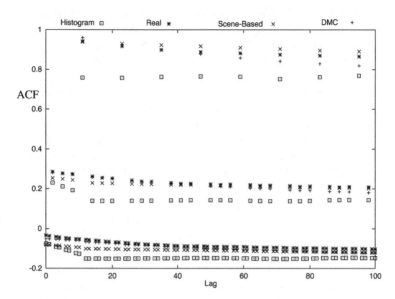

FIGURE 9.12
ACF for IPB frames (generated and actual sequence).

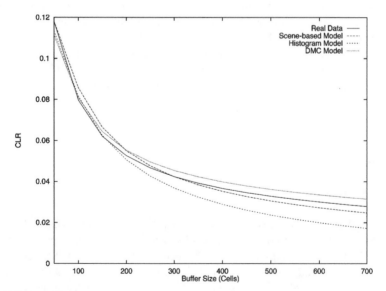

FIGURE 9.13
CLR performance evaluation (fixed link capacity).

multiplexer using the generated (synthetic) sequence based on the proposed model. We showed that the constructed sequence (I,P and B) gives close impact on the system performance when multiple streams are multiplexed at an ATM multiplexer.

Acknowledgment

We would like to thank O. Rose for providing the data sets for the MPEG video sequences. We wish to thank K. Djemame, R. Wade and S. Hussain for useful discussions during the preparation of this manuscript.

References

[1] M. Bunzel and S. Morris, *Multimedia Applications Development,* McGraw-Hill Inc, 1994.

[2] M. Conti, E. Gregori and A. Larsson, Study of the Impact of MPEG-I Correlations on Video Sources Statistical Multiplexing, *IEEE J. Selected Areas in Communications,* Vol. 14, No. 7, September 1996.

[3] V. Frost and B. Melamed, Traffic Modelling For Telecommunications Networks, *IEEE Communications Magazine,* March 1994.

[4] R. Groeneveld, *Introductory Statistical Methods: An Integrated Approach Using Minitab,* PWS-KENT, 1988.

[5] D. Heyman, A. Tabatabai and T. Lakshman, Statistical Analysis and Simulation Study of Video Teleconference Traffic in ATM Networks, *IEEE Transactions on Circuits and Systems for Video Technology,* Vol. 2, No. 1, March 1992.

[6] D. Heyman and T. Lakshman, Source Models for VBR Broadcast-Video Traffic, *IEEE/ACM Transactions on Networking,* Vol. 4, No. 1, February 1996.

[7] M. Izquierdo and D. Reeves, A survey of Source Models for Variable Bit Rate Encoded Video, *Multimedia Systems Journal,* August 1996.

[8] M. Kara and A. Mashat, Statistical Analysis and Modelling of MPEG Sources for Workload Characterization of Distribution Multimedia Ap-

plication, 5th IFIP workshop on Performance Modelling and Evaluation of ATM Networks, July 1997.

[9] M. Krunz and S. Tripathi, Scene-Based Characterization of VBR MPEG-Compressed Video Traffic, Technical Report TR-3573, Institute for Advance Computer Studies, Department of Computer Science, University of Maryland, 1996.

[10] A. Lazar, G. Pacifici and D. Pendarakis, Modeling Video Sources for Real-time Scheduling, Technical Report 324-93-03, Columbia University, Department of Electrical Engineering and Center for Telecommunications Research, April 1993.

[11] W. Mendenhall and T. Sincich, *Statistics For Engineering and The Science,* Fourth Edition, Prentice-Hall Inc, 1994.

[12] A. Mashat and M. Kara, The Impact of Synchronising MPEG Streams on Bandwidth Allocation, The 14th UK Performance Engineering Workshop, July, 1998.

[13] A. Mashat and M. Kara, Scene Change Scale: An Indicator of A CLR of Multiplexing MPEG Streams Over ATM Networks, 6th IFIP workshop on Performance Modelling and Evaluation of ATM Networks, July 1998.

[14] P. Pancha and M. El Zarki, Bandwidth Allocation Schemes for Variable Bit Rate MPEG Sources in ATM Networks, *IEEE Trans. Circuits and Systems For Video Tech.,* Vol. 3, No. 3, June 1993.

[15] O. Rose, Statistical properties of MPEG video traffic and their impact on traffic modeling in ATM systems, Report No. 101, Institute of Computer Science, University of Wurzburg, February 1995.

[16] O. Rose, Simple and Efficient Models for Variable Bit Rate MPEG Video Traffic, Report No. 120, Institute of Computer Science, University of Wurzburg, July 1995.

[17] G. Stamoulis and M. Anagnostou, Traffic source models for ATM networks: a survey, *Computer Communications,* Vol. 17, n. 6, June 1994.

[18] R. Venturin, Traffic Source Modelling of Multimedia Application for ATM, *Informacija Telekomnni Kacije Automati,* Vol. 14, Iss 1–3, 1995.

[19] ftp://ftp-info3.informatik.uni-wuerzburg.de/pub/MPEG/

Part III

Traffic-Based System and Network Design

Chapter 10

Buffering vs. Smoothing for End-to-End QoS: Fundamental Issues and Comparison

Tao Wu and Edward W. Knightly

Rice University

Abstract   Smoothing traffic flows at the network edge to reduce their burstiness has been shown to have significant benefits for video-on-demand systems and deterministic services. In this paper, we investigate the relative abilities of smoothing and buffering to improve a network's admissible region for end-to-end delay-bounded statistical services. In single multiplexer systems, we show that buffering outperforms smoothing for any delay bound and loss probability. We find that this behavior is due not only to statistical buffer sharing, but also to heterogeneity of the traffic flows' time scales. In multi-node scenarios, key issues for buffering and smoothing are user QoS requirements, traffic characteristics, and route length. For example, we find that as the number of hops traversed increases, the advantages of buffering diminish due to node-to-node buffer partitioning; and while smoothing is asymptotically superior, we find that in practice, the "critical route length" required to realize a smoothing gain is so large that buffering results in larger admissible regions, even in many multi-node scenarios.

Keywords: traffic smoothing, traffic shaping, end-to-end QoS, statistical service.

[1] This research is supported by Nokia Corporation, NSF CAREER Award ANI-9733610, and NSF Grant ANI-9730104. The author can be reached via http://www.ece.rice.edu/networks.

10.1   Introduction

In guaranteed quality-of-service communication, one expects that the greater a source's burstiness in terms of peak-to-average rate ratio, temporal correlation, etc., the greater its network resource requirements. This intuitive observation motivates *traffic smoothing*, in which a flow's burstiness is reduced at the network edge to achieve a variety of goals, including the reduction of network resource demands.

Indeed, in the literature, smoothing has been shown to be beneficial in a number of scenarios. For example, for deterministic QoS guarantees, smoothing can have significant advantages in multi-hop rate-controlled networks [8, 12]. Moreover, smoothing can also have significant benefits in video-on-demand systems in which traffic patterns are known in advance, clients may "work ahead" and prefetch video frames, and delay requirements are not strict [5, 14, 16, 19, 20]. Finally, networks in which traffic flows are smoothed but not buffered are more tractable than buffered networks, and a number of studies have considered such scenarios [4, 9, 15]. However, despite such potential advantages of smoothing, it is not yet clear what the services and scenarios are in which smoothing can improve a network's admissible region.

In this paper, we investigate the effectiveness of traffic smoothing in end-to-end delay-bounded statistical and deterministic services. Towards this end, we conduct a comparative study of two systems: (1) a *smoothing system* in which traffic flows are smoothed at the network edge with a maximum delay D and then are serviced by a network of bufferless multiplexers, and (2) a *buffering system* in which the same traffic flows are *not* smoothed, and are serviced by a network of buffered multiplexers, which also provide a maximum end-to-end delay D. For a given end-to-end delay requirement D and loss probability P_l (which may be 0 for the special case of deterministic service), we compare the admissible regions of the two systems and identify the key factors that influence their relative performance.

A fundamental issue for smoothing and buffering is the relative extent to which network resources are partitioned vs. shared. First, in the smoothing system, each flow's smoothing buffers are individually partitioned, while in the buffering system, flows share a common buffer. Thus, an obvious property of the buffering system is that it can attain a statistical multiplexing gain from statistically sharing a common resource. However, we will show that there is a further advantage of the buffering system that is not immediately evident, namely, a gain due to sources with different *critical time scales* sharing a resource. A key observation is that this gain derives solely from time scale heterogeneity and is therefore available in both deterministic and statistical buffering systems, i.e., it is not an artifact of statistical sharing. We illustrate this aspect of buffer sharing using deterministic delay calculus [2] and show how heterogeneous sources can obtain a buffering gain under deterministic services in which statistical multiplexing gains are not available.

Consequently, due to the aforementioned advantages of resource sharing, we show using sample path analysis that in the case of a single multiplexer, the buffering system has a greater admissible region than the smoothing system for any end-to-end delay bound and loss probability, including a loss probability of zero for deterministic service. We experimentally quantify the buffering system's advantages using simulations and admission control experiments with both periodic on-off sources and long traces of compressed video. As an illustrative example with on-off sources and a delay of 70 msec, we find that the buffering system achieves an admissible region 30% larger than the smoothing system's, while the advantage is 10% for video sources.

We next turn to multiple node networks. Here again at issue is partitioning vs. sharing of network resources: in multi-node scenarios, a flow's end-to-end delay budget and hence, buffering is *partitioned* among network nodes. Consequently, the significant advantages of buffering found in the single-node case are lessened in multi-node scenarios. We formally establish this property by showing that under certain conditions, there exists a *critical route length H^** such that if the number of hops traversed is less than H^*, the buffering system's admissible region is larger than that of the smoothing system, whereas at H^* hops and beyond, either the admissible regions are equivalent or smoothing is superior. We experimentally investigate this result and find that the flows' traffic characteristics strongly influence H^*: for periodic on-off sources, H^* tends to be moderate, on the order of 6 to 9 hops in typical examples of Section 10.4; in contrast, for more bursty video sources, we find H^* to be so large that smoothing is unable to improve the admissible region for end-to-end statistical services.

Finally, in addition to traffic characteristics, we find that user QoS requirements also play a key role in the relative merits of smoothing and buffering. We formalize this by using envelope-based admission control tests [11] to show that the critical route length H^* is a non-decreasing function of the loss probability P_l. Indeed, with the most stringent QoS requirement of $P_l = 0$ for deterministic service, H^* can be one. This concurs with previous studies of *deterministic* services which demonstrated that smoothing traffic at the network edge can produce significant utilization gains in many multi-hop scenarios [8, 12].

Thus, we study the relative merits of the two systems from the perspective of partitioning vs. sharing of network resources. By employing a number of analytical techniques, including deterministic delay calculus, sample path analysis, and statistical traffic envelopes, we show that statistical resource sharing, heterogeneity of time scales, and node-to-node buffer partitioning play key roles in these systems' admissible regions. Moreover, we explore the impact of several important system parameters such as route length, QoS requirements, and traffic characteristics on the smoothing/buffering systems. We find that in stark contrast to deterministic services and video-on-demand systems, smoothing for delay-bounded statistical services is of limited utility, and in many cases is detrimental towards improving a network's admissible region.

The remainder of this paper is organized as follows. In Section 10.2 we describe the smoothing and buffering systems. Next, in Section 10.3 we consider partitioning and sharing issues in the case of a single network multiplexer, while in Section 10.4 we consider multi-node networks. In both cases, we perform experimental investigations. Finally, in Section 10.5, we conclude.

10.2   System Description

In this paper, we compare the relative merits of smoothing and buffering for end-to-end QoS by studying the performance of two related systems: a *smoothing system* S, and a *buffering system* B. Denoting a traffic flow's maximum allowable end-to-end delay as D, the smoothing system allocates the delay budget to traffic shapers at the network edge, while the buffering system allocates all of the delay budget to buffers inside the network.

10.2.1   The Smoothing System

In the smoothing system S, each traffic flow is smoothed or shaped at the network edge and is serviced by a network of bufferless multiplexers. The delay incurred in the smoothing element can be bounded as follows. Denoting the arrivals of traffic flow j in the interval $[s, s+t]$ as $A_j[s, s+t]$, a non-decreasing subadditive function $b_j(t)$ is said to be a deterministic envelope of flow j [2] if $A_j[s, s+t] \leq b_j(t)$ $\forall s, t > 0$.

The smoothing element can be characterized by an envelope $\hat{b}_j(t)$ such that by delaying packets as required, traffic flow j's arrivals are bounded by $\hat{b}_j(t)$ at the output of the smoother. The delay incurred by smoothing a traffic flow with envelope $b(t)$ to one with envelope $\hat{b}(t)$ is bounded by $D = \max_{s \geq 0}\{(\hat{b}^{-1}(b(s)) - s)^+\}$, which can be interpreted as the maximum horizontal distance between the two envelopes b and $\hat{b}$ [3, 8, 12]. In this paper (and in [12, 15]), a traffic flow is smoothed with a buffered first-come first-serve server with rate

$$c_j = \max_{t \geq 0} \frac{b_j(t)}{t + D}, \tag{10.1}$$

which is the minimum smoothing rate such that the smoothing delay is no larger than D.

Observe that with bufferless multiplexers inside the network, the maximum end-to-end delay is also bounded by D. Moreover, without network buffers, loss occurs in a multiplexer whenever the aggregate input rate exceeds the multiplexer's link capacity. Throughout this paper, we will study the loss probability and end-to-end delay behavior of this system.

10.2.2 The Buffering System

In the buffering system $\mathcal{B}$, traffic is transmitted into the network without incurring any delays due to smoothing (or one can view that the traffic smoother has an envelope with $\hat{b}_j(t) = b_j(t)$ for all t, and hence, the traffic is not delayed by the smoother). In this case, the user's end-to-end delay budget D is allocated to queuing delays inside the network's buffers.

In this system, backlogged traffic is serviced in first-come-first-serve order, and each network node employs delay-jitter control [6]. A delay-jitter controller at the hth hop holds packet k of connection j for $D_j^{h-1} - \delta_{j,k}^{h-1}$ seconds before queuing it, where D_j^{h-1} is connection j's delay bound at node $h-1$ and $\delta_{j,k}^{h-1}$ is the actual delay incurred by packet k of connection j at node $h-1$. Consequently, if traffic flow j's arrivals in $[s, t]$ are $A_j[s, t]$ at the entrance of the network, they are $A_j[s - \sum_{h=1}^{H} D_j^h, t - \sum_{h=1}^{H} D_j^h]$ at the entrance of the Hth queue. Because the arrival sequence at the Hth queue is a constant-delayed version of the original sequence, we can analyze networks of buffered multiplexers using the same properties of A at each network node.

While consideration of buffered networks without delay-jitter control is beyond the scope of this paper, our techniques can be extended to *rate*-controlled servers [18] using techniques such as in [11], or to more general classes of networks using other techniques for end-to-end performance evaluation, e.g., [1, 13].

10.2.3 Experimental Workload

Throughout this paper we use two sources for admission control and simulation experiments: a periodic on-off source and a 30 minute trace of an MPEG-compressed video of an action movie. The periodic on-off source can be characterized by three parameters, i.e., the on period T_{on}, the off period T_{off}, and the peak rate R. The parameters that we use are $T_{on} = 83$ msec, $T_{off} = 750$ msec, and $R = 5.87$ Mbps. The MPEG video trace exhibits rate variations over multiple time scales and has an average rate of 583 Kbps and a peak rate of 5.87 Mbps. Finally, we consider networks of FCFS servers with 45 Mbps link capacity in all simulations and admission control tests.

10.3   Smoothing vs. Buffering: The Single Node Case

Here, we show analytically and demonstrate experimentally that for the single node case, the buffering system attains a higher (or same) admissible region than the smoothing system for any end-to-end delay bound D and loss probability P_l. Our analysis is based on sample path behavior and addresses both deterministic and statistical services within the same framework. We find that heterogeneity of the sources' time scales and statistical multiplexing gains account for buffering's relative advantage to smoothing. We quantify these results using simulation and admission control experiments.

10.3.1   Loss in Delay-Bounded System

We next use sample path analysis to show that for any arrival sequence the loss in the buffering system is less than that in the smoothing system. By demonstrating this for any sample path, the result is quite general and applies to both deterministic and statistical services.

To show this, we first note that the busy period of a finite buffer FCFS server is smaller than that of an infinite buffer FCFS server when loss occurs, and the duration of this busy period is dependent on the buffer size B. We refer to such a busy period in a finite buffer FCFS server as a *finite buffer busy period* and denote it by F. We are interested only in the buffer dynamics within finite buffer busy periods since this is where loss occurs. Without loss of generality, we assume a finite buffer busy period of interest, F, starts at time 0. The aggregate arrival from the beginning of F up to time t is denoted by $A(t)$, and the link capacity of the server is C.

LEMMA 10.1

In a single node buffering system $\mathcal{B}$, the loss in any finite buffer busy period F, $L_{\mathcal{B}}(F)$, is $L_{\mathcal{B}}(F) = \max\left(\sup_{t \in F}(A(t) - Ct) - B, 0\right)$.□

The proof can be found in [17]. Roughly, this lemma states that if there is a loss in a finite buffer FCFS server, the size of the loss is determined by maximizing $A(t) - Ct - B$ for t in the corresponding busy period. Figure 10.1(a) illustrates Lemma 10.1 by depicting a sample path of a finite buffer and an infinite buffer queue. Note that while there is loss of size L_1 at time t_1, $L_{\mathcal{B}}(F)$ is achieved at $t^* > t_1$ where L_1 is also accounted for. This result provides an analytical tool to obtain Theorem 10.1 as follows.

THEOREM 10.1

In a single node system in which all flows have delay bound D, the admissi-

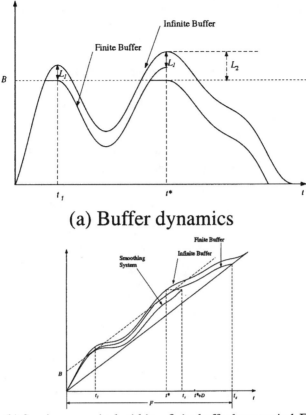

(a) Buffer dynamics

(b) Service vs. arrival within a finite buffer busy period F

FIGURE 10.1

Illustration of Lemma 10.1 and Theorem 10.1. (a) Buffer dynamics. (b) Service vs. arrival within a finite buffer busy period F.

ble region of the buffering system $\mathcal{B}$ is larger than or identical to that of the smoothing system $\mathcal{S}$, for both deterministic and statistical services.

PROOF   We prove the theorem on a sample path basis. Since the link capacity is C, the buffer size of $\mathcal{B}$ is $B = CD$. For each finite buffer busy period F where loss occurs, let t^* be the maximizing t in Lemma 10.1. The ending time of F, which we denote by t_e, satisfies $t_e \geq t^* + D$ since the buffer is full at t^*.

Note that $A(t^*)$ in $\mathcal{B}$ is smoothed to $A_s(t_s)$ in $\mathcal{S}$, i.e., $A_s(t_s) = A(t^*)$. We also have $t^* \leq t_s \leq t^* + D$ since A_s is deterministically smoothed, and thus $t_s \leq t_e$.

Denote the loss during $[0, t_s]$ in S by $L_S(t_s)$. The service S provides during $[0, t_s]$ is upper bounded by $C t_s$. Then we have $L_S(t_s) \geq A_s(t_s) - C \cdot t_s$ since S has a bufferless multiplexer. Furthermore, $L_S(F) = L_S(t_e) \geq L_S(t_s) \geq A_s(t_s) - C \cdot t_s = A(t^*) - C \cdot t_s$.

On the other hand, according to Lemma 10.1, the loss in B in F is $L_B(F) = A(t^*) - C \cdot t^* - B$. We thus have $L_S(F) - L_B(F) \geq B + C \cdot t^* - C \cdot t_s \geq B - C \cdot D = 0$.

We have shown that for each finite buffer busy period where loss occurs in B, there is a loss of equal or larger size in S in the same period. Since this is true for each sample path, B is capable of admitting more (or the same number of) flows than S for both deterministic and statistical services.   ∎

10.3.2   Heterogeneity-of-Time-Scales Gain of Buffering

An apparent explanation for Theorem 10.1 is that the statistical multiplexing gain in the buffering system B outweighs any advantages of smoothing. However, this explanation fails for deterministic services, in which resources are allocated according to the *worst case* scenario, and statistical sharing cannot be exploited since no loss can occur for deterministic service. Here, we show using deterministic delay calculus [2] that heterogeneity of the traffic flows' time scales partially accounts for the superiority of the buffering system.

Consider a single node buffering system B and smoothing system S and a deterministic service with delay bound D. Suppose there are N flows, each with traffic envelope $b_j(t)$, $j = 1, 2, \ldots, N$. From Eq. (10.1), the required link capacity of the bufferless multiplexer in S, C_S, is

$$C_S = \sum_{j=1}^{N} c_j = \sum_{j=1}^{N} \left\{ \max_{t \geq 0} \frac{b_j(t)}{t + D} \right\}. \tag{10.2}$$

We denote the maximizing ts in Eq. (10.2) by t_j^*, $j = 1, 2, \ldots, N$, and refer to t_j^* as source j's "critical time scale."

In the buffering system, the minimum link capacity needed to support the same set of sources is $C_B = \max_{t \geq 0} \left\{ \frac{\sum_{j=1}^{N} b_j(t)}{t + D} \right\}$. Observe that $C_B \leq C_S$ since $\max_{t \geq 0} \sum_{j=1}^{N} \frac{b_j(t)}{t+D} \leq \sum_{j=1}^{N} \max_{t \geq 0} \frac{b_j(t)}{t+D}$. Thus, to support the same set of sources, smoothing requires higher bandwidth. Note that *equality* holds only when the critical time scales t_j^* of all sources are the same (homogeneous traffic satisfies this condition).

We now provide a simple example to illustrate the heterogeneity gain of buffering. Suppose there are two dual leaky bucket flows with delay requirement $D = 1$ and traffic envelopes $b_1(t) = \min(5t, 4+t)$ and $b_2(t) = \min(3t, 4+t)$. From Eq. (10.2), $c_1 = 2.5$ and $c_2 = 2$. On the other hand, if we multiplex the two sources, the envelope for the aggregate traffic is $b(t) = \min(8t, 4+4t, 8+$

$2t$), and the capacity required for the buffering system for the same delay bound is $C_B = 4$, while $C_S = c_1 + c_2 = 4.5$.

10.3.3   Experiments

Here, we perform a set of simulations and admission control experiments to quantify the extent to which the buffering system outperforms the smoothing system in the single node case.

Figure 10.2 shows the results for periodic on-off sources. For Fig. 10.2(a), we use simulations to experimentally determine these systems' admissible regions by finding the maximum number of traffic flows that can be supported for a given QoS requirement. The figure depicts this number of flows (scaled to average utilization) vs. delay bound for a loss probability of 10^{-3}. As expected from Theorem 10.1, the figure shows that the buffering system achieves a larger admissible region than the smoothing system, with the two curves converging at low delays, since with $D \approx 0$, both systems behave as a single bufferless multiplexer. We also note that for larger delay bounds, the buffering system's utilization is significantly higher than the smoothing system's; for example, the difference is approximately 30% when the delay bound is 70 msec.

For Fig. 10.2(b), we fix the number of flows in both systems such that the utilization is 67.4% and depict loss probability vs. delay bound. Here, the loss probability of the buffering system is one to two orders of magnitude below that of the smoothing system for delay bounds above 40 msec.

Figure 10.3 depicts the results of analogous experiments using traces of MPEG-compressed video. For Fig. 10.3(a), observe that the buffering system again has a larger admissible region, although the shapes of these curves differ from those of Fig. 10.2(a). In particular, here the admissible region for the buffering system increases sharply for delays of up to 10 msec and then flattens considerably. This behavior indicates that while short time scale frame-to-frame rate variations are easily absorbed by network buffers, buffering is ineffective at absorbing longer time scale scene-to-scene rate variations and hence, the admissible region flattens [10].

Comparing the buffering and smoothing curves, the difference between the two admissible regions is approximately 10% utilization.

In Fig. 10.3(b), we fix the utilization to 89.5% and depict the experimental loss probability. As was the case for on-off sources, the buffering system's loss probability is significantly lower than the smoothing system's.

Thus, the above experiments quantify the advantages of the buffering system outlined in Sections 10.3.1 and 10.3.2 for single multiplexer networks, and indicate that in practice, the buffering system can achieve utilizations of 10% to 30% greater than the smoothing system depending on the characteristics of the traffic flows.

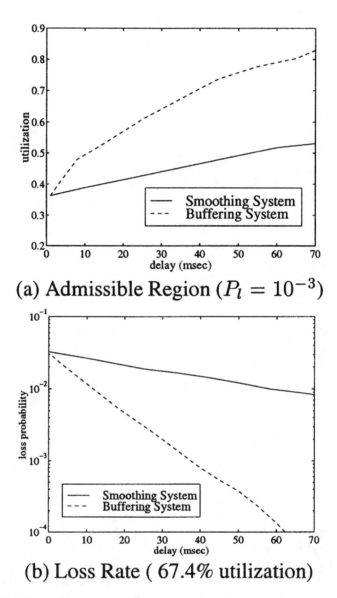

(a) Admissible Region ($P_l = 10^{-3}$)

(b) Loss Rate (67.4% utilization)

FIGURE 10.2

Simulation results for periodic on-off sources. (a) Admissible region ($P_l = 10^{-3}$). (b) Loss rate (67.4% utilization).

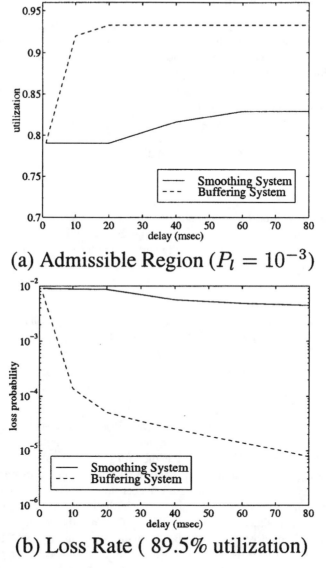

(a) Admissible Region ($P_l = 10^{-3}$)

(b) Loss Rate (89.5% utilization)

FIGURE 10.3
Simulation results for video traces. (a) Admissible region ($P_l = 10^{-3}$).
(b) Loss rate (89.5% utilization).

10.4   Buffering, Smoothing, and Multi-Hop Networks

In single node networks, we showed that buffering systems always achieve larger admissible regions than smoothing systems. However, this is not necessarily the case in multi-node scenarios. Here, we show that due to node-to-node partitioning of a flow's delay budget, the advantages of buffering over smoothing are reduced as an increased number of hops are traversed. In particular, we demonstrate the existence of a *critical route length* H^* such that for networks of at least H^* hops, *smoothing* achieves a larger admissible region than buffering. We then investigate the impact of the quality of service parameters and traffic characteristics on the critical route length.

10.4.1   Critical Route Length H^*

The proposition below establishes whether a larger admissible region is achieved by allocating an end-to-end delay budget entirely to traffic smoothing at the network edge or by equally partitioning the delay budget to queuing delays in the network's multiplexers.

PROPOSITION 10.1

For identical traffic flows with delay bound D traversing H multiplexers with capacity C, there exists a critical route length H^* *such that for H < H^*, B has a larger admissible region than S; for all H ≥ H^* the admissible region of B is smaller than (or the same as) that of S.*

PROOF   Since the traffic is reshaped by a delay jitter controller at each node, loss along the path that a flow traverses occurs independently. The loss and the end-to-end loss and delay-bound violation probability P_l is given by $P_l = 1 - (1 - P_{l,n})^H$, where $P_{l,n}$ is the loss probability at a single node [7]. Expanding the expression and neglecting all higher order terms yields $P_l \approx H \cdot P_{l,n}$. Hence, if P_l and D are fixed, the per-node admissible regions for both B and S will decrease with increasing H. Furthermore, the buffer size at each node in B will also decrease since $B = \frac{D}{H}C$. Thus the per-node admissible region of B would asymptotically be that of the smoothing system if the sources of both systems were the same. However, S admits smoothed streams, and thus asymptotically outperforms B. On the other hand, according to Theorem 10.1, B is superior to S in single node, thus there exists an H^* where the two systems' admissible regions cross.   ∎

With the existence of H^* established, the key issues for smoothing and buffering in multi-node networks are (1) what is the expected range of H^* in practice, and (2) how do user QoS requirements and traffic characteristics impact H^*? We address these issues below.

10.4.2 H^* and Loss Probability

Here, we show that the critical route length is a non-decreasing function of loss probability, so that as user QoS constraints become more restrictive, the smoothing system obtains a relative advantage. In the extreme case of $P_l = 0$ for deterministic service, H^* can be one such that for two or more nodes, smoothing is superior to buffering. However, for statistical services with $P_l > 0$, we find that H^* can be quite large.

To explore these issues, we first introduce background on admission control for statistical services and buffered multiplexers. We employ an algorithm that determines the per-node delay-bound-violation probability using rate-variance traffic envelopes [10], and use $P_l \approx H \cdot P_{l,n}$ as discussed above for end-to-end calculations. In particular, we characterize a traffic flow by the stochastic envelope

$$\sigma_j^2(t) = Var\left(\frac{A_j[s, s+t]}{t}\right) \tag{10.3}$$

and approximate the loss probability in a single node as

$$P_{l,n} \approx \max_t \Psi\left(\frac{C(t+D) - t\sum_j m_j}{t\sqrt{\sum_j \sigma_j^2(t)}}\right), \tag{10.4}$$

where m_j is source j's mean rate, and $\Psi(x)$ is the Gaussian tail probability $\Psi(x) = \frac{1}{\sqrt{2\pi}}\int_x^\infty e^{-t^2/2}dt$.

THEOREM 10.2

For identical traffic flows with maximum end-to-end delay bound D, the critical route length H^* is a non-decreasing function of P_l for any traffic envelope $\sigma^2(t)$.

PROOF   Suppose the critical route length is H when the end-to-end QoS requirements are (D, P_1). Consider a flow W traversing exactly H hops, with QoS requirements (D, P_1). Then the admissible regions for a single node in both $\mathcal{B}$ and $\mathcal{S}$ along the path W are the same and denoted by N_1. Without loss of generality, we assume $\mathcal{B}$ and $\mathcal{S}$ provide the same node loss probability, i.e., $P_{1,\mathcal{B},n} = P_{1,\mathcal{S},n}$.

Now suppose the end-to-end QoS requirements change to (D, P_2), and $P_2 < P_1$. The admissible region of $\mathcal{S}$ has to change to N_2 to satisfy the QoS change, and we have $N_2 \leq N_1$. To prove the theorem, it is equivalent to prove that $\mathcal{S}$ provides a lower node loss probability than $\mathcal{B}$ for W when admitting N_2 flows, i.e., $P_{2,\mathcal{S},n} \leq P_{2,\mathcal{B},n}$.

From Eq. (10.4), we have $P_{1,\mathcal{S},n} \approx \Psi\left(\frac{C-mN_1}{\sqrt{N_1}\sigma_\mathcal{S}}\right)$, where m is the mean rate of the flow and $\sigma_\mathcal{S}^2$ is the variance of the smoothed trace. Similarly, $P_{2,\mathcal{S},n} \approx \Psi\left(\frac{C-mN_2}{\sqrt{N_2}\sigma_\mathcal{S}}\right)$ and $P_{1,\mathcal{B},n} \approx \Psi\left(\frac{C+\frac{B}{t^*}-mN_1}{\sqrt{N_1}\sigma_\mathcal{B}(t^*)}\right)$, where $B = \frac{D}{H}C$, and $\sigma_\mathcal{B}^2(t)$ is the rate-variance function of interval length t in Eq. (10.3), and t^* is the maximizing t in Eq. (10.4).

With these relationships established, $P_{1,\mathcal{B},n} = P_{1,\mathcal{S},n}$ is equivalent to

$$\frac{C - mN_1}{\sqrt{N_1}\sigma_\mathcal{S}} = \frac{C + \frac{B}{t^*} - mN_1}{\sqrt{N_1}\sigma_\mathcal{B}(t^*)} \ . \tag{10.5}$$

Since $N_2 \le N_1$, we have $\frac{C-mN_2}{C-mN_1} \ge \frac{C-mN_2+B/t^*}{C-mN_1+B/t^*}$. And from Eq. (10.5), we have $\frac{C-mN_2}{\sqrt{N_2}\sigma_\mathcal{S}} \ge \frac{C+\frac{B}{t^*}-mN_2}{\sqrt{N_2}\sigma_\mathcal{B}(t^*)}$.

Since t^* may not be the maximizing t for N_2 flows, t',

$$P_{2,\mathcal{B},n} \approx \Psi\left(\frac{C + \frac{B}{t'} - mN_2}{\sqrt{N_2}\sigma_\mathcal{B}(t')}\right) \ge \Psi\left(\frac{C + \frac{B}{t^*} - mN_2}{\sqrt{N_2}\sigma_\mathcal{B}(t^*)}\right)$$

$$\ge \Psi\left(\frac{C - mN_2}{\sqrt{N_2}\sigma_\mathcal{S}}\right) \approx P_{2,\mathcal{S},n} \ .$$

Hence, the theorem is established.   ∎

We explore this result further by experimentally investigating the extent to which loss probability impacts the critical route length. Figure 10.4 depicts H^* vs. P_l for on-off and video sources using the admission control algorithm described above. Observe that both curves have the critical route length increasing with P_l, supporting Theorem 10.2. Moreover, note that even for stringent loss probability requirements, the critical route length for the video trace is quite large (greater than 30), indicating that buffering is preferable in a wide range of scenarios.

10.4.3   The Impact of Traffic Characteristics on H^*

In this section, we further evaluate the impact of the traffic characteristics on H^*. Figure 10.5(a) depicts node utilization vs. path length for periodic on-off sources with a loss requirement of 10^{-3} and an end-to-end delay budget of 125 msec. While the buffering system's utilization is significantly higher for a single hop, the difference decays quickly with H, so that H^*, the number of hops beyond which smoothing is equivalent or superior, is 6 hops.

Results for similar experiments with video traces with a loss probability requirement of 10^{-3} and a delay budget of 100 msec are shown in Fig. 10.5(b). We see the same trend as for on-off sources, but H^* is significantly larger, between 40 to 50 hops.

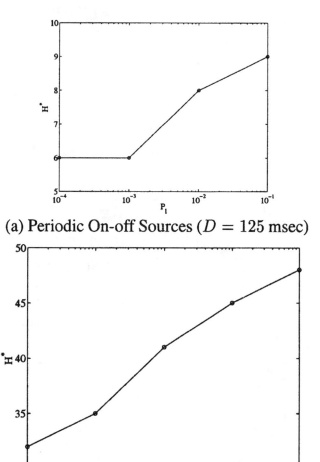

(a) Periodic On-off Sources ($D = 125$ msec)

(b) Video Traces ($D = 100$ msec)

FIGURE 10.4

H^* vs. P_l. (a) **Periodic on-off sources** ($D = 125$ **msec). (b) Video traces**
($D = 100$ **msec).**

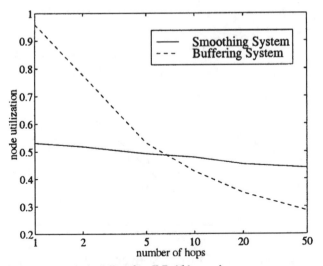

(a) Node Utilization:
Periodic On-off Sources

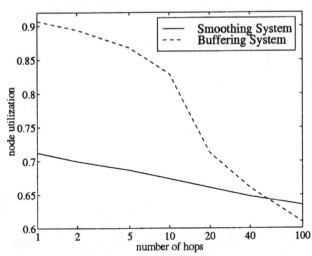

(b) Node Utilization:
Video Traces

FIGURE 10.5
Admissible region and utilization ratio. (a) Node utilization: periodic on-off sources. (b) Node utilization: video traces.

Thus, while both Figs. 10.5(a) and (b) support Proposition 10.1, it is note-worthy how widely H^* varies for these two sources due to the different nature of their traffic characteristics.

10.4.4 Utilization Ratio of Smoothing and Buffering Systems

In the experiments depicted in Fig. 10.5(c), we further compare the smoothing and buffering systems by investigating the *ratio* of their admissible regions as a function of the number of hops traversed. The two curves represent the respective admissible regions of deterministic service, computed using [2], and statistical service, as in the experiments above. Notice that the point at which the ratio becomes greater than or equal to 1 is H^*, the route length at which the smoothing system becomes equivalent or superior. We make the following observations about the figure.

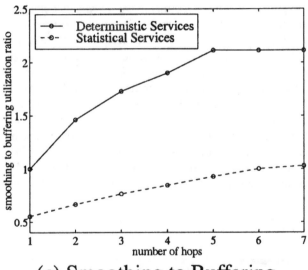

(c) Smoothing to Buffering
Utilization Ratio

FIGURE 10.5

Admissible region and utilization ratio. (c) Smoothing to buffering utilization ratio.

First, note that for one hop, the smoothing-to-buffering utilization ratio does not exceed 1 for both deterministic and statistical services, in agreement with Theorem 10.1. Moreover, for deterministic service the two systems attain the same utilization with one hop. The reason for this is that this experiment considers homogeneous sources which have identical critical time scales so that buffering's heterogeneity-of-time-scales gain (Section 10.3.2) is not available.

Second, notice that the curves for both deterministic and statistical services in Fig. 10.5(c) have positive slopes. This is in agreement with Proposition 10.1, which states that buffering's advantages over smoothing diminish as the number of hops traversed increases.

Finally, observe that the critical route lengths for deterministic and statistical services are quite different. As Theorem 10.2 points out, H^* is a non-decreasing function of the loss probability and in these experiments $H^* = 1$ for deterministic service and $H^* = 6$ for statistical service.

10.5   Conclusions

In this paper, we conducted a comparative study of smoothing and buffering for end-to-end QoS. For a single multiplexer network, we demonstrated that buffering is superior to smoothing for both deterministic and statistical services due to the flows' heterogeneity of time scales, and for statistical services, a further gain from statistical buffer sharing. For multi-node networks, buffering's superiority diminishes as the number of hops traversed increases, and there is a "critical route length" beyond which smoothing is preferable. We further explored the impact of other system parameters, including QoS requirements and traffic characteristics on the relative merits of smoothing and buffering. We found that in contrast to video-on-demand systems and deterministic services, for delay-bounded statistical services, a traffic flow's end-to-end delay budget is often better spent in network buffers than in traffic smoothers at the network edge.

References

[1] C. Chang. Sample path large deviations and intree networks. *Queuing Systems, Theory and Applications,* 20(1-2),7–36, 1995.

[2] R. Cruz. A calculus for network delay, part I: network elements in isolation. *IEEE Transactions on Information Theory,* 37(1), 114–121, January 1991.

[3] R. Cruz. Quality of service guarantees in virtual circuit switched networks. *IEEE Journal on Selected Areas in Communications,* 13(6), 1048–1056, August 1995.

[4] A. Elwalid and D. Mitra. Traffic shaping at a network node: theory, optimum design, admission control. *Proc. IEEE INFOCOM '97,* Kobe, Japan, April 1997.

[5] W. Feng and J. Rexford. A comparison of bandwidth smoothing techniques for the transmission of prerecorded compressed video. *Proceedings of IEEE INFOCOM '97,* Kobe, Japan, April 1997.

[6] D. Ferrari. Design and applications of a delay jitter control scheme for packet-switching internetworks. *Computer Communications,* 15(6), 367–373, July 1992.

[7] D. Ferrari and D. Verma. A scheme for real-time channel establishment in wide-area networks. *IEEE Journal on Selected Areas in Communications,* 8(3), 368–379, April 1990.

[8] L. Georgiadis, R. Guérin, V. Peris, and K. Sivarajan. Efficient network QoS provisioning based on per node traffic shaping. *IEEE/ACM Trans. Networking,* 4(4), 482–501, August 1996.

[9] M. Grossglauser, S. Keshav, and D. Tse. RCBR: A simple and efficient service for multiple time-scale traffic. *IEEE/ACM Trans. Networking,* 5(6), 741–755, December 1997.

[10] E. Knightly. Second moment resource allocation in multi-service networks. *Proc. ACM SIGMETRICS '97,* pages 181–191, Seattle, WA, June 1997.

[11] E. Knightly. Enforceable quality of service guarantees for bursty traffic streams. *Proceedings of IEEE INFOCOM '98,* San Francisco, CA, March 1998.

[12] E. Knightly and P. Rossaro. On the effects of smoothing for deterministic QoS. *Distributed Systems Engineering Journal: Special Issue on Quality of Service,* 4(1), 3–15, March 1997.

[13] J. Kurose. On computing per-session performance bounds in high-speed multi-hop computer networks. *Proc. ACM SIGMETRICS '92,* pages 128–139, Newport, RI, June 1992.

[14] J. McManus and K. Ross. Video-on-demand over ATM: constant-rate transmission and transport. *IEEE J. Selected Areas in Comm.,* 14(6), 1087–1098, August 1996.

[15] M. Reisslein, K. Ross, and S. Rajagopal. Guaranteeing statistical QoS to regulated traffic: the multiple node case. *Proc. 37th IEEE Conf. Decision and Control,* Tampa, FL, December 1998.

[16] J. Salehi, Z. Zhang, J. Kurose, and D. Towsley. Supporting stored video: Reducing rate variability and end-to-end resource requirements through

optimal smoothing. *IEEE/ACM Trans. Networking,* 6(4), 397–410, August 1998.

[17] T. Wu. *Efficient Statistical Service Provisioning in Broadband Networks.* M.S. Thesis, Rice University, May 1999.

[18] H. Zhang and D. Ferrari. Rate-controlled service disciplines. *Journal of High Speed Networks,* 3(4), 389–412, 1994.

[19] J. Zhang and J. Hui. Applying traffic smoothing techniques for quality of service control in VBR video transmissions. *Computer Communications,* 21(4), 375–89, April 1998.

[20] Z. Zhang, J. Kurose, J. Salehi, and D. Towsley. Smoothing, statistical multiplexing, and call admission control for stored video. *IEEE J. Selected Areas in Comm.,* 15(6), 1148–66, August 1997.

Chapter 11

Analysis of a Time Division Multiplexing Method with Priorities

Csaba Antal

Ericsson Traffic Analysis and Network Performance Laboratory

József Bíró

Technical University of Budapest

Abstract

This paper is concerned with a time division multiplexing method with two priority classes applicable for Dynamic Transfer Mode (DTM) networks. The method is useful to better utilize the capacity of DTM channels while the requirements of delay and delay sensitive traffic sources are also satisfied. A discrete-time model is performed to analyze the queuing behavior of low priority traffic streams. The model uses the important observation that from the viewpoint of low priority messages the system behaves as a queuing system subjected to periodic server interruption. The probability generating function (pgf) of the system time of low priority messages is expressed in closed form. Tail probabilities of system content and system time are derived by applying an efficient approximation technique. Finally, we give a simple illustration for the performance evaluation.

Keywords: discrete-time queuing, multiplexing, DTM.

11.1 Introduction

Dynamic Synchronous Transfer Mode (DTM) is a fast circuit switching technology [5]. It is designed with the assumption that processing capacity would be the bottleneck in communication networks. It uses unidirectional physical medium with multiple access, which is typically a fiber dual-bus. The whole communication channel on the physically shared medium is realized by a time division multiplexing scheme.

Due to the circuit switched property of DTM, network resources have to be reserved prior to the usage and remain unused between bursts of information. Burst switching can be used to utilize the channel between bursts. In order to be able to switch bursts, DTM has to support fast connection establishment and release. Performance characteristics of DTM relevant to burst switching like blocking probability and connection set-up delay were analyzed by simulation [9, 4, 3, 2] and by mathematical means [8].

In this paper, we present another type of solution: a multiplexing method that allows multiple sources to transmit data into the same DTM channel. The support of integrated services was considered in the specification of the multiplexing method, as it supports two priority levels. Real-time traffic is to be transmitted as high priority traffic while non-real-time data traffic is handled as low priority traffic.

The mean values of the system content and system time are analyzed in [1] in case the high priority source could be characterized with the Bernoulli arrival process. In this paper a more general model is developed, because both high and low priority traffic is characterized by general distributions. The results are also more general in this paper, because the probability generating function (pgf) of system time is derived here and the pgf of system content is already known from [6]. This paper also analyzes the tail probability distributions of system time and system content based on the generating functions.

The paper is structured as follows. Section 11.2 describes the multiplexing method applicable for DTM and introduces the mathematical model for the priority system. In Section 11.3, performance characteristics derived from the models are presented. A simple example is given to illustrate the derived expressions in Section 11.4. Finally, Section 11.5 draws the conclusions of the paper.

11.2   Time Division Multiplexing on Two Time-scales with Priorities

In DTM, the communication channel is divided into fixed length intervals (125 microsec), called cycles. Cycles contain 64-bit long slots. DTM channels are formed from the same slots of successive cycles. The multiplexing scheme presented here defines a new structure, which is called a frame. A frame is composed from M successive cycles. It is assumed that one high priority and several low priority sources share a DTM channel. High priority sources can transmit in any slot (i.e., in any cycle) of the DTM channel. Low priority (LP) sources can only use one slot in every frame (i.e., one cycle is every frame), and they are allowed to transmit in their slot when the high priority (HP) source is idle. That is, low priority sources are multiplexed using time-division multiplexing (TDM).

Figure 11.1 represents the concept of a queuing model of the system. Each source has its own queue. Lines in the figure show when sources are allowed to transmit. $U_{2,i,k}$ is the system content that belongs to low priority (priority 2) source i in cycle k and $A_{2,i,k}$ is the number of messages arrived to the low priority queue (priority 2) of source i in cycle k. $U_{1,k}$ denotes the system content that belongs to the high priority (priority 1) source in cycle k.

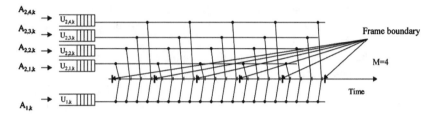

FIGURE 11.1
Concept of the queuing model for the TDM solution.

The system is described by means of discrete time queuing theory. In discrete time queuing discipline, the time axis is divided to fix size intervals (time-units). The length of these intervals is normalized. The time-unit in our model is the cycle. The discrete model used in this paper only considers the integer part of the system time, so the time between the arrival time instant and the next cycle boundary is not taken into consideration.

Based on the description of the multiplexing system, two new random variables are to be defined for each low priority source, the length of the availability interval (or A-time) T_A and the length of the blocking interval (or B-time) T_B. The availability interval is the number of successive cycles when the output channel is available for the source. Blocking interval is the number of successive cycles when the output channel is blocked for the source. Figure 11.2 displays the availability and blocking time of the first low priority queue.

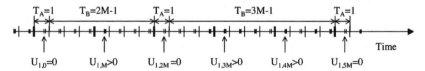

FIGURE 11.2
Availability and blocking times.

The evolution equations for the system content of the high and low priority queues in case of one-slot DTM channels can be written based on Fig. 11.1.

$$U_{1,k+1} = (U_{1,k} - 1)^+ + A_{1,k} \tag{11.1}$$

$$U_{2,i,k+1} = \begin{cases} (U_{2,i,k} - (1 - U_{1,i,k})^+)^+ + A_{2,i,k} & \text{if } k = Mn + i \\ U_{2,i,k+1} = U_{2,i,k} + A_{2,i,k} & \text{otherwise} \end{cases}$$

The analysis of the high priority queue is straightforward. If the number of messages arrived in a cycle form a sequence of independent and identically distributed random variables, a GI-D-1 model can be used to describe the behavior of the system. A more general model, which allows the analysis of high priority sources in case of multi-slot DTM channels, is also researched. The analysis of the GI-D-c queuing system suitable for c-slot DTM channels can be found in e.g., [6].

It can be seen from expression for the system content that low priority sources are independent from each other. The characteristics of the high priority source are independent of any other source [see Eq. (11.1)]. Thus it is enough to analyze one of the low priority sources, and the results can be applied to all of them. In the next section we show how to apply the server interruption model for solving the queuing model presented above.

11.3   Performance of Low Priority Sources

The server interruption model is directly based on the distribution T_A and T_B. In [6, pp.98–130] the server interruption model is analyzed in the case when both random variables have general independent distribution. The model of the TDM multiplexing method is a special case of the general model because the length of the availability interval is always 1 cycle ($T_A = 1$). The independence of the B-times is also satisfied due to the independence assumption on the arrival process of the high priority source. We further assume that the system reaches a stochastic equilibrium (stable state) under which the performance characteristics are to be investigated.

Now, we present a numerical approach to calculate the probability mass function and generating function of the length of blocking intervals. A given low priority source is allowed to transmit once in every frame. Therefore, B-time must be $Mi - 1$ cycles long (where i is any positive integer). In this way, only the probabilities $P(T_B = Mi - 1) = b(Mi - 1)$ should be expressed, any other length has zero probability.

The unknown probability can be expressed using the length of the high priority queue at different time-instants as $b(Mi - 1) = P(U_{1,iM} \neq 0, U_{1,(i-1)M} \neq$

$0, \ldots, U_{1,M} \neq 0 | U_{1,0} = 0$). This equation can be transformed to a simpler form. Let us denote the conditional probability $P(U_{1,iM} = 0 | U_{1,0} = 0)$ with $x_M(i)$, where iM is the number of cycles elapsed from the zero time-instant for all $i > 0$ and $M > 1$. The following recursive formula can be used to compute the probability mass function of the length of the B-times [2]: $b(Mi - 1) = x_M(i) - \sum_{j=1}^{i-1} b(Mj - 1)x_M(i - j)$, where the conditional probability $x_M(i)$ can be obtained numerically from the evaluation equation of the high priority queue. The probability mass function of the length of the B-times can be computed, which can be used to numerically determine the probability generating function of B-times.

For the system content a general pgf formula is derived in [6]. Here we only analyze the tail probabilities, which can be expressed from the generating function. For recalling here we note that the generating function of a nonnegative integer valued random variable X is $X(z) = E(z^X)$.

The pgf of the system content of low priority queue i, when the system reaches its equilibrium, is

$$U_{2,i}(z) = \frac{\left(1 - \left(1 + P_B'(1)\right)A_{2,i}'(1)\right)A_{2,i}(z)(1-z)\left(1 - A_{2,i}(z)P_B(A_{2,i}(z))\right)}{\left(1 + P_B'(1)\right)\left(A_{2,i}(z) - 1\right)\left(z - A_{2,i}(z)P_B(A_{2,i}(z))\right)}, \quad (11.2)$$

where $P_B(z) = E(z^{T_B})$. The moments of the probability distribution can be obtained from the derivatives of the generating function at $z = 1$.

The tail of the probability mass function of the system content is very important, because it can be used to calculate the probability of having longer queue than a specified value. The following theorem shows that the tail probability of the system content of any low priority source can be approximated with an exponential function if the conditions of stability are fulfilled.

THEOREM 11.1

If the stability condition is fulfilled, the tail probability mass function of the system content of low priority source i can approximately be expressed as

$$P(U_{2,i} > n) \approx$$
$$\frac{\left(1 - A_{2,i}'(1)(1 + P_B'(1))\right)A_{2,i}(z_0)(1 - z_0)}{(1 + P_B'(1))(A_{2,i}(z_0) - 1)\left(1 - A_{2,i}'(z_0)\left(P_B(A_{2,i}(z_0)) + A_{2,i}(z_0)P_B'(A_{2,i}(z_0))\right)\right)} z_0^{-n-1} \quad (11.3)$$

where z_0 is the real pole of generating function $U_{2,i}(z)$ with the smallest absolute value outside the unit circle.

Proof Sketch As $U_{2,i}(z)$ is the generating function of the system content, it is analytic inside the complex unit circle, which also involves that the absolute values of its poles are greater than 1. In [7] it was shown that if the generating function $X(z)$ of the integer valued random variable X has one positive real pole outside the unit circle and it has the form $X(z) = W(z)/Y(z)$, where $W(z)$ and $Y(z)$ are polynomials, then $P(X = n) \approx -cz_0^{-n-1}$ and $P(X > n) \approx cz_0^{-n-1}/(1 - z_0)$ where $c = W(z_0)/Y'(z_0)$ and z_0 is the positive real pole of $X(z)$.

It can be shown that $U_{2,i}(z)$ has exactly one positive real pole outside the unit circle. For this it is enough to show that its denominator has exactly one positive zero greater than 1, and at this value the numerator is not equal to 0.

The first derivative of $G(z) = z - A_{2,i}(z)P_B(A_{2,i}(z))$ at $z = 1$ is always greater than zero because the assumed stability condition for the system is $A'_{2,i}(1)(1 + P'_B(1)) < 1$. The second derivative of $G(z)$ is negative $\forall z > 0$. It means that $G'(z)$ becomes negative for sufficiently large z, thus, there is another zero of $G(z)$ in addition to $z = 1$. It is easy to see that it also means that there is exactly one real-valued zero of the denominator of $U_{2,i}(z)$. For this zero, denoted by z_0, it holds that

$$z_0 = A_{2,i}(z_0)P_B(A_{2,i}(z_0)) \quad \text{and} \quad z_0 > 1 \,. \tag{11.4}$$

The numerator of $U_{2,i}(z)$ at $z = z_0$ is strictly positive due to Eq. (11.4). Now we can state that z_0 is a real valued pole of $U_{2,i}(z)$. The parameter c in the approximation of tail probability can be computed now, allowing us to write Eq. (11.3). ∎

Now, we can proceed to the derivation of the generating function of the system time. An approximation of the tail probability of the system time is also analyzed based on the corresponding generating function.

The derivation for the generating function of system time is similar to that of the system content presented in [6]. First, the pgf of the system time is expressed *separately* for messages arrived in different cycles of the blocking and availability intervals. Then, based on the theorem of total probability, the pgf of the system time for an arbitrarily chosen message can be obtained as the linear combination of the separate pgf's.

The detailed derivation of the probability generating functions can be found in [2]. The variables for which the pgf should be derived are system time of messages arrived after the kth cycle of an A-time ($V_{A,k}$), system time of messages arrived after the kth cycle of a B-time ($V_{B,k}$), system time of messages arrived in an arbitrary cycle within an A-time (V_A), system time of messages arrived in an arbitrary cycle within a B-time (V_B), system time of messages arrived in an arbitrary cycle (V).

$V_B(z)$ can be derived from $V_{B,k}(z)$ using the theorem of total probability and using that the probability mass function of the position of an arbitrarily chosen cycle within the blocking interval (K_B) is [6] $P(K_B = k) = \sum_{j=k}^{\infty} b(j)/P'_B(1)$. The length of an A-time is 1, so $V_A(z) = V_{A,1}(z)$.

Finally, the pgf $V(z)$ can be written as a weighted sum of $V_A(z)$ and $V_B(z)$ where the weights are the probability of availability and blocking state of the output channel. Using the indexes referring to the priority and the identity of the low priority source, the final result is

$$V_{2,i}(z) = \frac{z\left(1 - (1 + P'_B(1))A'_{2,i}(1)\right)}{(1 + P'_B(1))A'_{2,i}(1)} \frac{A_{2,i}(zP_B(z)) - 1}{z - A_{2,i}(zP_B(z))}. \tag{11.5}$$

From this the mean value of the system time of a low priority message can be expressed:

$$V'_{2,i}(1) = 1 + \frac{A'_{2,i}(1)\left(P''_B(1) + 2P'_B(1)\right) - A''_{2,i}(1)\left(1 + P'_B(1)\right)^2}{2A'_{2,i}(1)(1 + P'_B(1))\left(1 - A'_{2,i}(1)(1 + P'_B(1))\right)}$$

$$= \frac{U'_{2,i}(1)}{A'_{2,i}(1)}. \tag{11.6}$$

The mean, which can be obtained from Eq. (11.2) and Eq. (11.6) is in accordance with Little's theorem.

Equation (11.5) can also be used to calculate higher moments of the distribution like the variance. With abbreviated notations the variance of the system time is

$$var(V_{2,i}) = \frac{3R''(1) + 2R'''(1)}{6R'(1)(1 - R'(1))} + \frac{3(R''(1))^2(1 - 2R'(1))}{4(R'(1)(1 - R'(1)))^2}, \tag{11.7}$$

where $R(z) = A_{2,i}(zP_B(z)) - 1$ and $R'(1)$, $R''(1)$, $R'''(1)$ are the derivatives of $R(z)$ at $z = 1$.

The last characteristic to be expressed from the generating function of the system time is a good approximation of the tail probability. It is very important if one wants to know the probability of waiting longer for a message than a specified threshold. The following theorem shows that this approximation of tail probability has exponential decay as expected.

THEOREM 11.2

Assuming the system has a stochastic equilibrium, the tail probability distribution of the system time can be approximated from Eq. (11.5) in the following form:

$$P(V_{2,i} > n) \approx$$

$$\frac{\left(1 - (1 + P'_B(1)A'_{2,i}(1))\right)(1 - z_0)}{(1 + P'_B(1))A'_{2,i}(1)\left(A'_{2,i}(z_0 P_B(z_0))(P_B(z_0) + z_0 P'_B(z_0)) - 1\right)} z_0^{-n}$$

where z_0 is the (real) pole of generating function $V_{2,i}(z)$, which is one of the solutions of equation $z = A_{2,i}(zP_B(z))$.

Proof Sketch   The proof is similar to that in Theorem 11.1. It is to be shown that $V_{2,i}(z)$ has only one positive real pole, which is greater than 1. The proof is based on the fact that denominator of $V_{2,i}(z)$ has one real zero in addition to the $z = 1$ point. (Note that $z = 1$ is not a pole of $V_{2,i}(z)$ because this function is analytic inside the unit circle.)   ∎

11.4   Example

The following simple example assumes that the high priority source can be characterized with a Bernoulli arrival process with generating function $A_1(z) = 1 - p + pz$, and all of the low priority sources have Batch Bernoulli arrival processes with batch-size 30 and pgf $A_{2,i}(z) = 1 - q + qz^{30}$. It is also assumed that the load coming from low priority sources equals to the load coming from the high priority source.

As at most 1 message arrives from the high priority source during a cycle and the server capacity is 1 message in each cycle, no queue builds up at the high priority source. In other words, the system content has also Bernoulli distribution. Due to the independence of system contents in successive cycles, it can be written that $b(Mi - 1) = pb(M(i - 1) - 1)$. From this equation the pmf and pgf of $P_B(z)$ can be obtained. So if the high priority source can be characterized with a Bernoulli process, the generating function for the system content and the system time of a given low priority source can be expressed directly from the arrival distributions:

$$U_{2,i}(z) = \frac{\left(1-p-MA'_{2,i}(1)\right)A_{2,i}(z)(1-z)(1-(A_{2,i}(z))^M)}{M(A_{2,i}(z)-1)\left(z(1-p(A_{2,i}(z))^M)-(1-p)(A_{2,i}(z))^M\right)} \qquad (11.8)$$

$$V_{2,i}(z) = \frac{z\left(1-p-MA'_{2,i}(z)\right)}{M(A'_{2,i}(1))} \frac{A_{2,i}(z^M(1-p)/(1-pz^M))-1}{z-A_{2,i}(z^M(1-p)/(1-pz^M))} \cdot \qquad (11.9)$$

Based on the tail probabilities two important parameters can be calculated: the limit of the queue length which is exceeded with a small probability (e.g., 10^{-4} or 10^{-6}), and the probability that the delay is greater than a critical value (e.g., 100 ms). Although our model assumes infinite buffers, it was shown in [7] that the probability $P(U > U_0)$ is a good estimation of the message loss probability of a finite queue with $U_0 + c$ size, where c is the number of servers (in this case it is 1). The size of the buffers is dimensioned so that the message loss probability should be below a certain value. Figure 11.3 shows the required buffer size if the maximum message loss rate is 10^{-4} and 10^{-6}, respectively.

In Fig. 11.4 the probabilities that the queuing delay is greater than 100 ms and 400 ms can be seen, respectively. As it can be noticed the number of low priority sources greatly influences the tail probability of the delay. This kind of characteristic can be used, for instance, to determine the optimal number of low priority sources for given delay bounds, loads, and high priority traffic.

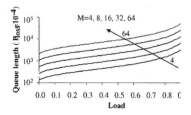
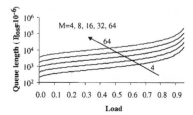

FIGURE 11.3
Buffer size dimensioning for loss rates.

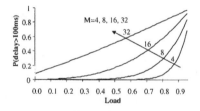
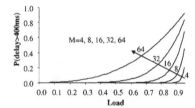

FIGURE 11.4
Buffer size dimensioning for delays.

11.5   Conclusions

In this paper a time division multiplexing method supporting priorities is analyzed. The method allows one to multiplex one high priority and several low priority traffic streams. This is useful for better utilization of DTM channels while the requirements of delay and delay sensitive sources can also be satisfied.

For analyzing the queuing behavior of the low priority traffic in the multiplexing method under question a discrete-time queuing model is applied. The model utilizes the important observation that from the viewpoint of low priority messages the system behaves as a queuing system subjected to periodic (random) server interruptions. It can be shown that the intervals between the service of consecutive messages belonging to the same low priority class, which is called the blocking-time (B-time), are independent and identically distributed random variables.

First a numerical method is developed for the calculation of pgf of B-time. Then closed-form expressions for the pgf of the system time are derived. The tail probabilities of the system content and system time are expressed using a well-known efficient approximation technique. These metrics are necessary for designing efficient DTM multiplexers and switches and evaluating their performance. The performance evaluation is illustrated with a simple numerical example.

Further research is needed for extending the models for non-independent arrival processes in case of the presented multiplexing method, and developing and investigating other multiplexing disciplines applicable for DTM.

References

[1] Cs. Antal, Servicing Bursty Sources Efficiently via a Fast Circuit Switched System, *International Conference for Computer Communication '97,* 19–21 November 1997, Cannes, France.

[2] Cs. Antal, Performance Evaluation of a Fast Circuit Switched Networking Technology, *Ph.D. dissertation,* Budapest, Hungary 1999.

[3] Cs. Antal, J. Molnár, S. Molnár, G. Szabó, Performance Study of Distributed Channel Reallocation Techniques for a Fast Circuit Switched Network, *Computer Communications, Special Issue on the Stochastic Analysis and Optimization of Communication Systems,* 1998.

[4] C. Bohm, Circuit Switching — A Viable Solution for High Capacity Integrated Services Networks, *Ph.D. dissertation,* ISRN-KTH/IT/R-96/10-SE, Stockholm, Sweden, 1996.

[5] C. Bohm, M. Hidell, P. Landgren, L. Ramfelt, P. Sjödin, Fast Circuit Switching for the Next Generation of High Performance Networks, *IEEE J. Selected Areas of Comm.,* Vol. 14, No. 2, February 1996.

[6] H. Bruneel, B.G. Kim, *Discrete-Time Models for Communications Systems Including ATM,* Kluwer Academic Publishers, Dordrecht, 1993.

[7] H. Bruneel, B. Steyaert, E. Desmet, G.H. Petit, Analytic derivation of tail probabilities for queue lengths and waiting times in ATM multiserver

queues, *European Journal of Operational Research,* 76, pp. 563–572, 1994, North-Holland.

[8] C.J. Chang, A.A. Nilsson, Analytical Model for DTM Access Nodes, technical report, http://www2.ncsu.edu/eos/info/ece_info/www/ccsp /tech_reports/abs/abs9806.html, North Carolina State University, Raleigh, USA, TR-98/06, 1998.

[9] P. Lindgren, Multi-Channel Network Architecture Based on Fast Circuit Switching, Ph.D. dissertation, Royal Institute of Technology, ISRN KTH/IT/R-96/08-SE, Stockholm, Sweden, 1996.

Chapter 12

Web Traffic Modeling and Performance Comparison Between HTTP1.0 and HTTP1.1

Z. Liu, N. Niclausse and C. Jalpa-Villanueva

INRIA Centre Sophia Antipolis

Abstract

In this work we propose a stochastic model for describing the Web traffic at request level. We concentrate on the HTTP requests to the same Web server and we are interested in the typical behavior of the clients' hypertext navigation. The mathematical model is defined by a stochastic marked point process which describes when clients arrive and how they browse the server. We have developed a benchmark tool of Web servers: WAGON. It comprises a generator of Web traffic, a robot which sends and analyzes requests and a monitoring tool. It can generate different types of traffic requests, which, in turn, can be sent out to the server from different machines with different (simulated) delays and bandwidth constraints. Using such a tool we have carried out experiments and compared the performance between HTTP1.0 and HTTP1.1 under different configurations. Our results indicate that HTTP1.1 almost always outperforms HTTP1.0, and this is true even if the latter uses more parallel connections and slightly larger bandwidth. The difference in request response time becomes more significant when the network is heavily loaded. The response time of clients using HTTP1.0 with a single connection could be ten times larger than those using HTTP1.1.

Keywords: web traffic modeling, heavy-tail distribution, long range dependence, HTTP, web hypertext.

12.1   Introduction

The World Wide Web has become a major way of publication and information search on the Internet during the last several years. It is now the dominant source of the Internet traffic. The exponential increase of the number of servers and of the number of users causes performance problems of access to Web objects, due to the saturation of Web servers and of the communication network.

One of the main preoccupations of Web server administrators is to propose a fast and reliable service to satisfy their clients. The tremendous success of the Web makes this task difficult to accomplish. Indeed, not only is it necessary to provide an efficient service for a given time instant, but also it is required to anticipate traffic growth in order to maintain the quality of service for short or medium term.

It is thus important to understand the statistical properties of the Web traffic and to develop appropriate traffic models for the performance evaluation of Web servers and Web applications.

SURGE [1] is a benchmark tool that tries to imitate a stream of HTTP requests originating from a fixed population of Web users. A user is modeled by an ON/OFF process (User Equivalent) who during the ON period makes requests for Web files and during the OFF period lies idle. Within an ON period there are active OFF time periods corresponding to the time between transfer of components of a page. Inactive OFF time periods correspond to the user think time. The workload is generated using an analytic approach to capture properties observed in real Web workloads concerning file sizes (what is stored in the file system), request sizes (what is transferred over the network from the server), file popularity and temporal locality. Distributional models for the file size, the active OFF times and the embedded references were developed using a client trace data set.

Several other Web benchmarks exist [10, 9, 6] which periodically generate simple HTTP requests to a small set of pages. In hbench:Web [5], the workload is generated according to empirical distributions based on server log files.

In our work, we propose a stochastic model for describing the Web traffic at request level. We concentrate on the HTTP requests to the same Web server and we are interested in the typical behavior of the clients' hypertext navigation. The mathematical model is defined by a stochastic marked point process which describes when clients arrive and how they browse the server.

HTTP request stream is dependant on both the protocol (depending on the use of parallel connections or persistent ones) and on the navigator (graphical or textual browser for instance). What is typical of Web user's behavior is hypertext browsing (click on links, read pages, and so on). Therefore, our goal was to design the protocol and implementation independent patterns of Web traffic, browsing behavior. Other components (server contents and embedded objects requests) are left to the benchmarking tool. Our model focus on user's behavior while they browse a server: the number of clicks and the time elapsed between each click.

We have developed a benchmark tool of Web servers: WAGON (Web trAffic GeneratOr and beNchmark). It comprises a generator of Web traffic, a robot which sends and analyzes requests and a monitoring tool. It can generate different types of traffic requests, which, in turn, can be sent out to the server from different machines with different (simulated) delays and bandwidths. Using such a tool we have carried out experiments and compared the performance between HTTP1.0 and HTTP1.1 under different configurations.

Our results show in particular that HTTP1.1 almost always outperforms HTTP1.0, and this is true even if the latter uses more parallel connections and slightly larger bandwidth. The difference becomes more significant when the pipeline mechanism is used in HTTP1.1 and when the propagation delay is large.

The paper is organized as follows. In section 12.2 we describe the traffic model we proposed and we report the statistical analysis results. In section 12.3 we present the experimental results obtained using WAGON.

12.2 Traffic Model and Statistical Analysis

12.2.1 Traffic Model

We propose a stochastic model of HTTP traffic. We confine ourselves to HTTP requests to the same Web server. We are interested in the typical behavior of clients traversing the hypertext of a Web server, namely, when they arrive and how requests are generated. This can actually be well described by the notion of session: a sequence of clicks of a client on the hyperlinks of the same server.

The traffic model we propose can be described by a stochastic marked point process. The arrival times correspond to the beginning times of session. Each arrival is associated with the following random variables (the marks):

- The number of clicks during the session;

- The times elapsed between successive clicks;

- The addresses of the successively required pages, i.e., the addresses of the first page and the successively clicked hyperlinks.

Note that in this traffic model for benchmarks, the embedded objects (icons, images, animations, audio, etc.) are not specified and are requested automatically by clients, by parsing HTML files.

It turns out that the arrival process of sessions is well described by a Poisson process; see results below. This permits a simple way to parameterize the traffic intensity. The distribution functions of the number of clicks and of the interclick times most often belong to the classes of Pareto, lognormal, Inverse Gaussian and Weibull distributions. The page addresses are samples of the weighted directed graph representing the hypertext structure of the server. These weights correspond to the visit frequencies and the routing probabilities (i.e., the probabilities of following the hyperlinks).

12.2.2 Statistical Analysis Results

Statistical analyses have been carried out on different log files, in particular, those of the Web servers at W3C,[1] INRIA[2] and www.clark.net.[3] Some characteristics of these server traces are in Table 12.1.

Table 12.1 Characteristics of the Servers www.w3.org, www.inria.fr, www.clark.net

	www.w3.org	www.inria.fr	www.clark.net
Time period:	Feb 97	Oct 96	Sep 95
Duration:	24h	24h	18h
Total number of requests:	275000	50000	150000
Total number of pages:	4726	7773	9294
Average page size:	23kB	15kB	13kB

The results of the statistical analyses and the parameter identifications are summarized in Table 12.2.

Previous results in the literature concerning the analysis of HTTP and IP traffic have rejected the Poisson hypothesis; see for example [8, 2]. However, if one looks at the arrival process of sessions instead of the arrival process of requests or packets, the Poisson assumption turns out to be valid.

The numbers of clicks of sessions form a renewal process whose increments have a heavy-tail distribution. For the traces we analyzed, this heavy-tail distribution is either inverse Gaussian or Pareto.

Our analyses indicate that the interclick times are positively correlated, although the coefficient of auto-correlation is very small. There also seems to be long-range dependence with a small Hurst parameter, see Fig. 12.1.

---

[1] http://www.w3.org/

[2] http://www.inria.fr/

[3] http://ita.ee.lbl.gov/html/contrib/ClarkNet-HTTP.html

Table 12.2 Distributions of Servers www.w3.org, www.inria.fr, www.clark.net

Random Variable	Matching with Hypothesized Distribution	Mean	Standard Deviation
Distributions for the server www.w3.org			
Session arrivals	Poisson process ($\lambda = 0.39$)	2.5s	2.7s
Number of clicks per session	Pareto ($a = 0.748$; $\beta = 0.807$)	3.1	4
Interclick time	LogNormal ($m = 2.84$; $\sigma = 1.68$)	63s	138s
Distributions for the server www.inria.fr			
Session arrivals	Poisson process ($\lambda = 0.037$)	27s	31s
Number of clicks per session	Inverse Gaussian ($\mu = 5.96$; $\sigma = 3$)	6	11.5
Interclick time	LogNormal ($m = 3.26$; $\sigma = 1.36$)	68s	121s
Distributions for the server www.clark.net			
Session arrivals	Poisson process ($\lambda = 0.21$)	4.7s	5s
Number of clicks per session	Pareto ($a = 0.94$; $\beta = 1.16$)	3.3	4.4
Interclick time	LogNormal ($m = 3.8$; $\sigma = 1.3$)	101s	152s

12.3 Experimental Results

12.3.1 WAGON

We have developed a benchmark tool of Web servers: WAGON. It comprises a generator of Web traffic, a robot which sends and analyses requests and a monitoring tool. It can generate different types of traffic requests, which, in turn, can be sent out to the server from different machines with different (simulated) delays and bandwidths. For this, a user can specify server features (server name or IP address, home page address of the server, server log files, etc.), client features (laws and parameters of the random variables in the traffic model; transport protocols and parameters used) and experiment configuration (local client caching, sampling rate, client machines and bandwidth constraint and routing delay on these machines, etc.).

During a benchmark, various performance measures can be obtained and observed on-line through the monitoring tool of WAGON. Of particular interest are request latency and user perceived throughput.

12.3.2 Long-Range Dependence and the Traffic Model

In our traffic model, we use mutually independent random variables for the marks of the point process. However, the resulting traffic is long-range dependent, and thus asymptotically self-similar, as illustrated in Fig. 12.2.

This result is actually not really surprising. As is already shown in [3], when one superposes an infinitely many on-off sources where the "on" times have a heavy-tail distribution, the resulting process is long-range dependent.

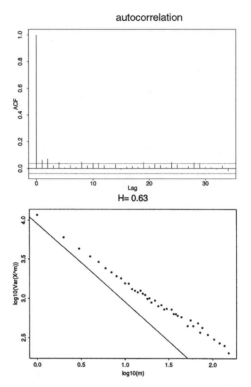

FIGURE 12.1
Dependence analysis of interclick times.

12.3.3   Performance Comparison between HTTP1.0 and HTTP1.1

At the time HTTP1.1 was proposed, a comparison study between HTTP1.0 and HTTP1.1 was carried out [7]. The effect of persistent connections, pipelining, document compression, bandwidth and latency on the performance was investigated using a single Web page containing 42 embedded images. A work to characterize Web response time is presented in [4]. Four proxy logs files are used, they are replayed using a URL re-player multi-process program. The workload is replayed by reading a log file of URLs, sending HTTP requests, and timing the transfer. Ten experiments were done to investigate the effects of proxy caching, network bandwidth, traffic load and persistent connections. The periodicity of the response times was also studied.

We investigate the following four types of connections: modems, T1 links, WAN (transatlantic) and satellite connections. In order to simulate such connections, we put the delay and bandwidth constraints as in Table 12.3.

The parameters used for generating Web traffic are illustrated in Table 12.4. We have chosen two types of Web server contents, both of which are sub-

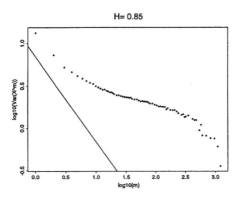

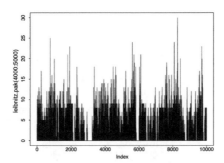

FIGURE 12.2
Variance-time plot of the observed traffic generated by WAGON.

Table 12.3 Delay and Bandwidth Constraints

	delay	bandwidth
modem	300 ms	33kb/s
T1	40ms	1.5Mb/s
WAN	180ms	100kb/s
satellite	500ms	2Mb/s

sets of the Web server INRIA.[4] Server 1 consists of many large pages (mostly PostScript files). Server 2 consists of HTML files in majority with more embedded images. Their characteristics are summarized in Table 12.5.

---

[4]http://www.inria.fr

Table 12.4   Clients Parameters Used in the Experimentations

Variable	Law	Mean	Std deviation
Session arrival	Poisson Process ($0.0005 < \lambda < 0.03$)		
Number of clicks	Inverse Gaussian ($\mu = 5; \lambda = 3$)	5	1.28
Interclick time	LogNormal ($m = 3; \sigma = 1.1$)	36.8s	56.4s

Table 12.5   Characteristics of the Web Servers Used in the Experimentations

	server1	server2
Total number of pages:	778	2353
Average size:	58kB	6.5kB

The Apache server (Version 1.3)[5] is used to serve the requests. The server accepts both HTTP1.0 and HTTP1.1 requests. The time out for persistent connections is set to be 30 seconds.

The comparison results are illustrated in Figs. 13.3 and 13.4. We considered four configurations of HTTP control parameters: HTTP1.0 with 1 connection per client, HTTP1.0 with 4 parallel connections per client, HTTP1.1 with 1 connection per client without pipeline, HTTP1.1 with 1 connection per client with pipeline. Recall that in the current implementation, the bandwidth constraint is applied per connection instead of per client. Thus, a client using HTTP1.0 with 4 parallel connections can actually have larger available bandwidth.

These results indicate that HTTP1.1 almost always outperforms HTTP1.0, and this is true even if the latter uses four parallel connections while the former just one connection. In most cases, HTTP1.1 with pipeline outperforms HTTP1.1 without pipeline, and HTTP1.1 without pipeline outperforms HTTP1.0 with four parallel connections, and the latter outperforms HTTP1.0 with a single connection. The difference in request response time becomes more significant when the network is heavily loaded. The response time of clients using HTTP1.0 with a single connection could be ten times larger than those using HTTP1.1.

These results are coherent with those of [7]. In our experiments, the number of packets generated by HTTP1.0 (103101 in one of the experiments) is almost twice of that by HTTP1.1 (58896 for the same experiment without pipeline and 57617 with pipeline). This saving in the number of packets by HTTP1.1 explains the significant difference in response times when the network is heavily loaded.

---

[5]http://www.apache.org

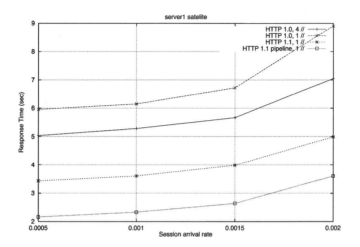

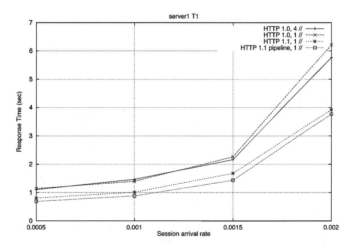

FIGURE 12.3a
Performance comparison between HTTP1.0 and HTTP1.1 on server 1.

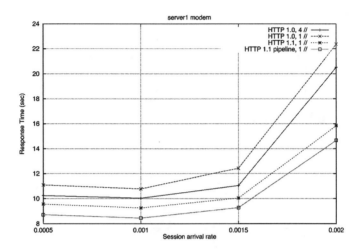

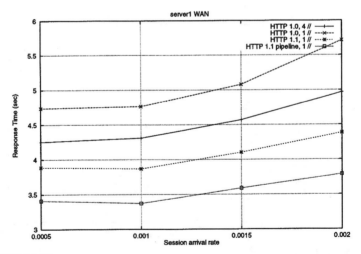

FIGURE 12.3b
Performance comparison between HTTP1.0 and HTTP1.1 on server 1.

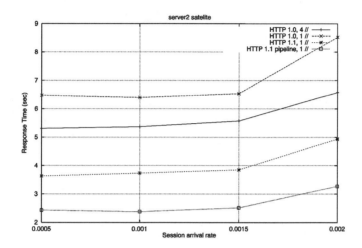

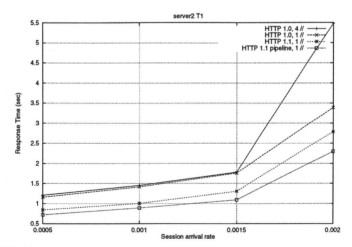

FIGURE 12.4a
Performance comparison between HTTP1.0 and HTTP1.1 on server 2.

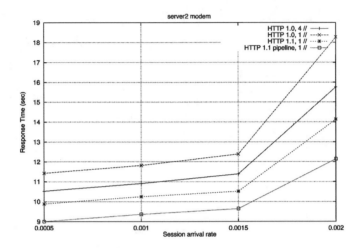

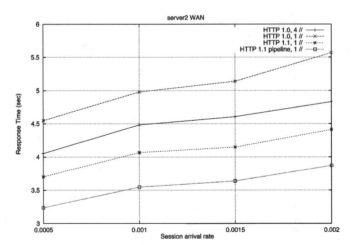

FIGURE 12.4b
Performance comparison between HTTP1.0 and HTTP1.1 on server 2.

References

[1] Paul Barford and Mark E. Crovella, Generating representative Web workloads for network and server performance evaluation. *Proc. ACM Sigmetrics'98,* 1998.

[2] Mark E. Crovella, Murrad S. Taqqu, and Azer Bestavros, Heavy-tailed probability distributions in the World Wide Web. To appear in the book: A Practical Guide To Heavy Tails: Statistical Techniques for Analysing Heavy Tailed Distributions, 1996.

[3] N. Likhanov, B. Tsybakov, and N.D. Georganas, Analysis of an ATM buffer with self-similar input traffic. *Proc. Infocom'95,* April 1995.

[4] Binzhang Liu, Characterizing Web response time. Master's thesis, Virginia Polytechnic Institute and State University, April 1998.

[5] S. Manley, M. Courage, and M. Seltzer, A self-scaling and self-configuring benchmark for Web servers. Technical report, Harvard University, 1998.

[6] David Mosberger and Tai Jin, httperf–a tool for measuring Web server performance. *Workshop on Internet Server Performance (WISP'98),* Madison, WI, June 1998.

[7] H. Frystyk Nielsen, J. Gettys, A. Baird-Smith, E. Prud'hommeaux, H. Lie, and C. Lilley, Network performance effects of http/1.1, css1, and png. *Proc. ACM SIGCOMM '97,* Cannes, France, September 1997.

[8] V. Paxson and S. Floyd, Wide-area traffic: The failure of Poisson modeling. *Proc. ACM/Sigcomm'94,* pages 257–268, September 1994.

[9] SPEC, An explanation of the specweb96 benchmark, 1996.

[10] Gene Trent and Mark Sake, Webstone: The first generation in http server benchmarking, 1995.

Chapter 13

Average Bandwidth and Delay for Reliable Multicast

Rajarshi Gupta and Jean Walrand
University of California

Abstract   The problem of ensuring reliability in a one-to-many multicast scheme has been approached from various angles and a number of protocols have been created to address this issue. We consider a nack-based and tree-based reliable multicast scheme which utilizes special agents (called Designated Receivers) for accumulation of nacks and caching of data to handle retransmissions. We evaluate the average bandwidth utilized per link in a uniform tree in order to transmit a single packet to all the hosts. We also calculate the average delay per packet for a host and verify the analytical results using simulations.

Keywords: reliable multicast, delay, bandwidth, analytical results.

13.1   Introduction

The number of real-time applications that use multicasting [3] has been increasing rapidly over the past few years. These applications have tight delay requirements but tolerate packet errors. Other applications, such as software or news distribution, would benefit from reliable one-to-many multicasting (see e.g., [4, 2]). The necessity therefore is for a protocol that ensures reliability for multicasting in a scalable and efficient manner. In this paper, we study the bandwidth utilization and delays involved in the correction of errors in one-to-many multicasting.

We begin with a discussion of a promising class of such strategies. In the scheme outlined in RMTP [4], certain hosts/routers act as specialized agents called *Designated Receivers (DR)* that have the purpose of accumulating nacks and maybe handling retransmissions. These DRs are spread throughout the tree, and every host is assigned a 'parent DR.'

Non-caching Scheme: In this simpler DR scheme, the DRs act only as nack processors. When a host detects a lost packet, it sends a nack (possibly after waiting for a timeout). However, instead of sending the nack to the sender of the packet, the nack is sent to the designated DR for the host. The DR waits for the other hosts in the subtree to nack for the same packet and sends only a *single* nack to its parent DR. This process continues until the source receives a nack, and retransmits the packet. The advantage is that the sender only receives a few nacks, and the nack implosion is avoided.

Caching Scheme: In a more advanced system, the DRs cache the data that passes through them. Depending on the size and duration of the session, they may cache the entire session, or a portion thereof. If a DR receiving nacks does not have the packet, it acts as before — sending a single nack up to its parent. However, when it has the requested packet cached, the DR handles the retransmission itself, without propagating the nack upwards.

13.2   Average Bandwidth

We are trying to find theoretical expressions for the average bandwidth utilized per packet per link and the average delay experienced per packet by a host in the Designated Receiver scheme. Note that in an ideal case (when *no* packets are lost), the average bandwidth utilized per packet per link is exactly 1, since a single copy of the packet is sent on every link. And the expected delay for a host per packet is simply the distance of the host from the source of the packet. Furthermore, we want to evaluate these expressions both for a Caching and a Non-Caching DR scheme. We assume a perfectly uniform multicast tree with equally likely and independent losses on the links.

Notation

Before we present the derivations, certain notations need to be clarified. Note that we assume a perfectly uniform multicast tree with equally likely and independent losses on the links. We use the following notations:

p = loss probability on each link;

w = order of the tree, i.e., every node has w children;

h = distance between DRs, i.e., every h^{th} level from the host consists of DRs;

b = total depth of the tree in levels of DRs, i.e., actual depth of the tree is $b \times h$;

$k \in [1, h]$ is a variable used to denote the distance of the host under consideration from its DR;

$i \in [0, b-1]$ is a variable used to denote the position of the DR being considered;

Thus, when a host is designated by (i, k) its actual distance from the source is then $ih + k$.

13.2.1 Number of Transmissions Required to Transmit Packet to All Receivers $\alpha(H, w, p)$

As an important measure, we calculate the expected number of transmissions required to transmit a single packet to *all* receivers in the multicast tree. We utilize the models devised in [1] and [5] but generalize their specialized tree to a general uniform tree with w children of each node. Every link has a loss probability of p, and the losses are independent.

Denote by $T(n)$ the number of transmissions required for a packet to arrive at node n and all its children, given that the packet arrives at the parent of node n at each time.

Let $F_n(i) = P(T(n) \leq i)$, for $i \geq 1$. If we let s denote the source, then $F_s(i) = P(T(s) \leq i)$.

Let the hosts that are one level away from the source be called children $c1$, the hosts two levels away called $c2$ and so on. Also, note that any host (source included) has exactly w children. Then,

$$F_s(i) = \prod_{c1 \in child(s)} F_{c1}(i) = (F_{c1}(i))^w$$

$$F_{c1}(i) = \sum_{j=o}^{i-1} \binom{i}{j} p^j (1-p)^{i-j} \prod_{c2 \in child(c1)} F_{c2}(i-j)$$

$$= \sum_{j=o}^{i-1} \binom{i}{j} p^j (1-p)^{i-j} (F_{c2}(i-j))^w .$$

The recursion eventually finishes when it reaches the leaf nodes, where $F_l(i) = 1 - p^i$.

Hence, the expected number of transmissions required to transmit a single packet to *all* the receivers in the multicast tree is denoted by

$$\alpha(H, w, p) = E[T(s)] = \sum_{i=0}^{\infty} (1 - F_s(i)) .$$

13.2.2 Calculating the Caching Average Bandwidth ρ_{avg}^C

In our calculation for the average bandwidth per packet, we first calculate the bandwidth experienced at some DR (located i levels away from the source) and average this across all the DRs at all levels. Since the DRs themselves are hosts, and the tree is uniform with DRs located in every h^{th} level, averaging the bandwidth across all the levels of DRs gives us a true estimate of the average.

Let $\rho^C(i)$ denote the expected bandwidth utilized per packet at a DR located i levels away from the source. The bandwidth utilized incorporates the sum of all the packets and nacks that pass through this DR, including both incoming and outgoing ones. We calculate $\rho^C(i)$ as the sum of five quantities that we explain below:

$$\rho^C(i) = N_1 + N_2 + N_{3A} + N_{3B} + N_4 \, .$$

Averaging this over all the levels of DRs,

$$\rho^C_{avg} = \frac{\sum_{i=0}^{b-1} \rho^C(i) \cdot w^{ih}}{\sum_{i=0}^{b-1} w^{ih}} \, .$$

N_1 = Number of copies of the packet that pass through DR

As soon as the DR gets one copy of the packet, it caches it. In case it sees other copies of the same packet, they are dropped and so need not be considered in our calculations. Thus, $N_1 = 1$.

N_2 = Number of nacks the DR forwards

For every transmitted copy of the packet that the DR sees a nack — it either needs to respond, or send a retransmission. Once it receives a copy of the packet, it caches it and responds to subsequent nacks. Furthermore, in the ideal case assumed, it forwards exactly *one* nack for every copy of the packet transmitted, until it gets some copy. So the number of nacks forwarded by the DR is exactly the number of drops experienced by the packet until it reaches the DR. Modeling the process required for the packet to reach the DR as a Markov Chain, we get

$$N_2 = \frac{i(1 - (1 - p)^h)}{(1 - p)^h} \, .$$

N_{3A} = Number of nacks seen by DR until the packet reaches DR

Until the DR receives its first copy of the packet, *every* host below it does not have the packet either. Consequently, all the children hosts of the DR nack to it asking for the packet. All its children DRs also send one nack each for the packet. This goes on until the first copy is received (after N_2 transmissions). Therefore,

$$N_{3A} = N_2 \cdot \frac{w^{h+1} - 1}{w - 1} = \frac{i(1 - (1 - p)^h)}{(1 - p)^h} \cdot \frac{w^{h+1} - 1}{w - 1} \, .$$

N_{3B} = Number of nacks seen by DR after the packet reaches DR

We calculate this by considering a loss at level k downstream from the DR and evaluating its effects on the number of nacks generated. A loss at level k causes all the hosts below that point to nack together, with one nack each from all the

DRs from that subtree.

$$N_{3B} = \sum_{k=1}^{h} (\text{\# level } k \text{ links }) \cdot (\text{lossprob at } k) \cdot (\text{\# nacks for level } k \text{ loss})$$

$$\approx \frac{p}{w-1} \frac{w^{h+1} [h(1-p)(w-1)-1]}{w(1-p)-1} \text{ For } p \ll 1 \implies (1-p)^h$$

$$\approx 1 - hp .$$

$N_4 = $ Number of packets the DR retransmits

A DR has to keep retransmitting a packet to every host below it until the next level of DRs gets the packet. It suffices to calculate the number of transmissions required till the next level of DRs gets the packets, since this implies every host above it having got the packet too.

There are h levels till the next line of DRs, and the probability of losing any packet at any link is p. Thus, $N_4 = \alpha(h, w, p)$.

13.2.3 Calculating the Non-Caching Average Bandwidth ρ_{avg}^{NC}

Similar to our calculation for ρ_{avg}^{C} (Section 13.2.2) we first calculate the bandwidth experienced at some DR (located i levels away from the source) and average this across all the DRs at all levels.

Let $\rho^{NC}(i)$ denote the expected bandwidth utilized per packet at a DR located i levels away from the source. We calculate $\rho^{NC}(i)$ as the sum of the same five quantities as in Section 13.2.2. Thus, $\rho^{NC}(i) = N_1 + N_2 + N_{3A} + N_{3B} + N_4$.

Again, averaging over all the levels of DRs,

$$\rho_{avg}^{NC} = \frac{\sum_{i=0}^{b-1} \rho^{NC}(i) \cdot w^{ih}}{\sum_{i=0}^{b-1} w^{ih}} .$$

$N_1 = $ Number of copies of the packet that pass through DR

Since the DRs do not cache any packets, it is up to the host to keep retransmitting copies of the packets until *every* host in the multicast tree gets it. Furthermore, since all packets are multicast by the host, potentially every packet sent out is received by every host. There are bh layers in all and each link loses each packet with a probability p. Thus,

$$N_1 = \alpha(bh, w, p)(1 - p)^{ih} .$$

$N_2 = $ Number of nacks the DR forwards

One nack is forwarded up by the DR for every copy of the packet transmitted, and this is carried on until every host below *this* DR receives the packet. Equivalently, we need to calculate how many transmissions are required till every one of the hosts in the last layer of the subtree rooted at this DR gets the packet.

Since all the packets sent do not actually reach the DR under consideration, we need to use a variation of the recursion scheme used in Section 13.2.1. Using the same notation, let n be this DR and let q be the probability that any packet sent by the host is lost on the path to DR n. Then $q = 1 - (1-p)^{ih}$ and $(b-i)h$ is the height of the subtree rooted at node n. Hence,

$$N_2 = E[T(n)] = \sum_{i=0}^{\infty} (1 - F_n(i))$$

$$F_n(i) = \sum_{u=o}^{i-1} \binom{i}{u} q^u (1-q)^{i-u} (F_c(i-u))^w .$$

The expression for $F_c(i-u)$, for a child node, is calculated as in Section 13.2.1.

N_{3A} = **Number of nacks seen by DR until the packet reaches DR**
N_{3A} for the non-caching case is identical to the N_{3A} term calculated for the caching case in Section 13.2.2.

$$N_{3A} = \frac{i(1 - (1-p)^h)}{(1-p)^h} \cdot \frac{w^{h+1} - 1}{w - 1} .$$

N_{3B} = **Number of nacks seen by DR after the packet reaches DR**
Following the analysis for the N_{3B} for ρ^C (Section 13.2.2) we get the value for the number of nacks seen by the DR due to the hosts below it. However, in the non-caching case, there may be nacks coming from below the next level of DRs due to packet losses further down. We incorporate the above phenomenon into our calculation by adding a term $w^h p'$, where w^h is the number of children DRs and p' is the probability of seeing a nack due to a loss below the next level of DRs. Then,

$$N_{3B} = \frac{p}{w-1} \frac{w^{h+1} [h(1-p)(w-1) - 1]}{w(1-p) - 1} + w^h p'$$

$$= \frac{p}{w-1} \frac{w^{h+1} [h(1-p)(w-1) - 1]}{w(1-p) - 1} + w^h \left[1 - (1-p)^{\frac{w^{bh-ih-h+1} - 1}{w-1}} \right] .$$

N_4 = **Number of packets the DR retransmits**
Since a non-caching DR does not cache, it is incapable of retransmission. Hence, $N_4 = 0$.

13.3 Average Delay

13.3.1 Calculating the Average Caching Delay τ_{avg}^{C}

For the caching case, the delay incurred in reaching a particular host consists of two parts — the delay incurred in reaching the DR for that host, and the delay incurred while traveling from the DR to the host. So for a host located at height $ih + k$, we calculate the expected delay as the sum of two parts as calculated below:

$$E[\tau_{avg}^{C}(ih + k)] = E[\tau_i] + E[\tau_k] .$$

τ_i = **delay incurred in reaching parent DR**
While trying to calculate the delay, we let D denote the number of times the packet gets dropped. Each time the packet is dropped, retransmission starts at the last DR to have received it, but after waiting for a timeout T. Let there have been D drops on the way. Then,

$$E[\tau_i] = ih + \frac{i(1 - (1 - p)^h)}{(1 - p)^h} T .$$

(Since $D = N_2$ as calculated in Section 13.2.2)

τ_k = **delay incurred in going from parent DR to host**
When the packet is transmitted from the final DR to the host, there is no further caching involved, and the successful transmission must cross all the intermediate links. Again, each time there is a drop, a timeout worth of delay is incurred. Let d denote the number of drops and T the timeout. Probability that there is a drop = $1 - (1 - p)^k$. This gives us

$$E[\tau_k] = E[E[\tau_k|D]] = \frac{2k + T}{(1 - p)^k} - k - T .$$

13.3.2 Calculating the Average Non-Caching Delay τ_{avg}^{NC}

$\tau_{1D}^{NC}(M)$ **for One-Dimensional tree**
Our assumption is of a one-dimensional multicast tree with every link having an independent loss probability of p. Whenever a packet is lost, a nack is generated by the highest host that is yet to get the packet. We are interested in the expected delay experienced by the host at level M, denoted by $\tau_{1D}^{NC}(M)$ (the subscript '$1D$' denotes one-dimensional).

Assuming a timeout T each time the packet gets dropped, and that there are D drops,

$$\tau_{1D}^{NC}(M) \simeq DT + M + 2\sum_{k=1}^{D} T x_k$$

$$E\left[\tau_{1D}^{NC}(M)\right] \simeq E\left[DT + M + 2E\left[(Tx_1 + \ldots + Tx_D)|D\right]\right] .$$

Tx_k is the distance from which the nack is sent after k transmissions. This is the maximum height that is yet to receive the packet. So, $E[Tx_k|D] \simeq \frac{1}{pf}ln(k)$. Then,

$$E\left[\tau_{1D}^{NC}(M)\right] \approx TD^* + M + \frac{2}{pF}ln(D^*!) ,$$

where $D^* = E[D] = \frac{1}{(1-p)^M} - 1$ and $F = 1 - (1-p)^{M-1}$.

$\tau_{avg}^{NC}(M)$ for the General Tree

Using the same argument as in the one-dimensional case, and assuming D drops,

$$\tau_{avg}^{NC}(M) = DT + M + 2\sum_{k=1}^{D} Tx_k .$$

However, in the case of the general tree, the Tx_js depend on the exact location of the losses. This is because the retransmissions are triggered by the nack from the host closest to the source that is yet to get the packet, and so there is no simple relationship between the Tx_js.

To solve the system, we can note that the system is a Markov process since the next state of the tree depends only on the current state. We can then apply existing algorithms to solve the system once it has been modeled. However, the state space for this problem is often unmanageably large, and we are working on an elegant solution to the Markov model.

13.3.3 Simulation Results

We used simulation studies of the system to verify the delay results obtained. In the simulation model, any packet was lost at any link with a loss probability p. In the caching model, each time a packet got lost, it was retransmitted by the last DR to have received it. For the non-caching model though, every retransmission began at the source. A counter kept track of the total number of steps taken by the packet to reach the destination. This value was averaged over 1.000 packets to determine τ^C and τ^{NC}.

We plotted the value of the average delay in reaching the last level as the depth of the tree grew from 5 to 25, for link loss probabilities of 0.001, 0.01, 0.05 and 0.1. Timeout was chosen as a constant value of 10 for all the simulations. In the graphs plotted here (Figs. 13.1 and 13.2), the distance between adjacent levels of DRs was chosen as 5 (i.e., $h = 5$). Simulations using $h = 4$, $h = 6$ and $h = 10$ also yielded similar results.

This is to be compared with the theoretical values plotted on the same graphs (Figs. 13.1 and 13.2). A comparison shows that the simulated values mirror the calculated ones quite well, the difference being of the order of 15%, and

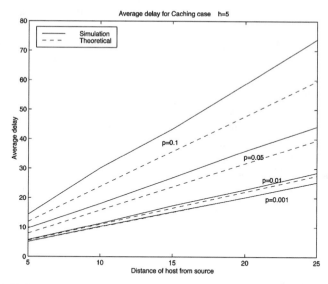

FIGURE 13.1
Caching average delay.

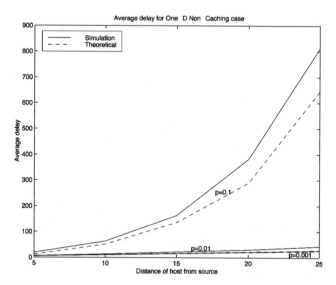

FIGURE 13.2
Non-caching average delay.

remaining fairly constant across all loss probabilities. As can be seen from the graphs, the simulation results are always *more* than the theoretical results. In the theoretical calculations, the delay experienced by each unsuccessful transmission of the packet is considered only up to the last DR it reaches, while the packet may actually travel a few more steps before being dropped at an internal host. These extra steps are also taken into account in the simulation model, accounting for the excess delay.

Further comparison of the delay graphs across the caching and the non-caching cases (comparing Figs. 13.1 and 13.2) shows the delay in the non-caching case to be considerably more than the caching case. Furthermore, as the height of the tree and the link loss probability increases, the delay in the caching scheme increases linearly, while the non-caching delay increases exponentially. Thus, in poor network conditions, and for large multicast trees, it becomes imperative to use caching DRs in order to ensure efficient and reliable performance.

13.4   Conclusion

We have presented our analysis of the bandwidth and delay for a large class of Reliable Multicast protocols. We identified the class of protocols to analyze — a nack-based and tree-based reliability scheme which utilizes nack-accumulating and caching agents (called Designated Receivers) to handle retransmission.

Having modeled the multicast tree as a uniform tree with equal and independent link loss probabilities, we estimated the bandwidth utilized over a single link at a DR for transmitting a single packet to all the members of the multicast group. This expected value was then averaged over all possible DRs to yield the average bandwidth per packet per link. The average delay experienced by a host per packet was then evaluated for the same tree. The calculations were carried out for both the caching and the non-caching cases. Simulation results were also used to support the delay calculations.

The chief contribution of this paper is to handle a large class of Reliable Multicast protocols and analyze the cost involved in implementing such methods — in terms of the excess bandwidth used by the retransmission packets and the extra delay incurred by the hosts. This is of critical importance to reliable multicast applications which need to function under various limitations on bandwidth and delay. Given the bandwidth and delay constraints imposed by the application, we can use the results presented here to evaluate the utility of using this class of solutions for a multicast session requiring reliability. This analysis shows the trade-offs involved in ensuring reliability over multicast, and quantifies the "costs" that have to be incurred to achieve this.

The complete paper, including all the derivations for the results presented here, is available at *http://www.path.berkeley.edu/~guptar/Gupta2706.ps.gz.*

References

[1] P. Bhagwat, P. P. Mishra and S. K. Tripathi, Effect of Topology on Performance of Reliable Multicast Communication, *Proc. INFOCOM'94,* vol. 2, pp. 602–609, Toronto, Ontario, Canada, June 1994.

[2] B. DeCleene, S. Bhattacharya, T. Friedman, M. Keaton, J. Kurose, D. Rubenstein and D. Towsley, Reliable Multicast Framework (RMF): A White Paper, available as http://www.tascnets.com/mist/RMF/RMFWP.ps.

[3] S. Deering and D. Cheriton, Multicast Routing in Datagrams, Internetworks and Extended LANs, *ACM Trans. Computer Systems (TOCS),* vol. 8, no. 2, pp. 85–110, May, 1990.

[4] J.C. Lin and S. Paul, RMTP: A Reliable Multicast Transport Protocol, *IEEE INFOCOM '96,* March 1996, pp. 1414–1424.

[5] J. Nonnenmacher and E.W. Biersack, Reliable Multicast: Where to use Forward Error Correction, *Proc. 5th Workshop on Protocols for High Speed Networks,* pp. 134–148, Sophia Antolis, France, Oct.1996, available as http:/www/eurocom.fr/~nonnen/my pages/FECgain.ps.gz.

[6] D.Towsley and J.Kurose, A Comparison of Sender-Initiated and Receiver-Initiated Reliable Multicast Protocols, to appear in *IEEE J. Selected Areas in Comm.*

Vitae

Rajarshi Gupta received his M.S. from the Department of Electrical Engineering and Computer Science at the University of California, Berkeley in December, 1998. Prior to that, he received his B.S. in Electrical Engineering and Computer Science (double major) in 1997, having pursued his undergraduate education at the Indian Institute of Technology, Bombay and the University of Maryland at College Park. His current research interests include communication networks, network protocols, multicasting and Digital Signal Processing.

Rajarshi is a member of IEEE, Tau Beta Pi and Eta Kappa Nu. His web address is http://www.eecs.berkeley.edu/~guptar.

Jean Walrand received his Ph.D. from the Department of Electrical Engineering and Computer Science at the University of California at Berkeley, where he is a professor. His research interests include stochastic processes, queuing theory, communication networks, and control systems. He is a recipient of the Lanchester Prize and a Fellow of the IEEE and the Belgian American Educational Foundation.

He is the author of "An Introduction to Queuing Networks" (Prentice-Hall, 1988) and of "Communication Networks: A First Course" (Second Edition, McGraw-Hill, 1998), and co-author of "High-Performance Communication Networks" (Morgan Kaufmann, 1996). See http://www.eecs.berkeley.edu/~wlr.

Chapter 14

Time-Slot Allocation in Wireless TDMA

S.C. Borst,[1] **E.G. Coffman, E.N. Gilbert, P.A. Whiting and P.M. Winkler**
Bell Labs, Lucent Technologies

Abstract   An important design issue in implementing Dynamic Channel Assignment in Time Division Multiple Access (TDMA) wireless networks is whether resource allocation can be done efficiently at the time slot level. Allocation at this level is seriously hampered by the lack of synchronization between base stations in distinct cells. We present simple *greedy packing* algorithms which overcome this obstacle by clustering calls in adjacent time slots. The results suggest that the algorithms are nearly optimal, and that little extra performance can be gained either by allowing the rejection of calls or by repacking.

Keywords: mobile communications, wireless networks, TDMA wireless systems, dynamic channel allocation.

14.1   Introduction

The use of wireless services has been expanding at a tremendous rate. The dramatic growth is fueled not only by the proliferation of traditional voice users, but also the introduction of new high-speed data services. The capacity expansion of cellular networks has not kept pace with the demand, creating a strong incentive to squeeze the most out of the existing network resources, in particular the available radio spectrum. With further growth anticipated, the drive for improved spectral efficiency will certainly persist, since the available spectrum for wireless communications is quite limited, while the cost of new infrastructure is substantial.

---

[1]Current affiliation: Center for Mathematics and Computer Science, Amsterdam.

Most digital cellular services are being provided by one of two Time Division Multiple Access (TDMA) systems: GSM [4], used widely in Asia and Europe, and IS-136 [2], used in North America. TDMA systems divide the allocated spectrum into a number of frequency bands, or carriers, which are time-slotted and, in the vast majority of systems, statically assigned to cells. Mobiles in the same cell may share a carrier by accessing it during distinct time slots. A mobile's communication channel is thus determined by the carrier it is using and its time slot. The number of slots per frame (cycle), which we denote by n, fixes the maximum number of mobiles that can share a carrier. For example, in GSM $n = 8$ and in IS-136 $n = 3$.

Since the number of cells is much larger than the number of carriers, each carrier is reused in cells sufficiently far apart that interference between the cells is held at acceptable levels; see [3]. This way of allocating channels to mobiles within a given group of carriers dedicated to a cell is known as Fixed Channel Assignment (FCA). FCA has the drawback that channels cannot be diverted in response to fluctuations in the traffic offered to each cell in the network. In contrast, if Dynamic Channel Assignment (DCA) is employed, this can be done, contingent on each mobile's signal-to-interference requirements being met. Thus, the radio spectrum is utilized as a network-wide sharable resource yielding significant efficiency gains. To achieve maximal flexibility in matching resources to offered traffic, it is preferable in DCA to allocate spectrum at the finest possible level of granularity, i.e., time slots. However, base stations in TDMA systems are not synchronized at the time slot level. As a result, one time slot at a particular base station typically interferes with two time slots at each neighboring base station. Thus if the calls are scattered over isolated slots, much of the carrier will be unavailable to neighboring base stations, and therefore less efficiently used.

One can avoid this problem by using time-slot allocation algorithms that cluster calls belonging to different base stations into disjoint sequences of consecutive or nearly consecutive slots. In this paper, we devise such algorithms and provide results that help balance the additional implementation complexity of these algorithms against their potential efficiency gains.

We consider two neighboring cells sharing the time slots of a single carrier. Let A and B name the cells and their base stations. For convenience, assume that base station B lags base station A, and to fix ideas consider the example in Fig. 14.1 for $n = 6$. If slot $i > 1$ is assigned to a call by base station A, base station B cannot pack a call in slot $i - 1$ or i in the same frame; and if base station A has packed a call in slot 1, base station B cannot have packed a call in slot n of the preceding frame nor can it pack a call in slot 1 of the same frame. This assertion holds *mutatis mutandis* when A lags B.

In the example of Fig. 14.1, there are no calls currently in progress in cell B, but base station A has calls packed in time slots 1 and 4. If the next event is a call arrival in cell B, then slots 2 and 5 at base station B are the only ones where the new call can be packed; they are the only unassigned slots at base station B not overlapping a slot at base station A that is already assigned to a call.

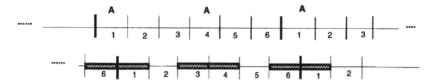

FIGURE 14.1

The nonoverlapping-slot constraint, $n = 6$. The upper and lower time lines apply to base stations A and B, respectively. The hatched intervals indicate the unused time slots at base station B that are not available to cell-B calls because of overlap with slots already assigned to cell-A calls.

An initial decision that must be taken when admitting a call is whether any *repacking* is to be allowed, i.e., whether the time-slot allocations of calls in progress can be changed. Figure 14.1 illustrates how repacking leads to greater efficiency; if the second A call were repacked in the slot next to the first A call, then there would only be 3 rather than 4 overlapping slots put out of action in cell B. But repacking has the possible adverse consequence of increasing call dropping, since every call moved from one time slot/carrier to another (as in inter-cell hand-offs) risks being dropped or causing other calls to be dropped. (DCA algorithms usually do not take into account the interference that is caused to mobiles in moving a call from one time slot to another.)

The next section begins by introducing notation. It then defines the mathematical model of call arrivals and holding times, and hence, the underlying call assignment process for a given call assignment algorithm. Section 14.3 describes in detail call clustering algorithms that are compared numerically in Section 14.4. Section 14.5, the final section, discusses our assumptions, states our major conclusions, and lists some directions for further research.

14.2   Preliminaries

Whether base station A lags base station B or vice versa will be immaterial to us, so a convenient graphic for the carrier state is the ring illustrated in Fig. 14.2 for $n = 8$. The outside of the ring gives the time slots at base station A and the inside of the ring gives the time slots at base station B. The relative displacement has been fixed, as shown, at half a slot duration. This loses no generality, as the existence but not the extent of the overlap is significant. Segments shaded black and gray indicate the time slots assigned to calls in cells A and B, respectively. Any shading, such as those shown, that does not have overlapping slots carrying an A in the outer ring and a B in the inner ring, is a valid shading. We will say that a slot at one base station is *available* if it is empty at one base station and does not overlap a slot assigned at the other base station.

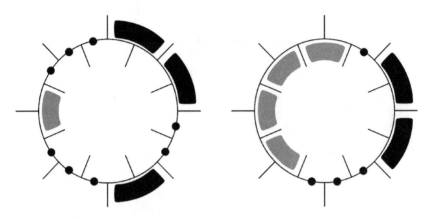

FIGURE 14.2
States $\langle AA..A...B...\rangle$ and $\langle B.AA...BBB\rangle$.

A convenient in-line notation for states is simply the bracketed sequence of labels and dots illustrated in the figure for $n = 8$, each dot corresponding to a half-slot not overlapping a slot assigned to a call in either cell. The $2n$ half-slots will be numbered 1 through $2n$ and the n slots will be identified by pairs of half-slots $(i, i+1)$, $1 \leq i \leq 2n$, where the $i+1$ is taken mod $2n$; the ith slot is denoted by $(2i-1, 2i)$ at base station A and $(2i, 2i+1)$ at base station B. Thus, since an A and a B are not allowed to overlap, they must be separated by at least one dot. For definiteness, the A slot at the top of the wheel representation is slot $(1,2)$ and all state sequences begin by characterizing half-slot 1, i.e., they begin with a B if $(16,1)$ is assigned to a call, an A if $(1,2)$ is assigned to a call, and a dot if half-slot 1 does not overlap a call assignment. Since every A and B occupies two half-slots, twice the total number of As and Bs plus the number of dots must be $2n$.

We adopt a standard traffic model. Calls arrive in independent Poisson streams at rates λ_A and λ_B in cells A and B. Call holding times are independent of the arrival processes and form an i.i.d. sequence of exponentially distributed random variables; the rate parameter for cells A and B is μ. (Our methods are trivially extended to the case where the cells have different departure rate parameters.) These assumptions yield a continuous-time, finite-state stochastic process Y on the set of carrier states defined above. A transition of the process occurs at an arrival or departure, the latter represented simply by the removal of a single call from the current state. An arrival transition is determined by the call admission algorithm; the current state remains unchanged if the new call is not admitted; otherwise, the next state reflects the packing of the new call in some available slot of the current state. The problem at the heart of this paper is the design and analysis of call admission algorithms that determine which calls to admit, and where to pack those that are admitted. We confine ourselves to admission algorithms that are defined by mappings from the current-state, new-call pair to the index of an available slot if the new call is to be admitted. Thus, because of the exponential assumptions, Y will be a Markov process for all of the algorithms presented in the next section.

If a rotation of the ring in Fig. 14.2 carries a state S into a new state S', then S and S' are in the same rotational symmetry class. Treating such states equivalently is a desirable feature of call admission algorithms. By "equivalently," we mean that an assignment in state S' should be the same as the assignment obtained by rotating S' to S, making the assignment called for in S, and then rotating back to S'. If S and S' differ only by a reflection, then we should be able to make the same assertion with rotation replaced by reflection. Together, the rotation and reflection symmetries define the *dihedral* symmetry group.

In the remainder of the paper, our focus will be on *greedy* admission algorithms. Such algorithms never reject a call when there is at least one available slot where it can be packed. Note that optimal algorithms, i.e., algorithms that minimize lost traffic, need not always make greedy decisions. To see this, it is only necessary to consider the system with sufficiently heavy traffic in cell A. In such cases, it is optimal to reserve the carrier for the exclusive use of base station A; the unavoidable wasted time created by a state that mixes even one B with As would increase the overall blocking probability. We return to this algorithm in Section 14.4 and quantify "sufficiently large traffic."

14.3 Algorithms

Strategies that unnecessarily mingle A and B assignments among the n slots are inefficient, as they lead to the wasted time required to separate As and Bs. A natural first choice among algorithms that tend to collect the As and Bs in separate clusters is as follows.

Algorithm C_n

A call arriving at a time when the current state has no slot available to the call's cell is rejected. Otherwise, the call is packed in the first available slot found in a scan of the current state clockwise from slot $(1,2)$ if the call is in cell A and counterclockwise from slot $(2n-2, 2n-1)$ if the call is in cell B.

This clustering method is essentially a (bidirectional) first-fit approach, and as such it lacks certain properties that have obvious appeal. One such property is invariance under the symmetries of the system mentioned in Section 14.2. For example, with $n = 8$, the states $\langle A.B..BB.....\rangle$ $\langle ...BB..B.A..\rangle$ $\langle ..A.B..BB...\rangle$ are all in the same dihedral class and should be considered equivalent from the point of view of packing a new call. Thus, a new A call should be assigned to the available slot adjacent to the A in every case.

Another desirable property of call packing algorithms is a consistent preference for the smaller gaps bounded by the same call type as the call to be assigned; this is best-fit rather than first-fit behavior. For example, a new A call should be assigned to the gap $\langle A..A\rangle$ in states like those in the dihedral classes of $\langle A..A....A.B.\rangle$ and $\langle A..A.....BB.\rangle$ with $n = 8$.

The algorithm defined below for $n = 8$ is designed to have both the best-fit and symmetry preserving properties. It is chosen from the class of *weighting algorithms* defined as follows. First, we augment the state so that each slot carries a weight. According to a weighting algorithm, a new call is packed in a slot of the same type with maximum non-negative weight, if one exists; otherwise, if all slots of the same type have negative weights, the call is rejected.

A specific weighting algorithm is defined by two weight-increment vectors $(\delta_0, \ldots, \delta_{\lfloor n/2\rfloor})$ and $(\delta'_1, \ldots, \delta'_{\lfloor n/2\rfloor})$. Weights are changed at arrival and departure events as follows. Suppose we have just assigned a new A call to an available slot; the case for B calls is entirely symmetric. The weight of the slot where the new call is assigned is incremented by δ_0, the slots to each side of that slot have their weights incremented by δ_1, the slots at distance 2 have their weights incremented by δ_2, and so on with the slots a distance $\lfloor n/2\rfloor$ incremented by $\delta_{\lfloor n/2\rfloor}$. If n is even, the slots encountered going a distance $\lfloor n/2\rfloor$ clockwise and counterclockwise are one and the same antipodal slot.

The two B slots straddled by the A slot just assigned have their weights incremented by δ'_1; the weights of the B slots at equal distance are then incremented by $\delta'_2, \ldots, \delta'_{\lfloor n/2\rfloor}$ as one moves away from the new A call. Finally, whenever a call departs, the increments made at the call's arrival time are decremented accordingly.

The system can be set up to begin with fractional weights associated with its slots, which we assume are all initially empty. These weights will break ties in symmetric situations. However, without these fractional values (all weights are initially 0), the increments are designed so that there will never be a tie between two slots of the same type unless the corresponding states are in the same dihedral class. Thus, the assignment algorithm preserves symmetry classes.

We consider only greedy weighting algorithms. Thus, the increment vectors must be such that in every reachable state with an available slot, the weight of some available slot must be non-negative. Moreover, there can be no reachable state in which the slot with maximum non-negative weight is unavailable. An example for $n = 8$ that we shall analyze in detail is:

Algorithm W$_8$

This algorithm is the best-fit weighting algorithm for $n = 8$, with

$$\delta_0 = -41, \quad \delta_1 = 12, \quad \delta_2 = 6, \quad \delta_3 = 2, \quad \delta_4 = 0$$

$$\delta_1' = -41, \quad \delta_2' = 0, \quad \delta_3' = 2, \quad \delta_4' = 3 \,.$$

Note that a δ_i sequence decreasing for $i \geq 1$ and a δ_i' sequence increasing for $i \geq 1$ promote clustering and an antipodal positioning of the clusters.

As As, build up to the left and right of an empty slot, the slot's weight can increase by at most $2 \cdot 12 + 2 \cdot 6 + 2 \cdot 2 = 40$, so setting $\delta_0 = \delta_1' = -41$ guarantees that an unavailable slot must always have negative weight.

In most states, it is obvious which slot (or equivalence class of slots) would be selected by an optimal algorithm, and in those states the algorithm chooses correctly. In a few cases the correct slot choice depends on traffic intensities. An example is the state $\langle .AA..A..A.B \rangle$ where the question is whether an arriving A call should be placed in the slot to the left or right of the isolated A (a calculation shows that these slots have weights 32 and 26, respectively). Similarly, when in the state $\langle ....AAA.B.A \rangle$, the question is whether to put a new A call into the available slot (of weight 29) next to the string of 3 As or into the available slot (of weight 22) next to the remaining A. But in all such states, the algorithm opts to make a large contiguous block of ongoing calls of the same type, which is reasonable and consistent behavior even under those circumstances when it may not be optimal. In [1], we prove that, for $n \leq 6$, we can find a weighting algorithm that is optimal.

To do significantly better than W$_8$ within the class of greedy algorithms, we need to be able to repack calls in other time slots whenever this permits a new-call admission that could not otherwise occur. The algorithm presented next is obviously optimal when repacking is allowed, so it provides a bound on the performance of algorithms not allowed to repack calls.

Repacking Algorithm R$_n$

This algorithm works just like C$_n$ except when a new call arrives and finds no available slot of its type. In that case, if there are fewer than $n - 1$ calls in the system, the A and B calls are compacted into separate clusters (strings) beginning at odd and even half-slots, respectively. This makes at least one slot available to the new call, which is then admitted.

We leave R's precise compaction algorithm unspecified, but note that compaction need only take place until the first available slot is created.

For the analysis of algorithm R$_n$, let $a(t)$, $b(t)$ be the respective numbers of A and B calls in the system at time t. Then $\{(a(t), b(t)), t \geq 0\}$ is a Markov process on the set of states $\{(0, n), (n, 0)\} \cup \{(i, j) : 0 \leq i, j; i + j \leq$

$n - 1\}$. Were it not for the states $(0, n)$, $(n, 0)$, the process would be the classical one of an Erlang queue with two classes of customers, a process that has local balance, as is easily verified. In spite of the added peculiarity of states $(0, n)$, $(n, 0)$, the process continues to have local balance and a product-form stationary distribution $q(i, j) := \lim_{t \to \infty} \Pr\{(a(t), b(t)) = (i, j)\}$. In particular,

$$q(i, j) = G^{-1} \frac{\rho_A^i}{i!} \frac{\rho_B^j}{j!} , \tag{14.1}$$

where the normalization constant $G = \sum_{i,j} \frac{\rho_A^i}{i!} \frac{\rho_B^j}{j!}$ is a sum over all states. Blocking probabilities are computed over the states

- $(n - 1, 0)$ which blocks only B calls,

- $(0, n - 1)$ which blocks only A calls, and

- $(n, 0), (n - 2, 1), \ldots, (1, n - 2), (0, n)$, which block both A and B calls.

Thus, the nonblocking states are just those states (i, j) with $i + j < n - 1$.

14.4 Comparisons

For our purposes, i.e., for small n, numerical comparisons of the various algorithms can be obtained by computational as well as simulation methods. Computations are based on the numerical solutions of finite Markov chains and are only feasible for n up to about 10. Simulations were easily implemented and gave insights into transient behavior as well as the stationary regime. Except in the case of R_n where formula (14.1) is available, we used simulations since the loss in accuracy was small enough to be of no concern. However, to verify the (probable) correctness of our simulation program for Algorithm W_8, we computed numerically the stationary loss probabilities of the corresponding Markov chains for the cases $\rho_A = \rho_B$. Further details are given in [1], where we exploit the symmetries of weighting algorithms like W_8 to minimize the size of the state space needed for the Markov chain analysis.

A comparison of algorithms C_n, W_n, and R_n is given in Table 14.1 for $n = 8$ with the notation: $\rho_A = \lambda_A/\mu$, $\rho_B = \lambda_B/\mu$; p_A, p_B are the traffic intensities and blocking probabilities for cell A and B calls, respectively. The overall fraction of lost calls is then

$$p = \frac{\lambda_A p_A + \lambda_B p_B}{\lambda_A + \lambda_B} .$$

Results are given for all integer traffic intensities summing to 6, and range from about 1 rejection out of every 200 calls to about 1 out of every 5.

Table 14.1 Blocking Probabilities for C_8, W_8, and R_8

		Algorithm C_8			Algorithm W_8			Algorithm R_8		
ρ_A	ρ_B	p_A	p_B	p	p_A	p_B	p	p_A	p_B	p
1	1	.0048	.0047	.0048	.0043	.0042	.0043	.0034	.0034	.0034
1	2	.0353	.0234	.0274	.0333	.0226	.0262	.0221	.0209	.0213
1	3	.1060	.0572	.0694	.0950	.0574	.0668	.0657	.0573	.0596
1	4	.2107	.1003	.1224	.1871	.1012	.1184	.1315	.1065	.1115
1	5	.3233	.1473	.1766	.2978	.1493	.1741	.2105	.1605	.1688
2	2	.0772	.0784	.0778	.0743	.0744	.0744	.0625	.0625	.0625
2	3	.1605	.1297	.1420	.1495	.1250	.1348	.1215	.1183	.1196
2	4	.2581	.1771	.2041	.2411	.1753	.1972	.1894	.1787	.1823
3	3	.2103	.2113	.2108	.2028	.2034	.2031	.1845	.1845	.1845

As expected, uniformly over all parameter values, W_8 gives lower overall lost traffic than C_8, and R_8 gives lower overall lost traffic than W_8. Note, however, that the same *cannot* be said of the individual blocking probabilities p_A and p_B, when the difference between traffic intensities is sufficiently large. In these cases, a lower overall blocking probability is achieved at the expense of a slight increase in blocking at the base station with more traffic. This holds in both the comparison of C_8 and W_8 and the comparison of W_8 and R_8. However, for each of the algorithms we also observe that, in all cases of unequal traffic, the blocking at the more heavily loaded station is smaller than that for the more lightly loaded station. A related property that can be seen in the data is that for a fixed total intensity $\rho_A + \rho_B$, the lost traffic decreases as the difference $|\rho_A - \rho_B|$ increases, i.e., as more and more traffic is being concentrated in one of the cells.

In [1], optimal algorithms with and without the greedy constraint are computed using dynamic programming. The results show that W_8 performs very nearly as well as an optimal greedy algorithm, and loses only a little extra in the comparison with optimal algorithms not required to be greedy.

We observed earlier that, with traffic intensities sufficiently large, a non-sharing algorithm (i.e., non-greedy algorithm confined to the calls of just one of the cells) becomes optimal. To get some idea of what "sufficiently large" means, we computed the overall blocking probability p in the equal-intensity case and found that freezing out one of the cells completely gives lower p only for $\rho_A = \rho_B \geq 10$. But in this case, over 2/3 of the calls are rejected on average. Thus, in the practical regimes where lost traffic is small to moderate, only greedy sharing algorithms are likely to be of interest.

14.5   Conclusions

We identified a synchronization-type problem encountered in allocating the time slots of a carrier shared by neighboring cells in a wireless TDMA network. We presented easily implemented greedy packing algorithms, which accept calls whenever possible, and attempt to cluster calls in adjacent slots. The results suggest that the algorithms perform nearly optimally, in the sense that rejecting calls or rearranging slot allocations does not produce any substantial performance gains. In view of the potential risk of call dropping, the small performance improvement does not seem to warrant the additional implementation complexity involved in repacking calls.

Admittedly, in the present paper we examined the simplest possible scenario of just two base stations sharing a single carrier. Realistic networks usually consist of several base stations deploying multiple carriers. Based on the results we obtained, we expect that greedy packing algorithms will continue to perform nearly optimally in those scenarios. This deserves further substantiation, presumably through simulation experiments, judging from the inherent difficulty of the simple scenario investigated here.

In the present paper we considered essentially centralized algorithms with perfect knowledge of the state of the system. Practical algorithms would probably have to be distributed in nature, and rely on local information, possibly augmented with limited knowledge of the state of neighboring cells obtained through signal strength measurements. An additional complication in networks is that the feasibility constraints may no longer be binary, but may involve the extent of overlap among time slots, the location of base stations, as well as the position of the users. The weighting algorithms which we proposed seem particularly suitable under these circumstances.

References

[1] Borst, S.C., Coffman, E. G., Gilbert, E. N., Whiting, P.A., and Winkler, P.M., Optimal Time-Slot Allocation in Wireless TDMA, Bell Labs, Lucent Technologies (in preparation), 1999.

[2] Harte, L., Smith, A., and Jacobs, C.A., *IS-136 TDMA Technology, Economics, and Services,* Artech House, Boston, 1998.

[3] Lee, W.C.-Y., *Mobile Cellular Telecommunication Systems,* McGraw Hill, New York, 1989.

[4] Mouly, M. and Pautet, M., *The GSM System for Mobile Communications,* Palaiseau, France, 1992.

Vitae

Sem Borst received an M.Sc. degree in applied mathematics from the University of Twente, The Netherlands, in 1990, and a Ph.D. degree from the University of Tilburg, The Netherlands, in 1994. During the fall of 1994, he was a visiting scholar at the Statistical Laboratory of the University of Cambridge, England. In 1995, he joined the Mathematics of Networks and Systems department of Bell Laboratories, Lucent Technologies in Murray Hill, USA, as a member of technical staff. Since the fall of 1998, he has been a senior member of the Probability, Networks, and Algorithms department of the Center for Mathematics and Computer Science (CWI) in Amsterdam. He also has a part-time appointment as a professor at Eindhoven University of Technology. His main research interests are in the performance evaluation of communication networks and computer systems.

Edward G. Coffman received a Ph.D. in engineering from the University of California at Los Angeles in 1966. He is currently a member of technical staff at Bell Laboratories in Murray Hill, New Jersey, where he has been engaged in basic research since 1979. Prior to 1979, he was on the computer science faculties of Princeton, Pennsylvania State, and Columbia Universities, and of the University of California at Santa Barbara. His research focuses on the performance analysis of computer and communication systems and on the analysis of computer algorithms and structures. He is a Fellow of ACM and of IEEE.

Edgar N. Gilbert was born in Woodhaven, N.Y. in 1923. He received a B.S. degree in physics from Queens College, Flushing, N.Y. in 1943 and a Ph.D. in mathematics from Massachusetts Institute of Technology, Cambridge, Mass. in 1948. In 1943 he taught physics at the University of Illinois, Urbana, Ill. In 1944–1946 he worked on radar antennas at the MIT Radiation Laboratory. From 1948 till his retirement in 1996 he was a member of technical staff in the Mathematics Research Center at Bell Laboratories in Murray Hill, N.J. There his work was mainly on communication theory and combinatorial or probabilistic problems.

Chapter 15

Maintaining Connectivity for Mobile Computing Applications in Cellular Systems with Multiple Traffic Classes and Mixed Platform Types[1]

Yunsang Park and Stephen S. Rappaport

State University of New York

Abstract   A scheme is proposed for cellular communication systems that support both voice and data sessions. During a session a mobile user has access to network resources, although this access may be shared with others. Upon the failure of a link to a mobile data user, the scheme attempts to maintain connectivity to the network through transparent reconnection attempts. The approach allows periods of independent autonomous operation by mobile data terminals. Preemptive priority is used to guarantee transparency for voice sessions. An analytically tractable model that allows consideration of mixed platform types, (such as pedestrians, vehicles, etc.), having different mobility characteristics and mixed traffic classes (such as voice, data, etc.), is developed. These features are important in the context of wide area mobile computing applications.

Keywords: cellular communications, mobile computing, communications traffic performance analysis.

---

[1]The research reported in this paper was supported in part by the U.S. National Science Foundation under Grant no. NCR 94-15530. Additional research support from Hughes Network Systems is gratefully acknowledged. Dr. Yunsang Park is currently with Hughes Network Systems.

15.1   Introduction

Because of the time insensitive nature of many data traffic types, some delay during communication is not critical. However, a lost connection which results in the termination of a session is significant, since it waste valuable wireless resources. Therefore, the question of "how to maintain connectivity of a mobile user to the network?" is an important issue. Some strategies for management of data calls in the background of voice traffic are considered in [1, 2]. Here we consider the issue of maintaining session connectivity. A scheme that uses automatic and transparent reconnection attempts is considered in [3], where a system with only a single traffic class consisting of time insensitive data, was treated.

Here we consider a system that supports widely disparate call traffic types as well as platforms with different mobility characteristics. A session-oriented approach is used. A session is typified as either a voice session or a data session. Preemptive priority is used to guarantee transparency for voice sessions. For data sessions, the scheme attempts to maintain a connection to the network. Data calls that are preempted or disconnected during the hand-off process are allowed a fixed number of reconnection attempts. Only after a given number of such attempts to reconnect have failed is the data session deemed to have failed. The strategy attempts to maintain connectivity for mobile data users in a way that is transparent to them. This allows, for example, mobile computing users to continue functioning autonomously (though not indefinitely) in an off-line mode.

We examine the combined effect of mixed call traffic types in the same system [2] and quantify the performances of each type. We consider mixed platform types having different mobility characteristics [4]. In addition, cut-off priority is used to reserve some resources for voice sessions, since they are especially susceptible to hand-off failures.

The model for traffic performance can be cast in the analytic framework that has been developing in recent years [2, 3, 4, 6]. The approach, which uses multidimensional birth-death processes, allows numerical computation of relevant state probabilities. These probabilities are then used to compute important traffic performance measures.

15.2   Session Management Strategy

When the physical link between a mobile terminal that has an active data session and the network fails, the data session is *suspended*. The mobile terminal will attempt to reconnect by successive reconnection requests made at random time intervals. These are called **reconnection attempts.** A maximum number, N, of reconnection attempts is allowed for each suspended session. If a reconnection has not been secured after this maximum is reached, the session is considered to have failed and is cleared from the system.

In order to support suspended sessions and reconnection attempts for data sessions, the system should have allocated necessary control channels for signaling. Since the control channels also need wireless resources, we assume there is a maximum number, H, of suspended sessions that the system will allow in each cell. If a platform with a suspended session on board leaves its current cell, a reconnection attempt is made to establish a link in the new call. This hand-off attempt counts towards the limit, N. If, in the target cell, there are no available channels to accommodate the arriving data session, and if there are already H suspended sessions in the target cell, the arriving data session cannot be admitted in the target cell. So, even if a suspended session has not exhausted the allowable number of reconnection attempts, it will be forced into termination if (owing to the existence of H suspended sessions in the target cell) it fails its hand-off attempt.

Since *voice* sessions must be transmitted or received on a real time basis, reconnection attempts are not allowed. Instead, voice sessions have preemptive priority over data sessions for using channel resources. When a voice session arrives and finds all channels occupied, an active data session (if any are present) will be either suspended or terminated to accommodate it. The choice of which data session to be suspended or be terminated is assumed to be random. If there are no active data sessions that can be preempted to service the incoming voice session the voice arrival will not be accommodated. That is, it will be blocked if it is a new call, or terminated if it is a hand-off.

There are two possible reasons that cause an active data session to be suspended. One is failure of a hand-off attempt. Specifically, if a data session attempts a hand-off when the channels in the target cell are fully occupied but, in the target cell, there are fewer than H data sessions suspended, the hand-off attempt will fail but the session will wait for another connection opportunity as a suspended session. The other reason for suspension arises when an active data session is preempted by an arriving voice session. When a voice session arrives in a cell in which all channels are occupied and fewer than H sessions are in suspension, and at least one active session is of data type, an arriving voice session will obtain a connection but an active data session will be suspended.

In the following we let g be an index that defines the platform type and mobility. Consider a suspended session that has already failed k-1 reconnection attempts. The next attempt is called the "k-reconnection attempt" where $1 \leq k \leq N$. It is important to emphasize that there are two driving processes that generate **reconnection attempts**. One is the **retry** process, which consists of successive statistically independent realizations of a random variable, $T_r(k, g)$, to generate epochs for retry attempt times for a suspended session. The other is the **hand-off** departure process — because *hand-off attempts always try to establish a link and therefore count as reconnection attempts.* The random variable, $T_r(k, g)$, gives the time from the previous **reconnection event** (either hand-off or retry) to the next anticipated **retry attempt**. The random variable, $T_r(k, g)$, can in general depend on k. Thus, the minimum rate of reconnection attempts depends on the number of attempts that have already been made. Of course, if the supporting platform leaves its current cell before the anticipated retry epoch, a hand-off attempt (to establish a link) will be made at that time and the value of k will be adjusted. If the session is in a suspended state after this attempt, a new random variable (for a retry epoch) will be generated. The random variable, $T_r(k, g)$, generated after the k-1 reconnection attempt, represents the maximum time to the next anticipated retry attempt. This is called the "k-trial time." The next reconnection attempt will be made either at this time or at the time that the supporting platform leaves the cell, whichever is the shortest. A suspended session that has not reestablished a link after k-1 reconnection trials and is waiting for the next (kth) reconnection attempt, is called a "k-suspended session."

15.3   Model Description

In the following description, we freely borrow concepts and phraseology put forth in [4, 6]. It is suggested that readers review those papers. We consider a large cellular system with many mobile platforms of several types. Each mobile can potentially generate a voice session or a data session. However, each platform can support at most one connection at any give time and each connection needs one channel (resource) to communicate. The platform types differ primarily in their mobility characteristics. The maximum number of simultaneous connections that each base station can support is C.

When a platform with either an active or suspended session moves to another cell, a hand-off is needed. We assume hand-off detection and initiation are perfect. For a voice session, a hand-off attempt will succeed to gain a connection in the target cell if there are fewer than C voice sessions in that cell. A voice session that fails to gain a connection will lose its wireless link and be cleared from system. For a data session, a hand-off attempt will gain access to a connection in the target cell if there are less than C sessions, either of voice type or data type, in progress in that cell. When a hand-off of a data session fails, a session will be suspended if the reconnection counter in the terminal indicates less than N and no more than H suspended sessions are in the same cell.

Platform mobility is characterized using the concept of *dwell time* [2, 4] — a random variable which is defined as the duration of time that a two-way communication link of satisfactory quality can be maintained between a platform and its current base, for whatever reason [4]. The amount of time that a session must use a channel for satisfying communication is modeled using the concept of *unencumbered session duration.* The unencumbered session duration is a random variable, which is the amount of time that the call would spend in service if there were no suspensions or forced termination. Similarly, the k-trial time is a random variable. A k-suspended session will execute a retry attempt after the epoch of the k-trial time unless it moves to another cell. If a k-suspended session moves to another cell before the epoch of the k-trial time, a hand-off attempt will be made.

15.3.1 Example Problem Statement

The system supports G types of mobile platforms, indexed by $\{g = 1, 2, 3 \ldots G\}$ having different mobility characteristics. Potentially, a non-communicating platform generate two types of sessions, voice and data, however, no more than one session can be supported by a platform at any given time. The voice session origination rate from a non-communicating g-type platform is denoted $\Lambda_v(g)$. We define $\alpha(g) = \Lambda_v(g)/\Lambda_v(1)$. Similarly the data session generation rate from a non-communicating g-type platform is denoted $\Lambda_w(g)$ and we define $\beta(g) = \Lambda_w(g)/\Lambda_v(g)$. The number of non-communicating g-type platforms in any cell is denoted by $v(g, 0)$. Therefore, the total voice session generation rate for g-type platforms in any cell can be denoted $\Lambda_{nv}(g) = \Lambda_v(g) \times v(g, 0)$ and the total data session generation rate for g-type platforms in a cell can be denoted $\Lambda_{nw}(g) = \Lambda_w(g) \times v(g, 0)$. An infinite population model is assumed [4].

A model that considers resource use based on connection type is developed in [5]. Here, it is assumed that each active connection, either for a data session or a voice session, requires the same amount of resources. Each cell or gateway can support a maximum of C connections. There are no quotas for either specific mobility platform types or specific session types. We consider cut-off priority for hand-off arrivals (either voice or data sessions) and for reconnection attempts of suspended data sessions. Thus, C_h connections in each cell are reserved for hand-off attempts (for either voice sessions or data sessions) and for reconnection attempts of *suspended data sessions in the cell.* A connection will be established for a *new voice session only* if there are less than $C - C_h$ *active voice sessions* in the cell. For an arriving data session, a connection will be made if there are fewer than C sessions, either of voice type or data type, in the cell. A hand-off attempt of a voice session will fail if there are C *voice sessions* in the cell.

A voice session that fails in a hand-off attempt will be terminated and cleared from the system. A hand-off attempt of a data type session will fail if there are C *active* sessions, *either of voice type or data type,* in the cell. A data session that fails in a hand-off attempt will be suspended if there are fewer than H suspended sessions the cell, and the session has not exceeded the maximum allowable number (N) of reconnection attempts. A platform is considered to "leave" the cell at the expiration of its current (random) dwell time. A communicating platform that leaves a cell generates a hand-off arrival to some other cell. The dwell time in a cell for a g-type platform is a ned random variable, $T_D(g)$, having a mean $\bar{T}_D(g) = 1/\mu_D(g)$. More general dwell time distributions can be treated, at the cost of increased dimensionality of the state space [8, 9]. The unencumbered voice session duration on a g-type platform is a ned random variable, $T_v(g)$, having a mean $\bar{T}_v(g) = 1/\mu_v(g)$. The unencumbered data session duration on a g-type platform is a ned random variable, $T_w(g)$, having a mean $\bar{T}_w(g) = 1/\mu_w(g)$. The k-trial time of a suspended session on a g-type platform is ned random variable, $T_r(g)$, having a mean $\bar{T}_r(k, g) = 1/\mu_r(k, g)$, where $1 \leq k \leq N$, and $\mu_r(k, g)(k = 1, 2, \ldots, N; g = 1, \ldots, G)$ is the parameter that determines the reconnection attempt rate for a *k-suspended session* on a g-type platform.

15.3.2   State Description

Considering a single cell, we define the **cell state** by a sequence of non-negative integers. When a maximum of N reconnection attempts are permitted for a suspended data session, the state of the cell can be written as G n-tuples as follows

$$
\begin{array}{ccccccc}
v_1 & w_1 & r_{1,1} & r_{1,2} & r_{1,3} & \cdots & r_{1,N} \\
v_2 & w_2 & r_{2,1} & r_{2,2} & r_{2,3} & \cdots & r_{2,N} \\
\vdots & \vdots & \vdots & \vdots & \vdots & \vdots & \vdots \\
v_G & w_G & r_{G,1} & r_{G,2} & r_{G,3} & \cdots & r_{G,N}
\end{array}
\tag{15.1}
$$

where $v_g\{g = 1, 2, \ldots, G\}$ is the number of active voice sessions on g-type platforms, $w_g\{g = 1, 2, \ldots, G\}$ is the number of active data sessions on g-type platforms, and $r_{g,k}\{g = 1, 2, \ldots, G; k = 1, 2, \ldots, N\}$ is the number of k-suspended sessions on g-type platforms. For convenience, we order the states using an index $s = 0, 1, \ldots, S_{\max}$. Thereafter, v_g, w_g, and $r_{g,k}$ can be written explicitly dependent on the state. That is, $v_g = v(s, g)$, $w_g = w(s, g)$, and $r_{g,k} = r(s, g, k)$.

When the cell is in state s, the following characteristics can be determined. The number of voice sessions is

$$
v(s) = \sum_{g=1}^{G} v(s, g) .
\tag{15.2}
$$

The number of active data sessions is

$$w(s) = \sum_{g=1}^{G} w(s, g) .$$ (15.3)

The number of suspended sessions, regardless of platform type, is

$$r(s) = \sum_{k=1}^{N} \sum_{g=1}^{G} r(s, g, k) ,$$ (15.4)

and, the total number of sessions in progress in a cell is

$$J(s) = v(s) + w(s) .$$ (15.5)

There are constraints on permissible cell states. These include that the total number of active sessions in a cell must be fewer than or equal to maximum supportable connections, $J(s) \leq C$; and the total number of suspended sessions in a cell must be fewer than or equal to the maximum number of suspended sessions allowed in a cell, $r(s) \leq H$.

There are nine driving processes. These are: (1) generation of voice sessions, (2) generation of data sessions, (3) completion of voice sessions, (4) completion of data sessions, (5) hand-off arrival of voice sessions, (6) hand-off arrivals of data session (either active or suspended), (7) hand-off departure of voice sessions, (8) hand-off departure of data sessions (either active or suspended), and (9) retry attempts. To allow solution within the multidimensional birth-death process framework, Markovian assumptions are used [3, 4, 6, 8].

15.3.3 Flow Balance Equations and Hand-off Arrival Parameters

The total transition flow into state s from any permissible predecessor state x is denoted as $q(s, x)$. Then, the total flow out of state s is denoted $q(s, s)$ and is given by

$$q(s, s) = - \sum_{\substack{k=0 \\ k \neq s}}^{S_{max}} q(k, s) .$$ (15.6)

The statistical equilibrium solution for the state probabilities can be found using the flow balance equations. This is a set of $S_{max} + 1$ simultaneous equations for the unknown state probabilities,

$$\sum_{j=0}^{S_{max}} q(i, j) \times p(j) = 0, \qquad i = 0, 1, \ldots \ldots , S_{max} - 1$$ (15.7)

$$\sum_{j=0}^{S_{max}} p(j) = 1 ,$$ (15.8)

in which, for, $i \neq j$, $q(i, j)$ is the net transition flow into state i from state j, and $q(i, i)$ is the total transition flow out of state i.

Hand-off parameters can be determined from the dynamics of the process itself. An iterative method can be used [4]. The average hand-off departure rate of voice sessions on g-type platforms, $\Delta_{hv}(g)$, can be expressed as

$$\Delta_{hv}(g) = \sum_{s=0}^{S_{\max}} \mu_D(g) \cdot v(s, g) \cdot p(s) . \tag{15.9}$$

Thereafter, the overall average hand-off departure rate of voice sessions, Δ_{hv}, can be written as

$$\Delta_{hv} = \sum_{g=1}^{G} \Delta_{hv}(g) . \tag{15.10}$$

The average hand-off departure rate of active data sessions on g-type platforms, $\Delta_{hw}(g)$, can be expressed as

$$\Delta_{hw}(g) = \sum_{s=0}^{S_{\max}} \mu_D(g) \cdot w(s, g) \cdot p(s) . \tag{15.11}$$

Thereafter, the overall hand-off departure rate of active data sessions, Δ_{hw}, can be written as

$$\Delta_{hw} = \sum_{g=1}^{G} \Delta_{hw}(g) . \tag{15.12}$$

The average hand-off departure rates of k-suspended sessions on g-type platforms, $\Delta_r(g, k)$, can be expressed as

$$\Delta_r(g, k) = \sum_{s=0}^{S_{\max}} \mu_D(g) \cdot r(s, g, k) \cdot p(s) . \tag{15.13}$$

Also, the overall average hand-off departure rates of k-suspended sessions, $\Delta_r(k)$, can be written as

$$\Delta_r(k) = \sum_{g=1}^{G} \Delta_r(g, k) . \tag{15.14}$$

From these equations, we find that the fraction of hand-off departures of voice sessions that are on g-type platforms, F'_{vg}, is

$$F'_{vg} = \Delta_{hv}(g)/\Delta_{hv} , \tag{15.15}$$

the fraction of hand-off departures of active data sessions that are on g-type platform, F'_{wg}, is

$$F'_{wg} = \Delta_{hw}(g)/\Delta_{hv} , \tag{15.16}$$

and, the fraction of hand-off departures of k-suspended sessions on g-type platforms, $F'_{rg}(k)$, is

$$F'_{rg}(k) = \Delta_r(g, k)/\Delta_r(k) . \tag{15.17}$$

For a homogeneous system in statistical equilibrium the hand-off arrival and departure rates per cell must be equal [4]. We must have $F_{vg} = F'_{vg}$, $F_{wg} = F'_{wg}$, $F_{rg}(k) = F'_{rg}(k)$, $\Lambda_{hv} = \Delta_{hv}$, $\Lambda_{hw} = \Delta_{hw}$, and $\Lambda_r(k) = \Delta_r(k)$, where $1 \leq k \leq N$.

15.4 Performance Measures

15.4.1 Carried Traffic and Average Number of k-Suspended Sessions

An important performance measure from a system point of view is the carried traffic. Since the traffic of data sessions is transparent to user of voice sessions, the carried traffic of voice sessions is same regardless of the amount of data sessions in the system. The carried traffic of voice sessions for g-type platforms, $A_{cv}(g)$, is

$$A_{cv}(g) = \sum_{s=0}^{S_{\max}} v(s, g) \cdot p(s) , \tag{15.18}$$

Clearly, the traffic of data sessions strongly depends on the traffic of voice sessions in the system. The carried traffic of data sessions for g-type platform, $A_{cw}(g)$, is

$$A_{cw}(g) = \sum_{s=0}^{S_{\max}} w(s, g) \cdot p(s) . \tag{15.19}$$

The average number of k-suspended sessions for g-type platforms, $A_{cr}(g, k)$, is

$$A_{cr}(g, k) = \sum_{s=0}^{S_{\max}} r(s, g, k) \cdot p(s) . \tag{15.20}$$

15.4.2 Blocking Probability

The blocking probability for voice sessions is the average fraction of newly generated voice sessions that are denied access to a channel. Since there are no quotas for specific type of mobility platform, the blocking probability is the same for all types of platforms. Blocking of newly generated voice sessions occurs when the cell is in one of the states in L_{Bv}, for which the number of active voice sessions is $C - C_h$ or more, i.e., $L_{Bv} = \{s : v(s) \geq C - C_h\}$. And, the blocking probability of voice session, P_{Bv}, is expressed as

$$P_{Bv} = \sum_{s \in L_{Bv}} p(s) . \tag{15.21}$$

The blocking probability for data sessions is the average fraction of newly generated data sessions that are denied access to a channel. A newly generated data session will be blocked if it finds all channels are occupied (by either by voice or data sessions). Blocking of newly generated data sessions occurs when the cell is in one of the states in the set, L_{Bw}, where $L_{Bw} = \{s : J(s) = C\}$. So, the blocking probability, P_{Bw}, for a data session is given by

$$P_{Bw} = \sum_{s \in L_{Bw}} p(s) . \tag{15.22}$$

15.4.3   Hand-Off Failure Probability

The hand-off failure probability of voice sessions, P_{Hv}, is the average fraction of voice-session hand-off attempts that are denied admission into the target cell because all channels are already occupied by voice sessions in the cell. A voice-session hand-off failure occurs when the cell is in a state belonging to L_{Hv}, where $L_{Hv} = \{s : v(s) = C\}$. So, the hand-off failure probability of voice sessions is given by

$$P_{Hv} = \sum_{s \in L_H} p(s) . \tag{15.23}$$

The hand-off failure probability of a data session, P_{Hw}, is the average fraction of hand-off attempts for data sessions that are denied admission into the target cell because all channels are occupied and H suspended sessions are into the cell. A data session, either active or suspended, that is denied admission in the target cell due to the lack of resources will be forced into termination and cleared from the system. A data-session hand-off attempt will fail if it occurs when the system is in one of the states belonging to the set $L_{Hw} = \{s : v(s) = C, r(s) = H\}$. So, the hand-off failure probability of data sessions is given by

$$P_{Hw} = \sum_{s \in L_{WH}} p(s) . \tag{15.24}$$

15.4.4   Forced Termination Probability

A voice session that fails in a hand-off will be forced into termination. As in [4, 8], the forced termination probability of voice sessions on g-type platform, $P_{FTv}(g)$, is defined as the probability that a g-type voice session that is not blocked is interrupted due to hand-off failure *during its lifetime.* It can be shown that the forced termination probability of a voice type session is given by

$$P_{FTv}(g) = \frac{\mu_D(g) \times P_{Hv}}{\mu_v(g) + \mu_D(g) \times P_{Hv}}. \qquad (15.25)$$

The forced termination probability of a data session on a g-type platform, $P_{FTw}(g)$, is defined as the probability that a data session that is not blocked is forced into termination *during its lifetime.* Space limitations preclude a complete discussion here. Interested readers are referred to [7] for a complete derivation and a more comprehensive discussion.

15.5 Discussion of Results

Numerical results were generated using the approach described in this paper. For Figs. 15.1 through 15.5, a mean unencumbered voice-session duration of 100s was assumed and a mean unencumbered data-session duration of 20s was assumed. Two platform types, low mobility and high mobility, were considered. A mean dwell time of 500s was assumed for a low mobility platform and 100s was assumed for a high mobility platform. A homogeneous system was assumed. The mean k-trial time of a g-type k-suspended session was chosen to be 10s for $1 \leq k \leq N$. The abscissas for Figs. 15.1 through 15.5 reflect call demands with the assumptions stated above. In these, the abscissa is the new voice session origination rate for platform type 1 [denoted $\Lambda_{nv}(1)$]. The ratio of new voice-session generation rates from other platform types to that of type 1 platforms were held fixed with parameters $\alpha(g)$. Also, the new data-session generation rate for platform type g was determined with respect to the new voice session origination rate using parameters, $\beta(g)$. For all calculations in this paper, $\alpha(g) = \beta(g) = 1$ is assumed.

Figures 15.1 and 15.2 show voice traffic performances. Since the traffic of data sessions is transparent to users of voice session, the traffic performance of voice sessions with data traffic is identical to that without data traffic. Figure 15.1 shows the blocking probability of voice session. As the number of reserved channels, C_h, is increased, obviously more newly generated voice session cannot be accommodated.

Figure 15.2 shows the forced termination probability of voice session. As the number C_h increase, fewer voice sessions are forced into termination with the cost of blocking of more newly generated voice sessions. Clearly, voice sessions on fast mobile platforms have higher forced termination probability than that on slow mobile platform. This is because voice sessions on fast mobile

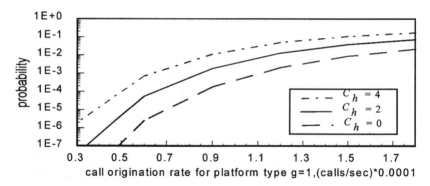

FIGURE 15.1

Blocking probability of voice-type sessions: $C = 15$, $v(1, 0) = v(2, 0) = 300$.

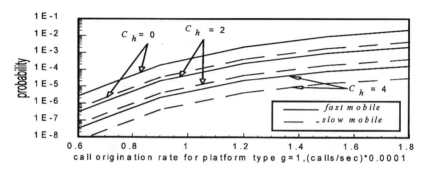

FIGURE 15.2

Forced termination probability of voice-type sessions: $C = 15$, $v(1, 0) = v(2, 0) = 300$.

platforms are most likely to experience more hand-offs during the lifetime of a session.

Figure 15.3 shows the forced termination probability of data sessions for various values of C_h used for cut-off priority. When we increase C_h, clearly, forced termination probability of data sessions decreased. It is also seen that data sessions on slow mobile have smaller forced termination probability. This is because a data session on slow mobile can finish its session with relatively fewer hand-offs during its lifetime. Figure 15.4 shows the dependence of forced termination probability of data sessions on the number of maximum allowable reconnection attempts, N. As we can see, increasing N results in fewer data sessions being forced to terminate during their lifetime. Figure 15.5 shows the dependence of forced termination probability of data sessions on the number of maximum supportable suspended sessions, H. With increasing H, clearly, the less the forced termination probability of data session is expected.

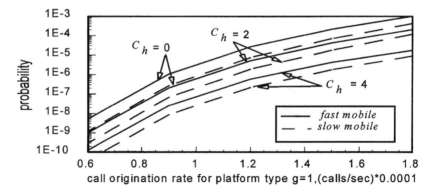

FIGURE 15.3
Forced termination probability of data-type sessions with various C_h : $C = 15, v(1, 0) = v(2, 0) = 300, N = 3, H = 3.$

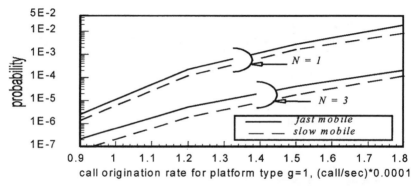

FIGURE 15.4
Forced termination probability of data-type sessions with various N : $C = 15, v(1, 0) = v(2, 0) = 300, C_h = 2, H = 3.$

15.6 Conclusions

With rapidly growing interest in the area of multimedia and mobile computing, the issue "how to accommodate diverse traffic types in wireless network"
must be solved. In this paper, we propose a scheme in which each type of media
is managed with different strategy according to the characteristics. For time
insensitive data sessions, the system allows users to continue in a temporary
off-line mode while awaiting an active network connection in the background.
For time sensitive voice sessions, the system gives preemptive priority over data
traffic so that the transparency of data traffic is guaranteed to voice users. We

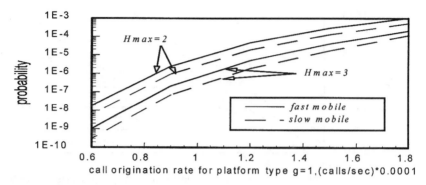

FIGURE 15.5
Forced termination probability of data-type sessions with various $H : C = 15, \nu(1,0) = \nu(2,0) = 300, C_h = 2, N = 3.$

develop the framework, using a suitable state description and multidimensional birth-death process representation, to compute traffic performance characteristics of a proposed system. Consideration of mixed platform mobilities is accommodated in the model. Traffic performance depends strongly on the amount of priority given for hand-off attempt of voice sessions and the limit on the number of allowable reconnection attempts for data sessions. Relevant traffic performance measures can be calculated for given system parameters.

References

[1] W.D. Grover, W.A. Krzymien, J.C. Chin, Strategies for Management of Connection-Oriented Data Sessions Employing the Idle Times in Cellular Telephony, *IEEE Trans. Vehicular Tech.*, vol. 44, no. 2, pp. 244–252, May 1995.

[2] Y. Park and S.S. Rappaport, Cellular Communication Systems with Voice and Background Data, D.J. Goodman and D. Raychaudhuri (Eds.), *Mobile Multimedia Communications,* Plenum Press, New York, pp. 33–42, 1997.

[3] Y. Park and S.S. Rappaport, Performance Analysis of Session Oriented Data Communications for Mobile Computing in Cellular Systems, Kin Leung and Branimir Vojcic (Eds.), *Multiacess, Mobility and Teletraffic for*

Wireless Communications: Vol. 3, Kluwer Academic Publishers, Boston, pp. 59–74, 1999.

[4] S.S. Rappaport, Blocking Hand-off and Traffic Performance Analysis for Cellular Communication System with Mixed Platforms, *IEE (British) Proc.,* Part I, Communications, Speech and Vision, vol. 40, no. 5, pp. 389–401, October 1993.

[5] C. Purzynski and S.S. Rappaport, Prioritized Resource Assignment for Mobile Cellular Communication Systems with Mixed Services and Platform Types, *IEEE Trans. on Vehicular Tech.,* vol. 45, no. 3, pp. 443–458, Aug. 1996.

[6] D. Hong and S.S. Rappaport, Traffic Model and Performance Analysis for Cellular Mobile Radio Telephone Systems with Prioritized and Non-Prioritized Hand-off Procedures, *IEEE Trans. on Vehicular Tech.,* vol.VT-35, no. 3, pp. 77–92, Aug. 1986.

[7] Y. Park and S.S. Rappaport, A Session Oriented Strategy for Multiple Traffic Classes in Cellular Communication Systems, *CEAS Technical Report no. 760.* College of Engineering and Applied Sciences, State University of New York, Stony Brook, NY 11794.

[8] S.S. Rappaport, The Multiple-Call Hand-off Problem in High-Capacity Cellular Communication Systems, *IEEE Trans. on Vehicular Tech.,* vol. VT-40, no. 3, pp. 546–557, Aug. 1991.

[9] P.V. Orlik and S.S. Rappaport, Traffic Performance and Mobility Modelling of Cellular Communications with Mixed Platforms and Highly Variable Mobilities, *IEEE Proc.,* Special Issue on Mobile Radio Centennial, vol. 86, no. 7, July 1998, pp. 1464–1479. See also IEEE Proceedings, Oct. 1998.

Chapter 16

A Parallel Branch-and-Cut Algorithm for Capacitated Network Design Problems

Oktay Günlük[1]

AT&T Labs

Abstract   For computationally difficult large-scale integer programming problems branch-and-cut, and more recently, parallel branch-and-cut, has proved to be a viable solution strategy. In this paper we present a parallel branch-and-cut algorithm to solve capacitated network design problems based on [9].

We discuss the following issues: fine-grain vs. coarse-grain parallelization of branch-and-cut; effect of multiple level branching on the size of the enumeration tree; central process management vs. distributed process management; a simple and effective load balancing scheme for the distributed case; comparison of different distributed computing platforms, namely, a network of (Sun-Ultra) workstations and a massively parallel distributed memory machine (SP2).

Keywords: optimization, integer programming, computing, parallel processing.

16.1   Introduction

In a previous paper [9] we presented a branch-and-cut algorithm to solve a mixed-integer programming formulation of the *Capacity Expansion Problem* (CEP). Applications of this problem (or its variants) arise in the telecommunications industry for both service providers (i.e., long-distance carriers) and

---

[1]Research partially supported by NSF grant DMS-9527124, when the author was at Cornell University.

their customers. For service providers the problem is to expand the capacity of the existing transport network, whereas, for their customers, the problem corresponds to designing a private line network by leasing data transmission lines from service providers. In both cases, transmission facilities are installed or leased in integral multiples of several modularities (such as OC1-OC48). We note that CEP is strongly NP-hard, as it contains the fixed-charge network design problem, and thus, the Steiner tree problem as a special case.

For computationally difficult large-scale integer programming problems such as the *Traveling Salesman Problem* or the *Set Partitioning Problem*, branch-and-cut has proved to be a viable solution strategy. The branch-and-cut algorithm can be parallelized in a very natural way, as one has to solve many independent subproblems to obtain a global optimal solution to the original problem. The main challenge is to find procedures to coordinate the processors so that they are utilized efficiently (both in terms of idle-time and quality of the work-load). Since the total work-load cannot be estimated and distributed to the processors at the beginning of the computation, dynamic procedures are needed to achieve this.

In this paper we present a parallel branch-and-cut algorithm for CEP and discuss some computational issues such as: (i) Fine-grain vs. coarse-grain parallelization of branch-and-cut. (ii) Effect of multiple level branching on the size of the enumeration tree. (iii) Central process management vs. distributed process management. (iv) A simple and effective load balancing scheme for the distributed case. (v) Implementation on different distributed computing platforms.

16.1.1 Parallel Branch-and-Cut

Given an integer programming problem: $z = \min\{cx : x \in P\}$, the main idea in branch-and-cut is to recursively partition the solution space $P = \cup_{i \in \pi} P_i$ and solve relaxations of the associated subproblems: $z_i^R = \min\{cx : x \in P_i^R\}$, where $P_i \subseteq P_i^R$. Clearly, $z \geq \min_{i \in \pi}\{z_i^R\}$. The refinement of the solution space P continues until a partition $P = \cup_{i \in \bar{\pi}} P_i$ with $\min_{i \in \bar{\pi}}\{z_i^R\} = \hat{z}$, where $\hat{z}$ is the value of a known integral solution to the problem.

The only difference between branch-and-bound and branch-and-cut is how the relaxations P_i^R are obtained. In branch-and-bound, the continuous relaxation of the problem is used to obtain P_i^R, whereas in branch-and-cut the continuous relaxation is strengthened with valid inequalities.

Since the subproblems associated with each P_i^R are independent, they can be processed simultaneously in a parallel environment. Furthermore, processing a subproblem can also be divided into smaller tasks and these tasks can be executed in parallel. The first approach is called the *coarse-grain parallelization* and the second one is known as the *fine-grain parallelization* approach.

16.2 Problem Formulation and Valid Inequalities

Given a capacitated network $G = (V, E)$ and a set of traffic demands to be routed between certain pairs of nodes of the network, the problem is to install more capacity on the edges and route traffic (simultaneously) in the resulting network so that the total capacity installation plus routing cost is minimized. Capacity can be installed in discrete multiples of various modularities. Polyhedral structure of this problem has been studied in [3] and closely related problems have been studied in [1, 4, 2, 6] and [12]. A variant of this problem where the initial capacities are assumed to be zero is also known as the *network loading problem*.

16.2.1 A Mixed Integer Programming Formulation

The demand data consists of a matrix $T = \{t_j^i\}$ where t_j^i is the amount of (directed) traffic that should be routed from $i \in V$ to $j \in V$. This demand can be sent via several directed paths. It is assumed that capacity can be installed in multiples of two modularities (such as OC3 and OC12) and capacity generated by the larger one is equivalent to the capacity generated by $\lambda \in Z_+$ small ones. Without loss of generality, we assume that the small batch size has capacity 1.

If we define $K = \{i \in V : \sum_{j \in V} t_j^i > 0\}$ to denote the set of nodes with positive supply, then we can describe the convex hull of feasible solutions by using the following (aggregate) multicommodity flow formulation:

$$\text{Min } z = \sum_{e \in E} \alpha_e x_e + \sum_{e \in E} \beta_e y_e + \sum_{\{i,j\} \in E} \gamma_{i,j} \sum_{k \in K} \left(f_{ij}^k + f_{ji}^k \right),$$

subject to:

$$\sum_{\{j,v\} \in E} f_{jv}^k - \sum_{\{v,j\} \in E} f_{vj}^k = t_v^k \qquad v \in V, \; k \in K$$

$$\sum_{k \in K} f_{ij}^k \le x_e + \lambda y_e + C_e$$

$$e = \{i, j\} \in E$$

$$\sum_{k \in K} f_{ji}^k \le x_e + \lambda y_e + C_e$$

$$f_{ij}^k, f_{ji}^k \ge 0 \qquad \{i, j\} \in E, \; k \in K$$

$$x_e, y_e \ge 0, \text{ and integer } \quad e \in E \;.$$

In this formulation, for every edge $e \in E$, integer variables x_e and y_e, respectively, denote the capacity installed on the edge using the small and large batch sizes. Note that a node $k \in K$ is the unique supplier of commodity k and a flow vector f gives a feasible (aggregate) routing of the traffic when it satisfies the (i) flow-balance constraints and (ii) capacity constraints simultaneously. It is easy to extract an individual routing for each $t_j^i > 0$ by disaggregating f.

16.2.2 Valid Inequalities

In our algorithm we use three families of valid inequalities: (i) the partition inequalities, (ii) mixed-integer rounding (MIR) inequalities and (iii) mixed-partition inequalities.

The partition inequalities are obtained as follows: First the node set of the graph is partitioned into a small number of subsets and the collection of edges Δ (the multi-cut) separating these subsets is identified. Next, a lower bound $\Theta(\Delta)$ on the total traffic load of these edges is computed. The final step is to round up this lower bound and obtain the following valid inequality:

$$\sum_{e \in \Delta} x_e + \lambda \sum_{e \in \Delta} y_e \geq \lceil \Theta(\Delta) \rceil . \tag{16.1}$$

These inequalities are facet defining when the partition is chosen carefully.

The second family of valid inequalities is obtained by applying simple mixed-integer rounding to (16.1). Let $r(\Theta) = \Theta(\Delta) - (\lceil \Theta(\Delta)/\lambda \rceil - 1)$, then the MIR inequality associated with (16.1) is:

$$\sum_{e \in \Delta} x_e \geq r(\Theta) \left(\lceil \Theta(\Delta)/\lambda \rceil - \sum_{e \in \Delta} y_e \right) . \tag{16.2}$$

These inequalities are also known to be facet defining under mild conditions. The mixed partition inequalities are obtained by combining a collection of partition inequalities.

16.3   The Underlying Branch-and-Cut Algorithm

The main modules of the underlying (serial) branch-and-cut algorithm are shown in Fig. 16.1. All of these modules, except the LP-solver, are implemented by us.

At the beginning of the algorithm, we generate a list of valid inequalities that consists of some simple partition inequalities. Throughout the algorithm, these inequalities are checked for possible violation before generating new cuts. Cut generation is performed heuristically since the associated separation problems are NP-hard.

The solution space is partitioned using variable dichotomies and we select the branching variable using the "maximum weighted integer infeasibility" rule, (where the integer infeasibility of a variable is multiplied by its cost coefficient to obtain the weight). We search the solution space using the best-bound strategy and thus process the subproblems in the work-pool in increasing order of lower bound.

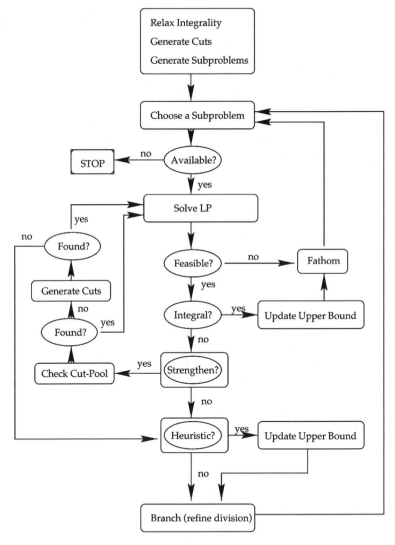

FIGURE 16.1
The branch-and-cut algorithm.

16.4   Fine-Grain vs. Coarse-Grain Parallelization

As briefly discussed above, branch-and-cut algorithms can be easily parallelized by processing the subproblems on different processors. It is also possible to break the subproblem processing module into smaller tasks such as cut generation, cut-pool search, LP-solver, etc. and execute these tasks on different processors. Furthermore, upper bound heuristics can also be executed in parallel. The first approach is known as the *coarse-grain* parallelization approach and the latter one as the *fine-grain* parallelization approach (see [8] and [10]).

The choice between the two approaches depends on the expected size and breadth of the enumeration tree. Our prior experience with capacitated network design problems suggests that even problem instances with roughly 20 nodes and 50 edges can be quite challenging and could require thousands of subproblem evaluations for optimality.

In this section we provide some computational results which support the coarse-grain approach for CEP.

16.5   Multiple Level Branching

As discussed above, the branch-and-cut algorithm starts with a single subproblem, which corresponds to a relaxation of the original integer program, and gradually generates more subproblems by partitioning the solution space. Therefore, at the beginning of the algorithm most of the processors are bound to stay idle, or, in other words, "starve." In one of the earlier papers on parallel branch-and-cut ([5], appeared in 1990), the authors suggest partitioning the solution space faster by employing a multiple-level branching strategy at the beginning of their algorithm.

We study several multi-level branching strategies and present computational results which do not support multi-level branching.

16.6   Process Control

In a distributed memory environment (which is more common and can be created by combining workstations), storage and sharing of the subproblems is the most important issue. The main concern here is load balancing, not only in terms of quantity, but also in terms of quality.

A possible solution to the load balancing issue is to set aside a dedicated processor for orchestrating the other processors and to store a single pool of unexplored subproblems. This approach is known as the *centralized control,* or, *the master-worker* approach.

Another possibility is to employ a non-hierarchical approach and achieve load balancing by means of communication between the processors throughout the algorithm. In this case, processors have to operate with incomplete information about the global work-load. We propose a combination of randomized procedures (see [11] and [7]) and re-balancing schemes to offset this and show that a *distributed control* or *peer-to-peer* approach can be very efficient. The idea is to have processors perform "local" best-first searches and send out new subproblems to other processors in a random fashion. Possible discrepancies are then taken care of by means of periodic and need-based redistribution of subproblems.

We present a computational comparison of these two approaches and attempt to establish rules based on the number of processors and the difficulty of the problem to decide which approach to take.

References

[1] F. Barahona, Network design using cut inequalities. *SIAM J. on Optimization,* 6, 1996.

[2] D. Bienstock, S. Chopra, O. Gunluk, and C-Y. Tsai, Minimum cost capacity installation for multicommodity network flows. *Math. Programming,* 81, 177–199, 1998.

[3] D. Bienstock and O. Gunluk, Capacitated network design - polyhedral structure and computation. *INFORMS Journal on Computing,* 8, 243–259, 1996.

[4] B. Brockmuller, O. Gunluk, and L.A. Wolsey, Designing private line networks – polyhedral analysis and computation. *CORE Discussion Paper,* 9647, 1996.

[5] T. Cannon and K. Hoffman, Large scale 0/1 linear programming on distributed workstations. *Annals of Operations Research,* 22, 181–217, 1990.

[6] G. Dahl, A. Martin, and M. Stoer, Routing through virtual paths in layered telecommunication networks. *Preprint,* 1995.

[7]   J. Eckstein, Control strategies for parallel mixed integer branch-and-bound. In *Proceedings of Supercomputing '94, IEEE Computer Society Press,* 1994.

[8]   M. Eso, L. Ladanyi, T. Ralphs, and L. Trotter, Fully parallel generic branch-and-cut. Technical report, Cornell University, 1996.

[9]   O. Gunluk, A branch-and-cut algorithm for capacitated network design problems. Technical report, Cornell University, 1996 (to appear in *Math. Programming*).

[10] M. Junger and P. Stormer, Solving large scale traveling salesman problems with parallel branch-and-cut. Technical report, Zentrum fur paralleles rechnen, Universitat zu Koln, 1995.

[11] R. Karp and Y. Zhang, Radomized parallel algorithms for backtrack search and branch-and-bound computation. *J. of the Association for Computing Machinery,* 40(3), 765–789, 1993.

[12] T. Magnanti and P. Mirchandani, Shortest paths, single origin-destination network design and associated polyhedra. *Networks,* 23, 103–121, 1993.

Vitae

Dr. Günlük is a senior member of technical staff at the Network Design and Performance Analysis Department of AT&T Labs in New Jersey, USA. His research is mainly focused on integer programming and computing with applications to telecommunications networks.

He holds degrees from Boðgaziçi University (BS, MS) and Columbia University (M.Phil. and Ph.D. [1994]). He has spent a year at CORE, Université Catholique de Louvain, Belgium and two years at the School of Operations Research and Industrial Engineering, Cornell University before joining AT&T.

Chapter 17

A Unified Approach to the Analysis of Large-Scale Teletraffic Models

Nihat Cem Oğuz and Khosrow Sohraby[1]

University of Missouri-Kansas City

Abstract Performance evaluation of computer and communication networks gives rise to teletraffic models of potentially large numbers of states. Computational analysis of such large-scale models is very demanding in terms of both CPU time and memory requirements. This paper summarizes a unifying and parallelizable system-theoretic approach to efficient solution of a diversity of teletraffic problems, and presents preliminary timing results comparing the sequential and parallel realizations of the approach. These indicate appreciable speed-ups making analysis of large-scale teletraffic problems feasible.

Keywords: teletraffic analysis, queuing systems, GI/G/1, MAP/G/1, fluid flow.

17.1 Introduction

Performance assessment problems arising in telecommunication networks basically consist of two components: traffic modeling and queuing analysis. Traffic is the driving force for telecommunication networks and their models are of crucial importance for evaluating network performance [13]. Probability models for traffic streams are needed to the extent that they are able to predict system performance measures to a reasonable degree of accuracy. The fundamental systems, of which traffic is the major constituent, are *queuing systems,*

---

[1]This work was partially supported by DARPA/ITO under grant A0-F316 and by NSF under grant NCR-950814.

and their numerical analyses provide the system performance measures once adequate traffic models are available.

Consider the scenario of a high-speed packet-switched network in which variable bit-rate (VBR) multimedia sources are statistically multiplexed over the network links. Engineering such a network to provide quality-of-service guarantees to different applications requires development of traffic models (either multiplexed or single source models). These models are useful in traffic engineering problems including link dimensioning, bandwidth allocation, and call admission control [8]. However, traditional models based on the assumption of Poisson call arrivals and exponential call holding times, which have performed successfully in the design of circuit-switched telephone networks, are no longer effective for high-speed networks. Furthermore, the VBR video traffic exhibits non-trivial higher-order statistics which are difficult to measure, characterize, and exploit. So does high-speed data, e.g., LAN-to-LAN interconnection traffic. Once adequate models are developed, computationally efficient queuing analysis techniques are needed.

The existing numerical techniques for efficient queuing analysis are tailored to a given class of probability models, e.g., Quasi-Birth-and-Death (QBD) processes, fluid flow models, etc. This paper summarizes a unifying algorithmic approach for general queuing analysis, which is numerically efficient, reliable, and parallelizable. The analysis of discrete-time models such as M/G/1-type Markov chains via this approach has been previously discussed along with performance comparisons with existing methods [1, 2]. Here, we focus on the treatment of continuous-time queuing models, and present preliminary results of timing comparisons between the sequential and parallel realizations of our approach. The results indicate appreciable speed-ups even for moderate problem sizes.

17.2   Analysis Framework and Examples

In this section, we will first cover setting up a unified and generic mathematical framework for continuous-time queuing models. Then, GI/G/1 and MAP/G/1 queues and Markov-modulated fluid flow models will be treated within this framework as examples.

17.2.1   Generic Solution of Continuous-Time Models

We view the problem of solving a queuing system as one of determining the output of a linear, finite-dimensional dynamical system [6] whose initial conditions are to satisfy certain stability constraints. To be more specific, we show that a large class of continuous-time teletraffic models can be put in the following mathematical form:

$$\frac{d}{dx}z(x) = Az(x), \quad z(0) = By_0, \quad w(x) = Cz(x), \quad \lim_{x \to \infty} w(x) = 1 . \quad (17.1)$$

This differential equation is in standard state-space form [6, 9], where $z(x)$ is the $n \times 1$ state vector of the dynamical system, and A, B, and C are *known* constant matrices of sizes $n \times n$, $n \times m$, and $1 \times n$, respectively. The $m \times 1$ vector y_0 is the *unknown* boundary vector which is to be determined. We note that, in the above formulation, $w(x)$ usually denotes the Cumulative Density Function (cdf) of a random variable W of interest, e.g., waiting time or unfinished work in a queuing system.

Note that, once the boundary vector y_0 is obtained, the unique solution to the linear differential equation (17.1) takes the simple matrix-exponential form

$$w(x) = Ce^{Ax}By_0 . \quad (17.2)$$

This form of solution, however, is not generally recommended for numerical computations. Before we provide a number of example queuing systems which can be put in the above mathematical form, we give a computationally efficient algorithmic method for the solution of (17.1).

Central to our solution methodology is decomposing the matrix A as

$$U^{-1}AU = \begin{bmatrix} A_u & 0 \\ 0 & A_s \end{bmatrix}, \quad (17.3)$$

where all n_u eigenvalues of the $n_u \times n_u$ matrix A_u lie in the closed right-half plane (i.e., they have non-negative real parts), and all n_s eigenvalues of the $n_s \times n_s$ real matrix A_s lie in the open left-half plane (i.e., they have strictly negative real parts). We note that finding such a decomposition is a fundamental subject of numerical linear algebra, and there are a number of efficient and numerically robust methods that do not require explicit determination of the eigenvalues of A (see [7] for example). This point will be briefly revisited in Section 17.3.

In what follows, we assume that the above decomposition is obtained, and proceed to formulating the solution to (17.1). Define the $n \times 1$ vector $g(x)$ such that $z(x) = Ug(x)$. Then, it follows from (17.1) and (17.3) that $g(x)$ satisfies the differential equation

$$\frac{d}{dx}g(x) = U^{-1}AUg(x) . \quad (17.4)$$

Now, partitioning $g(x)$ into two vectors of n_u and n_s elements, respectively, i.e., writing $g(x) = [\, g_u(x) \ g_s(x) \,]$, we get two un-coupled differential equations from (17.4):

$$\frac{d}{dx}g_u(x) = A_u g_u(x) \quad \text{and} \quad \frac{d}{dx}g_s(x) = A_s g_s(x) . \quad (17.5)$$

Since all the elements of $g(x)$ should remain bounded as $x \to \infty$, the only nonzero solution to the first d.e. in (17.5) is ku_*, where the vector u_* satisfies $A_u u_* = 0$ and k is a scalar to be determined, as discussed in the sequel.

Next, partitioning the matrix U in a similar way as $U = [\; U_1 \;\; U_2 \;]$, where U_1 and U_2 are of sizes $n \times n_u$ and $n \times n_s$, respectively, we obtain

$$z(x) = kU_1 u_* + U_2 e^{A_s x} g_s(0) . \tag{17.6}$$

Note that the second term of (17.6) diminishes as $x \to \infty$ since A_s has all its eigenvalues in the open left-half plane. Also since we need $Cz(\infty) = 1$, the scalar k should be chosen such that $kCU_1 u_* = 1$. Once $z(\infty)$ is found (this usually is known or obtained independently from the particular model at hand), it follows from (17.1) and (17.6) that $By_0 - U_2 g_s(0) = z(\infty)$, which can be expressed as a system of linear equations in the unique unknowns y_0 and $g_s(0)$. Solving this equation, we finally have

$$w(x) = 1 + C\; U_2 e^{A_s x} g_s(0) . \tag{17.7}$$

Note here that this result on $w(x)$ allows simple calculation of moments. Specifically, we have

$$E[W^k] = k!CU_2(-A_s)^{-k-1} g_s(0), \quad k \geq 1 . \tag{17.8}$$

In the following, we provide three example teletraffic problems which are put in the general form of (17.1).

17.2.2   GI/G/1 Queue

The system under consideration is one in which inter-arrival and service times are independently drawn from arbitrary distributions $A(x)$ and $B(x)$, respectively. We assume that there is a single server operating on a first-come-first-served basis [10]. We define the Laplace-Stieltjes Transforms (LSTs) of the probability density functions of the inter-arrival and service times as $\hat{A}(s)$ and $\hat{B}(s)$, respectively, and assume that they are rational functions of s so that we can write $\hat{A}(s) = \hat{p}_a(s)/\hat{q}_a(s)$ and $\hat{B}(s) = \hat{p}_b(s)/\hat{q}_b(s)$ for some polynomials $\hat{p}_a$ and $\hat{q}_a$ of degree a and polynomials $\hat{p}_b$ and $\hat{q}_b$ of degree b. Defining the cdf of the waiting time as $w(x)$ and its LST as $\hat{w}(s)$, we can now write the transform expression for $\hat{w}(s)$ based on [10]:

$$\hat{w}(s) = \frac{\hat{x}(s)\hat{q}_b(s)}{\hat{q}_a(-s)\hat{q}_b(s) - \hat{p}_a(-s)\hat{p}_b(s)} . \tag{17.9}$$

Here, the polynomial $\hat{x}(s)$ is of degree $a - 1$, and $\hat{x}(s)$ is to be determined so that the transform expression for $\hat{w}(s)$ becomes analytic in the open right-half plane. It is well known that, for a stable queue, the denominator polynomial $\Delta(s) = \hat{q}_a(-s)\hat{q}_b(s) - \hat{p}_a(-s)\hat{p}_b(s)$ has b roots in the open left-half plane,

$a - 1$ roots in the open right-half plane, and a single root at the origin. Without loss of generality, we assume the highest-degree coefficient of $\Delta(s)$ is unity. Following [10], if we obtain a factorization for $\Delta(s)$ as $\Delta(s) = \Delta_l(s)\Delta_r(s)$ with the roots of $\Delta_l(s)$ and $\Delta_r(s)$ lying in the closed left-half and open right-half planes, respectively, the choice of $\hat{x}(s) = k\Delta_r(s)$ with any constant k yields $\hat{w}(s)$ being analytic in the open right-half plane. Here, the constant k is to be chosen simply to provide $w(\infty) = 1$.

Now we give a state-space realization for $\hat{w}(s)$ in the form (17.1). We first define the following:

$$c = a + b, \qquad\qquad \Delta(s) = \alpha_1 s + \alpha_2 s^2 + \cdots + \alpha_{c-1}s^{c-1} + s^c ,$$
$$\hat{q}_b(s) = q_0 + q_1 s + \cdots + q_b s^b, \quad \hat{x}(s) = x_0 + x_1 s + \cdots + x_{a-1}s^{a-1} .$$

Then, through the observable canonical realization for $\hat{w}(s)$ given in [6, pp. 240–242], one can obtain the following matrices (with their sizes also given):

$$
A = \begin{bmatrix} 0\,0\cdots 0 & 0 \\ 1\,0\cdots 0 & -\alpha_1 \\ 0\,1\cdots 0 & -\alpha_2 \\ \vdots\;\vdots\quad\;\; \vdots & \vdots \\ 0\,0\cdots 1 & -\alpha_{c-1} \end{bmatrix}_{c\times c}, \quad
B = \begin{bmatrix} q_0 & & & \\ q_1 & q_0 & & \\ \vdots & q_1 & q_0 & \\ q_b & \vdots & q_1 & \ddots \\ & q_b & \vdots & \ddots & q_0 \\ & & q_b & & q_1 \\ & & & \ddots & \vdots \\ & & & & q_b \end{bmatrix}_{c\times a},
$$

$$C = [\,0\;0\;\cdots\;1\,]_{1\times c}, \quad y_0 = [\,x_0\;x_1\;\cdots\;x_{a-2}\;x_{a-1}\,]^T_{a\times 1} .$$

These constitute a state-space realization of the form (17.1) for the transform input-output relationship given in (17.9). We also note a well-known fact from linear system theory: the poles of $\hat{w}(s)$, i.e., the roots of $\Delta(s)$, coincide with the eigenvalues of A. Therefore, the matrix A has b eigenvalues in the open left-half plane, $a - 1$ eigenvalues in the open right-half plane, and one simple eigenvalue at the origin.

We also note that, with this formulation of GI/G/1 queues, the state-space dimension is $c = a + b$. This may provide a significant advantage over matrix-geometric methods proposed for PH/PH/1 queues [12] in the context of QBD chains. In QBD methodology, the state-space dimension is the product ab, that is, the dimension is multiplicative rather than being additive.

17.2.3 MAP/G/1 Queue

The Markovian Arrival Process (MAP) is introduced in [11] in which the reader can find a detailed description of the MAP, its use in traffic modeling, and related issues.

The MAP is characterized by two matrices D_0 and D_1. Here, D_0 and D_1 are $m \times m$ matrices, D_0 has negative diagonal elements and non-negative off-diagonal elements, D_1 is non-negative, and $D = D_0 + D_1$ is an irreducible infinitesimal generator. Let the service time for the MAP/G/1 queue have a distribution function $B(x)$, with rational LST, $\hat{B}(s) = \hat{p}(s)/\hat{q}(s)$, where the polynomials $\hat{p}(s)$ and $\hat{q}(s)$ have degrees n and l, respectively, with $n < l$ and the highest-degree coefficient of $\hat{q}(s)$ being unity. Hereafter, we assume that the parameters of the incoming MAP are normalized so that the mean service time is unity. Let $x_0 = [\, x_{01} \;\; x_{02} \;\; \ldots \;\; x_{0m} \,]$ be defined so that x_{0j} is the stationary probability that, at an arbitrary time, the arrival process is in phase j and the queue is empty. Also let

$$\hat{H}(s) = (sI + D_0)\hat{q}(s) + D_1\hat{p}(s) = H_d s^d + H_{d-1}s^{d-1} + \cdots + H_1 s + H_0 ,$$

for some constant matrices $H_i, i = 0, 1, \ldots, d$ where $d = l + 1$ and

$$\hat{q}(s) = q_{d-1}s^{d-1} + q_{d-2}s^{d-2} + \cdots + q_1 s + q_0 .$$

Based on these definitions, the following choice of matrices A, B, and C can be shown to constitute a state-space realization of the for (17.1) for the virtual waiting time distribution in the MAP/G/1 queue:

$$A = \begin{bmatrix} 0 & 0 & \cdots & 0 & -H_0 \\ I & 0 & \cdots & 0 & -H_1 \\ 0 & I & \cdots & 0 & -H_2 \\ \vdots & \vdots & & \vdots & \vdots \\ 0 & 0 & \cdots & I & -H_{d-1} \end{bmatrix}^T , \quad \begin{array}{l} B = [\, B_1 \;\; B_2 \;\; \cdots \;\; B_d \,]^T, \\ C = [\, e^T \;\; 0 \;\; \cdots \;\; 0 \,], \\ \text{and} \;\; y_0 = x_0^T , \end{array}$$

where e denotes a column vector of ones, and

$$B_1 = I, \quad B_i = q_{d-i}I - \sum_{j=1}^{i-1} B_j H_{d-i+j}, \quad i = 2, 3, \ldots, d.$$

17.2.4 Fluid Flow Models

Let the fluid arrival rate into a buffer be $\lambda[\mathbf{S}(t)]$, where $\mathbf{S}(t)$ is the state of a finite irreducible Markov process at time t, and c denotes the service (drain) rate. Also let $X(t)$ be the amount of fluid in the buffer at time t. Within this framework, the behavior of $X(t)$ is described by

$$\frac{d}{dt}X(t) = \begin{cases} \lambda(\mathbf{S}(t)) - c, & \text{if } X(t) > 0 \text{ or } \lambda[\mathbf{S}(t)] \geq c, \\ 0, & \text{otherwise.} \end{cases}$$

Assuming, without loss of generality, that the state variable $s \in \mathbf{S}$ is integer-valued, i.e., $\mathbf{S}(t) \in \{1, 2, \ldots, m\}$, we define

$$W(s, x) = \lim_{t \to \infty} Pr\{\mathbf{S}(t) = s, \; X(t) \leq x\} .$$

Let Λ be the infinitesimal generator matrix of the underlying Markov chain on s modulating the fluid arrival rate. Also defining the drift matrix D as $D = diag\{\lambda(1) - c, \lambda(2) - c, \ldots, \lambda(m) - c\}$, a state-space realization of the form (17.1) for $w(x) = \sum_s W(s, x)$, the stationary cdf of the unfinished work (amount of fluid in the buffer), follows with the following choices of matrices A, B, and C [4]: $A = D^{-1}\Lambda^T$, $C = e^T$, and B is an m-by-r matrix where r is the number of under-load states, i.e., $\{s \mid \lambda(s) < c\}$. Assuming that the states are enumerated so that the first r states are underload states, the matrix B takes the form $B = [\ I_r \ \ 0_{r,m-r}\ ]^T$. Otherwise, the matrix B should be modified in an obvious manner.

17.3 Parallel Implementation of the Method

In this section, we focus on parallel realization of the approach of Section 17.2, and provide some preliminary timing results. We first outline the algorithm we use to obtain the state-space decomposition (17.3).

17.3.1 State-Space Decomposition

For continuous-time models, given the matrix A in (17.1), the task is to find U that yields the decomposition (17.3) of A, where A_u and A_s comprise the unstable (non-negative real parts) and stable (negative real parts) eigenvalues of A, respectively. Among many alternative methods for this, the matrix-sign function method is our choice for it is suitable to parallelization. The matrix iteration

$$Z_0 = A, \quad Z_{k+1} = (Z_k + Z_k^{-1})/2, \ \ k \geq 0 , \tag{17.10}$$

is conceptually the simplest way to compute $sgn(A)$, the matrix-sign of A, and its convergence rate is quadratic. By computing $sgn(A)$, one is indeed mapping all eigenvalues of A with negative (positive) real parts to -1 (to 1). Consequently, $sgn(A) + I$ has all its eigenvalues clustered at 2 and 0, and by a rank-revealing QR decomposition on $sgn(A) + I$, one obtains a basis for the unstable subspace of A. That is, $sgn(A) + I$ is decomposed as

$$sgn(A) + I = Q_u R_u \Pi_u , \tag{17.11}$$

where Q_u is an orthogonal matrix, R_u is an upper-triangular matrix with diagonal elements decreasing in magnitude, and Π_u is a permutation matrix. Then, the basis U_1 for the unstable subspace is obtained as the n_u leading columns of Q_u, where n_u is the number of eigenvalues of A with positive real parts. Another rank-revealing QR decomposition on $sgn(A) - I$ similarly yields a basis for the stable subspace of A: U_2 is the n_s leading columns of Q_s in

$sgn(A) - I = Q_s R_s \Pi_s$. We obtain U in (17.3) as $U = [\ U_1 \quad U_2\ ]$. One practical problem here is that A should have no eigenvalues on the imaginary axis for $sgn(A)$ to be defined and for iteration (17.10) to converge. As was argued in Section 17.2, A in the common context of queuing problems we are interested in has one unstable eigenvalue at the origin. The remedy to this is to move this eigenvalue to the right-half plane by adding a certain rank-1 matrix to A. That is, we modify A as $A := A + \alpha\beta/(\beta\alpha)$, where α and β are right and left eigenvectors of A corresponding to the zero eigenvalue, respectively. These eigenvectors are usually readily available from the problem definition or obtained at little additional cost.

17.3.2 Preliminary Timing Results

In implementation, we rely exclusively on well-known numerical linear algebra library LAPACK (Linear Algebra PACKage) [3] and its scalable (or parallel) version ScaLAPACK [5], which is designed for distributed-memory message-passing (MIMD) computers and networks of workstations. These libraries provide a large set of high-performance routines for carrying out numerous matrix algebra and decomposition tasks. Matrix inversion and rank-revealing QR decomposition along with basic matrix algebraic operations are what we essentially need to implement the decomposition algorithms discussed above, and these are all available in ScaLAPACK library.

In ScaLAPACK, a matrix is distributed according to a block cyclic scheme over a process grid. This distribution scheme provides a means to achieve a good load balance over processes while at the same time making efficient use of block matrix operations provided by the lower level BLAS (Basic Linear Algebra Subroutines) library [3]. The blocking factor, defined as the number of contiguous rows and columns that are stored by a given process, is the optimization parameter here. The larger the blocking factor is, the more benefit is made from the efficiency of BLAS routines, but the worse the load balance will be. Conversely, a small blocking factor will lead to a better load balance while rendering BLAS routines ineffective. In [5], it is argued that a blocking factor of 32 to 64 is optimum for most parallel machines, and in our experiments we have used 32.

Also argued in [5] is that a rectangular process grid is the most beneficial way to structure the parallel machine. Hence, we considered a 2×2 process grid, a 233 MHz DEC Alpha processor residing at each vertex.

The preliminary timing results we have obtained are given in Table 17.1. The results are for a fluid flow example (see Section 17.2.4) with a utilization of 85% and with varying number of fluid sources, n. (Note here that, for the fluid flow model, the number of sources n is also the size of matrix A to be decomposed.) As timing comparisons are insensitive to the type of model considered, we do not consider other examples here. These results indicate appreciable speed-ups

Table 17.1 Timing Comparison of Sequential and Parallel Implementations. The Example is a Fluid Flow Problem with n Fluid Sources. The Times Given are in Seconds, and η is the Speed-Up Factor Defined as the Ratio of the Sequential CPU Time to the Parallel Real Time

n	Sequential CPU Time	Parallel CPU Time	Real Time	η
256	42.02	26.27	87.03	0.48
512	372.2	136.6	293.3	1.30
768	1300	372.0	654.2	1.98
1024	3400	790.5	1235	2.75

even for moderate matrix sizes from 500 to 1.000. One should expect even better speed-ups for larger size problems.

References

[1] N. Akar and K. Sohraby. An invariant subspace approach in M/G/1 and G/M/1-type Markov Chains. *Stochastic Models,* 13(3), 1997.

[2] N. Akar, N.C. Oguz, and K. Sohraby. Matrix-geometric solutions of M/G/1-type Markov chains: a unifying generalized state-space approach. *IEEE J. on Select. Areas in Comm.,* 16(5), 1998.

[3] E. Anderson et al. *LAPACK Users's Guide, 2nd ed.,* 1994. Also available at the URL http://www.netlib.org.

[4] D. Anick, D. Mitra, and M.M. Sondhi. Stochastic theory of a data handling system with multiple sources. *Bell Syst. Tech. J.,* 61, 1871–1894, 1982.

[5] L.S. Blackford et al. *ScaLAPACK Users's Guide,* 1997. Also available at the URL http://www.netlib.org.

[6] C.T. Chen. *Linear System Theory and Design,* Holt, Rinehart and Winston, Inc., New York, 1984.

[7] G.H. Golub and C.F. Van Loan. *Matrix Computations,* The Johns Hopkins University Press, Baltimore, 1989.

[8] D. Heyman, A. Tabatabai, and T.V. Lakshman. Statistical analysis and simulation study of video teleconference traffic in ATM networks. *IEEE Trans. Circuits Syst. Video Technol.*, 2(1), 49–59, 1992.

[9] T. Kailath. *Linear Systems,* Prentice-Hall Inc., Englewood Cliffs, NJ, 1980.

[10] L. Kleinrock. *Queuing Systems Volume 1: Theory,* Wiley-Interscience Publication, 1975.

[11] D. M. Lucantoni, K. S. Meier-Hellstern, and M. F. Neuts. A single-server queue with server vacations and a class of non-renewal arrival processes. *Adv. Appl. Prob.,* 22, 676–705, 1990.

[12] M. F. Neuts. *Matrix-geometric Solutions in Stochastic Models,* Johns Hopkins University Press, Baltimore, MD, 1981.

[13] W. Willinger. Traffic modeling for high-speed networks: theory versus practice. In F. P. Kelly and R. J. Williams, editors, *Stochastic Networks,* Springer-Verlag, Berlin, 1995.

Chapter 18

MRE: A Robust Method of Inference for Finite Capacity Queues[1]

Demetres Kouvatsos, Rod Fretwell and Charalambos Skianis

Computer and Communication Systems Modeling Research Group

Abstract

The information theoretic principle of minimum relative entropy (MRE) is applied, as a method of inference, to the general problem of estimating the finite buffer stationary queue length distribution (*qld*) given, as a prior estimate, the *qld* of the corresponding infinite buffer queue. Following a classical theoretic investigation into necessary and sufficient conditions for "parallel" *qld*s satisfying an explicit buffer size dependent proportionality relationship, the MRE method is shown to yield exact results for particular classes of queues while in all cases the results are asymptotically correct.

18.1 Introduction

Classical queuing theory provides a conventional and powerful framework for formulating and solving models of discrete flow systems such as computer systems, communication networks and flexible manufacturing systems. However, in many cases, simplifying assumptions are employed in order to produce tractable solutions, while approximate methods are required to analyze more complex, and thus, more realistic models. Since the mid-1960s, alternative ideas and tools, analogous to those applied in the field of Statistical Mechanics, have been proposed in the literature [1, 2, 3].

---
[1]This work is supported in part by the Engineering and Physical Sciences Research Council (EPSRC), UK, under grant GR/K/67809.

In this paper, the information theoretic principle of minimum relative entropy (MRE) is applied, as a method of inference [4, 5], to determine the finite buffer stationary queue length distribution (qld) given, as a prior estimate, the qld of the corresponding infinite buffer queue. Over recent years, this principle has been applied towards the analysis of finite queues and arbitrary queuing networks with or without server vacations with generalized exponential (GE) processes, which are completely described by their first two moments (c.f., [6, 7]). At the single infinite GE-type queue level, the MRE solution is exact while at the GE-type network level, relative entropy minimization provides cost-effective queue-by-queue decomposition algorithms (c.f., [6, 7]). These earlier analytic results serve further to establish the MRE inference technique and motivate its application towards the analysis of a wider class of queuing systems and networks with more complex interarrival and service time processes.

Section 18.2 first provides a review of MRE and its formalism and then presents the application of MRE as a method of inference to derive the qld of a finite buffer queue given, as a prior estimate, the corresponding infinite buffer qld.

Section 18.3 describes some finite buffer queues and carries out a classical theoretic investigation into the necessary and sufficient conditions for "parallel" qlds satisfying an explicit buffer size dependent proportionality relationship. These queues provide the examples for Section 18.4 in which the MRE method is demonstrated to yield the exact finite buffer qld given, as a prior estimate, the infinite buffer qld.

Conclusions and the direction of future work are given in Section 18.5.

18.2   Minimum Relative Entropy

Let x be the state of a system with a set D of feasible states. Let D^* be the set of all the probability density functions (pdf) p on D such that $\forall x \in D\ p(x) \geq 0$ and

$$\int_D p(x)\, dx = 1 . \tag{18.1}$$

Suppose that the system under consideration is described by a true but unknown density function $p^* \in D^*$ and that $q \in D^*$ is a prior density that is a current estimate of p^*, such that $\forall x \in D\ q(x) > 0$. In addition, new information for the system places a number of constraints on p^*, in the form of expectations $\{\langle a_i \rangle\}_{i=1}^{k}$ defined on a set $\{a_i(x)\}_{i=1}^{k}$ of k suitable functions, namely

$$\int_D a_i(x) p(x)\, dx = \langle a_i \rangle, \quad i = 1, \ldots, k , \tag{18.2}$$

where k is less than the number of feasible states. Since the above set of constraints (18.1) and (18.2), denoted by $I = (p^* \in \Phi)$, do not determine the form of $p^*(x)$ completely, they are satisfied by a set of *pdf*s $\Phi \subseteq D^*$.

The principle of MRE states that, of all *pdf*s that satisfy constraints I, the least biased one is the posterior *pdf* $p \in \Phi$ that minimizes the relative entropy function $H(p', q)$, $p' \in \Phi$, namely

$$H(p, q) = \min_{p' \in \Phi} H(p', q) = \min_{p' \in \Phi} \int_D p'(x) \log \frac{p'(x)}{q(x)} \, dx \, . \tag{18.3}$$

By applying the Lagrange method of undetermined multipliers the form of the posterior *pdf* is [4, 5]

$$p(x) = e^{-\beta_0} \, e^{-\beta_1 a_1(x)} \ldots e^{-\beta_k a_k(x)} \, q(x) \, , \tag{18.4}$$

where β_0 and $\beta_1, \ldots, \beta_k$ are the Lagrangian multipliers whose values are determined by the constraints (18.1) and (18.2). If the integral in (18.2) is solved analytically, closed form expressions could be derived for $\beta_1, \ldots, \beta_k$ in terms of the mean values $\langle a_1 \rangle, \ldots, \langle a_k \rangle$. When D is a set of discrete system states, densities are replaced by discrete probability mass functions and integrals by sums in the usual way. Note that in the presence of a uniform prior density, the principle of MRE reduces to that of Maximum Entropy [8, 9].

Formally, the relative entropy minimization procedure may be seen as an information operator $\circ$ which takes two arguments, a prior distribution q and new constraint information I of the form (18.1) and (18.2), yielding a posterior MRE distribution p, i.e., $p = q \circ I$. To this end it can be shown that minimizing $H(p, q)$ uniquely determines distribution p, satisfying the four consistency inference criteria [4]. In particular, it has been shown that ME and MRE solutions are uniquely correct distributions and that any other functional used to implement operator $\circ$ will produce the same distribution as the entropy and relative entropy functionals, otherwise it would be in conflict with the consistency criteria.

18.2.1 Inferring Finite Buffer *QLD* from Infinite Buffer *QLD*

Let the finite buffer queue have capacity N and let the stationary *qld* be given by $p_N(n)$, $n = 0, \ldots, N$ for the finite buffer system and by $p_\infty(n)$, $n = 0, 1, \ldots$ for the infinite buffer system.

Let the finite buffer information be given in the form of the following constraints:

Normalization:

$$\sum_{n=0}^{N} p_N(n) = 1 \, ; \tag{18.5}$$

Full buffer state probability $p_N(N) = \varphi, 0 < \varphi < 1$:

$$\sum_{n=0}^{N} f(n) p_N(n) = \varphi, \qquad f(n) = \begin{cases} 0 & n < N, \\ 1 & n = N. \end{cases} \qquad (18.6)$$

Then the MRE solution to the finite buffer *qld* $p_N(\cdot)$, given $p_\infty(n)$ as the prior *qld*, is obtained by minimizing the relative entropy function $H(p_N, p_\infty)$ subject to the finite buffer constraints (18.5) and (18.6). This solution may be determined by applying Lagrange's method of undetermined multipliers and yields the form

$$p_N(n) = \frac{1}{Z_N} p_\infty(n) \, y^{f(n)}, \qquad (18.7)$$

where Z_N is the normalizing constant and y is the Lagrangian coefficient corresponding to constraint (18.6), satisfying the flow balance condition

$$\lambda(1 - \pi) = \mu U, \qquad (18.8)$$

where λ is the mean arrival rate, π is the marginal probability of any customer being blocked, μ is the mean service rate and $U = 1 - p_N(0)$ is the server utilization.

Clearly, MRE solution (18.7) is applicable to both continuous and discrete time domains and, in all cases it is asymptotically correct since as $N \to \infty$, $\pi \to 0$ and from (18.7) and (18.8) it follows that

$$\frac{1}{Z_N} = 1 + \frac{\rho}{1-\rho} \pi \to 1. \qquad (18.9)$$

As a result Eq. (18.7) can now be written as

$$p_N(n) = p_\infty(n) \quad \text{as } N \to \infty. \qquad (18.10)$$

18.3   Queues with "Parallel" Distributions

The stationary *qld* of the M/M/1/N queue is (apart from scale and range) independent of the buffer size N, i.e., if $p_N(n)$ is the marginal probability that the M/M/1/N queue contains n customers then $p_{N+1}(n) = c_N p_N(n)$ for $n = 0, \ldots, N$ and some constant c_N of proportionality. It might be said that the M/M/1/N queue length distribution at one buffer size is "parallel" to that at other buffer sizes.

In the first part of this section some established results on parallel queue length distributions are reviewed. In the queues which are considered, the arrivals exhibit no count correlation. The second part is an investigation into conditions for parallel *qld* in discrete time censored $GI^G/D/1/N$ DF queues, in which arrivals are from a batch renewal process having both count correlation and correlated interarrivals.

18.3.1 $M^G/G/1/N$ and $Geo^G/G/1/N$ Queues

The $M^G/G/1/N$ and $Geo^G/G/1/N$ queues denote single server queuing systems at equilibrium with finite capacity N, general (G) service times and batch Poisson (M^G) and batch Bernoulli (Geo^G) arrival processes, respectively. The arrivals are censored, i.e., it is assumed that all those customers that, upon arrival, find the buffer full are turned away.

It is known [10] that $p_N(n)$ satisfies the following relation for $n = 0, \ldots, N-2$ and all $N > 2$:

$$p_N(n) = \alpha(n)p_N(0) + \sum_{k=0}^{n} \alpha(n-k)p_N(k+1), \qquad (18.11)$$

where $\alpha(n)$ is the probability of n arrivals during a service period. Then, assuming $\alpha(0) > 0$, the ratio $p_N(n)/p_N(0)$ is independent of N given only that $N > 2$. In particular,

$$p_{N+1}(n) = c_N p_N(n) \qquad n = 0, \ldots, N-1, \qquad (18.12)$$

where $c_N = p_{N+1}(0)/p_N(0)$.

18.3.2 $GI^G/D/1/N$ Queues

In a batch renewal arrivals process the intervals between batches of simultaneous arrivals are independent and identically distributed (*iid*) and the batch sizes are iid.

In the discrete time censored $GI^G/D/1/N$ DF queue GI^G denotes a batch renewal arrivals process, the service time is fixed at one slot per customer and an arrival at an epoch may occupy the place being released by a departure at that epoch (DF = "departures first").

The stationary *qld* may be established [11] from consideration of two (related) Markov chains embedded at arrival epochs.

- For the first chain (chain "A"), the state is the number of customers in the queue after allowing for any departure at that epoch but discounting the new arrivals at that epoch. Let $p_N^A(n)$ be the probability that the state is $n, n = 0, \ldots, N-1$ (where N is the capacity of the queue).

- For the second chain (chain "D"), the state is the number of customers in the queue after allowing for any departure at that epoch but including the new arrivals. Let $p_N^D(n)$ be the probability that the state is n, $n = 1, \ldots, N$.

Equivalently, one might treat the departures as *actually* occurring before arrivals and focus on the two points 1) at which the departures have already gone and the arrivals have not yet come, 2) immediately after the arrivals.

Then the two chains are related by

$$
p_N^D(n) = \begin{cases} \displaystyle\sum_{k=0}^{n-1} p_N^A(k)\, b(n-k) & n = 1, \ldots, N-1 \\[2ex] \displaystyle\sum_{k=0}^{N-1} p_N^A(k) \sum_{r=N-k}^{\infty} b(r) & n = N \end{cases} \tag{18.13}
$$

$$
p_N^A(n) = \begin{cases} \displaystyle\sum_{k=1}^{N} p_N^D(k) \sum_{t=k}^{\infty} a(t) & n = 0 \\[2ex] \displaystyle\sum_{k=n+1}^{N} p_N^D(k)\, a(k-n) & n = 1, \ldots, N-1 \end{cases} \tag{18.14}
$$

and the stationary *qld* is given by

$$
p_N(0) = 1 - \frac{1}{a} \sum_{k=0}^{N-1} p_N^A(k) \left(\sum_{r=1}^{N-k} r b(r) + \sum_{r=N-k+1}^{\infty} (N-k) b(r) \right) \tag{18.15a}
$$

and, for $n = 1, \ldots, N$,

$$
p_N(n) = \frac{1}{a} \sum_{k=0}^{n-1} p_N^A(k) \sum_{r=n-k}^{\infty} b(r), \tag{18.15b}
$$

in which $a(t)$ is the *pmf* of intervals between batches with mean a and $b(n)$ is the *pmf* of batch sizes with mean b.

18.3.2.1 Conditions for Parallel GI^G/D/1/N QLD

This subsection addresses conditions under which the property of parallel *qld* may be exhibited in censored GI^G/D/1/N DF queues. To be precise, assume that for some batch renewal process there exist some integer $J \geq 0$ and some constant c_N of proportionality such that

$$
p_{N+1}(n) = c_N p_N(n) \qquad n = 1, \ldots, N-J \tag{18.16}
$$

for all $N > J$, where $p_N(n)$ is the marginal probability that the censored GI^G/D/1/N DF queue contains n customers. Note that parallel queue length distributions may arise in a trivial way if, for example, there is an upper bound B to batch size together with a lower bound $A \geq B$ on interval between batches: in that example, queue length never exceeds B regardless of buffer size. To avoid such trivialities, assume that there be no *taboo* queue lengths, i.e., $p_N(n) > 0$ for all $n = 0, \ldots, N$.

The following analysis shows that relation (18.16) implies conditions on the form of the *pmf* $a(\cdot)$ of the intervals between batches and, for $J = 0$ or $J = 1$, these conditions are sufficient to ensure (18.16).

Using Eq. (18.15b) with $n = 0$ and then by complete induction for $n = 1, \ldots, N-1$ shows that $p_N^A(n)$ is a linear combination of $p_N(1), \ldots, p_N(n+1)$ in which the weights are independent of the buffer size N (although naturally the weights depend upon the batch renewal process). Therefore relation (18.16) implies

$$p_{N+1}^A(n) = c_N p_N^A(n) \qquad n = 0, \ldots, N-J-1 . \tag{18.17}$$

From Eq. (18.13) with $n = 1, \ldots, N-1$, it may be seen that (18.17) implies

$$p_{N+1}^D(n) = c_N p_N^D(n) \qquad n = 1, \ldots, \min(N-J, N-1) . \tag{18.18}$$

Now, using Eq. (18.14) with $n = 1, \ldots, N-1$ gives

$$p_{N+1}^A(n) - c_N p_N^A(n)$$

$$= \sum_{k=n+1}^{N} \left(p_{N+1}^D(k) - c_N p_N^D(k) \right) a(k-n) + p_{N+1}^D(N+1)a(N-n+1) , \tag{18.19}$$

which, together with (18.17) and (18.18) yields

$$0 = \left(p_{N+1}^D(N) - c_N p_N^D(N) \right) a(N-n) + p_{N+1}^D(N+1)a(N-n+1)$$
$$J = 0 \tag{18.20a}$$

$$0 = \sum_{k=N-J+1}^{N} \left(p_{N+1}^D(k) - c_N p_N^D(k) \right) a(k-n) + p_{N+1}^D(N+1)a(N-n+1)$$
$$J > 0 \tag{18.20b}$$

for all $N > J+1$ and for all $n = 1, \ldots, N-J-1$.

Case 1: $J = 0$

Write α_N for $\left(c_N p_N^D(N) - p_{N+1}^D(N) \right) / p_{N+1}^D(N+1)$. Then (18.20a) gives

$$a(N-n+1) = \alpha_N a(N-n) \qquad n = 1, \ldots, N-1 \quad \text{for all } N > 1 \tag{18.21}$$

or, equivalently,

$$a(t) = \alpha_N^{t-1} a(1) \qquad t = 1, \ldots, N . \tag{18.22}$$

However, since the arrivals process does not depend upon the buffer size N, the rate α_N must be the same for all N and, in consequence, the intervals between batches is geometric. In other words, a *necessary* condition for (18.16) to apply with $J = 0$ is that the batch renewal arrivals process be a batch Bernoulli process. But, as is well known, that condition is *sufficient* also.

Case 2: $J = 1$

Equation (18.20b) for $J = 1$ is the same as Eq. (18.20a) for $J = 0$ except for the applicable range for n. Thus

$$a(t) = \alpha_N^{t-2} a(2) \qquad t = 2, \ldots, N \tag{18.23}$$

where, clearly, α_N does not depend upon N. To give Eq. (18.23) in conventional notation, α_N would be written as $1 - \tau$ and $a(2)$ would be written as $\sigma\tau$, i.e.,

$$a(t) = \begin{cases} 1 - \sigma & t = 1 \\ \sigma\tau(1-\tau)^{t-2} & t = 2, 3, \ldots, \end{cases} \tag{18.24}$$

which is a shifted GGeo distribution (i.e., Generalized Geometric shifted by one slot).

That the intervals between batches are distributed as a shifted GGeo is a *sufficient* condition for "parallel" queue length distribution (Eq. (18.16) with $J = 1$) is seen by showing that the form of $p_N^A(\cdot)$ is independent of N and then referring to Eq. (18.15b).

From (18.14) with $a(\cdot)$ given by (18.24),

$$(1-\tau)p_N^A(1) - \tau p_N^A(0) = (1-\sigma-\tau)p_N^D(2) - \tau p_N^D(1) \tag{18.25a}$$

and, for $n = 2, \ldots, N-1$,

$$(1-\tau)p_N^A(n) - p_N^A(n-1) = (1-\sigma-\tau)p_N^D(n+1) - (1-\sigma)p_N^D(n) . \tag{18.25b}$$

Then, utilizing (18.13), Eqs. (18.25a) and (18.25b) yield

$$\left(1-\tau - (1-\sigma-\tau)\right)p_N^A(1) = \left((1-\sigma-\tau)b(2) + \tau - \tau b(1)\right)p_N^A(0) \tag{18.26a}$$

and, for $n = 2, \ldots, N-1$,

$$\left(1-\tau - (1-\sigma-\tau)\right)p_N^A(n) = p_N^A(n-1)$$
$$+ \sum_{k=0}^{n-1}\left((1-\sigma-\tau)b(n-k+1) + (1-\sigma)b(n-k)\right)p_N^A(k) , \tag{18.26b}$$

so there exist $\{c(n)\}_{n=0}^{\infty}$, independent of N, such that

$$p_N^A(n) = c(n)p_N^A(0) . \tag{18.27}$$

Consequently relation (18.17) holds with $c_N = p_{N+1}^A(0)/p_N^A(0)$ and then (18.15b) implies (18.16).

In conclusion, relation (18.23) is a necessary and sufficient condition for the $GI^G/D/1/N$ DF queue length distribution to be "parallel" for $n = 1, \ldots, N-1$ and for all $N > 2$.

Case 3: $J > 1$

From Eq. (18.20b) with $J > 1$ it can be seen that necessary conditions for parallel *qld* include a $J+1$-term recurrence relation in $a(\cdot)$. However, that condition is not sufficient to guarantee parallel *qld*, as is seen from the following example.

Consider a batch renewal process in which the batches are of fixed size K. Then, for all buffers of size N such that $N \le K$, Eq. (18.15b) for the stationary *qld* becomes

$$p_N(n) = \frac{1}{a} \sum_{t=N-n+1}^{\infty} a(t), \quad n = 1, \ldots, N-1, \qquad (18.28)$$

and the "parallel" queue condition (18.16)

$$p_{N+1}(n) = c_N p_N(n) \qquad n = 1, \ldots, N-J$$

then implies

$$a(t) = c_N{}^{t-J-1} a(J+1), \quad t = J+1, \ldots, N, \qquad (18.29)$$

and

$$\sum_{t=K}^{\infty} a(t) = \frac{c_N{}^{K-J-1}}{(1 - c_N)} a(J+1). \qquad (18.30)$$

These conditions are clearly inconsistent with there being a $J+1$-term recurrence relation in $a(\cdot)$ for any $J > 1$.

18.3.3 The MRE Solution for the Queues with "Parallel" Distributions

Focusing on expressions (18.6) and "parallel" relationships (18.12) and (18.16) it is clearly implied that the MRE solution captures the exact *qlds* for the particular classes of queues under investigation.

18.4 Exact MRE Results

18.4.1 $M^G/G/1/N$ and $Geo^G/G/1/N$ Queues

From Eq. (18.7) it is immediate that

$$p_N(n) = \frac{p_N(0)}{p_\infty(0)} \, p_\infty(n) \, y^{f(n)}, \tag{18.31}$$

where $f(n)$ is defined as in (18.6), with $1/Z_N$ given by $p_N(0)/p_\infty(0)$, while the unknown Lagrangian coefficient y can be evaluated by using the set of constraints (18.5) and (18.6) and the flow balance condition (18.8).

18.4.2 sGGeo/D/1/N

A batch renewal process is called a sGGeo process if both the batch sizes and the intervals between batches have shifted GGeo distributions. In this case, both the count covariances and the intervals covariances decline strictly geometrically. The process may be parameterized by the geometric rates β_a and β_b of the count covariances and intervals covariances, respectively, together with the mean batch size b and the mean interval a between batches.

It is known [11] that the stationary qld is given by

$$p_N(n) = \begin{cases} \dfrac{1}{Z_N}(1-\lambda) & n = 0 \\[2ex] \dfrac{1}{Z_N}\lambda\,\dfrac{1-x}{1-\beta_b} & n = 1 \\[2ex] \dfrac{1}{Z_N}\lambda\,\dfrac{b-1}{1-\lambda}\dfrac{1-\beta_a\beta_b}{1-\beta_a}\dfrac{(1-x)^2}{1-\beta_b}x^{n-2} & n = 2,\ldots,N-1 \\[2ex] \dfrac{1}{Z_N}\dfrac{b-1}{a-1}\dfrac{1-x}{1-\beta_a}x^{N-2} & n = N, \end{cases} \tag{18.32}$$

where $\lambda = b/a$,

$$x = 1 - \frac{(1-\lambda)(1-\beta_a)(1-\beta_b)}{(b-1)(1-\beta_a\beta_b) + (1-\lambda)(1-\beta_a)}, \tag{18.33}$$

and the normalizing constant is

$$Z_N = 1 - \frac{b-1}{a-1}x^{N-1}. \tag{18.34}$$

As in the previous example, it is immediately apparent that Eq. (18.32) conforms exactly to the MRE solution (18.7) with

$$y = \frac{x}{1 - x\beta_a}. \tag{18.35}$$

18.5 Conclusions and Future Directions

The principle of MRE is applied, as a method of inference, to the general problem of estimating the finite buffer stationary *qld*, given, as a prior estimate, the *qld* of the corresponding infinite buffer queue. Moreover, focusing on the $M^G/G/1/N$, $Geo^G/G/1/N$ and $GI^G/D/1/N$ queues, a classical theoretic investigation is carried out into the necessary and sufficient conditions for "parallel" *qld*s satisfying an explicit buffer size dependent proportionality relationship. The MRE method is shown to yield exact results for the aforementioned queues, while in all cases the results are asymptotically correct.

The MRE principle provides an interesting information theoretic interpretation of the *qld*s for particular classes of queues. Moreover, it reveals a *qld* of closed form [c.f., (18.7)] – which classical queuing theory does not – in terms of the exact prior distribution estimate and appropriate Lagrangian coefficients. As a consequence, the MRE solution can be used as a cost-effective building block for the approximate analysis of arbitrary queuing networks.

Further work is required both to

- identify more subtle constraints that would give exact finite buffer *qld* for other types of queues with more complex interarrival and service processes, and

- analyze conditions for prescribed degrees of accuracy of approximate MRE solutions applicable to other cases of finite capacity queues where the "parallel" condition does not hold.

References

[1] V.E. Benes, *Mathematical Theory of Connecting Networks and Telephone Traffic,* Academic Press, New York, 1965.

[2] A.E. Ferdinand, A Statistical Mechanical Approach to Systems Analysis, *IBM J. Res. Dev.,* 14, pp. 539–547, 1970.

[3] E. Pinsky, Y. Yemini, A Statistical Mechanics of Some Interconnection Networks, *Performance '84,* North-Holand, pp. 147–158, 1984.

[4] J.E. Shore, R.W. Johnson, Axiomatic Derivation of the Principle of Maximum Entropy and the Principle of Minimum-Cross Entropy, *IEEE Trans. on Information Theory,* vol. IT–26, pp. 26–37, 1980.

[5] J.E. Shore, R.W. Johnson, Properties of Cross Entropy Minimisation, *IEEE Trans. on Information Theory,* vol.IT–27, pp. 472–482, 1981.

[6] D.D. Kouvatsos, Entropy Maximisation and Queuing Network Models, *Annals of Operations Research* 48, pp. 63–126, 1994.

[7] C.A. Skianis, D.D. Kouvatsos, Arbitrary Open Queuing Networks with Server Vacation Periods and Blocking, *Annals of Operations Research,* 79, pp. 143–180, 1998.

[8] E.T. Jaynes, Information Theory and Statistical Mechanics I, *Physical Review,* vol.106, pp. 620–630, 1957.

[9] E.T. Jaynes, Information Theory and Statistical Mechanics II, *Physical Review,* vol.108, pp. 171–190, 1957.

[10] H. Takagi, Queuing Analysis: A Foundation of Performance Evaluation, Volume 2: Finite Systems, North-Holland, 1993.

[11] D.D. Kouvatsos, R. Fretwell, Closed Form Performance Distributions of a Discrete Time $GI^G/D/1/N$ Queue with Correlated Traffic, *Enabling High Speed Networks,* (Ed. S. Fdida and R.O. Onvural), IFIP publication, Chapman and Hall, ISBN 0 412 73250 5, pp. 141–163, October, 1995.

Part IV

Advances in System Performance Methodologies

Chapter 19

PNiQ — A Concept for Performability Evaluation

Matthias Becker and Helena Szczerbicka

University of Bremen

Abstract   Integrated performance and dependability analysis, called *performability,* has been receiving considerable attention in the design of complex, fault-tolerant systems.   We present **P**etri **N**ets **i**ncluding **Q**ueuing Networks (PNiQ) a novel high-level modeling technique, which is particularly appropriate for performability evaluation. The definition integrates concepts of generalized stochastic Petri nets (GSPN) and Queuing Networks on the modeling level and specifies interfaces between them. Steady state solution is based on aggregation of queuing networks and replacing them with GSPN constructs that model the delays of tokens introduced by queuing nets. The resulting GSPN model can be analyzed with state of the art methods and tools. This process can be carried out automatically.   Applicability of PNiQ for evaluation of performability is shown in an example.

Keywords: combined modeling, Petri, queuing, aggregation, performability.

19.1   Introduction

Evaluation of computer and communication systems plays an important role in all phases of their life cycle. Performance typically refers to quality of the system under the assumption that the system is failure free. On the other hand dependability (according to the definition of Laprie [7]) is that property that allows reliance to be justifiably placed on the service it delivers. In the classical view of quantitative system evaluation, performance and dependability have been distinguished. As a consequence, for both performance and dependability different evaluation techniques suited to each concept have been developed. A model-based general framework for evaluation of performance of systems subject to failures or maintenance has been introduced as "performability" in the early eighties by Meyer [8]. Following the definition by Meyer the performability of a system S with performance Y is the probability measure $Perf$ induced by Y where, for any measurable set B of accomplishment levels ($B \subseteq A$), $Perf(B) = P[Y \in B]$ is the probability that S performs at some level in B. Whereby, the performance of S over a specified utilization period T is a random variable Y taking values in a set A. Elements of A are the accomplishment levels (performance outcomes) that might possibly be attained by S. A variety of contributions to methods for evaluation of performability were made during the last period (see [12]). Probably the most significant was to introduce solution methods based on reward models (e.g., [9]). This concept incorporates two processes: reward process and performance process.

In our approach **Petri Nets** including **Queuing** Networks (PNiQ) are used for performability modeling. Queuing nets included in PNiQ allow convenient performance modeling, including concise graphical description of the service station, queue plus queuing discipline, and stochastic routing. Efficient analysis algorithms for large systems have been developed over the years. Dependability aspects like blocking/locking, fork/join, failure, and synchronization can be modeled using the generalized stochastic Petri net (GSPN) part of PNiQ. Our approach furthermore takes the interactions between the different performance levels into account instead of solving isolated performance models for each level of performance.

In the following section we briefly review the literature on combination of GSPN and queuing networks. **Petri Nets** including **Queuing** Nets (PNiQ) are introduced formally as well as by example. Then we describe a steady state solution algorithm. The approach uses efficient queuing net analysis algorithms and notation where possible and GSPN notation where needed. Finally, an example of a performability model of a manufacturing system is given to demonstrate the applicability of PNiQ.

19.2   Related Approaches

If a system cannot be modeled by queuing nets (for instance if fork/join operations must be modeled), performance analysis of the queuing net-model is often extended directly by a continuous time Markov chain CTMC [5] or combined with GSPN, which offer a graphical description for such operations and allow automated generation of the underlying CTMC. There are some examples for the combination of GSPN and queuing nets as a solution for special modeling problems (as in [1, 11]), mostly based on replacing one type of net by a flow-equivalent. However, neither a general definition of a combined net structure nor a methodological modeling and solution approach, which would allow easy and correct modeling of other problems, is given. The underlying model of the Dynamic Queuing Network [6] concept is a Markov reward model. Rewards are calculated in parameterized queuing models and used for the generation of the state space of the Markov reward model. The performability model of a Dynamic Queuing Network consists of separate models for dependability and performance. Bause developed Queuing Petri Nets [2], where in special places called *queuing places* a queuing discipline can be modeled, according to which tokens are being served. Differing from our approach, the solution is based on the solution of the derived CTMC. Therefore the complexity of large models still remains a problem. Moreover neither existing algorithms for analysis of queuing nets nor the graphical description of queuing *networks* are exploited.

19.3 Combined Modeling

The goal of the PNiQ concept is to provide a formalism for the aggregation of queuing nets in GSPN. Combined modeling and analysis of general systems with PNiQ is possible for modelers without prior knowledge of the technique of aggregation. Informally a PNiQ is a live and bounded GSPN extended by a third node type, which represents mono-class queuing networks consisting of a number of queues. Tokens from the GSPN can enter a queuing net from transitions at one specific queue called the *input queue* of the queuing net. Tokens in one queuing net can move from queue to queue within this net or to places of the GSPN or to input queues of other queuing nets. Inhibitor arcs can be input or output arcs of a whole queuing net as well. Next, the formal definition of a PNiQ is given. A PNiQ is a tuple $(P, T, S, I, O, H, W, \Pi, m_0)$ where

- P is the set of places, T is the set of transitions.

- S is the set of mono-class queuing nets.
  Each queuing net $qn_i \in S$ consists of

    · a set of queues $Q_i = \{q_{i,0}, \ldots, q_{i,k_i}\}$,
      $q_{i,0}$ is called *input queue*, $k_i + 1$ is the number of queues in qn_i.
      The type of queues which may be used depends on the analysis algorithm.

    · $Q^0 := \{q_{i,0} | i = 1, \ldots, |S|\}$ is the set of all input queues.

    · $Q := \bigcup_i Q_i$ is the set of all queues.

> · $p_i(x, y)$; $q_{i,x}, q_{i,y} \in qn_i$ are the routing probabilities within qn_i.
> $p_i(x, p)$; $q_{i,x} \in qn_i$, $p \in (P \cup Q^0)$ are the routing probabilities
> that a job leaves qn_i after service at queue $q_{i,x}$ and moves into place
> or input queue p.
> r_i is the number of queues from which tokens can leave qn_i. These
> queues are referred to as *output queues*.

- $I : T \rightarrow bag(P)$ is the input function

  (arcs from places to transitions).

- $O : T \cup Q \rightarrow bag(P) \cup Q^0$ is the output function (represented by arcs
  from transitions and queues to places and input queues).

- $H : T \cup S \rightarrow bag(P \cup S)$ is the inhibition function (circle-headed arcs
  from places or queuing nets to transitions or queuing nets).

- $W : T \rightarrow \mathbf{R}$ defines the negative exponentially distributed firing rate in
  the case of timed transitions and the "weight" in the case of immediate
  transitions.

- $\Pi : T \cup Q \rightarrow \mathbf{N}$ is the priority function. Timed transitions and queues
  have priority level 0, immediate transitions have a priority level > 0.

- $m_0 : P \cup S \rightarrow \mathbf{N}$ is the initial marking. The initial marking of a queuing
  net is defined as the initial *total* number of tokens in the queuing net.

From the definition of the output function it follows that arcs from transitions
or queues to the input queue have multiplicity one. That means that tokens from
transitions or queues may enter a queuing net one by one at only one queue, the
input queue. From a queue a served token can proceed to only *one* destination
out of several possibilities given by the routing probabilities. That is, queues
cannot double tokens in the sense that for one served token two tokens are sent
to *different* destinations like transitions can do. Furthermore it follows that
arcs from queues to places have two labels, the arc multiplicity and the routing
probability. If such an arc has a multiplicity greater than one, then for every
token which leaves the queue to a place, a number of tokens according to the
multiplicity is placed in the destination place.

The explanation of the semantics of the inhibition function is the following:
If an inhibitor arc from a queuing net to a transition exists, then the transition
can only fire if the total population of the queuing net is strictly below the arc
multiplicity of the inhibitor arc. If a queuing net is inhibited by an inhibitor arc,
then no token in the queuing net can be moved, every action within the queuing
net is inhibited. The initial marking of a queuing net denotes the initial total
population of the queuing net. The initial distribution of these tokens among
the queues of one queuing net is not relevant for the behavior of the PNiQ.
Some arcs are forbidden by the definition of a PNiQ, e.g., arcs from a place to

a queue, arcs from a queue to a transition, and inhibitor arcs from or to a single queue are not allowed.

19.4 Analysis

The structure of a PNiQ allows one to perform an efficient steady state quantitative analysis and also to use techniques for structural analysis known from Petri nets. First the informal idea of the analysis is introduced: The combined model is transformed into a pure GSPN in which the queuing nets are substituted by GSPN subnets. These GSPN subnets are said to be *flow equivalent* to the queuing nets, because the subnet models the delay that the flow of tokens experiences in the queuing net. The flow equivalent GSPN subnet for a queuing net qn_i consists of one input place ip_i, one output place op_i, $r = 1, \ldots, r_i$ immediate routing transitions $rt_{i,r}$, and one timed transition fet_i with marking dependent firing rate. The firing rate equals the throughput of the queuing net containing a certain number of jobs and depends on the number of tokens of the input place. The number of tokens in ip_i represents the population of qn_i. The tokens leaving qn_i are gathered in op_i. They can leave the output place by immediate routing transitions $rt_{i,r}$ whose weights are adjusted according to the visit ratio and routing probabilities of output queue r. The visit ratio of an output queue is the same for different populations of the queuing net, therefore the weights of routing transitions are not marking-dependent. Immediate transitions do not contribute to the size of the state space. Even if complex dependencies or control structures are modeled with immediate transitions in the GSPN–part of a PNiQ this does not increase the computational complexity as much as the complex graphical appearance of this structures might suggest. The substitution of a subnet by a flow equivalent is only exact in product form queuing nets, but based on the concept of near-independence the error of the substitution in non-product form nets is expected to be small in many cases [4].

Next we show formally how the substitution of the queuing net is done. In order to solve the PNiQ for steady state, the GSPN PN' is derived from PNiQ $(P, T, S, I, O, H, W, \Pi, m_0)$ by substitution of the queuing net by GSPN elements:

$$PN' = (P', T', I', O', H', W', \Pi', m_0') \text{ with}$$

- $P' = P \cup \{ip_i | i = 1, \ldots, |S|\} \cup \{op_i | i = 1, \ldots, |S|\}$ is the set of places extended by one input place ip_i and one output place op_i for each qn_i.

- $T' = T \cup \{fet_i | i = 1, \ldots, |S|\} \cup \{rt_{i,r} | i = 1, \ldots, |S|, r = 1, \ldots, r_i\}$ is the set of transitions extended by one flow equivalent transition (fet_i) and immediate routing transitions ($rt_{i,r}$) for each qn_i.

- $I' = I \cup \{(fet_i, ip_i)|$ for $i = 1, \ldots, |S|\} \cup \{(rt_{i,r}, op_i)|i = 1, \ldots, |S|, r = 1, \ldots, r_i\}$.

- $O' =$
  $\{O|O \in (T \times bag(P))\}$
  $\cup \{(t, ip_i)|(t, q_{i,0}) \in O, t \in T, q_{i,0}\} \in Q^0 \cup \{(rt_{i,r}, ip_l)|(q_{i,r}, q_{l,0}) \in O\}$
  $\cup \{(fet_i, op_i)|i = 1, \ldots, |S|\}$ $\cup \{(rt_{i,r}, p)|(q_{i,r}, p) \in O, p \in P\}$.

- $H' =$
  $\{H|H \in (T \times bag(P))\}$ $\cup \{(fet_i, ip_j)|(qn_i, qn_j) \in H\}$
  $\cup \{(fet_i, p)|(qn_i, p) \in H, p \in P\} \cup \{(t, ip_i)|(t, qn_i) \in H, t \in T\}$.

- $W' : T' \to \mathbf{R}$
  The population dependent firing rate of fet_i is:
  $W'(fet_i,$ if $\#ip_i = k) := \lambda_i(k), i = 1, \ldots, |S|, k = 1, \ldots, maxpop_i$
  where $\lambda_i(k)$ is the mean throughput of qn_i with a total population of k and $maxpop_i$ is the maximal population of qn_i.
  The weights of the routing transitions are calculated according to:
  $W'(rt_{i,r}) := e_{i,r} \cdot p(q_{i,r}, p_r)$. $p_r \in (P \cup Q^0)$ is the place or queue to which the tokens leave from output queue $q_{i,r}$. (The calculation of $e_{i,r}$, $\lambda_i(k)$ and $maxpop_i$ is explained later.)

- $\Pi' : T' \to \mathbf{N}$ is the priority function.
  $\Pi'(fet_i) = 0, \Pi'(rt_{i,j}) = 1, i = 1, \ldots, |S|, j = 1, \ldots, k_i$.

- $m_0' : P' \to \mathbf{N}$ is the initial marking.
  $m_0'(ip_i) := m_0(qn_i), m_0'(op_i) := 0, i = 1, \ldots, |S|$.

19.4.1   Analysis Algorithm

First the PNiQ is transformed into a GSPN PN' according to Section 19.4 without the calculation of the weight function W'. Then the P-invariants of PN' are determined, which can be done without knowing W'. The maximal population of qn_i is calculated from the P-invariants containing fet_i:

$$maxpop_i = \min\{k \mid fet_i \in \text{P-invariant, which is k-bounded}\}.$$

Then each qn_i is analyzed in isolation as closed queuing net from population $k = 1, \ldots, maxpop_i$ by short-cutting qn_i. Short-cutting means that a token that leaves qn_i from an output queue, reenters qn_i immediately at the input queue $q_{i,0}$. This is done by setting the routing probabilities $p_i(r, 0) := p_i(r, p_r)$, for all output queues $q_{i,r}, r = 1, \ldots, r_i$, of qn_i and $p_r \in (P \cup S)$. From the analysis of the shortcut queuing net we get the population dependent throughputs $\lambda_i(k)$ of each qn_i and visit ratios $e_{q_{i,j}}$ of each queue $q_{i,j} \in qn_i$. Now the values of

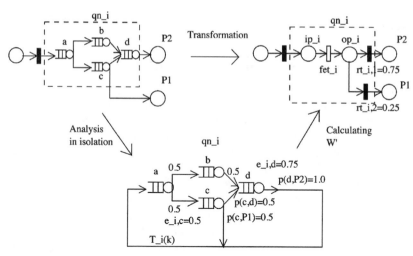

FIGURE 19.1
Illustration of the analysis algorithm.

W' can be calculated according to Section 19.4:

$$W'(fet_i, \text{ if } \#ip_i = k) := \lambda_i(k) \,.$$
$$W'(rt_{i,r}) := e_{i,r} \cdot p(q_{i,r}, p_r) \,.$$

PN' is now completely defined and structural and quantitative analysis can be done with any tool which can handle population dependent firing rates. Figure 19.1 gives an overview of the analysis procedure. Steady state analysis of PN' yields the throughput of transitions, the average population of places and the probability of finding k tokens in place p, $P(\#p = k)$. Therefore $P(\#ip_i = k)$ is the probability of finding a population of k in qn_i. Modeling with PNiQ preserves the capabilities of qualitative analysis exhibited in GSPNs. Since queuing nets in PNiQ preserve the number of tokens (in fact they play a role of delay), the structural properties of the PNiQ are the same as the resulting GSPN after replacement of queuing nets. We can analyze structural properties of the resulting GSPN to check whether the PNiQ model correctly represents the modeled system. For calculation of the performability we can transform the Meyer definition $Perf = \sum_{A_j} \sum_{B_i \in A_j} P[Y \in B_i] \cdot R_j$ into $Perf = \sum_{B_i} P(B_i) \cdot R'_i$, since we do not regard separate models for each performance level. $P(B_i)$ denotes the steady state probability of marking B_i, R'_i is the reward in this particular marking with $B_i \in A_j$, A_j is the corresponding accomplishment level.

19.5   Application Example of the Modeling Concept

In this section we illustrate the applicability of PNiQs for performability evaluation by an example from manufacturing systems. We consider a so–called kanban system consisting of three manufacturing cells where parts enter the system, pass through cell one and then either go through cell two or three and finally the finished parts exit. The kanban mechanism is a scheme for coordination of parts between the cells, where parts leaving a production cell trigger the production of new parts in the directly preceding production cell. Production control by kanban cards was first implemented by Toyota in Japan [10] and meanwhile is widely used all over the world. Figure 19.2 shows the corresponding PNiQ model of a kanban system in its initial marking. The system consists of three production cells. Within the system a number of pallets given in place P1 circulates. We assume infinite supply of raw parts, therefore every pallet in P1 means that a raw part is ready for entering the line. In each cell buffer space is a limited resource. Kanbans (literally: cards) circulate within each cell and control the inventory: Whenever a pallet wants to enter a cell, a free kanban must be available in the bulletin board (places BB1, BB2, BB3) of the cell. Only when a free kanban (= token in bulletin board) is available, the kanban is attached to the pallet and the pallet can enter the cell. The pallet proceeds through the cell and when it leaves the cell, the kanban returns to the bulletin board. The production steps in each cell are modeled by a product form queuing network. Some pallets proceed through cell one and two and return to P1 after the finished products are removed. In cell one a certain percentage of pallets leave cell one and proceed to cell three, where the parts undergo a different final production step.

Cells of a system can fail. A faulty cell is then switched off. Parts arriving at a faulty cell are then rerouted and distributed among non-faulty cells. For simplicity let us assume that only cell three is subject to failure. If a token is present in place "Failure," then cell three fails, where all machines are stopped. Parts waiting for admittance to cell three are rerouted to cell two, which takes a certain amount of time modeled by transition "Back." If cell three operates correctly the token in place "OK" inhibits transition "Back" so that no rerouting can occur. Transition "repair" models the duration of repair while "fail" models the time between two failure occurrences. Notice that the kanban system cannot be modeled with queuing networks because fork and join operations are required. When using GSPN to model the kanban system only small systems can be studied due to state space explosion. We study the influence of the mean time between failures on the performability (in terms of throughput) of the kanban system.

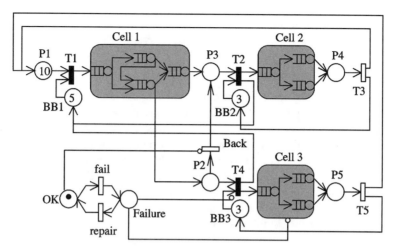

FIGURE 19.2
PNiQ model of a kanban system with failures.

19.6 Results

We analyzed the PNiQ from Fig. 19.2 for different values of the mean time between failures and compared the results with the results obtained from an exact GSPN model where the queues were modeled by a place, and a transition, the stochastic routing between the queues, was modeled by immediate transitions where the weights were set accordingly to the routing probabilities. The queuing discipline can assumed to be random, since no order of service is defined in a GSPN. We examined the approximation error which is inherent in the analysis algorithm of a PNiQ. After substituting the queuing nets the PNiQ model has 10304 tangible markings and one evaluation takes about 10 seconds, whereas the exact GSPN model has 330750 tangible markings and takes about 9 minutes on the same computer for obtaining the results. Note that the reduction of number of states is achieved without generating the complete state space of the exact solution. The reachability set of the exact GSPN model could not be generated for just a few more tokens in the initial marking whereas this is no problem using the PNiQ model. The base for a quantitative evaluation is the steady state distribution of markings of the GSPN model after elimination of queuing sub-models. The system operates at two performance levels $A_j; j = 0, 1$ (corresponding to on/off state of cell three). The performability of the system is characterized by its throughput λ, which can be computed as the firing rate of the transition "T1:"

$$\lambda = \sum_{B_i} P(B_i) \cdot W_i = \sum_{B_i} P(B_i) \cdot R_i' = Perf.$$

B_i are the markings in which the transition "T1" is enabled and W_i the weight of the transition in this marking (in our example $W_i = R_i' = 1$ for all i).

The throughput of the transition "Back" was selected as another performability measure of the system. This measure evaluates the process of rerouting of pallets after the failure of cell three. Table 19.1 shows the throughput of the whole system measured at "T1" and of the transition "Back" for the GSPN and the PNiQ for increasing time between failures. In the last two columns the relative error is given, which is remarkably low. We can observe that increasing the mean time between failures has almost linear effect on the rates of pallets which are re-routed (throughput of transition "Back").

Table 19.1   Results

Time betw. fail.	GSPN		PNiQ		% rel.err.	
	overall thr.	thr. Back	overall thr.	thr. Back	all	Back
25	0.7191	0.08508	0.7087	0.08491	1.45	0.20
50	0.7547	0.05299	0.7427	0.05299	1.59	0.00
100	0.7797	0.03017	0.7665	0.03021	1.69	0.13
200	0.7948	0.01620	0.7809	0.01623	1.75	0.19

19.7   Conclusion

We presented a formalism which describes the integration of GSPN and queuing net concepts especially suitable for performability modeling and analysis. All possible performance levels are part of the PNiQ model, transitions between performance levels are included as well. The approach allows modeling of the performance parts of systems with the concise description of queuing nets, which can be analyzed fast with available solution techniques. Dependability structures are modeled with GSPN elements. By providing a well defined interface between GSPN and queuing nets consistent modeling is achieved by PNiQ while the aggregation procedure for steady state analysis is transparent for the user. A further advantage is the possibility of qualitative analysis of the system (for deadlock, live-lock, boundedness, etc) using GSPN analysis algorithms.

Our approach allows to model large systems more concisely and makes larger systems analytically tractable. The advantage of our approach is its feasibility with regard to solution algorithms. Our method has proved to be a tool for practical, automated performability evaluation in several applications (e.g., [3]). Furthermore different solution methods and tools for GSPN and queuing nets can be integrated easily in our algorithm because of its clear modular structure. Future research is devoted to formalize the integration of multi-class queuing nets in GSPN and to provide a tool support for modeling and analysis.

References

[1] G. Balbo, S. C. Bruell, and S. Ghanta. Combining queuing networks and generalized stochastic Petri nets for the solution of complex models of system behavior. *IEEE Trans. Computers,* 37(10), 1251–1268, 1988.

[2] F. Bause. Queuing Petri nets: A formalism for the combined qualitative and quantitative analysis of systems. In *Proc. 5th International Workshop on Petri Nets and Performance Models,* pages 14–23, Toulouse, France, October 1993. IEEE-Computer Society Press.

[3] M. Becker and H. Szczerbicka. Modeling and optimization of ON/OFF-sources transmitting data over an unreliable network. In *Proc. IEEE Int. Conf. on Systems, Man and Cybernetics,* San Diego, USA, October 1998.

[4] P. Courtois. Decomposability, instabilities, and saturation in multiprogramming systems. *Communication of the ACM,* 18, 371–376, 1975.

[5] S. L. De Araújo, Y. Frein, and M. Di Mascolo. Efficient procedures for the design of kanban systems. *International Conference on Industrial Engineering and Production Management,* 1993.

[6] B. Haverkort and I. Niemegeers. Using dynamic queuing networks for performability modelling. *Proceedings of the European Simulation Multiconference 1990,* pages 184–191, 1990.

[7] J.-C. Laprie. Dependability: A unifying concept for reliable computing and fault tolerance. In T. Anderson, editor, *Dependability of Resilient Computers,* pages 1–28. BSP Professional Books, 1998.

[8] J. Meyer. On evaluating the performability of degradable computing systems. *IEEE Trans. Comput.,* 29(8), 720–731, 1980.

[9] J. Meyer. Closed form solutions of performability. *IEEE Trans. Comput.,* 31(7), 648–657, 1982.

[10] Y. Sugimori, K. Kusunoki, F. Cho, and S. Uchikawa. Toyota production system and kanban system materialization of just–in–time and respect–for–human system. *International Journal of Production Research,* 15(6), 553–564, 1977.

[11] H. Szczerbicka. A combined queuing network and stochastic Petri-net approach for evaluating the performability of fault-tolerant computer systems. *Performance Evaluation,* 14, 217–226, 1992.

[12] K. Trivedi, R. Sahner, and A. Puliafito. *Performance and reliability analysis of computer systems,* Kluwer Academic Publishers, 1996.

Vitae

Matthias Becker was born in Germany, in 1970. He received his diploma degree in computer science from the University of Würzburg, Germany in 1996. Since November 1996 he has worked as a Ph.D. student at the University of Bremen, Germany. His research interests comprise analysis and simulation of combined queuing nets and Petri nets, and analysis and simulation of JIT manufacturing systems.

Helena Szczerbicka received her M.S. in applied Mathematics and her Ph.D. in Computer science from the Technical University of Warsaw, Poland in 1974 and 1982, respectively. From 1985 to 1995 she has been with the Faculty of Computer Science at the University of Karlsruhe, Germany. Since 1994 she has worked as professor at the University of Bremen, Germany. Her research interests include performance and dependability modeling of computer systems, Petri nets, queuing networks, and simulation.

Chapter 20

Performance Analysis of Multiclass Data Transfer Elements in Soft Real-Time Systems Using Semaphore Queues[1]

Carlos Juiz and Ramon Puigjaner
Universitat de les Illes Balears

Harry G. Perros
North Carolina State University

Abstract   Usually, design methods for soft real-time systems do not provide any help in performance analysis and estimation of the system which is being designed. For this reason the main proposal of this paper is how can they be extended to cope with this subject. This paper presents several approximate analytical models of performance software elements, called multiclass channels and pools. These elements are used in the construction of large real-time software systems to complement automatically the system design, in order to obtain the desired average estimates for the soft real-time constraints.

Keywords: soft real-time systems design, multiclass data transfer elements, performance analysis, decomposition, semaphore queues.

20.1 Introduction

Real-time systems are those of which logical reliability is based on their correctness of the outputs and timeliness. A hard real-time system is a system

---

[1]This research is partially supported by CICYT under project number TIC96-0513, UNESCO code 120318.

that must satisfy explicit or bounded response-time constraints or risk severe consequences, including failure or human accidents [4]. Otherwise, in soft real-time systems some responsiveness is required, but deadlines are not critical as in the hard real-time systems. Soft real-time systems are normally defined as those which are having performance constraints on several time measures like response time, throughput or utilization of their components. Unfortunately, these constraints are considered only during the testing phase if conventional design and implementation techniques are used. Therefore, it might be worth-while to consider the savings on design effort and backtracking that can be achieved if performance modeling techniques were included during the early steps of the design process.

This paper includes several kinds of performance multiclass models of soft real-time elements, called Pools and Multiclass Channels. In every element a proposed approximate analytical model is provided, in which some numerical exactitude is given up in front to the exact known classical solution to reach to the simulated behavior, achieving quite balanced performance with faster execution.

20.2   Data Transfer Elements: Channels and Pools

A common operation in Soft Real-time systems is to transfer data between tasks without any need for task synchronization. Such data movements can be unidirectional or bi-directional, selective or non-selective. These requirements of communication have led to the use of two data transfer methods: Pools, for non-selective data transfer and Channels, for selective data transfer [8].

A Channel forms a pipe to carry data between tasks. The Channel itself provides temporary storage of the data. Thus, a simple channel is a data structure that consists of one buffer with two processes: the producer that puts information in the buffer if some slot is empty and the consumer that gets information from the buffer if anyone is available. The rules regarding this element are: (i) random arrival of petitions to put information in the buffer; (ii) one consumer that, immediately after getting an information from the buffer, tries to get another one; (iii) buffer of defined and finite size; (iv) consumer waits when the buffer is empty; (v) producer waits when the buffer is full; (vi) subsequent productions wait when the consumer is writing or held up. Items in the buffer are read in a FIFO manner. Insertion and extraction are done asynchronously. A simple Channel representation using Mascot method [1] is shown in Fig. 20.1.

The Pool is a data storage which can be written to and/or read from by any task, and at any time. It is a means of sharing data between a number of tasks. Senders write information into the store and receivers read such stored

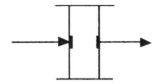

FIGURE 20.1
Channel.

information as a unit. Thus writers and readers need have no knowledge of each other. Reading has no effect on the stored data, however, writing is a destructive operation. Moreover, Pool usage is random. It is impossible to predict in advance when tasks will access the data. A Basic Pool representation in Mascot method is shown in Fig. 20.2.

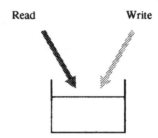

FIGURE 20.2
Pool.

20.3 Semaphore Queues

The Multiclass Channels and Pools modeling is based on the semaphore queue paradigm. A Basic Channel model is analyzed using the algorithm in [6] developed to study the window mechanism for the traffic control in a communication network. In this section, we describe Basic Channel model. This is generalized in later sections.

The management of a shared resource can be carried out efficiently using a semaphore. A semaphore station S consists of an input queue $f(S)$ (customer queue) and a token queue $e(S)$ (resource queue). A customer arriving at the semaphore queue requests a token. The customer departs immediately if there is a token available in queue $e(S)$. Otherwise, the customer is blocked and is forced to wait in the input queue $f(S)$ until a token becomes available. Therefore, if there are tokens in $e(S)$, then there are no customers in the input queue. On the other hand, if there are customers in the input queue, then $e(\mathbf{S})$ is empty.

A customer having received a token, leaves the input queue and enters the producer, as shown in Fig. 20.3. When it finally departs from the producer queue, the token is returned back to the token queue via the consumer. The total number of tokens available is C (the buffer capacity). At any time, the number of customers in the producer and the consumer is less than or equal to C. Producer and consumer are assumed to be both of the BCMP type (FIFO exponential). Customers arrive at the semaphore queue in a Poisson fashion at rate λ.

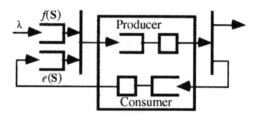

FIGURE 20.3
Semaphore queue in a Basic Channel.

In Fig. 20.3 symbols commonly used in Petri nets [2] are introduced in order to depict the fork and join operations. In particular, the join symbol of Fig. 20.4 depicts the following operation. At the instant that queues $f(\mathbf{S})$ and $e(\mathbf{S})$ contain a customer, both instantaneously depart from their respective queues and merge into a single customer. The fork symbol depicts the following operation. A customer arriving at this point is split into two siblings. These two symbols are used for descriptive convenience.

FIGURE 20.4
Join and fork operations.

An exact analysis of the network depicted in Fig. 20.3 is rather difficult. Therefore, it is proposed to analyze it using decomposition and aggregation [5]. In particular, the system shown in Fig. 20.4 is first analyzed assuming that the arrival process at queue $e(\mathbf{S})$ is described by a state dependent arrival rate $\gamma(k)$.

This queuing system depicts the semaphore operation described above. The arrival process at queue $f(\mathbf{S})$ is assumed to be Poisson distributed and there are C tokens. It is also assumed that the interarrival times available at queue $e(\mathbf{S})$ are exponentially distributed with a rate $\gamma(k)$ where k is the number of outstanding tokens, i.e., $C - k$ is the number of tokens in queue $e(\mathbf{S})$. The state of the system in equilibrium can be described by the tuple (i, j) where i is the number of customers in queue $f(\mathbf{S})$ and j is the number of tokens in queue $e(\mathbf{S})$. The rate diagram associated with this system is shown in Fig. 20.5.

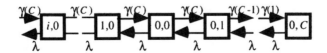

FIGURE 20.5
Birth-and-death rate diagram.

It is noticeable that this system is a birth-and-death process with an arrival rate λ and a state dependent service rate $\gamma(k)$ if $k \leq C$ and $\gamma(C)$ if $k > C$ where k is the number of customers in this queue. The random variables, i and j, are related to k as follows: $i = \max(0, k - C)$ and $j = \max(0, C - k)$. The solution of this system is obtained by a direct application of classical results. Thus,

$$p(i, 0) = \rho^i p(0, 0) \tag{20.1}$$

$$p(0, j) = \frac{\Pi(j)}{\lambda^j} p(0, 0) \tag{20.2}$$

where $\rho = \lambda/\gamma(C)$ and

$$\Pi(j) = \left\{ \begin{array}{ll} \prod_{k=0}^{j-1} \gamma(C - k) & j > 0 \\ 1 & j = 0 \end{array} \right\}. \tag{20.3}$$

The probability $p(0, 0)$ is chosen so that the equilibrium state probabilities add up to 1:

$$p(0, 0)^{-1} = \frac{1}{1 - \rho} + \sum_{j=1}^{C} \frac{\Pi(j)}{\lambda^j}. \tag{20.4}$$

However, all these expressions have been obtained assuming that $\gamma(k)$ is known. This can be approximately obtained by studying the closed queuing network of the producer and consumer as shown in Fig. 20.6. The analysis of this queuing network can be carried out easily since it has been assumed that this network is of the BCMP type. Therefore, the throughput of this network can be computed for different values of k, the number of customers, where $k = 1, 2, \ldots, C$.

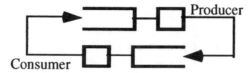

FIGURE 20.6
Closed queuing network.

Finally, this throughput is set equal to the arrival rate $\gamma(k)$ of tokens at the token queue $e(\mathbf{S})$. The solution existence condition is $\lambda < \gamma(k)$ where $\gamma(k)$ is the maximum throughput and $\rho < 1$.

20.4   Multiclass Channel

The simplest multiclass channel has the same data structure as the basic channel but the customers belongs to different classes [7]. This means that different customer classes could have different service requirements for the producer or the consumer. It also means that the customers could arrive to the input queue with different arrival rate per class. The remaining rules regarding the Multiclass Channel are the same of Section 20.3.

As in the Basic Channel, a semaphore station is used with different classes of customers. In order to simplify the presentation, first we consider two customer classes, and then we generalize it to $R \geq 2$ number of classes. Therefore, if only two classes are considered, customers arrive at the semaphore queue in a Poisson fashion at the rates λ_1 and λ_2, respectively.

As in the Basic Channel, an exact analysis of the network depicted is a great difficulty. In consequence it is proposed to analyze it using decomposition and aggregation. In particular, the structure of the solution changes due to the growing of the states space. It is also assumed that the interarrival times at queue $e(\mathbf{S})$ are exponentially distributed with a rate $\gamma(k, l)$ where k is the number of outstanding tokens used by class 1 customers and l is the number of outstanding tokens used by class 2 customers, i.e., $C - (k + l)$ is the number of tokens in queue $e(\mathbf{S})$, although there is no distinction between tokens since they are representing empty slots in the buffer. The state of the system in equilibrium could be described by the tuple (i, j, k, l) where i and j would be the number of customers for each class in queue $f(\mathbf{S})$ and k and l would be the number of outstanding tokens for each class, respectively.

Figure 20.7 shows the marginal states within the extended states of the semaphore queue, where every marginal state belonging to a diagonal has the same number of tokens. Let's define $F = i + j$ as the total number of customers in the input queue and $E = k+l$, the total number of outstanding tokens. Only outstanding tokens are represented because every token accompanies a customer in the producer queue (join), and there are only tokens at consumer queue (fork).

If Fig. 20.7 is observed, the initial state, where $F = 0$ and $E = C$, can be found, i.e., $i + j = 0$ and $k + l = C$. This state is either $(0, 0)$ in Fig. 20.8, or the diagonal $E = C$ in Fig. 20.7 where there are $C + 1$ marginal states, from $(C, 0)$ to $(0, C)$; as a result there are $C + 1$ different configurations of buffer full condition that force a new calculation of $\gamma(C)$.

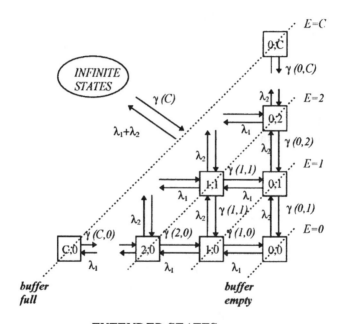

FIGURE 20.7
Rate diagram of the extended states.

This system of diagonals is a birth-and-death process with an arrival rate $\lambda = \lambda_1 + \lambda_2$ and a state dependent service rate $\gamma(k, l)$ if $k + l \leq C$ and $\gamma(C) = \sum \gamma(k, l)/C + 1$ if $k + l > C$, where $k + l$ is the number of customers in this queue. Therefore, the basic solution of Basic Channel can be applied.

Thus,

$$P(F, 0) = \rho^F P(0, 0) \tag{20.5}$$

$$P(0, C - E) = \Pi(E)P(0, 0) \tag{20.6}$$

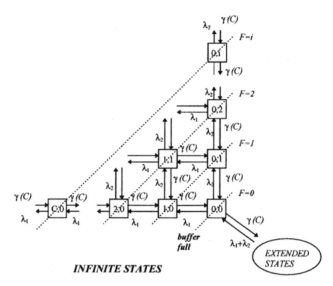

FIGURE 20.8
Rate diagram of the infinite states.

where $i + j = F$, $\rho = (\lambda_1 + \lambda_2)/\gamma(C)$ and

$$\Pi(m) = \begin{cases} \displaystyle\prod_{n=0}^{m-1} \Delta(C - n), m > 0 \\ 1, m = 0 \end{cases} \qquad (20.7)$$

$$\Delta(E) = \frac{1}{E} \left[\sum_{k=1, l=E-k}^{E-1} \gamma(k, l) + \frac{\lambda_1 \gamma(C, 0) + \lambda_2 \gamma(0, C)}{\lambda_1 + \lambda_2} \right]. \qquad (20.8)$$

As in the previous section, the probability $P(0, 0)$ is chosen so that the balance state probabilities add up to 1:

$$P(0, 0)^{-1} = \frac{1}{1 - (\rho_1 + \rho_2)} + \sum_{m=1}^{C} \frac{\Pi(m)}{(\lambda_1 + \lambda_2)^m}. \qquad (20.9)$$

Now every $P(F, E)$ can be derived from these formulas. Although to solve the queue length per class, the marginal probabilities $p(k, l)$ should be known. Thus, for extended states, $P(0, 0)$ is the probability of being in diagonal $E = C$ or the buffer full condition. Hence, for extended states, $P(0, C) = p(0, 0)$ and in every diagonal

$$p(k + l, 0) + \ldots + p(k - l, l) + \ldots + p(0, l) = P(0, k + l)$$

where $p(k, l)$ is the marginal probability of having k class 1 customers and l class 2 customers in the buffer.

In order to compute the mean queue length per class at extended part, it is only necessary either to solve global balance equations of marginal probabilities $p(k, l)$ or to assume local balance between diagonals on Fig. 20.8, if $\gamma(k, l) = \gamma(l, k)$. In this last case, every marginal probability within a diagonal is derived from the previous diagonal, beginning with $P(0, C) = p(0, 0)$ until $E = C$. The calculations are made taking into account the throughput relations of every marginal state due to the regularity flow between diagonals. In any case, let the mean queue length of class 1 customers be N_{C1} and the mean queue length of class 2 customers be N_{C2}.

On the other hand, the mean queue length per class on infinite states is calculated depending on the marginal probabilities of every state, $p(i, j)$.

In Fig. 20.7 the marginal states are described by the pair (i, j) where i is the number of class 1 customers and j is the number of class 2 customers in queue $f(S)$. It is interesting to remember that there are F customers within a diagonal. If local balance between diagonals is assumed on Fig. 20.7 it shows that every $p(i, j)$ is

$$p(i, 0) = (\lambda_1/\gamma(C))^i P(0, 0) \tag{20.10}$$

$$p(0, j) = (\lambda_2/\gamma(C))^j P(0, 0) \tag{20.11}$$

$$p(i, j) = \binom{i+j}{j} ((\lambda_1^i \lambda_2^j)/\gamma(C)^{i+j}) P(0, 0) . \tag{20.12}$$

Let $\rho_1 = \lambda_1/\gamma(C)$ and $\rho_2 = \lambda_2/\gamma(C)$, the mean queue lengths per class at infinite part should be calculated:

$$N_{\infty_1} = P(0, 0) \sum_{i+j=C+1}^{\infty} \sum_{i=0}^{i+j-C} (i + \alpha) \binom{i+j-C}{i} \rho_1^i \rho_2^j \tag{20.13}$$

$$N_{\infty_2} = P(0, 0) \sum_{i+j=C+1}^{\infty} \sum_{j=0}^{i+j-C} (j + \beta) \binom{i+j-C}{j} \rho_1^i \rho_2^j \tag{20.14}$$

then

$$N_{\infty_1} = P(0, 0) \left(\frac{\rho_1}{(1 - \rho)^2} + \alpha \frac{\rho}{1 - \rho} \right)$$

$$N_{\infty_2} = P(0, 0) \left(\frac{\rho_2}{(1 - \rho)^2} + \beta \frac{\rho}{1 - \rho} \right) \tag{20.15}$$

where $\rho = \rho_1 + \rho_2$ and the additional weights α and β must comply with $\alpha + \beta = C$, therefore,

$$\alpha = C \frac{\rho_1}{\rho} \qquad \beta = C \frac{\rho_2}{\rho} . \tag{20.16}$$

Reorganizing the sum terms, the proportional partition of total queue length into classes remains:

$$N_{\infty 1} = P(0,0) \frac{\rho_1}{(1-\rho)} \left(\frac{1}{1-\rho} + C \right) \qquad (20.17)$$

$$N_{\infty 2} = P(0,0) \frac{\rho_2}{(1-\rho)} \left(\frac{1}{1-\rho} + C \right). \qquad (20.18)$$

These queue lengths coincide with the calculations made on operational analysis. Since every customer arrives at input queue with frequency λ as the sum of λ_1 and λ_2, in the steady state they also have to leave the channel with same frequency. From both formulas it is possible to solve all the operational measures of the basic multiclass channel, as the throughput or the mean response time.

As in the Basic Channel without classes of customers, all these expressions have been obtained assuming that $\gamma(k,l)$ is known. This can be approximately obtained by studying the closed queuing network of the producer and consumer for different values of k, l, the number of customers, where $k+l = 1, 2, \ldots, C$, and is set equal to the arrival rate $\gamma(k,l)$ of tokens at the token queue $e(\mathbf{S})$. The solution existence condition can be simply expressed as $\lambda_1 + \lambda_2 < \gamma(k,l)$, where $k + l = C$, being the maximum throughput of the closed network. This complement subnetwork is solved either through Mean Value Analysis, if service times are identical, or the iterative Marie's method [9] in other cases.

20.4.1   Generalization of the Multiclass Channel with R Classes of Customers

The major difficulty of modeling a Multiclass Channel with R classes of customers is the R-dimension of the infinite and extended states representation. This means that all the binomial calculations on the two-class model would be replaced by the corresponding multinomial computations. However, in the steady-state the input and output customer flows through the channel must be equal, then it can be applied to the proportional partition of the total mean queue length:

$$N_{\infty} = \sum_i N_{\infty i} = \sum_i P(0,0) \frac{\rho_i}{(1-\rho)} \left(\frac{1}{1-\rho} + C \right). \qquad (20.19)$$

20.5   Priority Channel

The Priority Channel is the same data structure as in the previous section, but another rule of its behavior must be added: insertions and extractions are done according to their priority in a preemptive scheduling discipline. This new requirement modifies the arrival-departure flow (utilization) at state space and needs closer examination. In order to simplify the presentation, only two customer classes with different priority levels are considered, but it will be generalized to any number of classes in the next section. As in the previous sections, a semaphore station is used. However, the service of a lower class customer is interrupted in the input queue upon the arrival of a higher class customer (Fig. 20.9).

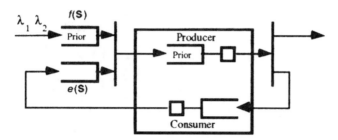

FIGURE 20.9
Semaphore queue in a Priority Channel.

The producer is a simple queue constituted by a service station with a single server and a preemptive-resume scheduling discipline and the consumer is assumed FIFO exponential. Customers arrive at the semaphore queue in Poisson fashion at rates λ_1 and λ_2, where λ_1 is the arrival rate for higher priority customers and λ_2 the arrival rate for lower priority customers. As in the Multiclass Channel, it is proposed to analyze it using decomposition and aggregation. In particular, the structure of the solution changes due to the different throughput between the extended states. It is also assumed that the interarrival times at queue $e(\mathbf{S})$ are exponentially distributed with a rate $\gamma(k, l)$ where k is the number of outstanding tokens used by higher priority class customers and l is the number of outstanding tokens used by lower priority class customers, i.e., $C - (k + l)$ is the number of tokens in queue $e(\mathbf{S})$. Figure 20.12 shows the marginal states within the extended states, where every marginal state belonging to a diagonal has the same E tokens.

The system of diagonals is identical to the Multiclass Channel and it is practically a birth-and-death process with an arrival rate $\lambda = \lambda_1 + \lambda_2$ with a state dependent service rate $\gamma(k, l)$ if $k + l \leq C$ and $\gamma(C, 0) = \gamma(0, C)$ if $k + l > C$, where $E = k + l$ is the number of customers in this queue. However, $\gamma(k, l)$ has different values because this throughput is obtained from a technique included in [11] to evaluate closed queues with preemptive priorities and finite source. In order to calculate the mean length of queue per class at extended part, it is necessary to solve global balance equations of marginal probabilities $p(k, l)$ (in this case assuming local balance between diagonals

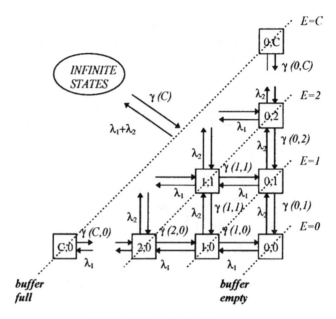

FIGURE 20.10
Marginal states in the extended states.

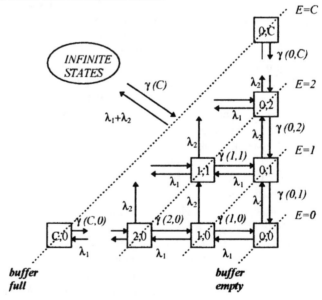

FIGURE 20.11
Marginal states in the infinite states.

is not permitted) in Fig. 20.10 and then to derive every marginal probability in the diagonal, from $P(0, C) = p(0, 0)$ to the diagonal where $E = C$. At infinite part a different assumption has to be taken, due to the difficulty of the calculations of the infinite series, as the Fig. 20.11 shows. The lack of the transitions from (i, j) to $(i, j - 1)$, with the exception of the $i = 0$ case, makes it necessary to solve the mean length queue at infinite part with some modification of Cobham's formulas [3]. The mean queuing time for higher priority class customers depends only on the precedent of their class, but lower priority class customers are overtaken by higher priority class customers while they are waiting for service. Therefore, the mean queue length at infinite part is decomposed in R non-proportional terms if there are R different priority classes.

Then, given an r customer class, its marginal mean length queue depends on the utilization of the R' classes of higher priority (including itself) and the $R' - r$ higher class customers' arrivals during its queuing time (excluding itself).

$$N_\infty = \frac{\rho}{1 - \rho} = \sum_{\forall R} \left[\frac{\rho_r}{1 - \sum\limits_{\forall R'} \rho_{r'}} \frac{1}{1 - \sum\limits_{\forall R'-r} \rho_{r'}} \right] \qquad (20.20)$$

However, the mean queue length of a multiclass channel at infinite part is computed from the buffer full condition. Therefore, there is a shift or translation of C states corresponding to the buffer capacity for both classes. Thus, the non-proportional partition of both queue lengths would be:

$$N_{\infty 1} = P(0, 0) \frac{\rho_1}{1 - \rho_1} \left(\frac{1}{1 - \rho} + C \right)$$

$$N_{\infty 2} = P(0, 0) \frac{\rho_2}{1 - \rho_1 - \rho_2} \frac{1}{1 - \rho_1} \left(\frac{1}{1 - \rho} + C \right) . \qquad (20.21)$$

20.5.1 Generalization of the Priority Channel with R Classes of Customers

The major difficulty of modeling a multiclass channel with R classes of customers is the R-dimension of the infinite and extended states representation. However, the non-proportional partition on the infinite states could be done as we have seen previously. If the priority scheduling was non-preemptive, first it would be necessary to find an analytical solution for the closed queuing network of producer and consumer queues. Thus, this decomposition scheme could have been applied and also the non-proportional partition of queue lengths at infinite with the modification of the Cobham's formulas for non-preemptive scheduling.

20.6 Pools

The Pool is a data storage which can be written to and/or read from by any task, and at any time. There are several variants of the reader's/writer's problem, but the basic structure is the same. Tasks are of two types: reader tasks and writer tasks. All tasks share a common variable or data object. Reader tasks never modify the object, while writer tasks do modify it. Thus writer tasks must mutually exclude all other reader and writer tasks, but multiple reader tasks can access the shared data simultaneously [10]. In this case either only one writer task can store information into the pool or up to C reader tasks can read it. We propose to analyze the pool with two semaphore queues sharing the server. Customers arrive at the semaphore queues in Poisson fashion at rates λ_w and λ_r, where λ_w is the arrival rate for writers and λ_r the arrival rate for readers. The service rate for writers is always μ_w and $k\mu_r$ is the service rate for kth reader at the input queue. Since there is limited simultaneous service for the readers at the pool, their service rate is inversely proportional to their number, i.e., from μ_r in the case of one reader, to $C\mu_r$, in the case of C readers [7]. Thus, if the maximum number of accepted readers being served in the pool is set equal to the limited number of simultaneous outstanding tokens, the rate diagram associated of the extended states of the pool is the classical Markov Chain of Fig. 20.12.

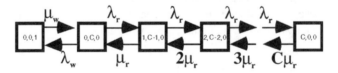

FIGURE 20.12
Flow rate diagram of the extended states in the pool server.

This simple finite chain is solved C times for all the possible number of simultaneous readers $n = 1, 2, \ldots C$. Then, we know C different probabilities of the outstanding tokens: $P_n(0, 0, 0)$, the probability of the initial state, where there is no reader or writer in the pool; $P_n(0, 0, 1)$, the probability of state of the pool being accessed by the exclusive writer; and finally, the k states of the nth Markov chain $P_n(k, C - k, 0)$, corresponding to the probabilities of the pool being accessed by k simultaneous readers.

However, the number of reader and writer tasks is not bounded, and they are arrival independent processes. Therefore, the writer's queue is a semaphore queue $\mathbf{W}$ constituted by its input queue $f(\mathbf{W})$ and its token queue $e(\mathbf{W})$, where there is a token available. The reader's queue is also a semaphore queue $\mathbf{R}$ constituted by its input queue $f(\mathbf{R})$ and its token queue $e(\mathbf{R})$, where there are C tokens available. Both semaphore queues have the same functional features described in Section 20.3. Although arrivals to $f(\mathbf{W})$ and $f(\mathbf{R})$ are independent, the arrival of tokens at queues $e(\mathbf{W})$ and $e(\mathbf{R})$ are described by two different state dependent rates, ω for the writer token and $\varepsilon(k)$ for the reader tokens. The semaphore queues are solved by decomposition and aggregation as we explained above in Section 20.4, taking into account that $\mathbf{W}$ only has one extended state while $\mathbf{R}$ has C. The solution existence conditions are expressed as $\lambda_{w<\omega}$ and $\lambda_r < \varepsilon(C)$, the corresponding maximum throughputs of $\mathbf{W}$ and $\mathbf{R}$.

For these last calculations, the infinite and the extended part at the steady state equations are obtained assuming that ω and the $\varepsilon(k)$ vector are known. These arrival rates ω of the tokens are given by:

$$\omega = \left[\sum_{n=1}^{C} (1 - P_n(0, 0, 1))/n \right] \mu_w$$

$$\varepsilon(k) = \sum_{n=1}^{k} \left[\sum_{i=1}^{C-k+1} (1 - P_n(k, C - k, 0))/k \right] \mu_r . \qquad (20.22)$$

From these expressions it is possible to solve all the operational measures of the pool as the throughput or the mean response time, following the performance calculations of Section 20.4.

20.7 Conclusions and Open Problems

This paper has shown the possibility of building analytic models of typical soft real-time design elements such as the Basic Multiclass Channel, the Priority Channel and the Basic Pool. The advantages of such types of performance models are the saving of human debugging time and machine computing time compared to these times in the simulation case.

By the use of the decomposition-aggregation method, anyone of these approximate analytical models avoids the need of using a simulation with a reasonable degree of accuracy. All these elements could be included by software developers in libraries to complement soft real-time system design methodologies. These libraries would be implemented in the corresponding performance tool.

Also this paper has given some clues to generalize the analytical modeling and evaluation of new elements with buffering or shared variables and no synchronization from the study of multiclass Channels and Pools. The application of the decomposing technique combined with some iterative, will increase the number of new modeled elements as available building blocks for developing a Performance Modeling Tool.

References

[1] G. Bate, Mascot 3: an Informal Introductory Tutorial, *Software Eng. J.,* (May. 1986) 95–102.

[2] F. Bause, P.S. Kritzinger, Stochastic Petri Nets: an Introduction to the Theory. *Advanced Studies in Computer Science,* Verlag, Vieweg, 1996.

[3] A. Cobham, Priority Assignment in Waiting Line Problems, *Operations Research,* 2, (1954) 70–76.

[4] J.E. Cooling, Real-Time Software Systems: An Introduction to Structured and Object-Oriented Design, International Thomson Computer Press, 1997.

[5] P.J. Courtois, Descomposability: Queuing and Computer System Applications, Academic Press, 1977.

[6] S. Fdida, H.G. Perros, A. Wilk, Semaphore Queues: Modeling Multilayered Window Flow Control Mechanisms, *IEEE Trans. Communications,* Vol. 38, No. 3. (Mar. 1990) 309–317.

[7] C. Juiz, R. Puigjaner, K. Jackson, Performance Evaluation of Channels for Large Real-Time Software Systems, *Proc. Int. Conf. Eng. of Computer-Based Systems,* (Jerusalem, Israel, Mar. 30- Apr. 3). IEEE Computer Society Press, 1998, pp. 69–76.

[8] P.A. Laplante, Real-time Systems Design and Analysis. 2nd edition. *IEEE Press,* 1997.

[9] R. Marie, An Approximate Analytical Method for General Queuing Networks. *IEEE Trans. Software Eng.,* Vol. 5, No. 3. (Sept. 1979) 538–538.

[10] R. Puigjaner, Third Set of Generic Performance Models of MASCOT Elements, *Complement Project Document* UIB64-1.0. (Nov.), 1993.

[11] M. Veran, Exact Analysis of a Priority Queue with Finite Source, Modeling and Performance Evaluation Methodology, *Lectures Notes in Control and Information Sciences,* Bacelli F. and Fayolle G. (eds.), Springer-Verlag, 60, (1984) 371–390.

Chapter 21

Hybrid Analysis of Non-Markovian Stochastic Petri Nets

Peter Buchholz

Technische Universität Dresden

Abstract   A new analysis approach for stochastic Petri nets with immediate, exponential and non-exponential transitions is presented. The technique can be applied for transient and stationary analysis. Analysis is based on a combination of discrete event simulation and numerical Markov chain analysis. Simulation is used to determine times when non-exponential transitions fire or when the enabling degree of non-exponential transitions changes. Numerical analysis is applied to determine the state distribution in the intervals between simulated time points. In this way it is possible to combine up to some extent the advantages of state based analysis and discrete event simulation.

Keywords: non-Markovian stochastic Petri nets, discrete event simulation, randomization.

21.1   Introduction

Stochastic Petri Nets (SPNs) are a very popular paradigm to describe and analyze discrete event systems from a wide variety of application areas. Different classes of stochastic Petri Nets have been proposed during the last decade, very popular are Generalized Stochastic Petri Nets (GSPNs) [2], including immediate transitions with zero firing delay and timed transitions with exponentially distributed firing delays. Well defined GSPNs with a reachability set of a moderate size can be mapped onto finite Continuous Time Markov Chains (CTMCs), which can be analyzed with known numerical techniques [11]. The main limitation of GSPNs comes from the restriction of firing delays to exponential distributions. Many activities in real life systems do not have an exponentially distributed duration. Non-exponential distributions can be approximated in GSPNs by phase type distributions [1], but the price for introducing phase type distributions is an enlargement of the state space. Additionally, several distributions cannot be appropriately approximated by phase type distributions with a moderate number of phases. The class of DSPNs [3] contains apart from exponential timed transitions also transitions with a constant and non-zero firing delay. If in a DSPN the number of concurrently enabled deterministic transitions is restricted to one, then the underlying stochastic process can still be analyzed numerically via the embedded Markov chain. Although analysis is more complex than analysis of GSPNs with exponential firing time distributions, state spaces of a moderate size can be analyzed with available solution techniques [8]. The solution approach has been extended to nets where at most one transition with a general firing time distribution is enabled. Recently, also for DSPNs with concurrently enabled deterministic transitions, numerical solution techniques have been published [6, 9]. However, these techniques are complex and require much effort, much more than necessary for numerical CTMC analysis. Thus, only very small examples have been analyzed with these techniques yet.

Apart from numerical analysis, discrete event simulation can be used to analyze SPNs. Simulation is applicable for nets with arbitrarily distributed firing delays. However, simulation requires often a huge effort and results are statistical in nature. In cases where numerical analysis and simulation both can be applied, numerical analysis is often preferable because it usually produces more reliable results with less effort. This holds especially for results based on rare events or small probabilities.

We consider in this paper a fairly general class of Petri nets with immediate transitions, exponential transitions and transitions with generally distributed firing times. Following [5], we denote these nets as Non-Markovian SPNs (NM-SPNs). For this general class of nets numerical analysis methods are unknown. We propose an analysis approach which combines discrete event simulation and numerical analysis. Analysis is based on the observation that states of the stochastic process underlying most NMSPNs with several exponential transitions can be partitioned into subsets such that a general process with a behavior depending only on the subset, but not on the state inside the subset, determines times when jumps between subsets occur. The behavior between two jump times is described by a finite CTMC. This observation is exploited in the analysis by using simulation to fix the jump times of the general process and by computing the behavior between two jumps with the randomization technique for the transient analysis of CTMCs [7, 11]. In this way we obtain an analysis technique combining numerical techniques and simulation. Like in discrete event simulation, we obtain statistical results, but the variability of the results is usually smaller than in simulation, because the use of randomization for the analysis of the behavior inside the subsets of the state space smoothes result measures. The approach is especially well suited for the determination of results accumulated during some finite interval, but can, like simulation, also be used to determine steady state measures.

The idea of combing simulation and randomization has been first applied in the context of CTMCs to avoid the state space explosion problem by describing a system as a set of small interacting CTMCs instead of a large CTMC [4]. As outlined above, interactions times between the interacting CTMCs are determined by simulation, whereas numerical analysis is used to analyze the behavior between interactions. Several examples in [4] show that the technique outperforms simulation, especially when rare events or measures based on states with a small probability have to be computed.

The outline of this paper is as follows. In the next section the basic class of NMSPNs is introduced. Afterwards, in Section 21.3, the time dependent behavior of a NMSPN is described. Section 21.4 introduces the new analysis approach.

21.2 Basic Definitions and Notations

We assume that the reader is familiar with Petri nets and refer for details to the literature (e.g., [2]).

DEFINITION 21.1 *A Non-Markovian Stochastic Petri Net is defined as $NMSPN = (P, T_I, T_E, T_G, I^-, I^+, I^H, M_0, \Lambda, \Delta, \Omega)$ where T_I, T_E and T_G are disjoint sets, $(P, T, I^-, I^+, I^H, M_0)$ with $T = T_I \cup T_E \cup T_G$ is a P/T net with inhibitor arcs, $\Lambda : T \to \mathbb{R}_+$ such that for $t \in T_I$: $\Lambda(t)$ describes a relative non-zero firing weight, and for $t \in T_E \cup T_G$: $\Lambda(t)^{-1}$ describes the mean firing delay, $\Delta : T \to Dist$ maps transitions onto distributions from some finite set of distributions $Dist$ such that $\Delta(t) = const(0)$ for $t \in T_I$ and $\Delta(t) = \exp(\Lambda(t))$ for $t \in T_E$, and $\Omega : T_G \to \{ena, age\}$ describes the enabling memory policy of transitions from the set T_G.*

For $t \in T$ we define $\bullet t = \{p \in P | I^-(p, t) > 0\}$, $t\bullet = \{p \in P | I^+(p, t) > 0\}$ and $\circ t = \{p \in P | I^H(p, t) > 0\}$, the sets of input -, output - and inhibition places. T_I contains immediate transitions, T_E exponential transitions and T_G transitions with general firing delay. The set of distributions $Dist$ has to include constant distributions if T_I is non-empty, it has to include exponential distributions if T_E is non-empty and it may include arbitrary distributions to characterize the firing delay of transitions from T_G. By the enabling rules defined below, transitions from T_I have strict priority over transitions from T_E

and T_G. We do not explicitly exclude exponential distributions for transitions from T_G, although these transitions are usually collected in T_E. Ω describes the enabling memory policy of transitions with a general firing time distribution. We consider enabling (ena) or age memory (age) (see [1]).

Markings of the net can be described by $|P|$-dimensional vectors such that $M(p)$ includes the number of tokens on place p. Transition t is enabled if $M(p) \geq I^-(p, t)$ for all $p \in \bullet t$, $M(p) < I^H(p, t)$ for all $p \in \circ t$ and if $t \in T_E \cup T_G$, then no transition from T_I observes the conditions according to I^- and I^H. If t fires in marking M, then the successor marking M' is defined as $M'(p) = M(p) - I^-(p, t) + I^+(p, t)$ for all $p \in P$. We will use the shorthand notation $M - t \rightarrow M'$. Transition firings follow the race model, i.e., the transition with the smallest delay fires first.

For an NMSPN the reachability set RS and reachability graph RG can be computed. RS contains all markings reachable from M_0 by firing sequences of transitions. RG is an arc labeled graph such that the vertices are described by the elements of RS and an edge labeled with $t \in T$ connects M and M' if and only if $M - t \rightarrow M'$. Observe that for the generation of RS and RG the firing time distributions for transitions from T_G are not taken into account according to the firing rules defined above. If all firing time distributions for transitions from T_G have an infinite support, then RS and RG characterize exactly the reachability set and graph of the NMSPN.

It is well known that for NMSPNs including immediate transitions RS can be decomposed into two subsets, one including all markings where only immediate transitions are enabled and a second where timed transitions are enabled. Markings belonging to the former set are denoted as vanishing and markings belonging to the second class are named tangible. The set of tangible markings is denoted as TRS. Define $Prob(M, M', t)$ for $M, M' \in TRS$ and all $t \in T_E \cup T_G$ that are enabled in M, as the conditional probability that if t fires in M, then M' is the next tangible marking. Implicitly we define $Prob(M, M', t) = 0.0$ if t is not enabled in M or M' is not reachable by firing t and a sequence of immediate transitions starting in M. Methods to compute $Prob(M, M', t)$ are known from the literature [2]. In the sequel we assume that TRS is a finite set such that it can be appropriately described by a set of integers $\{0, \ldots, n - 1\}$. Integer x describes marking M_x; we use both notations interchangeably. Furthermore, we assume that $M_0 \in TRS$ and initial firing delays for enabled transitions from T_G are drawn from the corresponding distributions (i.e., if $t \in T_G$ is enabled in M_0, then the first firing delay is determined by drawing a random number with distribution $\Delta(t)^1$).

Let $ENA(M) = \{t \in T_G | t$ is enabled in $M\}$ be the set of timed transitions with general firing time distribution enabled in marking M. TRS can be de-

---

[1] We implicitly assume that $\Delta(t)$ describes the complete distribution of the firing delay and can be used as input for a random number generator such that $DRAW(\Delta(t))$ gives a random number drawn from distribution $\Delta(t)$.

composed into subsets by collecting M and M' in the same subset if and only if $ENA(M) = ENA(M')$. Let N be the number of different subsets and denote by $TRS[X]$ all markings belonging to the X-th subset and let $ENA(X)$ be the subset of transitions from T_G which are enabled in the markings from $TRS[X]$. Let n_X be the number of markings in $TRS[X]$; obviously $n = \sum_{X=1}^{N} n_X$ has to hold. In the sequel we assume that transitions $t \in T_G$ with $\Omega(t) = ena$ are not immediately enabled after being disabled by firing some transition $t' \neq t$. According to the subsets $TRS[X]$, markings are reordered such that all markings from $TRS[X]$ receive numbers from $\sum_{Y=1}^{X-1} n_Y$ through $\sum_{Y=1}^{X} n_Y - 1$ in TRS.

The tangible reachability graph TRG is a graph with vertices TRS and edges labeled with transitions and probabilities. If $t \in T_E \cup T_G$ is enabled in $M \in TRS$ and $Prob(M, M', t) > 0.0$, then TRG contains an edge between M and M' which is labeled with $(t, Prob(M, M', t))$. TRG can be described by a set of matrices. Let $\mathbf{R}_t$ be a $n \times n$ matrix which contains $Prob(M_x, M_y, t)$ in position $\mathbf{R}_t(x, y)$. According to the partition of TRS, matrices $\mathbf{R}_t$ are decomposed into N^2 submatrices $\mathbf{R}_t[X, Y]$ of size $n_X \times n_Y$. For exponential transitions we define

$$\mathbf{Q} = \sum_{t \in T_E} \Lambda(t) \mathbf{R}_t ,$$

the rate matrix of exponential transitions. Like $\mathbf{R}_t$, $\mathbf{Q}$ can be decomposed into submatrices $\mathbf{Q}[X, Y]$.

21.3 The Timed Behavior of an NMSPN

We now consider the timed behavior of an NMSPN. A state is completely characterized by the marking plus a vector τ including the remaining firing times of all transitions from T_G. For $t \in T_G$ let τ_t be the remaining firing time. We define $\tau_t = \infty$ if t has no remaining firing time. This is always the case for transitions with enabling memory which are not enabled in the current marking. If t has age memory, then $\tau_t = \infty$ implies that t has not been enabled since it fired for the last time or it has never been enabled during the whole execution.

The state of the NMSPN changes continuously, because values τ_t for enabled transitions decrease linearly with the time. However, in discrete event simulation only those points are considered where a transition fires and the state changes discontinuously at these points. Here we go one step further and consider in a simulation those points where global transitions occur (i.e., where transitions from T_G fire or the subset $TRS[X]$ changes). The goal of our analysis approach is to analyze the behavior of the NMSPN inside a subset $TRS[X]$ using numerical techniques for the transient analysis of CTMCs. To do so, times of global transitions have to be known. Assume that the current state (M, τ) is known and $M \in TRS[X]$. Then $\min_{t \in ENA(M)}(\tau_t) = \min_{t \in ENA(X)}(\tau_t)$ determines the next (potential) firing time of a transition from T_G. However, before this firing occurs, an exponential transition may fire and change the enabling of transitions from T_G. Unfortunately, the firing rates of exponential transitions depend on the detailed marking M and not only on the subset $TRS[X]$. To obtain independence of the exponential firing times from the detailed marking, we use the idea of uniformizing or randomizing the CTMC [7]. The CTMC is represented by a Poisson process and a Discrete Time Markov Chain (DTMC). The Poisson process determines the times when jumps occur and the DTMC determines the successor state. Let

$$\alpha_X = \max_{x \in TRS[X]} \sum_{y \in TRS \setminus TRS[X]} \mathbf{Q}(x, y) \, ,$$

the maximum rate of exponential transitions leaving subset $TRS[X]$. Define $\mathbf{R}_{exp}[X, Y] = \mathbf{Q}[X, Y]/\alpha_X$ for $X \neq Y$ and $\mathbf{R}_{exp}[X, X] = \mathrm{diag}(e^T - \sum_{Y=1, Y \neq X}^{N} \mathbf{R}_{exp}[X, Y]e^T)$, where e is a row vector with all elements equal to 1 and $\mathrm{diag}(\mathbf{a}^T)$ for row vector $\mathbf{a}$ is a diagonal matrix with $\mathbf{a}(i)$ in position (i, i). Observe that $\mathbf{R}_{exp}$ is a stochastic matrix.

An exponential distribution with rate α_X determines the time points when the subset of states potentially changes due to firing an exponential distribution. However, if the NMSPN is in marking M_x, then with probability $\mathbf{R}_{exp}[X, X](x, x)$, the transition is a pseudo transition and the marking does not change. It is easy to show that the randomized and the original processes behave identical [7, 11]. Thus, the Poisson process defined by α_X determines a sequence of potential times which include the times when the subset $TRS[X]$ changes due to firing an exponential transition.

Instead of defining the state of the NMSPN by (M_x, τ), we define it by $(\pi[X], \tau)$, where vector π includes a probability distribution over the markings in $TRS[X]$. State (M_x, τ) with $M_x \in TRS[X]$ can be represented by $(\pi[X], \tau)$ where $\pi[X](x) = 1.0$ and $\pi[X](y) = 0.0$ for $x \neq y$. Assume that the state at some time ti is known to be $(\pi[X], \tau)$. The time when the next transition from T_G fires potentially is given by $ti + \delta_G$, where $\delta_G = \min_{t \in ENA(X)}(\tau_t)$. We assume that δ_G belongs to the firing of a unique transition $t \in T_G$. If several transitions have the same firing time, then one transition is chosen by some predefined mechanism. The time when the subset of states changes due to firing an exponential transition can be drawn from an exponential distribution with rate α_X. Let δ_E be the corresponding value and define $\delta = \min(\delta_G, \delta_E)$. Thus, $ti + \delta$ is the next time when vector τ needs to be updated and the subset $TRS[X]$ potentially changes. Since the behavior of the NMSPN in the interval $[0, ti + \delta)$ is completely determined by exponential transitions that do not leave $TRS[X]$, the distribution at time $ti + \delta$ immediately before the next global transition is given by

$$\pi'[X] = \pi[X]\exp((\mathbf{Q}[X, X] - \operatorname{diag}(\mathbf{Q}[X, X]\mathbf{e}^T)) \cdot \delta)$$

$$= \sum_{k=0}^{\infty}((\mathbf{Q}[X, X] - \operatorname{diag}(\mathbf{Q}[X, X]\mathbf{e}^T)) \cdot \delta)^k .$$

Matrix $\mathbf{G}[X, X] = (\mathbf{Q}[X, X] - \operatorname{diag}(\mathbf{Q}[X, X]\mathbf{e}^T)$ is the generator matrix of the CTMC for the behavior of the net in subset $TRS[X]$ under the condition that no global transition occurs. The above formula describes the transient analysis of a CTMC to compute the distribution after δ time units starting with distribution $\pi[X]$ [11].

Now assume that $t \in T_G$ is the transition that fires at time $ti + \delta$. With probability $\pi'[X]\mathbf{R}_t[X, Y]\mathbf{e}^T$ the successor marking is in subset $TRS[Y]$. The values define a probability distribution over the subsets $TRS[Y]$ $(Y = 1, \ldots, N)$. By drawing a uniform $[0, 1)$ distributed number, the successor subset Y can be determined via simulation. Under the condition that the successor marking is in subset $TRS[Y]$, the distribution after firing t equals

$$\pi[Y] = \pi'[X]\mathbf{R}_t[X, Y]/(\pi'[X]\mathbf{R}_t[X, Y]\mathbf{e}^T) . \tag{21.1}$$

Vector τ is updated as follows:

(1) if $t \in ENA(Y)$ then $\tau_t = DRAW(\Delta(t))$ else $\tau_t = \infty$,
(if t is also enabled in the successor marking, then a new firing time has to be drawn, otherwise no firing time is remaining)

(2) for $t' \in ENA(Y) \cap ENA(X)$ $(t' \neq t)$: $\tau_{t'} = \tau_{t'} - \delta$,
(for transitions that are enabled in the old and new markings, the remaining firing times are reduced by δ)

(3) for $t' \in ENA(Y) \backslash ENA(X)$ $(t \neq t')$ and $\tau_{t'} = \infty$: $\tau_{t'} = DRAW(\Delta(t))$,
(for newly enabled transitions without remaining firing time, a new firing time has to be drawn)

(4) for $t' \in ENA(X) \backslash ENA(Y)$ $(t \neq t')$ and $\Omega(t) = ena$: $\tau_{t'} = \infty$,
(for newly disabled transitions with enabling memory the remaining firing time is set to ∞)

(5) for $t' \in ENA(X) \backslash ENA(Y)$ $(t \neq t')$ and $\Omega(t) = age$: $\tau_{t'} = \tau_{t'} - \delta$, and
(for newly disabled transitions with age memory, remaining firing times are kept)

(6) all remaining values $\tau_{t'}$ keep unchanged.

Afterwards the current time equals $ti + \delta$ and the state equals $(\pi[Y], \tau)$. Now assume that the global transition results from the potential firing of an exponential transition. With probability $\pi'[X]\mathbf{R}_{exp}[X, X]\mathbf{e}^T$, the transition is a pseudo transition, which means that the NMSPN remain in subset $TRS[X]$ and the new distribution is computed via (21.1) after substituting $\mathbf{R}_t[X, X]$ by $\mathbf{R}_{exp}[X, X]$. By drawing a random $[0, 1)$ distributed number, it is determined whether the transition is a pseudo transition or not. If it is a pseudo transition, the values τ_t are set to $\tau_t - \delta$ for all $t \in ENA(X)$. Time is elapsed to $ti + \delta$ and the new state of the NMSPN equals $(\pi'[X], \tau)$. With probability $\pi'[X]\mathbf{R}_{exp}[X, Y]\mathbf{e}^T$, the state changes to subset $TRS[Y]$. The distribution after entering $TRS[Y]$ is computed via (21.1) after substituting matrices $\mathbf{R}_t[X, Y]$ by $\mathbf{R}_{exp}[X, Y]$. Values in τ are updated as described in the points 2–6 above.

21.4 A Hybrid Analysis Approach

The steps presented in the previous section can be combined to a hybrid analysis algorithm which generates the times when the process jumps from one subset to another and the successor subset by simulation, whereas the behavior inside a subset is analyzed numerically. For the numerical analysis randomization is used [7, 11]. Let $\pi_{ti}[X]$ be the distribution at some time ti, let $\pi_{ti+\delta}[X]$ be the distribution at time $ti + \delta$ and assume that in the interval $[ti, ti + \delta)$ only local transitions took place. Then $\pi_{ti+\delta}[X]$ can be computed from

$$\pi_{ti+\delta}[X] = \sum_{k=0}^{\infty} \pi_{ti}[X](\mathbf{G}[X, X]/\beta_X + \mathbf{I})^k \frac{(\beta_X \delta)^k}{k!} e^{-\beta_X \delta} , \qquad (21.2)$$

where $\beta_X = \max_s(|\mathbf{G}[X, X](s, s)|)$. For further details and implementation issues we refer to [11, 7].

To compute results related to rate rewards, it is necessary to determine the portion of time the process stays in each marking in the interval $[ti, ti + \delta)$. Let $\phi_\delta[X]$ be a vector including in position x the portion of time the process stays in marking $M_x \in TRS[X]$ in the interval $[ti, ti + \delta)$ when the initial distribution is $\pi_{ti}[X]$ and no global transition occurs in the interval (i.e., $\delta \cdot \phi_\delta[X](x)$ is the absolute amount of time the process stays in M_x in the interval $[ti, ti + \delta)$). Vector $\phi_\delta[X]$ satisfies the differential equation [12]:

$$\dot{\phi}_\delta[X] = \phi_\delta[X]\mathbf{G}[X, X] + \pi_{ti}[X] . \qquad (21.3)$$

Although (21.3) is an inhomogeneous system, randomization can as well be applied for the solution (see [10] for details). After $\phi_\delta[X]$ is known, rate based rewards accumulated in the interval $[ti, ti + \delta)$ are computed by multiplying $\phi_\delta[X]$ with the portion of the reward vectors which corresponds to states in $TRS[X]$.

Hybrid_analysis $(ti_{stop}, T_G, \mathbf{G}, \mathbf{R}_t$ for all $t \in T_G \cup \{\exp\}, ENA, \Delta, \pi_0[X])$

1. $ti = 0;$
2.   for all $t \in T_G$ do
3.   if $t \in ENA(X)$ then
4. $\tau_t = DRAW(\Delta(t))$;
5.   else
6. $\tau_t = \infty$;
7.   od
8.   while $ti < ti_{stop}$ do
9. $\delta = min(min_{t \in T_G} (\tau_t), DRAW(\alpha_X))$
10. $t = $ transition which fires at $ti + \delta$ (exp if a global transition from T_E potentially fires)
11.   if $ti + \delta > ti_{stop}$ then
12. $\delta = ti_{stop}$
13.   compute $\pi_{ti+\delta}[X]$ from (21.2) and $\phi_{ti+\delta}[X]$ from (21.3) using randomization
14.   update all result values using $\delta \cdot \phi_{ti+\delta}[X]$
15. $ti = ti + \delta$
16.   determine Y from the distribution $\pi_{ti}[X]\mathbf{R}_t[X, Y]\mathbf{e}^T$
17. $\pi_{ti}[Y] = \pi_{ti}[X]\mathbf{R}_t[X, Y]/(\pi_{ti}[X]\mathbf{R}_t[X, Y]\mathbf{e}^T)$
18.   if $t \neq \exp$
19.   if $t \in ENA(Y)$ then
20. $\tau_t = DRAW(\Delta(t))$
21.   else
22. $\tau_t = \infty$
23.   fi
24.   for all $t' \in T_G \setminus \{t\}$ do
25.   if $t' \in ENA(Y) \cap ENA(X)$ or $(t \in ENA(X) \setminus ENA(Y)$ and $\Omega(t) = age)$ then
26. $\tau_{t'} = \tau_{t'} - \delta$
27.   if $t' \in ENA(Y) \setminus ENA(X)$ and $\tau_{t'} = \infty$ then
28. $\tau_{t'} = DRAW(\Delta(t'))$
29.   if $t' \in ENA(X) \setminus ENA(Y)$ and $\Omega(t) = ena$ then
30. $\tau_{t'} = \infty$
31.   od
32.   od

FIGURE 21.1

Hybrid Analysis Algorithm for NMSPNs.

With the previous steps a hybrid solution algorithm is defined as shown in Fig. 21.1. The algorithm simulates the system starting with initial distribution $\pi_0[X]$ until time ti_{stop}. During the simulation reward values are updated such that a single simulation run determines the accumulated rewards in the interval $[0, ti_{stop})$. It is obviously also possible to evaluate the number of firings and mean times between firings of transitions from T_G. A single run determines one trajectory of the stochastic process; to obtain statistical meaningful results, several independent replications have to be performed such that confidence intervals for result measures can be computed with standard methods.

Advantages of the algorithm in Fig. 21.1 compared to conventional simulation result from the computation of the vectors π and ϕ using a numerical technique. We can expect good results whenever times between global transition firings are long and results are based on small probabilities such that numerical techniques outperform discrete event simulation. On the other hand, if most times global transitions fire or the behavior of the net is mainly determined by global transitions, we cannot expect benefits from the hybrid approach.

21.5   Summary and Conclusions

In this paper, we presented a new analysis approach for Non-Markovian Stochastic Petri Nets. The approach combines discrete event simulation and the randomization technique in a single solution approach. The central idea is to use discrete event simulation to determine the "non-Markovian" part of the behavior and to analyze the net between two simulated steps by means of randomization. The method has advantages whenever results are computed that are mainly based on the system behavior, which is analyzed via randomization. Additionally, established methods for symmetry exploitation at net or state space levels can be integrated in the new approach and allow the efficient analysis of symmetric systems.

References

[1] M. Ajmone-Marsan, G. Balbo, A. Bobbio, G. Chiola, G. Conte, and A. Cumani. The effect of execution policies on the semantics and analysis of stochastic Petri nets. *IEEE Transactions on Software Engineering,* 15(7), 832–845, 1989.

[2] M. Ajmone-Marsan, G. Balbo, G. Conte, S. Donatelli, and G. Franceschinis. *Modelling with generalized stochastic Petri nets.* Wiley, 1995.

[3] M. Ajmone-Marsan and G. Chiola. On Petri nets with deterministic and exponential firing times. In G. Rozenberg, editor, *Advances in Petri Nets 1987,* pages 132–145. Springer LNCS 266, 1987.

[4] P. Buchholz. A new approach combining simulation and randomization for the analysis of large continuous time Markov chains. *ACM Transactions on Modeling and Computer Simulation,* 8(2), 194–222, 1998.

[5] R. Fricks, A. Puliafito, M. Telek, and K. Trivedi. Application of non-Markovian stochastic Petri nets. *ACM Performance Evaluation Review,* 26(2) 15–27, 1998.

[6] R. German and C. Lindemann. Analysis of stochastic Petri nets by the method of supplementary variables. *Performance Evaluation,* 20, 317–335, 1994.

[7] D. Gross and D. Miller. The randomization technique as a modeling tool and solution procedure for transient Markov processes. *Operations Research,* 32(2), 926–944, 1984.

[8] C. Lindemann. An improved numerical algorithm for calculating steady-state solutions of deterministic and stochastic Petri net models. *Performance Evaluation,* 18, 75–91, 1993.

[9] C. Lindemann and G. Shedler. Numerical analysis of deterministic and stochastic Petri nets with concurrent deterministic transitions. *Performance Evaluation,* 27/28, 565–582, 1996.

[10] A. L. Reibman and K. S. Trivedi. Transient analysis of cumulative measures of Markov model behavior. *Communications in Statistics: Stochastic Models,* 5(4), 683–710, 1989.

[11] W. J. Stewart. *Introduction to the numerical solution of Markov chains.* Princeton University Press, 1994.

[12] K. Trivedi, J. Muppala, S. Woolet, and B. Haverkort. Composite performance and dependability analysis. *Performance Evaluation,* 14, 197–215, 1992.

Chapter 22

A Performance Model for SPADES Specifications

Peter Harrison and Kamyar Kanani

Imperial College

Abstract   The stochastic process algebra SPADES provides a simple yet powerful formal description technique that can be used to specify both the quantitative and qualitative properties of a system. We show how the quantitative behavior of certain SPADES systems can be captured by a generalized semi-Markovian performance model. This provides the designer with potential to model the performance of the system analytically, to optimize the process of simulating the system and to convert the SPADES model to other stochastic process algebra formalisms.

Keywords: stochastic process algebra, generalized distributions.

22.1   Introduction

Stochastic process algebras (SPA) [9, 17, 16, 2, 6] are a class of formalism that are well suited to specifying simultaneously the functional (*qualitative*) and performance (*quantitative*) properties of a system. They provide a programmatic paradigm which can be used to construct systems in a compositional manner. Therefore, not only is the process of constructing models an intuitive one, it also avoids the complexity problems that plague the construction of global specifications when the system being modeled becomes large e.g., using queuing networks or Petrinets.

Performance analysis using SPA is often achieved using the fact that a particular formalism has an underlying performance model. For example, SPAs that are classed as *Markovian* employ a (continuous-time) Markov chain (CTMC) as the underlying performance model. Once a system has been specified using the SPA the performance model is extracted and used as the basis for continuing performance analysis. Some SPA formalisms may not have an underlying performance model (e.g., [14]). Specifications constructed in these formalisms are simulated[1] and performance metrics are gathered directly from these simulation runs. Some SPAs (e.g., [8]) may require models[2] to be manipulated, using equivalence preserving rewrite rules, into some normal form from which a performance model can be derived.

SPADES[3] is a SPA introduced in [17]. It is a SPA based on CCS [15] that allows CCS-based specifications to be extended with generally distributed random delays and probabilistic resolution of choice. These constructs allow the designer to specify temporal and probabilistic properties of a system on top of its functional behavior. As a SPA, it currently falls into the class of those whose performance analysis is accomplished through direct simulation. However, [17] did introduce notions of equivalence between SPADES agents which could be used to indirectly model the performance of a system. Here the specification is transformed into one with known performance characteristics.

The aim of this paper is to show that, under appropriate circumstances, SPADES agents can be given an underlying performance model which is a *generalized semi-Markov process* (GSMP) [5]. The benefits of deriving this performance model are threefold. Firstly, the subsequent performance analysis of the system can take place within a framework with a wealth of established theory. Therefore, if the GSMP is realized to have particular properties, further simplifications of the performance model can be made which may provide an analytical means of solution (e.g., following the methodology presented in [13]). Secondly, since it has been shown that a SPADES agent can model a GSMP, the direct simulation of SPADES agents (e.g., as in [11, 3]) can benefit from the process of GSMP derivation. This is because GSMP derivation can be viewed as a process of reducing the SPADES agent such that qualitative behavior is abstracted in the compact notion of a GSMP transition — it will be seen that a single GSMP transition may be modeled by numerous transitions of the SPADES agent. Finally, being able to express a system as a GSMP provides a common link between many generalized SPAs. This fact can provide a means of transforming a specification presented in one generalized SPA framework into another. If the GSMP can be reduced to a CTMC, for example, then the system can be described by any SPA.

The remainder of the paper is organized as follows. In Section 22.2 the syntax and behavior of SPADES models are outlined. In Section 22.3 we show how the behavior of finite state SPADES agents can be captured as a *symbolic*

---

[1]These formalisms are acting as *simulation description languages.*

[2]henceforth referred to as "agents" or "processes."

[3]Not to be confused with the SPA of same name introduced in [16] but named in [1].

state transition graph. In Section 22.4 we continue by formally defining a GSMP and then proceeding to show how SPADES behavior can be analyzed to derive an underlying GSMP. This process is illustrated with several examples. In Section 22.5 we model an ATM switch using SPADES. From this model we extract an underlying GSMP which we simulate for performance analysis. In Section 22.7 we summarize by relating our work with others in the field of SPA and hinting at directions of future work.

22.2 The SPADES Formalism

We begin by briefly introducing the constructs used to specify SPADES agents and then go on to describe the behavior that is captured by those constructs.

22.2.1 The Language of SPADES

The basic language of SPADES is built upon CCS. Entities in SPADES are agents[4] which can perform *actions*. There are three types of SPADES actions.

1. Labelled Actions The actions which resemble the CCS style actions are referred to as *labeled* actions, which may either be *visible* or *invisible* (sometimes referred to as "silent"). Silent actions are indistinguishable from one another and are represented by the special action "τ." Labelled actions may be decorated by the *conjugate* operator, "$\bar{}$," with the convention that for the visible action, "a," $\bar{\bar{a}} = a$ and $\bar{\tau} = \tau$.

A *conjugate pair* of actions is a pair where one is the conjugate of the other. The labeled actions themselves come in two varieties: immediate, when such an action is enabled the passage of time cannot occur, and passive otherwise.

2. Delay Actions A *delay* action is denoted "(x)," where $x \in \mathbb{R}$ or a variable that represents an amount of delay.

3. Sample Action A special action is used to introduce the notion of random variables into SPADES. The construct "$\mathcal{R}[x \leftarrow f]$" is used to denote that fact that the variable, "x," is assigned a value drawn according to the density function, "f." The distribution function is a general one.

---

[4]Sometimes referred to as "processes".

The simplest SPADES agents are the related agents "nil," which represents the non-temporal deadlocked agent, and "**0**," which represents the temporal deadlocked process. Neither is able to perform any action but differ in their way of treating the passage of time. The non-temporal deadlock agent permits the passage of time whereas the temporal deadlock agent does not.

More complex SPADES agents can be constructed by *action prefixing* using the *prefix composition* operator ".". Therefore,

$$a.(2).\text{nil} \,,\ \mathcal{R}[x \leftarrow \exp(0.5)].(x).b.\text{nil} \,,\ \bar{a}.b.\text{nil}$$

are examples of valid SPADES agents[5].

Agents themselves may be combined together to form more complex agents. Let a, a_1, $a_2 \cdots$ denote SPADES agents and p_1, $p_2 \cdots$ denote probabilities. The constructs that deal with agent composition are

Sum choice Denoted by the binary operator "$a_1 + a_2$." Multiple summations are often represented as "$\sum_i a_i$."

Parallel composition Denoted by the binary operator "$a_1 | a_2$." Multiple parallel compositions are often represented as "$\prod_i a_i$."

Probabilistic choice Denoted by the operator "$[p_1]a_1 \dotplus [p_2]a_2 \dotplus \cdots$," often represented as "$\sum_i [p_i]a_i$."

Conditional choice Denoted by a construct of the form "if c then a_1 else a_2" where c represents a Boolean expression.

The final SPADES operators deal with action relabeling ("$a[S]$" where "S" is a relabeling function), action hiding ("$a \backslash \{L\}$" where "L" is a list of immediate, non-conjugate visible actions) and recursion ("**rec**$(X = a)$" where "X" is a process variable occurring free in the body of "a"). A SPADES program is a list of agent definitions.

22.2.2   The Behavior of SPADES Agents

The behavior of the various SPADES constructs is presented using an operational semantics that defines the *transition* from one process to another. There are three forms of transition that can occur between agents:

Labeled transition Denoting a CCS style transition with single actions firing or action pairs *synchronizing*.

Evolution transition Denoting the passage of a finite amount time.

---

[5]Trailing "nil's" are usually only implied.

Probabilistic transition Denoting the resolution of probabilistic choices or the sampling of random variables.

A complete symbolic semantics is presented in Appendix A. However, it is worthwhile to give some form of intuitive background to the defined behaviors.

A SPADES agent is meant to evolve in a way that mimics a simulation. An agent goes through cycles of evolution. Firstly it *fires* any possible probabilistic transition, resolving any probabilistic choice and sampling random variables to be utilized later. It then checks to see if it needs to perform any immediate actions (all synchronizations being immediate) and fires those. Once there are no more immediate actions to be fired (and no probabilistic transitions have become enabled) it can go through a period of evolution. Here, the (implicit) simulation time is advanced until another form of transition becomes enabled.

[17] gives an operational semantics for SPADES. The semantics define the conditions under which a SPADES agent can undergo the various forms of transition.

A labeled transition between SPADES agents P and Q via action α, say, is denoted

$$P \xrightarrow{\alpha} Q .$$

An evolution transition is denoted

$$P \xrightarrow{t} Q$$

where $t \in \mathbb{R}$. The intuition is that P idles for "t" units of time before becoming Q.

A probabilistic transition is denoted

$$P \xrightarrow{p}_l Q$$

where $p \in \mathbb{R}$ and l is an *index*. The index is a technical annotation used to collapse multiple inferences which we would like to think of as representing the same probabilistic transition into a single formal entity — a process carried out by the *label extension function*, $\mathrm{lf}(\cdot, \cdot)$. The index is the *measure* that sets up the notion of probability in SPADES theory.

The *process probability measure*, $\mu(P, S)$, (informally, the chance of P evolving to become a member of the set of processes S) is a probability measure defined over the indices involved in probabilistic transitions between P and members of S.

Example 22.1 SPADES transitions
The agent

$$A \stackrel{\text{def}}{=} (([\tfrac{1}{3}]a[].\text{nil} \dotplus [\tfrac{2}{3}]b[].\text{nil}) + \mathcal{R}[x \leftarrow f].(x).\text{nil}) \backslash \{a, b\}$$

can undergo the following transition sequence:

$$A \xrightarrow{f(5)/3}_l (a[].\text{nil} + (5).\text{nil})\backslash\{a, b\}$$
$$\xrightarrow{5} (a[].\text{nil} + \text{nil})\backslash\{a, b\}$$
$$\xrightarrow{a} (\text{nil} + \text{nil})\backslash\{a, b\}$$

where the index, l, is "[1]+(5)" denoting the fact that the probabilistic transition consisted of a sample being made (the sample having value "5") on the right-hand side of a sum and a resolution of a probabilistic choice (the first choice being taken) on the other. $\square$

SPADES agents have certain properties (proposed and proved in [17]) which impose an order on the sequence of transitions a process can undergo.

- *Action urgency*
  All synchronizations have to occur before time can progress:

$$\text{If } P \xrightarrow{\tau} \text{ then } P \not\xrightarrow{t}.$$

- *Probabilistic transitions fire first*
  A probabilistic agent, P cannot undergo labeled or evolution transitions:

$$\text{If } \text{Prob}(P) \text{ then } P \not\xrightarrow{\alpha} \text{ and } P \not\xrightarrow{t}.$$

22.3   Representing the Behavior

Following the approach introduced in [7], the behavior of a SPADES model can be captured concisely using a symbolic graph. On top of this, [11] shows how each process can have a separate notion of state associated with it.

Each symbolic SPADES process is decorated with a state function, $\mathcal{S}$, as well as a substitution function, σ, denoted $P^{\mathcal{S}}_{\sigma}$.

DEFINITION 22.1   *If the state of a symbolic SPADES process, P, is represented as a tuple of variables, $(v_1 \cdots v_n)$, then the state function, $\mathcal{S}$, is a function that associates an expression with each variable. The expression may contain symbols which act as place holders to be instantiated at a later point.*

A symbolic state transition graph captures the behavior of such processes.

DEFINITION 22.2   *A Symbolic State Transition Graph (SSTG) for the system is a six tuple:*

$$< N, act, tr_l, tr_e, tr_p, N_0 >$$

where N is a set of nodes
act is a set of actions
tr_l: *Node* $\times BExp \times act \rightarrow Node$, *is the labeled transition relation*
tr_e: *Node* $\times BExp \times Exp \rightarrow Node$, *is the evolution transition relation*
tr_p: *Node* $\times BExp \times Exp \rightarrow Node$, *is the probabilistic transition relation*
N_0 *is the start node representing* $SYSTEM_{\{\}}^{\rho_0}$
ρ_0 *represents the initial state of the system.*

BExp and Exp represent the class of Boolean and numerical expressions which may contain symbols.

If Node N_1 represents the agent $(P_{N_1})_\sigma^S$ and node N_2 represents the agent $(P_{N_2})_{\sigma'}^{S'}$, then

$$(N_1, b, \alpha, N_2) \in tr_l \iff (P_{N_1})_\sigma^S \xrightarrow{b,\alpha} (P_{N_2})_{\sigma'}^{S'}$$

$$(N_1, b, t, N_2) \in tr_e \iff (P_{N_1})_\sigma^S \overset{b,t}{\rightsquigarrow} (P_{N_2})_{\sigma'}^{S'} \not\rightarrow$$

$$(N_1, b, p, N_2) \in tr_p \iff (P_{N_1})_\sigma^S \overset{b,p}{\hookrightarrow}_l (P_{N_2})_{\sigma'}^{S'} \wedge \neg\mathrm{Prob}(P_{N_2})$$
$$\text{where } p = \mu(P_{N_1}, P_{N_2}) .$$

A link between two nodes represents either a labeled transition, or the longest evolution or probabilistic transition between the decorated agents represented by the nodes. A link is *enabled* only when the Boolean expression b which guards it is satisfied.

22.4 Derivation of GSMP Performance Model

DEFINITION 22.3   *A generalized semi-Markov process (GSMP) is a tuple* $(S, \mathcal{E}, E, C, R, T, F, s_0)$ *where*

- S *is the countable set of* states.

- $\mathcal{E}$ *is the finite set of* events.

- $E : S \rightarrow \mathcal{P}(\mathcal{E})$ *is the* event assignment function.

- $C : S \rightarrow \mathcal{P}(\mathcal{C})$ *is the* clock assignment function. $\mathcal{C}$ *is the set of clocks with each clock,* $c : \mathcal{E} \rightarrow \mathbb{R}$, *being uniquely associated with a single event* $\in \mathcal{E}$.

- $R : S \rightarrow \mathcal{E} \rightarrow \mathbb{R}$ *is the* rate assignment function.

- $T : S \rightarrow S \rightarrow \mathcal{E} \rightarrow [0, 1]$ *is the* transition probability assignment function. $T(s', s, e)$ *is the probability that the transition* $s \rightarrow s'$ *takes place on occurrence of event* e.

- $F : C \rightarrow (\mathbb{R} \rightarrow [0, 1])$ *is the* distribution assignment function.

- $s_0 \in S$ *is the* initial state *of the GSMP.*

A GSMP is a stochastic process with state space S. The time the process spends in a state s is governed by the set of *active clocks,* $C(s)$, in that state. The time to the next state transition $\Delta = \min_{e \in E(s)} \frac{c_e}{R(s,e)}$, where c_e is the clock associated with event e. The *trigger event,* denoted e^*, is the event whose clock expires first, i.e., $\Delta = \frac{c_{e^*}}{R(s,e^*)}$. A transition is caused by an event being triggered. To trigger an event, all clocks in a state are updated, $c^*(s) = \{c_i - c_{e^*} : c_i \in C(s)\}$. Clock lifetimes are distributed in a way such that no two expire at precisely the same time. A new state, s' is chosen with probability $T(s', s, e^*)$. The clocks that are active in state s' may be expressed as $C(s') = N(s'; s, e^*) \cup O(s'; s, e^*)$ where $O(s'; s, e^*) = C(s') \cap (C(s) \setminus \{c_{e^*}\})$ is the set of *old clocks* and $N(s'; s, e^*) = C(s') \setminus O(s'; s, e^*)$ is the set of *new clocks.* The lifetime of the old clocks is given by $c = c^*$ for $c \in O(s'; s, e^*)$. The lifetime of the new clocks are distributed according to F, i.e., $c \sim F(c)(t)$, for $c \in N(s'; s, e^*)$.

In deriving a GSMP performance model we use the intuition that SPADES agents behave in a cyclic fashion — like discrete event simulations. An agent performs computation by firing a number of immediate and probabilistic transitions before reaching a *stable* state. It then delays (evolves via an evolution transition — the longest one it can perform) before it carries out more computation.

To be able to map a system to a GSMP we need to make some assumptions about the nature of the system being analyzed. These will be referred to as the *basic criteria* and deemed to be the minimal criteria in order to derive the GSMP.

(1) The system is closed. The system has no external interface and thus requires no interaction with the environment to define its behavior.

(2) The system is free from *state* non-determinism. There is a defined probability that the system can reach one stable configuration from another.

With these criteria we systematically derive the state space components, S and s_0, the clock components, C, R and F, the event components, E, and the transition components, T, which make up the GSMP definition.

22.4.1 State

Every instance of the agent representing the evolution of the system has a state associated with it. Deadlocked states (either temporal or non-temporal) are represented by a single "sink" state in the GSMP and discarded from further analysis[6]. We partition the set of non-deadlocking agents making up the transition graph of the system into those that are *stable* and those that are *ephemeral*.

DEFINITION 22.4 *A process, P, is* stable, *denoted stable(P)* $\iff$ $P \overset{t}{\leadsto}$, $t > 0$. *P is* ephemeral, *denoted ephem(P) iff* $\neg stable(P)$.

The state associated with a stable process represents a GSMP state ($s \in S$). Ephemeral states (those states associated with ephemeral processes) represent the fleeting state of the system during the process of computation. The state space of the GSMP can therefore be extracted from that of the SPADES system by pruning out all the *implementation specific* ephemeral states.

The symbolic state space of the GSMP, S, is defined

$$S = \{\sigma^* s : P_\sigma^s \in SSTG \land stable(P)\}$$

where $SSTG$ is the symbolic state transition graph for the system and σ^* is the transitive closure of the symbolic substitution function σ. The initial state of the GSMP, s_0, is the state of the stable process reachable from the initial SPADES process. The basic criteria ensure that there is only one such stable process.

22.4.2 Clocks and Events

In each non-sink state, one of a number of events can occur that lead to a transition. The transition may take the GSMP to a new state or leave the state unchanged. This *event* is signaled by the expiration of one clock from a set (the basic criteria (3) disallows two or more clocks expiring at the same time). Each evolution transition out of a stable state represents the expiration of a clock. By examining the sequence of delays that represent the evolution transition, we identify the clocks whose expiration triggers an event.

---

[6]Initially they can be identified and since they have no outgoing transitions can be subsequently ignored.

Before proceeding, we lay down some preliminary definitions. Firstly, the evolution to a labeled or probabilistic transition, denoted $\leadsto^t_\alpha$, $\alpha \in$ Act and $\leadsto^t_\pi$, respectively:

DEFINITION 22.5

(1) $P \leadsto^t_\alpha Q \iff P \leadsto^t Q \wedge P \not\xrightarrow{\alpha} \wedge Q \xrightarrow{\alpha}$ *and* $P \leadsto^0_\alpha P \iff P \xrightarrow{\alpha}$.

(2) $P \leadsto^t_\pi Q \iff P \leadsto^t Q \wedge Q \hookrightarrow$ *and* $P \leadsto^0_\pi P \iff P \hookrightarrow$.

Example 22.2 Evolutions to labeled or probabilistic transitions
$$P \stackrel{\text{def}}{=} (x).a.P + (y).b.P + (z).\mathcal{R}[t \leftarrow f].P$$

$$P \leadsto^x_a a.P$$
$$P \leadsto^y_b b.P$$
$$P \leadsto^z_\pi \mathcal{R}[t \leftarrow f].P \ . \quad \square$$

We can relate the durations of those evolutions to sequences of delay actions in the body of the process:

DEFINITION 22.6   *A time sequence, denoted t^+, associated with a stable process P, is a sequence of delay actions, $(t_1)...(t_n)$, $n > 0$ such that (t_{i-1}) guards (t_i) in P. The duration of the time sequence is $\sum t_i$ and is denoted t.*

Example 22.3 Time sequences in a process
$$P \stackrel{\text{def}}{=} (x).((y).a.\text{nil} + (z).a.\text{nil})$$
gives rise to the time sequences $t_1^+ = (x).(y)$ (duration $x + y$) and $t_2^+ = (x).(z)$ (duration $x + z$). $\square$

The expiration of a clock is captured by a *maximal* evolution. This is the evolution of a stable process to an ephemeral one.

DEFINITION 22.7   *Process P evolves to Q maximally, with duration t, denoted by $P \leadsto^t_m Q$ if $P \leadsto^t Q \wedge ephem(Q)$.*

The duration of a maximal evolution, t, is that of either a single sequence t^+ or the maximum of two sequences t_1^+ and t_2^+. We can write $P \leadsto^{t^+}_m Q$ or

$P \overset{(t_1^+, t_2^+)}{\rightsquigarrow}_m Q$ without ambiguity. These represent the sequence (or sequence pair for an evolution leading to a synchronization) of delay actions that have to expire before an ephemeral agent Q is reached. In a stable process, each such sequence corresponds to an active clock whose time to expiration is the duration of the sequence. We define a function to identify the active clocks of a process:

$$Clocks :: Process \rightarrow \{TimeSequence\} .$$

DEFINITION 22.8   For stable(P)

$$Clocks(P) = \{t^+ \; : \; P \overset{t^+}{\rightsquigarrow}_m\} .$$

Here t^+ may be a sequence pair.

To be able to identify how the set of active clocks change going from one state to the next, we identify which new sequences become unguarded or removed (i.e., resolved out) during a state transition (for a given event).

The *Clocks* function identifies the active sequences in a process. Moving from one process to another we identify which sequences are just *remnants* of older sequences. Remnants are defined in terms of *residual sequences.*

DEFINITION 22.9   *A sequence, s^+, of the form $(h_s).tl_s^+$, is a d-residual of sequence t^+, of the form $(h_t).tl_t^+$ if*

$$tl_s^+ \equiv tl_t^+ \wedge h_s = h_t - d$$

with $d < h_t$. Otherwise s^+ is a $(d - h_t)$-residual of tl_t^+.

For example, the sequence "$(c).(d).(e)$" is a $(a + b)$-residual of the sequence "$(a).(b).(c).(d).(e)$."

DEFINITION 22.10   *A sequence d^+ in process Q is a remnant of a sequence s^+ in stable process P if $\exists P' P \overset{t \leq s}{\rightsquigarrow} P'\{\rightarrow \cup \hookrightarrow\}^* Q$ and, d^+ is a (t)-residual of s^+.*

Example 22.4 Remnant processes
In the symbolic process pair

$$P \overset{\text{def}}{=} (t).a \mid (x).((y).\tau + (z).b)$$
$$Q \overset{\text{def}}{=} (t - x - y).a \mid (z - y).b .$$

$(t - x - y)$ in Q is a remnant of (t) in P, $(z - y)$ in Q is a remnant of $(x).(z)$ in P. In both cases $P' \equiv (t - x - y).a|\tau + (z - y).b$ with the sequences being $(x + y)$-residuals.   ☐

A sequence pair is a remnant if its elements have this property individually. For example, the sequence pair "$((a).(b), (c).(d))$" is a remnant of the pair "$((a + x).(b), (c + x).(d))$" if the processes they come from are related by a path with an initial evolution of duration "x."

We now define two relationships between stable processes in terms of their clocks:

DEFINITION 22.11

$Old(P, Q) = \{c_Q : c_Q \text{ is a remnant of } c_P, c_Q \in Clocks(Q), c_P \in Clocks(P)\}$.
$New(P, Q) = Clocks(Q) \backslash Old(P, Q)$.

These represent the clocks not *disabled* and those *enabled* going from one configuration (that associated with P) to another (that associated with Q).

Example 22.5 Clocks of a process
In the symbolic process pair (assuming *in situ* substitution)

$$P \stackrel{\text{def}}{=} (r).a.(s).\overline{b} + (t).\tau|(x).\overline{a}.(y).b|(z).\tau$$
$$Q \stackrel{\text{def}}{=} (s).\overline{b}|(y).b|(z - r).\tau$$

we have

$$Clocks(P) = \{((r), (x)), (t), (z)\}$$
$$Clocks(Q) = \{((s), (y)), (z - r)\}$$
$$Old(P, Q) = \{(z - r)\}$$
$$New(P, Q) = \{((s), (y))\} .$$

Note that the clock associated with (t) was disabled, the one associated with $((r), (x))$ having expired.   ☐

The clock assignment function for the GSMP is calculated dynamically as the system evolves:

$$C(s) = N(s'; s, e^*) \cup O(s'; s, e^*) .$$

The initial clock assignment $C(s_0) = \{c_e : c_e = t , t^+ \in Clocks(P_0)\}$ where P_0 is the initial stable state of the system and e is the event associated with the transition $P_0 \stackrel{t^+}{\rightsquigarrow}$.

We now have

$$N(s'; s, e^*) = \{c_e \ : \ c_e = t \ , \ t^+ \in New(P, Q)\}$$

where s' is the state of process Q, s is the state of process P, e^* is the event that leads to the transition from P to Q and e is the event associated with the transition $P \stackrel{t^+}{\rightsquigarrow}$. Similarly,

$$O(s'; s, e^*) = \{c_e \ : \ c_e = t \ , \ t^+ \in Old(P, Q)\} \ .$$

The clocks associated with the set $N(.,.)$ are initialized according to the function F which is defined by the duration of the sequences (or sequence pairs) representing the clocks. In general the distribution is governed by a sum of the random variables associated with the delays composing the sequence (or maximum of a pair of sums).

Without loss of generality, all clock rates can be set to 1, i.e., $R(s, e) = 1$ for all states s and events e. A clock whose rate changes from state to state is modeled by a number of different clocks, each with a different initial value.

22.4.3 Transitions and Transition Probabilities

Transitions are modeled by the paths in the SSTG from one stable state to another. The first link along the path represents the (maximal) evolution modeling the delay to the trigger event. The remainder of the path represents the "computation" carried out during the transition that leads to the next GSMP state.

A GSMP transition for a given event/state defines the destination state and the probability associated with the choice of that state. The source and destination state of a transition is simply encoded in the path representing the event transition. Calculating the probability of the transition requires deeper analysis. We note the properties of the computation path followed, from one stable state to another.

(1) The SPADES transitions along the path denoting the computation steps are either probabilistic and represent

 - Introduction of a random variable
 - Making a probabilistic choice

 or represent a τ labeled transition.

(2) Non-deterministic paths between states must be confluent: concurrent computation can only be modeled by interleaving, but leads to the same result.

(3) For a given event, the stable processes that are the destinations of different transition paths must have different states associated with them.

The definition of the transition graph and the semantic properties of probabilistic transitions ($\mu(P, Q)$ is the probability density associated with moving from P to Q) enables the transition probabilities to be derived simply. First we identify the different transitions possible.

DEFINITION 22.12   *Under the basic criteria, for the graph $<N, act, tr_l, tr_e, tr_p, N_0>$, for $P, Q \in N$, the computation path from P to Q, denoted $CP(P, Q)$ is defined:*

$$CP(P, Q) = \emptyset \text{ if } P \equiv Q$$
$$CP(P, Q) = \{(P, a, b, P')_l.R : \exists P' tr_l(P, b, a) = P'\ R \in CP(P', Q)\}$$
$$CP(P, Q) = \{(P, p, b, P')_p.R : \forall P' tr_p(P, b, p) = P'\ R \in CP(P', Q)\}.$$

Example 22.6 Transition paths
$$P \stackrel{\text{def}}{=} \tau.nil|\tau.([\tfrac{1}{3}]Q \dotplus [\tfrac{2}{3}]R)$$

has transition graph:

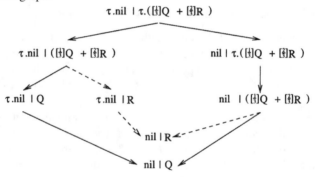

We have

$$CP(P, (nil \mid Q)) = \{l_1.l_2.l_3\}$$
$$l_1 = (P, \tau, true, nil|\tau.([\tfrac{1}{3}]Q \dotplus [\tfrac{2}{3}]R)(\equiv P'))_l$$
$$l_2 = (P', \tau, true, nil|[\tfrac{1}{3}]Q \dotplus [\tfrac{2}{3}]R(\equiv P''))_l$$
$$l_3 = (P'', \tfrac{1}{3}, true, (nil \mid Q))_p .$$

Note that there are two possible computation paths from P to the agent $(nil \mid Q)$ (denoted by the solid links in the diagram) due to the original nondeterministic choice between the two possible τ-transitions. CP returns only one of them.   ⬜

Having reached its head, a computation path has a certain probability of being followed during execution. We can split this probability into that of making each individual transition. Firstly we can show that a link denoting a labeled transition on a path is always taken [11]. Therefore, a link in a computation path that denotes a labeled transition can always be replaced by a probabilistic link with probability 1 and identical source and destination. As far as transitions and transition probabilities are concerned they are the same.

Links denoting probabilistic SPADES transitions, by their nature, are not crossed in every simulation. To derive the chance of a given link being crossed we have to aggregate over all possible simulation runs, i.e., symbol assignments $\rho' \subset \rho$ with the symbols restricted such that all guards for the simulation trace to that node are true. That is to say, the probability of the link being crossed is $\int \mu(P, Q) d\rho'$ for the link representing the transition $P \hookrightarrow Q$.

This analysis can be carried out systematically by examining the possible form of $\mu(P, Q)$ and, for the case of the subset of SPADES presented in this paper, can be simplified to the product of probabilities for a sequence of single step transitions.

The probability of a particular computation path as a whole being taken is now just the probability of every constituent link being taken.

Example 22.7 Probability of computation path

For the processes P,Q

$$P \stackrel{\text{def}}{=} \mathcal{R}[x \to f_x].([\tfrac{1}{3}]\tau.S \dotplus [\tfrac{2}{3}]R)$$

we have $P(p_{PS} \text{ taken})$ where $\mathcal{CP}(P, S) = \{p_{PS}\}$ is

$$1 \times 1/3 \times 1 = 1/3$$

where "$1 \times 1/3$" is the probability of taking the link denoting the transition $P \hookrightarrow \tau.S$ and the rightmost "1" denoting the probability of taking the link denoting the transition $\tau.S \to S$. ⬚

A transition path is just a computation path from the node after a maximal evolution out of a stable state to another stable state:

$$T = \{(s, s', e, p) : P \leadsto_m P', \mathcal{CP}(P', Q) \neq \emptyset\}$$

where s is the state associated with process P, s' is the state associated with process Q, e is the event associated with the maximal evolution $P \leadsto_m P'$ and p is the probability of taking a path leading from P' to Q.

22.5   Example: An ATM Switch

Here we derive the GSMP for a SPADES model of an ATM switch. The switch is based on a three stage Delta network and has 27 input and output ports. Customers (cells) arriving at the inputs provide the workload for the model. Each switching element buffers cells using a FIFO queuing discipline. The queues employ a repetitive service form of blocking whereby a cell repeats service at the head of the queue if there is no buffer space available for it in the next stage. Cells that arrive to a full buffer at the stage 0 are discarded. The interconnection of the switching elements is shown in Fig. 22.1.

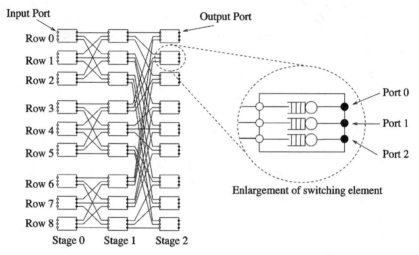

FIGURE 22.1

A 27×27 **switch.**

Arrival to each input port occurs in a *bursty* fashion. The size of each burst is assumed (arbitrarily) to be geometrically distributed and the interval between each burst is assumed (arbitrarily) to be exponentially distributed. Cells leaving stage 2 are never blocked. The route each cell takes through the network is chosen uniformly across the possible outputs; the route is a 2 digit base 3 number. The two digits specify which of three possible switching elements the cell should be forwarded to at stages 1 and 2, respectively.

22.5.1   The SPADES Model

The SPADES model specifies the system as an interaction between an environment and the switch. The environment provides the workload, generating arrivals at the input ports and removes departures generated at the output ports.

22.5.1.1   Workload

The workload generates the arrivals to stage 0 of the network. Arrivals occur in bursts. The arrivals to each input port are modeled by its own process $(CPP_{<row,port>})^7$. After a delay (for x units) a batch of n arrivals occurs. An arrival comes to stage 0 of the switch for a particular row and port. The arrival carries with it a route which that cell is to take through the switch.

$$CPP_{<row,port>} = \mathcal{R}[x \leftarrow f_e].\mathcal{R}[n \leftarrow f_g].(x).BATCH_{<n,row,port>}$$

$$BATCH_{<n,row,port>} = \mathcal{R}[route \leftarrow f_{Route}].$$
$$(\overline{arr}_{<0,row,port,route>}.\overline{accept}.BATCH_{<n-1,row,port>}$$
$$+ \overline{full}_{<0,row,port>}.\overline{drop}.BATCH_{<n-1,row,port>})$$

$$BATCH_{<0,row,port>} = CPP_{<row,port>}$$

$$ARRIVALS = \prod_{row=0}^{8} \prod_{port=0}^{2} CPP_{<row,port>}$$

f_e is the probability density function governing the arrival rate, f_g is the discrete probability mass governing the batch size and f_{Route} is the mass function governing the route a cell takes through the network. Here the actions *arr*, *accept*, *drop* and *full* synchronize with their conjugates (to be introduced in later processes) and denote events that occur in the system: arrival of a cell to the switch, acceptance of a cell at stage 0, dropping of a cell at stage 0 and signaling of a full buffer at stage 0, respectively.

Departures occurring at the output of the switch (arrivals to a hypothetical stage 3) are "absorbed" into the environment.

$$DEPARTURES = \sum_{r,p,t} arr_{<3,r,p,t>}.DEPARTURES$$

22.5.1.2   The Switch

The switch itself is a Delta network of queues. Each queue is made up of a buffer (*BUFF* with maximum capacity of eight cells) and a server (*SERVER*). The buffer holds the routes of the cells which have arrived. The notation $h:Q$ represents the list which differs from another list Q in that it has the value h attached to its head. The notation $Q : h$ has the symmetrical meaning. An empty queue is denoted [] with $h:[] = []:h = [h]$.

$$BUFF_{<n,s,r,p,h:Q>} = \left(\sum_{route} arr_{<s,r,p,route>}.BUFF_{<n+1,s,r,p,h:Q:route>} \right.$$

---

[7] Here the annotation $CPP_{<row,port>}$ denotes a family of agent names that only differ by assignment to the variables *row* (range $0 - 8$) and *port* ($0 - 2$).

$$+\overline{service}_{<s,r,p,h>}.BUFF_{<n-1,s,r,p,Q>} \, ,$$

for $0 < n < 8$

$$BUFF_{<0,s,r,p,[]>} = \sum_{route} arr_{<s,r,p,route>}.BUFF_{<1,s,r,p,[route]>}$$

$$BUFF_{<8,s,r,p,h:Q>} = \overline{full}_{<s,r,p>}.BUFF_{<8,s,r,p,h:Q>}$$

$$+\overline{service}_{<s,r,p,h>}.BUFF_{<7,s,r,p,Q>}$$

$$SERVER_{<s,r,p>} = \sum_{route} service_{<s,r,p,route>}.BUSY(s, r, p, route)$$

$$BUSY_{<s,r,p,route>} = \mathcal{R}[x \leftarrow f_s].(x).$$

$$\overline{(full_{<s+1,next\_row(s,r,p),digit(route,2-(s+1))>}.BUSY_{<s,r,p,route>}}$$

$$+\overline{arr}_{<s+1,next\_row(s,r,p),digit(route,2-(s+1)),route>}.SERVER_{<s,r,p>})$$

$$QUEUE_{<s,r,p>} = (SERVER_{<s,r,p>} \mid BUFF_{<0,s,r,p>})\backslash\{service\}$$

The density function f_s governs the service time distribution of a queue. The function $next\_row(s, r, p)$ calculates, for the queue at port p in a switching element in row r at stage s, which row in the next stage a cell should be routed to. The function $digit(n, i)$ returns the i'th ternary digit of the number n and dictates which queue of the switching element in the next stage the cell is routed to.

$$SWITCH = \prod_{stage=0}^{2} \prod_{row=0}^{8} \prod_{num=0}^{2} QUEUE_{<stage,row,num>}$$

The complete system consists of the switch placed in the environment (arrival and departure processes). Since we are going to monitor the probability of cell loss at arrival to the switch, a monitoring process is placed in parallel with the system to count the number of the occurrences of the *accept* and *drop* actions.

$$MONITOR_{<i,j>} = accept.MONITOR_{<i+1,j>} + drop.MONITOR_{<i,j+1>}$$

$$SYSTEM = (ARRIVALS \mid SWITCH \mid DEPARTURES \mid$$

$$MONITOR_{<0,0>}) \backslash \{arr, full, accept, drop\}$$

22.5.2   Deriving the GSMP

22.5.2.1   The State Space

The state of the process $MONITOR_{<i,j>}$ is defined as (i, j). A single queue is stable when $QUEUE_{<s,r,p>}$ is of the form

$$((x).(\overline{full}_{<\cdots>}.BUSY_{<\cdots>}$$

$$+\overline{arr}_{<\cdots>}.SERVER_{<\cdots>}) \mid BUFF_{<n,\cdots>})\backslash\{\cdots\} \tag{22.1}$$

for $n \geq 0$ (representing a busy server) or of the form

$$(SERVER_{<\cdots>} \mid BUFF_{<0,\cdots>})\backslash\{\cdots\} \tag{22.2}$$

which represents an empty queue waiting for an arrival. In the first case it is defined as having state $1 + n$ and in the second as 0.

The arrival process is stable only when each $CPP_{<...>}$ process is of the form

$$(x).BATCH_{<n,r,p>} \tag{22.3}$$

for some x and n. It does not contribute to the state.

The state space of the GSMP is defined as $S = \{(i, j, \mathbf{Q}) : \mathbf{Q}_{s,r,p} \geq 0, 0 \leq s \leq 2, 0 \leq r \leq 8, 0 \leq p \leq 2\}$ when *MONITOR* is in state (i, j) and $QUEUE_{<s,r,p>}$ is in state $\mathbf{Q}_{s,r,p}$.

22.5.2.2 The Clocks

The system is stable when each constituent process is stable. At such a point the active clocks are those associated with the delay action (x) in processes of the form (22.1) or (22.3).

22.5.2.3 The Transitions

A transition occurs when a clock expires. Due to the continuous distribution of the delays, no two clocks can expire at precisely the same time with non-zero probability. Only one destination state is available for each transition. For an expiration of the delay in a process of the form (22.1) (a descendant of $BUSY_{<s,r,p,route>}$), the GSMP remains in the same state if

$$\mathbf{Q}_{s+1,next\_row(s,r,p),digit(route,2-(s+1))} = 9$$

otherwise, it moves from state $(a, d, \mathbf{Q})$ to $(a, d, \mathbf{Q}')$ where $\mathbf{Q}'_{s,r,p} = \mathbf{Q}_{s,r,p} - 1$, $\mathbf{Q}'_{s+1,...} = \mathbf{Q}'_{s+1,...} + 1$ and $\mathbf{Q}'_{i,j,k} = \mathbf{Q}_{i,j,k}$ for $(i, j, k) \neq (s, r, p)$. If a transition occurs (either moving to a new state or remaining in the same state), all old clocks are carried over and the one that expired is replaced with one with duration governed by f_s if $\mathbf{Q}'_{s,r,p} > 0$.

If the delay in a process of the form (22.3) (a descendant of $CPP_{<row,port>}$) expires, the GSMP moves from state $(a, d, \mathbf{Q})$ to $(a', d', \mathbf{Q}')$ where $a' = a + x$, $d' = d + (n - x)$, $\mathbf{Q}'_{0,row,port} = \mathbf{Q}_{0,row,port} + x$, $x = min(n, 9 - \mathbf{Q}_{0,row,port})$ and n is a discrete random variable with probability mass governed by f_g. In this transition, all old clocks are carried over and the one that expired is replaced by a new one with duration governed by f_e.

22.5.3 Simulation Results

The GSMP was simulated and the probability of cell loss (steady state value of $j/(i+j)$ for GSMP state $(i, j, \mathbf{Q})$) for varying batch size and arrival rate gathered. The results are shown in Fig. 22.2 and are plotted with a 95% confidence interval.

Here f_e was an exponential distribution function with parameter (arrival rate) varying from 0.025 to 0.5, f_g was a geometric distribution function with parameter (1/mean batch size) varying from 0.05 to 0.5 and f_s was an exponential distribution function with fixed parameter of 1. Simulating the GSMP model of the system resulted in an order of magnitude speed-up over simulation of the model directly. This was due to the fact that sequences of instantaneous transitions (especially those resulting from a batch arrival) were amalgamated into single GSMP transitions.

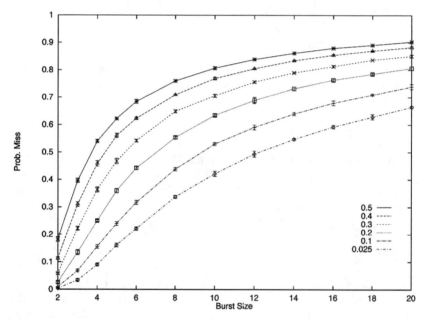

FIGURE 22.2
Simulation results.

22.6   Related Work

In [12], a GSMP was used to act as the underlying performance model for *stochastic event structures*. The GSMP was derived by systematically examining the relationship between state and transition entities defining the stochastic event structure and a GSMP. The process of derivation could only be carried out for the class of *deterministic* event structures. They defined a SPA that used stochastic event structures as a semantic model thereby bridging the route from a SPA to a GSMP performance model. In our method, the process of derivation is more direct. The GSMP model can be derived from the SPADES source directly. The use of the SSTG associated with the agent is not only for convenience of presentation but also as a step towards automating the process.

The process of deriving a GSMP can be viewed as a *reduction* process similar to that of [10]. There, the transition system associated with the SPA was separated into *tangible* and *vanishing* states which loosely correspond with our notion of stable and ephemeral states. The reduction method was then a combination of *in-depth* reduction; a process of amalgamating numerous instantaneous transitions in sequence, and *in-width* reduction; a process of amalgamating branching instantaneous transitions leading to the same state. This compares with the process used to construct transition paths. [10] did not define a performance model for their SPA. The process of reduction was introduced as a reduction strategy towards further, possibly automated, analysis.

[1] introduces a SPA coincidently named SPADES. Their process algebra mimics ours in that the notion of action and delay are now separated into two distinct specification constructs. Their SPA uses *stochastic automata* as a semantic model. They show the (close) relationship between stochastic automata and GSMP and come up with a simulation algorithm to extract performance metrics from their models. Notions of probability have to be modeled using the interaction between clocks. Were it not for the fact that the synchronization paradigm in their approach is a broadcast based one, their models could be viewed as a straightforward subclass of ours.

[2] used a class of *extended generalized semi-Markov processes* as the underlying performance model for their SPA. Their SPA captures the notion of weights and priorities associated with actions. Unfortunately their approach maintains the idea that actions and durations are modeled by a single specification construct. This leads to the necessity of somewhat obfuscating the syntactic and semantic presentation of the SPA with constructs that are used to deal with the fact that, in a generalized framework, action durations are no longer *memoryless*.

22.7 Conclusion

We have shown how a GSMP can be used as the underlying performance model for a class of SPADES models. In order to make the process of deriving the GSMP tractable we've had to make certain assumptions such as the basic criteria, which may occasionally limit the size of the class of models for which we can successfully derive a GSMP. Implementing algorithms based on the derivation process will serve not only to explicitly generate a performance model but also as an optimization technique for simulation of SPADES systems: the GSMP can be described as a compact SPADES model which can be simulated using existing tools.

The process of deriving the GSMP is an intuitive one based upon the nature of SPADES transitions and the operational nature of GSMPs. Since SPADES can be used to give an operational semantics to GSMP (by constructing a SPADES model corresponding to a GSMP) we can prove the derivation methodology sound. This requires constructing a notion of equivalence based upon the fact that two systems are to be indistinguishable from one another if they exhibit the same stochastic property of state. Formalizing these concepts is an area of further research.

Using axiomatizations based on the notion of equivalence above is thought to be a starting point for translating SPADES models into other SPA models directly. In particular the process of translating (simplified) SPADES models to PEPA [9] ones, which can be solved analytically using existing tools [4], seems an exciting one. Similarly the techniques presented in [13] can be used for the analytical solution of GSMP systems in which clock durations may be exponentially or deterministically distributed.

A Appendix: SPADES Symbolic Operational Semantics

The set of *process expressions,* **PExp**, is the least set including

$$
\begin{aligned}
\mathbf{PExp} = \ & X \\
& |\ \text{nil} \\
& |\ (r).P \\
& |\ \alpha.P \\
& |\ \alpha[s \leftarrow t].P \\
& |\ \mathcal{R}[s \leftarrow f].P \\
& |\ \sum_{i \in I} [q_i] P_i \\
& |\ P + Q \\
& |\ P \mid Q \\
& |\ P[S] \\
& |\ P \backslash A \\
& |\ \mathbf{rec}(X = P) \\
& |\ \text{if } b \text{ then } P \text{ else } Q
\end{aligned}
$$

where

- $X \in$ **PVar**.

- $P, Q \in$ **PExp**.

- $s \in$ **Var**.

- $b \in$ **BExp**, the set of Boolean expressions.

- $u, v \in$ **Sym**, the set of symbols.

- $t \in$ **SymExp**, the set of symbolic expressions.

- Λ is a set of actions not containing τ, $Act = \Lambda \cup \{\tau\}$, $\alpha \in Act$.

- I is a finite indexing set with the $P_i \in$ **PExp**.

- S is a relabeling function $S : \Lambda \to \Lambda$, $A \subset \Lambda$.

- q_i are probabilities.

- $\sigma :$ **Sym** $\to$ **SymExp** is the static symbolic substitution function associated with a closed symbolic process.

- $\{u/x\}$ is the syntactic relabeling function replacing free occurrences of x with the symbol (expression) u.

- *NewSymbol* is a function that generates a new symbol on each invocation.

A.1 Symbolic Labeled Transitions

$$\frac{}{(\alpha.P)_\sigma \xrightarrow{true,\alpha} P_\sigma} \qquad \text{Prefix1}$$

$$\frac{P_\sigma \xrightarrow{b,\beta} P'_{\sigma'}}{((u).P)_\sigma \xrightarrow{u=0 \wedge b,\beta} P'_{\sigma'}} \qquad \text{No} - \text{Delay}$$

$$\frac{P_\sigma \xrightarrow{b,\beta} P'_{\sigma'} \quad \neg\text{Prob}(Q) \quad Q_\sigma \xrightarrow{b,\beta} Q'_{\sigma'} \quad \neg\text{Prob}(P)}{(P+Q)_\sigma \xrightarrow{b,\beta} P'_{\sigma'} \qquad (P+Q)_\sigma \xrightarrow{b,\beta} Q'_{\sigma'}} \qquad \text{Sum}$$

$$\frac{P_\sigma \xrightarrow{b,\beta} P'_{\sigma'} \quad \neg\text{Prob}(Q) \quad Q_\sigma \xrightarrow{b,\beta} Q'_{\sigma'} \quad \neg\text{Prob}(P)}{(P|Q)_\sigma \xrightarrow{b,\beta} (P'|Q)_{\sigma'} \qquad (P|Q)_\sigma \xrightarrow{b,\beta} (P|Q')_{\sigma'}} \qquad \text{Parallel}$$

$$\frac{P_\sigma \xrightarrow{b,\alpha} P'_{\sigma'} \quad Q_\sigma \xrightarrow{b',\bar{\alpha}} Q'_{\sigma''}}{(P|Q)_\sigma \xrightarrow{b \wedge b',\tau} (P'|Q')_{\sigma' \cup \sigma''}} \qquad \text{Communicate1}$$

$$\frac{P_\sigma \xrightarrow{b,\beta} P'_{\sigma'}}{(P[S])_\sigma \xrightarrow{b,S(\alpha)} (P'[S])_{\sigma'}} \qquad \text{Relabel}$$

$$\frac{P_\sigma \xrightarrow{b,\beta} P'_{\sigma'}}{(P\backslash A)_\sigma \xrightarrow{b,\beta} (P'\backslash A)_{\sigma'}} \quad \alpha \notin A \text{ and } \overline{\alpha} \notin A \quad \text{Restrict}$$

$$\frac{(P\{\mathbf{rec}(X{=}P)/X\})_\sigma \xrightarrow{b,\beta} P'_{\sigma'}}{(\mathbf{rec}(X{=}P))_\sigma \xrightarrow{b,\beta} P'_{\sigma'}} \quad \text{Rec}$$

$$\frac{P_\sigma \xrightarrow{b,\beta} P'_{\sigma'}}{X_\sigma \xrightarrow{b,\beta} P'_{\sigma'}} \quad X \overset{\text{def}}{=} P \quad \text{Definition1}$$

A.2 Symbolic Single Step Evolution Transitions

$$\frac{P_\sigma \overset{b,t}{\leadsto_o} P'_{\sigma'}}{((u).P)_\sigma \overset{u=0\wedge b,t}{\leadsto_o} P'_{\sigma'}} \quad \text{No} - \text{Delay}$$

$$\frac{v=NewSymbol}{((u).P)_\sigma \overset{v>0,v}{\leadsto_o} P_{\sigma[v\mapsto u]}} \quad \text{End} - \text{Delay}$$

$$\frac{v=NewSymbol, \ t=NewSymbol}{((u).P)_\sigma \overset{t<u,t}{\leadsto_o} (v).P_{\sigma[v\mapsto u-t]}} \quad \text{Reduce}$$

$$\frac{v=NewSymbol, \ t=NewSymbol}{(\alpha[s\leftarrow f].P)_\sigma \overset{true,t}{\leadsto_o} \alpha[s\leftarrow v].P_{\sigma[v\mapsto f+t]}} \quad \text{Idle}$$

$$\frac{t=NewSymbol}{\mathbf{nil}_\sigma \overset{true,t}{\leadsto_o} \mathbf{nil}_\sigma} \quad \text{Nil}$$

$$\frac{P_\sigma \overset{b,u}{\leadsto_o} P'_{\sigma'} \quad Q_\sigma \overset{b',v}{\leadsto_o} Q'_{\sigma''}}{(P{+}Q)_\sigma \overset{u=v\wedge b\wedge b',u}{\leadsto_o} (P'{+}Q')_{\sigma'\cup\sigma''}} \quad \text{Sum}$$

$$\frac{\neg P|Q\xrightarrow{\tau} \quad P_\sigma \overset{b,u}{\leadsto_o} P'_{\sigma'} \quad Q_\sigma \overset{b',v}{\leadsto_o} Q'_{\sigma''}}{(P|Q)\sigma \overset{u=v,b\wedge b',u}{\leadsto_o} (P'|Q')_{\sigma'\cup\sigma''}} \quad \text{Parallel}$$

$$\frac{P_\sigma \overset{b,t}{\leadsto_o} P'_{\sigma'}}{(P[S])_\sigma \overset{b,t}{\leadsto_o} (P'[S])_{\sigma'}} \quad \text{Relabel}$$

$$\frac{P_\sigma \overset{b,t}{\leadsto_o} P'_{\sigma'}}{(P\backslash A)_\sigma \overset{b,t}{\leadsto_o} (P'\backslash A)_{\sigma'}} \quad \alpha \notin A \text{ and } \overline{\alpha} \notin A \quad \text{Restrict}$$

$$\frac{(P\{\mathbf{rec}(X{=}P)/X\})_\sigma \overset{b,t}{\leadsto_o} P'_{\sigma'}}{(\mathbf{rec}(X{=}P))_\sigma \overset{b,t}{\leadsto_o} P'_{\sigma'}} \quad \text{Rec}$$

$$\frac{P_\sigma \overset{b,t}{\leadsto_o} P'_{\sigma'}}{X_\sigma \overset{b,t}{\leadsto_o} P'_{\sigma'}} \quad X \overset{\text{def}}{=} P \quad \text{Definition1}$$

A.3 Symbolic Evolution Transitions

$$\frac{P_\sigma \overset{b,t}{\leadsto}_o P'_{\sigma'}}{P_\sigma \overset{b,t}{\leadsto} P'_{\sigma'}} \qquad \text{Any} - \text{Delay}$$

$$\frac{P_\sigma \overset{b,t}{\leadsto}_o P'_{\sigma'} \quad P'_{\sigma'} \overset{b',t'}{\leadsto} P''_{\sigma''}, \quad v{=}NewSymbol}{P_\sigma \overset{b\wedge b',v}{\leadsto} P''_{\sigma''[v\mapsto t+t']}} \quad \text{Add} - \text{Delay}$$

A.4 Symbolic Single Step Probabilistic Transitions

$$\frac{}{(\sum_{i\in I}[q_i]P_i)_\sigma \overset{true,q_i}{\underset{0}{\leadsto}}_{[i].\langle\rangle} (P_i)_\sigma} \qquad \text{Resolve}$$

$$\frac{t{=}NewSymbol}{(\mathcal{R}[s{\leftarrow}f].P)_\sigma \overset{true,f(t)}{\underset{0}{\leadsto}}_{(t).\langle\rangle} (P\{t/s\})_{\sigma[t\sim f]}} \qquad \text{Sample}$$

$$\frac{}{\text{(if } c \text{ then } P \text{ else } Q)_\sigma \overset{c,1}{\underset{0}{\leadsto}}_{\{\langle\rangle,0\}} P_\sigma \quad \text{(if } c \text{ then } P \text{ else } Q)_\sigma \overset{\neg c,1}{\underset{0}{\leadsto}}_{\{0,\langle\rangle\}} Q_\sigma} \qquad \text{Cond}$$

$$\frac{P_\sigma \overset{b,q}{\underset{0}{\leadsto}}_l P'_{\sigma'}}{((u).P)_\sigma \overset{u=0\wedge b}{\underset{0}{\leadsto}}_l P'_{\sigma'}} \qquad \text{No} - \text{Delay}$$

$$\frac{P_\sigma \overset{b,q}{\underset{0}{\leadsto}}_l P'_{\sigma'}}{(P{+}Q)_\sigma \overset{b,q}{\underset{0}{\leadsto}}_{l+\langle\rangle} (P'{+}Q)_{\sigma'}} \quad \frac{Q_\sigma \overset{b,q}{\underset{0}{\leadsto}}_l Q'_{\sigma'}}{(P{+}Q)_\sigma \overset{b,q}{\underset{0}{\leadsto}}_{\langle\rangle+l} (P{+}Q')_{\sigma'}} \qquad \text{Sum}$$

$$\frac{P_\sigma \overset{b,q}{\underset{0}{\leadsto}}_l P'_{\sigma'}}{(P|Q)_\sigma \overset{b,q}{\underset{0}{\leadsto}}_{l|\langle\rangle} (P'|Q)_{\sigma'}} \quad \frac{Q_\sigma \overset{b,q}{\underset{0}{\leadsto}}_l Q'_{\sigma'}}{(P|Q)_\sigma \overset{b,q}{\underset{0}{\leadsto}}_{\langle\rangle|l} (P|Q')_{\sigma'}} \qquad \text{Parallel}$$

$$\frac{P_\sigma \overset{b,q}{\underset{0}{\leadsto}}_l P'_{\sigma'}}{(P[S])_\sigma \overset{b,q}{\underset{0}{\leadsto}}_l (P'[S])_{\sigma'}} \qquad \text{Relabel}$$

$$\frac{P_\sigma \overset{b,q}{\underset{0}{\leadsto}}_l P'_{\sigma'}}{(P\backslash A)_\sigma \overset{b,q}{\underset{0}{\leadsto}}_l (P'\backslash A)_{\sigma'}} \qquad \text{Restrict}$$

$$\frac{(P\{\mathbf{rec}(X{=}P)/X\})_\sigma \overset{b,q}{\underset{0}{\leadsto}}_l P'_{\sigma'}}{(\mathbf{rec}(X{=}P))_\sigma \overset{b,q}{\underset{0}{\leadsto}}_l P'_{\sigma'}} \qquad \text{Rec}$$

$$\frac{P_\sigma \overset{b,q}{\underset{0}{\leadsto}}_l P'_{\sigma'}}{X_\sigma \overset{b,q}{\underset{0}{\leadsto}}_l P'_{\sigma'}} \ X \overset{\text{def}}{=} P \qquad \text{Definition1}$$

A.5   Symbolic Probabilistic Transitions

$$\frac{P_\sigma \xrightarrow[\langle\rangle]{b,p}{}_l P'_{\sigma'} \quad P'_{\sigma'} \xrightarrow[m]{b',q} P''_{\sigma''}}{P_\sigma \xrightarrow[\mathrm{lf}(l,m)]{b\wedge b',p.q} P''_{\sigma''}} \quad \text{Mult} - \text{Samples}$$

$$\frac{\neg \mathrm{Prob}(P)}{P_\sigma \xrightarrow[\langle\rangle]{1} P_\sigma} \qquad \text{No} - \text{Samples}$$

with the label extension function

$$\mathrm{lf}(\langle\rangle, m) = m$$
$$\mathrm{lf}(a.\langle\rangle, m) = a.m$$
$$\mathrm{lf}(l + l', m + m') = \mathrm{lf}(l, m) + \mathrm{lf}(l', m')$$
$$\mathrm{lf}(l \mid l', m \mid m') = \mathrm{lf}(l, m) \mid \mathrm{lf}(l', m')$$
$$\mathrm{lf}(\{l, 0\}, m) = \{\mathrm{lf}(l, m), 0\}$$
$$\mathrm{lf}(\{0, l\}, m) = \{0, \mathrm{lf}(l, m)\}$$

References

[1] P.R. D'Argenio, J.-P Katoen, and E. Brinksma. General purpose discrete event simulation using SPADES. In *Process Algebra and Performance Modeling, Sixth International Workshop,* 1998.

[2] M. Berbardo, M. Bravetti, and R. Gorrieri. Towards Performance Evaluation with General Distributions in Process Algebras. In *Proceedings of 9th Int. Conference on Concurrency Theory (CONCUR'98)* D. Sangiori and R. de Simone (Eds), LNCS 1466, pp 405–422, September 1998.

[3] A.J. Field, P.G. Harrison, and K. Kanani. Automatic generation of verifiable cache coherence simulation models from high-level specifications. *Australian Computer Science Communications,* 20(3), 261–265, March 1998.

[4] S. Gilmore and J. Hillston. The PEPA Workbench: A Tool to Support a Process Algebra-based Approach to Performance Modeling. In *Proceedings of the Seventh International Conference on Modeling Techniques and Tools for Computer Performance Evaluation,* number 794 in Lecture Notes in Computer Science, pp 353–368, Vienna, May 1994. Springer-Verlag.

[5] P. W. Glynn. A GSMP Formalism for Discrete Event Systems. In *Proceedings of IEEE,* 77(1), 14–23, 1989.

[6] N. Götz, U. Herzog, and M. Rettelbach. TIPP: A language for timed processes and performance evaluation. *Report internal, Universität Erlangen-Nürnberg,* March 1992.

[7] M. Hennessy and H. Lin. Symbolic bisimulations. *Theoretical Computer Science,* 138(2), 353–389, 20 February 1995.

[8] H. Hermanns, M. Rettelbach, and T. Weiss. Formal characterization of immediate actions in SPA with nondeterminism. *The Computer Journal,* 38, 530–541, July 1995.

[9] J. Hillston. A Compositional Approach to Performance Modeling. *Distinguished Dissertation in Computer Science.* Cambridge University Press, 1996.

[10] Z. Huzar and J. Maggot. Reduction method for transition system of a performance evaluation extension of LOTOS. In *Proceedings of the Fourth Process Algebra and Performance Modeling Workshop,* M. Ribaudo, editor, pp 95–119, Torino, Italy, July 1996. CLUT.

[11] K. Kanani. A Unified Framework for Systematic Quantitative and Qualitative Analysis of Communicating Systems. *PhD thesis,* Imperial College of Science, Technology and Medicine. University of London, August 1998.

[12] J.-P. Katoen, E. Brinksma, D. Latella, and R. Langerak. Stochastic simulation of event structures. In M. Ribaudo (Ed), *Proceedings of the Fourth Process Algebra and Performance Modeling Workshop,* pp 21–40, Torino, Italy, July 1996. CLUT.

[13] C. Lindemann. Performance Modeling with Deterministic and Stochastic Petri Nets. John Wiley, 1998.

[14] C. Miguel, A. Fernández, and L. Vidaller. A LOTOS based performance tool. *Computer Networks and ISDN Systems,* (25), 791–814, 1993.

[15] R. Milner. Communication and Concurrency. *International Series in Computer Science.* Prentice Hall, 1989. SU Fisher Research 511/24.

[16] J.-P. Katoen, P.R. D'Argenio, and E. Brinksma. A stochastic automata model and its algebraic approach. *CTIT technical report, process algebra and performance modeling,* Fifth International Workshop, University of Twente, June 1997.

[17] B. Strulo and P. Harrison. Stochastic process algebra for discrete event simulation. *Quantitative Methods in Parallel Systems,* Esprit Basic Research Series, pp 18–37. Springer-Verlag, 1995.

Vitae

Peter Harrison is currently Professor of Computing Science at Imperial College London, where he became a lecturer in 1983. He graduated at Christ's College Cambridge as a Wrangler in Mathematics in 1972 and went on to gain Distinction in Part III of the Mathematical Tripos in 1973, winning the Mayhew prize for Applied Mathematics. He obtained his Ph.D. in Computing Science at Imperial College in 1979. He has researched into analytical performance modeling techniques and algebraic program transformation for some twenty years, visiting IBM Research Centers for two summers in the last decade. He has written two books, had over 100 research papers published in his research areas and held a series of research grants, both national and international. The results of his research have been exploited extensively in industry, forming an integral part of commercial products such as Metron's Athene-Client-Server capacity planning tool. He has taught a range of subjects at undergraduate and graduate levels, including Operating Systems: Theory and Practice, Functional Programming, Parallel Algorithms and Performance Analysis.

Kamyar Kanani is currently a Research Associate in the Department of Computing at Imperial College, London. He graduated from Imperial in 1994 with a Master of Engineering degree in Software Engineering. He continued at Imperial with Ph.D. research into the development of a high level specification language based on stochastic process algebra. He was awarded his Ph.D. in October 1998 and has since been working on the COMPA research project aimed at developing the applications of stochastic process algebra.

Chapter 23

Analysis of Commercial Workload on SMP Multiprocessors

Xiaodong Zhang and Zhichun Zhu

College of William & Mary

Xing Du

University of Virginia

Abstract   A major challenge of studying architectural effects on the performance of a commercial workload is the lack of easy access to large scale and complex database engines running on a multiprocessor system with powerful I/O facilities. Experiments involving case studies have been shown to be highly time-consuming and expensive. We present an analytical model to address this issue. Our model characterizes both the memory access patterns of a commercial workload and the memory hierarchy of SMP multiprocessors. We use the commercial benchmark TPC-C as the workload. The model is able to predict the execution time of the workload, the number of cycles per instructions (CPI), and transaction throughput on SMPs. We have validated the model using the published performance results of the TPC-C workload measured by hardware counters on a Pentium Pro-based SMP server. We have also validated the model by running the TPC-C workload on a simulated SMP by SimOS. Our study demonstrates that this modeling approach is a feasible, cost-effective, and accurate way to evaluate the performance of a commercial workload on SMPs, and is complementary to the measurement-based experimental approaches.

Keywords: memory hierarchy, queuing models, SMP multiprocessors, workload locality, TPC-C commercial workload.

[1]This work is supported in part by the National Science Foundation under grants CCR-9400719 and CCR-9812187, by the Air Force Office of Scientific Research under grant AFOSR-95-1-0215, and by Sun Microsystems under grant EDUE-NAFO-980405.

23.1   Introduction

Symmetric multiprocessor systems (SMPs) have become a standard parallel processing platform for various applications. One important usage of such
systems is the execution of commercial workloads, which represent one of
the most rapidly growing market segments. In comparisons with scientific,
numeric-intensive, and engineering applications, commercial workloads contain more sophisticated system software activities. Performance of commercial
workloads is determined by so many factors (both hardware and software) that
it is hard and time-consuming to evaluate. Based on an intensive experimental
study conducted at Western Research Lab of Compaq, Barroso et al. [2] recently summarize the challenges and difficulties of the performance evaluation
of commercial workloads — the lack of experimental resources. It is difficult
and expensive to have a large scale and complex database engine running on a
multiprocessor system with powerful I/O facilities for performance evaluation.
In addition, the experiments for case studies have been shown to be highly
time-consuming. So far, all published results on performance evaluation of
commercial workloads on SMP multiprocessors are experimentally oriented
and measurement-based case studies (see e.g., [7, 8, 10]).

If performance models are tractable and sufficiently accurate for the evaluation of commercial workloads, it is certainly cost-effective and complementary
to the measurement-based experiments. In this paper, we present an analytical
model to study the SMP architectural impacts on performance of commercial
workloads. We use the TPC Benchmark C (TPC-C) [16], a standard commercial workload benchmark, as the workload. We characterize its computation
and communication requirements. The model predicts the average execution
time per instruction for the workload. It is derived from the workload's locality
property and the memory hierarchy of the targeted SMP.

We have evaluated the accuracy of the model using the published performance
results of the TPC-C workload measured by hardware counters on a Pentium
Pro-based SMP server. We have also validated the model by running the TPC-
C workload on a simulated SMP by SimOS. We show that modeling results
for execution time, CPI and other architecture related values are fairly close to
measured results and simulation results, which is acceptable for the performance
evaluation and prediction purpose. Our study also indicates that some detailed
architectural operations, such as branch behavior, are difficult to model. For
this type of detailed architectural information, measurement or simulation based
evaluation is a more suitable approach.

23.2 Characterizing TPC-C Workload and SMP Architecture

23.2.1 TPC-C Overview

The Transaction Processing Performance Council (TPC) is a non-profit organization founded to define commercial workload benchmarks and to disseminate its benchmark performance data to the industry. Its benchmarks are widely used by computer manufacturers and database providers to test, evaluate, and demonstrate the performance of their products. Currently, there are two benchmarks in the TPC benchmark suite: TPC-C and TPC-D, which represent two major categories of commercial applications: those supporting business operations and those supporting business analysis. TPC-C is an on-line transaction processing (OLTP) benchmark. It is a mixture of read-only and update intensive transactions that simulate a complete computing environment where a population of terminal operators executes transactions against a database.

Benchmark TPC-C contains representative transactions of an industry which must manage, sell, or distribute a product or service. Specifically, TPC-C simulates a wholesale company with a number of geographically distributed warehouses and their sales districts. Customers call the company to place a new order or request the status of an existing order. Orders are composed of 10 order lines (ordering 10 items at one time on the average).

The transactions are generated using emulated users. An emulated user selects a transaction type, inputs a transaction of that type (keying), waits for the output of the transaction, and thinks after getting the output on the screen. Multiple emulated users may generate transactions concurrently to work against the same database through a client-server mode. The TPC-C performance metric measures the total number of transactions of type I (New-Order) completed per minute in the server. It is expressed and reported in the unit of transactions-per-minute-C ($tpmC$).

23.2.2 SMP Architecture

Symmetric multiprocessors (SMPs) are by far the most popular server products for commercial applications. Generally speaking, an SMP consists of several identical processors. Each processor has its own cache and is connected to the shared main memory by a memory bus or a crossbar interconnection network. The number of processors varies from 2 to 8 for small scale SMPs. For multiprocessors with a small number of processors and large caches, the bus/network and the single memory can only satisfy a limited memory demand from each processor. I/O buses such as PCI or SCSI are used to connect I/O devices. An adaptor links the memory bus and an I/O bus. The memory bus or the crossbar network is used both by processors when they access memory and by I/O devices when they transfer data between memory and I/O devices. To simplify the discussion, we further assume that all disks are of the same type and of the same size.

23.2.3 Workload Characterization

The workload characterization on SMPs is mainly based on the probabilities of references to different levels of the memory hierarchy. The probability is determined based on *stack distance curves* taken directly from an address stream [5].

The work in [9] uses the same approach for evaluating the performance of memory hierarchies of uniprocessor systems. In general, the stack distance of datum A at one position of the address stream is the number of unique data items between this reference and the next reference to A. The distribution of stack distances can be expressed as a cumulative probability function, denoted $P(x)$, which represents the probability of references within a given stack distance of x. This fits an LRU-managed and fully-associative cache hitting rate well if x is considered as the cache size. The probability density function, denoted $p(x)$, describes the frequency of references at stack distance x. Similar to other related work [9, 13, 14], we model $P(x)$ and $p(x)$ in the form of

$$P(x) = 1 - \frac{1}{(x/\beta + 1)^{\alpha-1}}, \quad \text{and} \quad p(x) = \frac{\beta^{\alpha-1}(\alpha - 1)}{(x + \beta)^{\alpha}}, \qquad (23.1)$$

where $\alpha > 1$ and $\beta > 1$ are workload parameters to characterize locality of a program. The program locality improves with the decrease of β or the increase of α. The shared-memory of the SMP can be viewed as a large cache at a different access speed. Thus, the stack distance model discussed above is suitable for our performance evaluation of the SMP memory hierarchy.

The execution of the TPC-C workload on an SMP can be abstracted as a queuing model in Fig. 23.1, where the transactions are characterized as multiple database users simultaneously requesting services from the SMP, and the SMP is constructed by its 4 layers of memory hierarchies.

23.3 Analytical Model

23.3.1 Framework of the Model

We start the performance characterization from modeling average execution time per instruction of the workload. In comparisons with a scientific computing

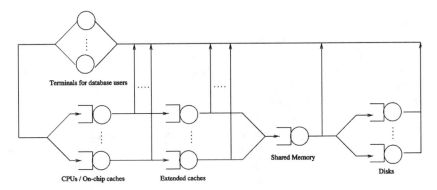

FIGURE 23.1
A queuing model for the TPC-C commercial workload running on an SMP multiprocessor.

workload, the TPC-C workload does not have coordination and synchronization activities among transactions running on different processors. Instructions involved in each transaction are executed in a dedicated processor. Based on Amdahl's Law, the average execution time per instruction is the sum of both computation and stall times as follows:

$$E(Instr) = T_{cpu} + T_{mem} , \qquad (23.2)$$

where T_{cpu} is an average CPU execution time per instruction, and T_{mem} is the associated memory access time of the instruction. The value of T_{cpu} is CPU power and type dependent. A multiple-issue processor launches multiple instructions per CPU cycle. However, experiments in [7] show that TPC-C commercial workload could hardly take advantage of this feature and make T_{cpu} close to one CPU cycle time. We will give further discussions when we quantify the value of T_{cpu} in the performance evaluation section.

The average memory access time per instruction, T_{mem}, is a complex and dynamic variable which plays the major role affecting the execution performance of the commercial workload. We adopt the framework used in [4, 6, 9], and [17] to predict the average memory access time:

$$T_{mem} = \sum_{i=1}^{k} P_i t_i = t_1 + t_2 \int_{s_1}^{\infty} p(x)dx + t_3 \int_{s_2}^{\infty} p(x)dx + \dots$$
$$+ t_k \int_{s_{k-1}}^{\infty} p(x)dx , \qquad (23.3)$$

where P_i and t_i are the access probability and the average access time, respectively, to the memory hierarchy at the ith level, $i = 1, \dots, k$. However, this model does not consider the overlapping effects from a pipeline facility in a modern processor design, which has been widely used in many commercial processors. In our targeted SMP, $k = 4$, t_1 is the access time to the L1 cache, t_2 is the access time to the L2 cache, t_3 is the access time to the memory, and t_4 is the access time to the disks. Simultaneous accesses to the shared-memory from several processors cause contention, and make the average access time to that level significantly higher than that without contention. The average access time varies due to variations of network architectures and of the number of simultaneous accesses. Because of the performance enhancement of the pipeline techniques, the L1 cache access time, t_1, can be almost overlapped with other operations. We will further discuss this in the next section when we validate the model based on measurement results on a Pentium Pro-based SMP.

Table 23.1 lists all notations used in the model and their descriptions in two groups: SMP parameters and workload parameters. In the group of SMP parameters, except t_i, $(i = 1, \ldots, k)$ and T_{mem}, all the other parameters are known for a given SMP and are machine dependent. In the group of workload parameters, for a given memory hierarchy, λ_i and P_i, $(i = 1, \ldots, k)$ are modeled based on the workload dependent parameters α and β which characterize the program locality. Another workload dependent parameter is average number of instructions in a transaction, I.

Table 23.1   Notations for the Model

SMP	Parameter descriptions
n	The number of processors in an SMP.
CR	CPU clock rate in MHz.
T_{cpu}	Average CPU execution time per instruction.
k	The number of levels in the memory hierarchy.
s_i	The memory size in bytes at the ith level, $i = 1, \ldots k$.
τ_i	Access time per instruction to the ith level without contention.
t_i	Access time per instruction to the ith level with contention.
T_{mem}	Average memory access time per instruction in the SMP.
Workload	Parameter descriptions
I	Average number of instructions in a database transaction.
λ_i	The access rate to the ith level of the memory hierarchy.
$P_i(\alpha, \beta)$	The probability of accessing the ith level.

For given SMP and workload parameters, the execution performance in (23.2) can be determined if the average memory access time T_{mem} is known. Therefore, T_{mem} is the key variable to be modeled in this study.

23.3.2   A Memory Access Time Model for SMPs

In an SMP multiprocessor ($n > 1$), each processor has its own cache and shares the main memory with other processors through a memory bus. The memory hierarchy consists of four levels: the L1 cache, the L2 cache, the shared-memory, and disks. Since both the L1 and the L2 cache are dedicated to each processor, the access times from its own processor (t_1 and t_2) can be considered as constants, and equal to the cache access times without contention (τ_1 and τ_2). The average access time to the memory (t_3) is determined by several factors. Assume the access rate to the memory from a processor is λ_3. (Without losing generality, we assume the access rates from different processors are identical.) The access time to the memory without contention is a constant (τ_3). The accesses to the memory by n processors can be modeled as a memoryless, general, and one-server (M/G/1) closed system with n customers [12]. A Markov diagram describing accesses to the shared-memory, which can be analyzed by the MVA method, is given in Fig. 23.2. The state represents the number of customers in the processors and the number of customers accessing the memory.

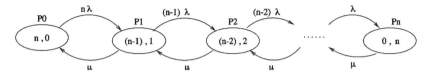

FIGURE 23.2
Markov diagram of memory access pattern.

The access rate to the memory λ_3 and the access rate to the disk λ_4 are determined by the access probability P_3 and P_4, respectively:

$$\lambda_3 = \frac{1}{E(Instr)} P_3 \qquad (23.4)$$

and

$$\lambda_4 = \frac{1}{E(Instr)} P_4 . \qquad (23.5)$$

Using the definition of $p(x)$ in (23.1), the probability of accesses to the ith memory level can be further derived into

$$P_i = \int_{s_{i-1}}^{\infty} p(x)dx = \frac{1}{(s_{i-1}/\beta + 1)^{\alpha-1}} . \qquad (23.6)$$

The remaining task is to obtain the value of t_3 by analyzing the Markov chain and to calculate the value of $E(Instr)$. But at the same time, we need to know the value of $E(Instr)$ in order to calculate t_3.

We use an iterative approach to solve this problem. Initially, setting $E(Instr) = 1$ cycle, we get the value of t_3, and a corresponding $E(Instr)$ in the end of the first iteration. The value of $E(Instr)$ is repeatedly used to calculate t_3 until it converges.

Using the modeled average execution time per instruction of the workload, $E(Instr)$, and other SMP and TPC-C workload dependent parameters, we can further determine the following important performance measures:

- Cycles Per Instruction (CPI): $CPI = E(Instr) \times CR$,

- execution time per transaction: $E(Tran) = E(Instr) \times I$, and

- total number of transactions completed per minute ($tpmC$): $tpmC = \dfrac{n}{E(Tran)}$,

where CR is the CPU clock rate, I is the average number of instructions per transaction, and n is the number of processors in the SMP.

23.4   Model Validation

A group of computer professionals from University of California at Berkeley and Informix Software, Inc. recently evaluated different architectural effects of a 4-processor Pentium Pro-based SMP on a TPC-C-like workload operated by an Informix database [7]. Their approach is purely experimental by using hardware counters, and the measured results are considered accurate. Using their measured workload locality data, and the Pentium Pro-based SMP architectural parameters, we have validated our model, and found that the modeled results are fairly close to the measured results on execution time, CPI, and throughput. Based on the model parameter notations in Table 23.1, we collect both the workload and SMP parameter values from [7] to be used in our model, and list them in Table 23.2.

The Pentium Pro-based SMP has four 200 MHz processors where a process is limited to a 2 GB of user space in the shared-memory. The average CPU execution time per instruction is 0.97 cycle. There are a total of 4 levels of memory hierarchy: L1 cache (on-chip) of 8 KB instructions and 8 KB data, 1 MB unified L2 cache (external cache), 4 GB of 4-way interleaved shared memory, and 90 Quantum 4.55 GB Ultra SCSI-3 disks. The access times to the L1 cache and L2 cache are 3 cycles and 7 cycles, respectively. The access time to the shared-memory without contention is 58 cycles. The average access time to the shared-memory with contention (t_3) will be predicted by our model, and so will the average time per instruction of the SMP, T_{mem}. The disks were not used for these experiments. Thus, we are unable to model the average access time per instruction to the disks, t_4.

The workload access probabilities to different levels provided by the experiments are 100% to the L1 cache, 14.1% to the L2 cache, and 0.7% to the shared-memory. The TPC-C-like workload does not change the structure of

Table 23.2 The Measured Locality Data and the Pentium Pro-Based SMP Parameters

Pentium Pro-based SMP	Parameter descriptions
$n = 4$	4 processors in the SMP.
$CR = 200$ MHz	CPU clock rate.
$T_{cpu} = 0.97$ cycle/instruction	Average CPU execution time.
$k = 4$	4 levels of the memory hierarchy.
$s_1 = 16$ KB	size of the L1 cache.
$s_2 = 1$ MB	size of the L2 cache.
$s_3 = 2$ GB	size of the shared-memory.
$s_4 = 360$ GB	size of the disks.
$\tau_1 = 3$ cycles/instruction	Access time to cache without contention.
$\tau_2 = 7$ cycles/instruction	Access time to cache without contention.
$\tau_3 = 58$ cycles/instruction	Access time to the shared-memory without contention.
$t_1 = \tau_1$	Access time to the L1 cache with contention.
$t_2 = \tau_2$	Access time to the L2 cache with contention.
t_3, to be modeled	Access time to the shared-memory with contention.
T_{mem}, to be modeled	Average memory access time in the SMP.
TPC-C-like workload	Parameter descriptions
$I = 625,000$	Average number of instructions per transaction.
$P_1 = 100\%$	The probability of accessing to the L1 cache.
$P_2 = 14.1\%$	The probability of accessing to the L2 cache.
$P_3 = 0.7\%$	The probability of accessing to the shared-memory.
$P_4 = $ NA	Accessing to the disks is not applicable.

the workload program itself, but only changes the way of submitting transactions by using two client machines to simulate thousands of remote terminal emulators, generating requests with no think time between requests. Since the average number of instructions per transaction, I, of the TPC-C and the TPC-C-like are the same, we collected the measurement results of $I = 625,000$ from [1].

In the Pentium Pro, there are three parallel decoders to translate the macro-instructions into triadic μops. In each cycle, multiple μops can be executed. The access times to the L1 cache are likely to be overlapped with other operations not only by the parallel decoders, but also by other pipeline hardware support, such as stream buffers. Both experiments in [3] and [7] show the strong effectiveness of the overlapping on the Pentium Pro processor. Considering this architectural effect, we set $t_1 = \tau_1 = 0$ in our model.

Applying the given P_1, P_2, and P_3 characterizing the locality of the TPC-C-like workload, and the given T_{cpu}, n, s_1, s_2, s_3, τ_1, τ_2, and τ_3, characterizing the Pentium Pro-based SMP, we use our model to quantitatively determine the following 4 variables: $E(Instr)$, t_3, λ_3, and T_{mem}. Table 23.3 gives comparisons between our modeled results and the measured results on CPI, average access time to the shared-memory, and the throughput of $tpmC$. The average shared-memory access time, t_3 is modeled from hardware memory hierarchy while the measured t_3 includes both hardware and the operating system effects. The 4.1% relative error reflects this difference of the two results. Using the modeled execution time per transaction, $E(Tran)$, we also predicted the throughput, $tpmC$, which is 11.55 transactions per minute, and is in the range of the measured $tmpC$: 9 — 12.7 transactions per minute.

Table 23.3   Comparisons Between the Modeled and Measured Performance Results of the TCP-C-Like Workload on the Pentium Pro-Based SMP

	Modeled Results	Measured Results	Relative Errors
t_3	98.9 cycles	95 cycles	4.1%
CPI	2.68	2.52	6.3%
$tpmC$	11.55	9-12.7	N/A

The comparisons between the modeled and measured results show that our model is sufficiently accurate to be used for evaluating the memory hierarchy effects on the commercial workload. Compared with the measurement approach, this modeling approach has two limits. First, some complex hardware operations, such as branch prediction behavior and μops retirement behavior, are difficult to model. Second, a commercial workload involves many operating system activities which are dynamic and also difficult to model. For more precise and detailed performance information, the models need support from simulation. Dynamic workload and system effects can be obtained through simulation experiments. The combination of analytical and experimental results provides a cost-effective and reliable performance evaluation for computer systems [18]. In the next section, we will present our study of using simulation to support our analytical model.

23.5   Workload Parameterization and Simulation

The purpose of the simulation is to characterize locality property of the workload (miss rates at different memory hierarchy levels) by running a smaller portion of the workload. The simulation involves detailed hardware operations and operating system activities, thus, major dynamic effects which are hard to capture in the models will be measured. Our principle of this study is to apply the analytical methods to capture as many deterministic performance factors as possible, and to use simulation to collect only necessary dynamic factors. The objective is to provide sufficiently accurate performance results and insights and to significantly reduce the evaluation time.

We integrate a simulation environment of commercial workload on an SMP for two purposes: (1) to run the TPC-C benchmark on the simulated SMP to collect the benchmark's parameters required by the model; (2) to support the model for more complex performance evaluation by collecting both hardware and system software dependent data which are dynamic and non-deterministic.

The SimOS [11] is used to simulate a bus-based cache coherent cache/memory system. SimOS is a machine simulation environment developed by Stanford University [11]. SimOS simulates the complete hardware of a computer system booting a commercial operating system and running a realistic workload, such as the TPC-C and its associated database system, on top of it. The simulator contains software simulation of all the hardware components of a computer system: processors, memory management units, caches, memory systems, as well as I/O devices such as SCSI disks, Ethernets, hardware clocks, and consoles. The current version of SimOS simulates the hardware of MIPS-based multiprocessors to run Silicon Graphics' IRIX operating system.

The simulated SMP is very similar to the one for measurement except for the cache and memory sizes. The simulated SMP consists of four 200 MHz R10000 processors. The access times to L1, L2 caches and the shared-memory are identical to those of the Pentium Pro-based SMP. The cache sizes and the memory size are scaled down to 8 times so does the database workload. This has significantly reduced the simulation time.

The database system running on the simulator is POSTGRES [15], which was developed at University of California at Berkeley. Although this is not a commercial database and it may have some different behavior compared with a commercial database, it is sufficient enough for our performance study because we are only interested in the characteristics of the TPC-C workload rather than the performance of a specific database system. Thus, the TPC-C performance results operated by the POSTGRES should not have any fundamental difference from that operated by a commercial database. In addition, using the POSTGRES for performance evaluation is cost-effective, because it is a public domain software. Figure 23.3 is the simulation environment showing the integration of TPC-C benchmark, POSTGRES, and the SimOS.

We collected the number of misses at each memory level and converted them to the miss rates. These miss rates from the simulation are reasonably close to the measured miss rates we presented in the previous section. The simulation allows us to collect necessary workload locality parameters for the model calculation. We also collected the CPI and throughput results from the simulation, which are close to the measured and modeled results. This again

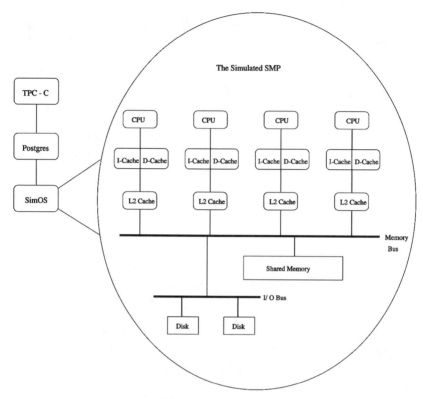

FIGURE 23.3
The integrated simulation environment: TPC-C benchmark is operated
by POSTGRES database, and executed on a simulated SMP by SimOS.

validates the model. Table 23.4 gives comparisons between our modeled results
and the simulated results.

Table 23.4   Comparisons Between the Modeled
and Simulated Results

	Modeled result	Simulated result	Relative error
t_3	103.6 cycles	100 cycles	3.6%
CPI	3.59	3.26	10.1%

The memory access patterns in the TPC-C-like workload in the measurement
and the TPC-C workload in our simulation are identical. Figure 23.4 compares
the memory access probability in memory hierarchy from simulation against the
measured probability. The comparison indicates that our simulation is able to

obtain accurate workload locality data without using expensive computing resources. The locality information is used as input of our model for performance evaluation.

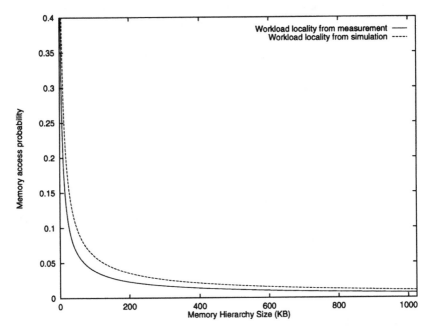

FIGURE 23.4
Comparisons between the memory access probability in memory hierarchy from the simulation and the measured probability.

23.6 Conclusions and Future Work

Performance evaluation is the first step toward improving the performance of commercial applications on SMPs. Experimentally-based evaluation requires significant computing resources and time. In this paper, we investigate the feasibility of using an analytical model supported by simulation to characterize commercial workloads on SMPs. Our study shows that the modeling results are sufficiently accurate and acceptable for characterizing the TPC-C workload on SMPs and for giving insights into SMP architectural effects on performance of commercial workloads. A unique feature of this approach is its efficiency in terms of timing and computing resources.

In this study, the focus was on the processor, cache, and memory systems.

However, the I/O system connected to the SMP is a potential bottleneck for a commercial workload. We are studying effective configurations of I/O systems in order to improve performance of commercial workloads. Since scalability is a major limit on bus-based shared memory multiprocessors, we are investigating other alternatives as well. With the availability of high speed networks and powerful workstations with large disk storage capability, networks of workstations are a cost-effective candidate for commercial applications. We are studying the performance of commercial workloads supported by a distributed database management system on networks of workstations.

Acknowledgment

We appreciate the discussions with J. Ding of Intel on the Pentium processor architecture. We wish to thank our colleague Zhao Zhang for preparing some data for us.

References

[1] G.A. Abandah, E.S. Davidson, Configuration independent analysis for characterizing shared-memory applications. *Proc. 12th IPPS,* pp. 485–491, 1998.

[2] L.A. Barroso, K. Gharachorloo, E. Bugnion, Memory system characterization of commercial workloads, *Proc. 25th ISCA,* pp. 3–14, 1998.

[3] L. Bhandarkar, J. Ding, Performance characterization of the Pentium Pro processor, *Proc. 3rd HPCA,* pp. 288–297, 1997.

[4] C.K. Chow, On optimization of storage hierarchies, *IBM Journal of Research and Development,* 194–203, 1974.

[5] E.G. Coffman, P.J. Denning, Operating System Theory, Prentice-Hall Inc., Englewood Cliffs, 1973.

[6] X. Du, X. Zhang, An analytical model for cost-effective cluster computing, Technical Report, College of William and Mary, 1998.

[7] K. Keeton, et al., Performance characterization of a Quad Pentium Pro SMP using OLTP workloads, *Proc. 25th ISCA,* pp. 15–26, 1998.

[8] J.L. Lo, et al., An analysis of database workload performance on simultaneous multithreaded processors, *Proc. 25th ISCA,* pp. 39–51, 1998.

[9] B.L. Jacob, P.M. Chen, S.R. Silverman, T.N. Mudge, An Analytical Model for Designing Memory Hierarchies, *IEEE Trans. Computers,* 45, 1180–1194, 1996.

[10] P. Ranganathan, et al., Performance of database workloads on shared-memory systems with out-of-order processors, *Proc. 8th ASPLOS,* pp. 307–318, 1998.

[11] M. Rosenblum, et al., Using the SimOS machine simulator to study complex computer systems, *ACM Trans. on Modeling and Computer Simulation* 7, 78–103, 1997.

[12] S.M. Ross, Introduction to Probability Models, Sixth Edition, Academic Press, San Diego, 1997.

[13] A.J. Smith, Cache Memories, Computing Survey 14, 473–530, 1982.

[14] H.S. Stone, High Performance Computer Architecture, Addison Wesley, 1993.

[15] M. Stonebraker, G. Kemnitz, The POSTGRES next generation database management system, *Communications of ACM* 34(10), 78–92, 1991.

[16] Transaction Processing Performance Council, TPC Benchmark C, TPC Benchmark C Standard Specification, Revision 3.3.3, April 16, 1998.

[17] T.A. Welch, Memory hierarchy configuration analysis, *IEEE Trans. on Computers,* 27, 408–415, 1978.

[18] Z. Xu, X. Zhang, L. Sun, Semi-empirical multiprocessor performance predictions, *Journal of Parallel and Distributed Computing* 39, 14–28, 1996.

Vitae

Xiaodong Zhang is a professor of computer science at the College of William & Mary. He received his Ph.D. from University of Colorado at Boulder in 1989. His research interests are parallel/distributed systems and performance evaluation.

Zhichun Zhu is a Ph.D. student of computer science at the College of William & Mary. She received her B.S. from Huazhong University of Science and Technology in 1992. Her research interests are computer systems and performance evaluation.

Xing Du is a research scientist at the University of Virginia. He received his Ph.D. from Nanjing University in 1991. His research interests are parallel/distributed systems and software engineering.

Part V

System Performance and Reliability

Chapter 24

Bayesian Belief Networks for Safety Assessment of Computer-Based Systems

Bev Littlewood, Lorenzo Strigini, David Wright, Norman Fenton and Martin Neil

City University

P.-J. Courtois

AV Nuclear

Abstract   Safety assessment for highly critical systems differs from other performance evaluation tasks in various respects. Statistical evidence is usually insufficient for assigning model parameters with any confidence before operation of a new system, and for a long time into the operation period itself. On the other hand, a high degree of confidence is sought that the system will perform as safely as required. The assessors use disparate forms of evidence to reach this confidence, usually via their own expert judgement, a process which is poorly understood and subject to well-documented problems. Explicit, probabilistic formal reasoning is a way for the assessors to control the risks of intuitive judgement. We report on an exercise in using the formalism of Bayesian Belief Networks to support such formal probabilistic reasoning, the various difficulties encountered and methods for resolving them.

Keywords: safety assessment, Bayesian belief networks, expert judgement, inference.

[1] This research was funded in part by the European Commission via the Long Term Research Project 20072 'DeVa' and the ESPRIT project 'SERENE' and by the UK EPSRC project 'IMPRESS.'

24.1   Introduction

Safety-critical equipment for regulated industries must undergo a formal safety assessment before it can be operated. This is a difficult task. The assessor must consider the possibility of design and realization faults that would impair safety. Especially the increasing dependence on software-based systems has increased concern about safety assessment with respect to design faults. Although equipment vendors may operate to the best known standards of practice, these are known not to guarantee freedom from design faults in every single case.

Safety assessment uses disparate evidence like known conformance to standards of design and methodology, demonstrated competence of the organizations involved in producing a system, results of verification and validation activities on various products of the design process. Deriving a single judgement of satisfactory safety from all this evidence is usually an informal process of "expert judgement," which may be unreliable and is difficult to analyze and verify. The "safety argument" — the reasoning that links the evidence to the final judgement — is mostly in the assessor's mind, and its descriptions on paper are typically limited to enumerations of items of evidence, without a detailed explanation of how these are assumed to support or counter one another.

We have looked for explicit, formal ways of describing safety arguments, and chosen "Bayesian belief networks" (BBNs), a probabilistic notation for describing relationships between many variables in terms of conditional distributions and conditional independence relations. We hope that the use of BBNs may make the hidden safety arguments visible, communicable and auditable. BBNs offer a formal mathematical language for describing reasoning in uncertain situations. Assessors can thus describe their "safety arguments" in a form that they can re-examine and "debug." They can describe the causal models they assume to apply to the situations considered. This description implicitly specifies the value of the evidence considered in predicting the safety of the product, and the inference process can be automatically performed by software tools. At the same time, the formal description allows experts to analyze and discuss the constituent parts of the "safety argument," devise empirical tests of their validity, and so on.

We summarize here a case study that was run as part of the European long-term research project "DeVa" (Design for Validation). A more detailed account can be found in two technical reports [1, 2]. This report concentrates on issues of elicitation and validation of a BBN, as evidenced in the case study.

In Section 24.2 we describe the essential characteristics of the BBN formalism; in Section 24.3 we recall the context of our case study and in Section 24.4 the BBN model we produced. In Section 24.5, we discuss issues of validation of the model, which we try to address in Section 24.6 by developing methods for feed-back to the assessors of various implications of the BBN model. A discussion of our results and future developments follows in Section 24.7.

24.2 Bayesian Belief Networks (BBNs)

A BBN is a directed acyclic graph, like the one in Fig. 24.1, associated with a set of probability values. We can use a BBN to represent our uncertain, probabilistic knowledge about a real-world situation. Each node has a set of possible "values" (or "states"), representing a partition on the set of outcomes of an experiment or observation, e.g., the values of a numerical random variable. Each node has a "node probability table" (NPT) associated with it. If the node has no incoming arcs (root node), its NPT lists the marginal probabilities of its values; if it has n incoming arcs, the NPT lists the probabilities of its values, conditional on each possible n-tuple of values of its "parent" nodes. This information represents the fact that knowledge about a (parent) node is useful for predictions about another (child) node, either through cause-effect relationships, or via more general correlation laws. The absence of an arc between two nodes, say A and B, represents conditional independence. Roughly speaking, it means that any way the knowledge of the state of A might influence our expectations about the probabilities of states of B is already represented by other nodes in the BBN, which do have arcs joining them to B.

After building a BBN, i.e., choosing a topology and filling the NPTs, one can use an automated tool (e.g., the Hugin tool, for which information is available at http://www.hugin.dk) to:

- calculate the probabilities of the values of all nodes with incoming arcs from the conditional and marginal probabilities of the values of their ancestor nodes;

- update all probabilities (using Bayesian inference) when actual values of one or more nodes are observed. This operation is called "propagation."

Applications of BBNs to safety and reliability issues are documented in [3, 4], and have been the subject of another European research project [5]. BBNs offer a formal probabilistic model in an easily assimilated visual form, together with efficient computational methods and tools for exploring model consequences. The model itself may be obtained from known physical/mathematical laws and statistical information, as possible, for instance, in applications to medical decision support systems. An example of such a BBN for software dependability assessment is in [3]. But another attractive feature of BBNs is that experts can represent laws that they conjecture or believe to be true, or even that they unconsciously apply. So, intuitive expert judgement can to some degree be opened to criticism, checked for consistency and challenged in terms of its constituent assumptions, and it can be integrated with other knowledge using the formal rules of probability calculus. Building, analyzing and in the end trusting these representations of expert judgement procedures clearly poses problems, and these were the focus of this case study.

24.3   Context of the Case Study

This case study dealt with the safety argument for a class of software-based systems used in nuclear plant for functions important to safety. The exercise involved a group of researchers on the application of BBNs to safety assessment and an expert of the class of equipment and safety problems concerned. We expect most uses of BBNs to require a similar collaboration between experts of the formalism and domain experts. For obvious reasons of professional discretion, the identity of the nuclear operators, manufacturers, systems and functions from which the expertise captured by the BBN is in part drawn has been kept confidential and not even revealed to co-authors.

To contain the effort required, we limited the exercise to describing a part of the safety argument. This BBN addresses the early part of the life cycle of [the computer part of] a nuclear safety system, during which two documents are produced, the "System Requirements Document" and the "Computer System Specification Document," and subjected to various analyzes. Its goal variable (the variable about which predictions are sought) is "Safety Adequacy of Computer System Specification." It is through this quality that the results of this phase of development affect successive phases. These two main documents are produced and modified through the interaction of three "personae" (each typically consisting of a team or subset of an organization): the *system manufacturer;* the *system licensee* (future user of the system) and the *independent assessor,* who works on behalf of a safety authority and is responsible for eventually recommending approval of the system from the safety viewpoint. In our scenario, the independent assessor has [partial] visibility (through access to documents and personnel) of the development process that produces and validates these documents, rather than being required to evaluate the finished product and documentation only.

In more detail, the two documents have these functions:

(1) the System Requirements Document describes the environment of operation as well as the functions of the safety system. It lists the system's foreseeable failure modes, with probabilities, criticality and intended lines of defence against each of them, and assesses the criticality of the system;

(2) the "Computer System Specification Document" specifies and justifies, among other things, the allocation of safety functions between hardware and software. It must demonstrate that the computer architecture satisfies the system and safety requirements, in particular concerning adequate levels of redundancy and diversity, and barriers between safety and non-safety functions. It should include a "failure modes and effects analysis" in terms of the software and hardware components, and specify methods and mechanisms of auto-detection by the system of its own failures.

24.4 The BBN Model and its Construction

Figure 24.1 shows the topology of the BBN produced. Its general structure strongly reflects the life-cycle model used, roughly divided into three subgraphs, divided by dotted lines in the figure. The three subgraphs concern (from bottom to top in the figure) the quality of the requirements document, the design process that leads from this to the computer system specification, and the quality of the specification document itself.

An important part of the safety argument is a detailed specification of the meaning of each node, which we omit for lack of space. A few conventions will help to interpret this BBN: i) the names of nodes are reasonably self-explanatory, *if read in the context* of the subgraph to which the node belongs; thus, for instance, the node named "Completeness & Correctness" in the bottom part of the figure refers to the completeness and correctness of the requirement document; ii) we have appended an asterisk to the names of those nodes that represent observable variables; iii) when a variable is defined in terms of subjective judgement or observation, the observer or judge is the independent assessor, unless otherwise specified. Defining a node or variable as 'observable' means that we expect that at some stage of applying the BBN model to the assessment of a system, the user will enter a value for that node (or even possibly an assignment of probabilities to its possible values — a "likelihood observation" in BBN jargon).

The possible states of a node in this BBN are usually ordered on a scale of increasing or decreasing "quality," e.g., in the "Requirements Document" sub-graph, **Quality of Requirements** may take the values *("Poor," "OK,"* and *"Good")*.

The BBN model was built by an iterative process: the construction broadly proceeded in "top-down" fashion from the definition of the nodes to that of the BBN topology to that of the NPTs, but elicitation at a later stage in this sequence often prompted reconsideration of previous stages and changes in the information that had been elicited at an earlier stage.

Eliciting the multi-dimensional NPT for the Design Process Performance node posed serious problems. The sheer size of the table (324 entries) makes it very difficult for experts to describe their beliefs as a complete, consistent probability table. To elicit this NPT, we obtained a smaller NPT (81 entries) by fixing the states of a pair of parent nodes, identified as least significant among the five parents. We then varied the states of the other nodes to cover every combination. To represent the effects of variation in the states of the two parent nodes believed to be least significant, we produced (by a simple parametric formula) a linear displacement consistent with a short list of rules which the domain experts believed to govern the influence of these two less significant parents.

24.5   Validation & Sensitivity Issues

Ideally, experts can use a BBN to express their beliefs about a complex problem in a formal probabilistic language. In practice we expect both that the experts may find the BBN they produced inadequate, and that the process itself of building and validating it may change these beliefs. This may be a positive effect — they may face questions that they had not previously thought of, and thus be led to deeper analyzes, confutation of previous beliefs, etc. On the down side, the experts may be led to give inaccurate descriptions of their beliefs, simply through the need to express themselves in an unfamiliar or inappropriate language.

Multiple validation issues thus arise, which are particularly pertinent in the nuclear application we treated, because empirical data are relatively sparse. In other fields in which BBNs have been used successfully, such as in medicine, there are large empirical data bases and the dependence upon the unaided expert (for selecting topologies and especially for specifying NPTs) is less.

A first set of validation issues concerns whether the BBN represents the experts' initial understanding of the way they apply judgement to safety assessment. Issues at this stage may include:

- slips and other errors of execution in using the formalism. Some but not all of these will be detected by the BBN support tools;

- lack of self-consistency of the experts' intuition. The set of "local" dependencies specified in the BBN may contradict some other aspect of their global beliefs, as evidenced in their judgements;

- insufficient familiarity with the subtleties of the BBN formalism;

- "normatively incorrect" reasoning by experts. A BBN can only describe a process of judgement that is a correct application of Bayesian rea-

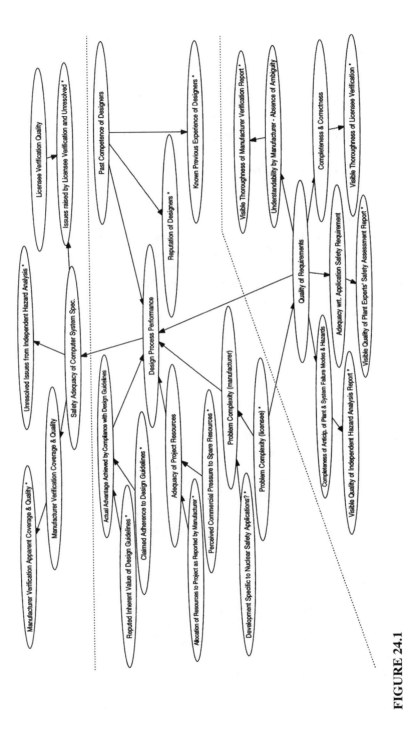

FIGURE 24.1
BBN topology. The dotted lines separate the three sub-graphs described in the text.

soning. Human judgement seldom approaches such formal perfection. Mismatches must to be resolved by the experts diagnosing errors in their previous intuitive judgement and/or their specification of the BBN;

- ambiguities in the definitions of the variables and their states, making it difficult for an expert to interpret them consistently over time, and to communicate their meanings to other experts to allow meaningful discussion of the safety argument;

- spurious precision in the BBN, as an artifact of demanding that the expert specify numerical probability values.

A second order of concerns is whether the experts, once satisfied that a BBN represents their current beliefs, will change these beliefs once they have a chance to analyze them thoroughly, using the BBN itself, and compare them to additional knowledge/beliefs, not represented in the BBN. Last, another interesting question is whether the captured intuition of the expert really does accurately express the real-world uncertainty. In cases where there is a lot of data it may be possible to address this question — it has been examined in some detail, for example, in software reliability growth modeling using tools such as Prequential Likelihood [6]. Such an investigation is, however, beyond the scope of the present work.

24.6   Support for Validation and Sensitivity Analysis

To check the validity of a BBN model they produced, experts need feedback from it. They need to see various (non-obvious) implications of the model to decide whether any of these are counter to their intuition. We see two main forms of feed-back: exploring the direct consequences of the BBN "as is," and sensitivity analysis with respect to observations or changes in the NPTs.

Mathematically, a BBN model can be seen as a function which maps vectors of *observations* onto finite vectors of *probabilities* of the states of unobserved nodes. Feedback to the experts may consist in showing them instances of this function: what the BBN "would infer" if given facts were observed, or what it implies in terms of prior probabilities in the absence of observations. The experts can compare these results from alternative NPTs, among which they are undecided. In particular, the NPT values may have been defined as parametric functions, as we did for the NPT of the Design Process Performance node; the experts can "tune" the parameters by observing their effects on the results of the BBN model. Many approaches are possible here. We show some examples.

24.6.1 Feedback from Numerical Calculation Using the Hugin Tool

As an illustration of how evidence affects model conclusions, we traversed the space of possible complete observations of the 15 variables which we intend typically to be observable, and plotted in Fig. 24.2 the resulting distribution of the main goal node *Safety Adequacy of Computer System Specification*. The path chosen is one of the possible paths that lead from an intuitively "least favorable" to a "most favorable" combinations of observations, by changing one node at a time to an intuitively more favorable state.

This graphical format clearly helps the viewer to note general trends and exceptions to them, and is especially appropriate for nodes whose states can be considered as ordered on a scale. For instance, the line under the region labelled "Good" in the upper half of the figure, if taken as a function plot in isolation, represents the probability that the state of the node is worse than "Good" and the dependency of this probability on observed evidence (within the set of observations represented on the x-axis).

In this particular figure, one would naturally expect every curve to be monotonically non-increasing. The "spike" in the left-hand side of the bottom graph is an obvious "irregularity," which would prompt an expert to re-analyze the pertinent NPTs. An expert may conclude that the irregularity is due to an error in building the NPTs, and correct this error; on the other hand, the expert may conclude that the perceived irregularity indicates a previously ignored, counterintuitive consequence of the beliefs that the NPTs (correctly) represent. So, graphs like these can be a powerful visual aid. Experts may even be surprised by features that do not violate any rule they may have specified beforehand, and yet require a re-analysis of the NPTs.

24.6.2 Complementary Symbolic Analysis Using Polytree Propagation Algorithm

Plots such as that in Fig. 24.2 raise many questions about the systematic relationships which must exist for the mathematical function which our model embodies. We wished therefore to give the experts feedback in an analytical form, more susceptible to systematic analysis than individual numerical results. An "analytical propagation engine" for BBNs would be extremely complex, but luckily the special topology of this BBN allowed a simpler solution. This topology can be treated as a *polytree* [7] provided we block one of the nodes in the only cycle present, by assuming its value has been observed. This way of conditioning on values of certain nodes to break loops in a BBN is discussed in [7, Section 4.4.2]. In our example, we expect the "Problem Complexity (licensee)" node to be observed by the assessor. We simply condition all our reasoning on its observed state. This creates a polytree topology.

We then devised a "symbolic propagation algorithm" for polytree BBNs [2], implemented with the Maple mathematical software. This gives us:

- Arbitrary (i.e., user specified) numerical precision.

- An ability to substitute any node observation or [part of] any NPT by a parametric function, and observe the functional form of model output.

- Greater ease of obtaining plots of functional relationships.

- Potentially better intuitive understanding from access to algebraic, as well as visual topological, representations of model assumptions and their consequences. We found that these different forms of representation of model output complemented each other well.

- Ease of investigating the effects of model inputs on model outputs, by differentiation to find maxima and minima.

24.7   Discussion and Conclusions

This special session is meant to compare different forms of "validation" and, specifically evaluation performed at the end of system development against early prediction followed eventually by evaluation of the completed system. From this viewpoint, safety validation in general has some peculiar characteristics. The comparison above suggests that evaluation "at the end of system development" is much more reliable than preliminary predictions for the as-yet unbuilt system. And indeed predictions about (for instance) system throughput can usually be validated as soon as a system is built, by running it with appropriate test loads. But safety requirements are of a negative nature, requiring some system behaviors to be extremely unlikely. Demonstrating that they are really so via statistical observation is usually considered unaffordable and is in many cases infeasible [8]. So, even at the end of system development, the system's conformance to the user's safety needs is difficult to ascertain with great confidence. Much "safety validation" activity deals with checking other qualities that are believed to be good indicators of safety. In many markets, this safety validation must not only convince the vendor and the buyer, but an independent regulatory authority (like the F.A.A.) and/or certification agency (like a TÜV) as well. To reduce the risk of products being rejected at this last validation stage, after long and expensive development processes, interactions have developed between the parties involved. Many design and management decisions during development are in practice pre-negotiated with the regulators, or dictated by guidelines they have approved. In this sense, safety validation is seldom performed on the finished product only. Even so, important unresolved issues remain: there is little evidence that the checks being performed actually

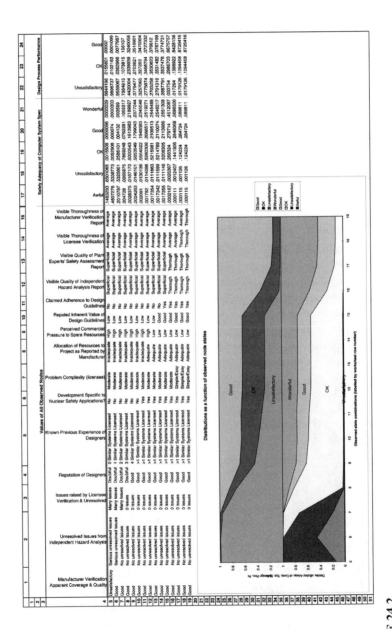

FIGURE 24.2

Updated distributions plotted as a function of some observation combinations.

deliver the required levels of safety. For instance, it seems self-evident that HAZOP (HAZard and OPerability analysis, essentially a systematic procedure for checking the ways that failures might cause accidents — several such systematic methods are in common use) will decrease the risk of the produced system causing accidents, and yet no-one knows how much the probability of such accidents is reduced by a HAZOP.

BBNs are an ideal tool for this continuing assessment. At the beginning of a project, a BBN like that in Fig. 24.1, without any observation having yet been entered, can describe the prior probability of the project producing acceptable results. "What if" analysis — entering various possible combinations of observations — can answer questions like: "What would I need to observe, at each successive stage of the project, in order to show that the chances of success are still acceptable — that the project is on track?", or "After observing some damning evidence, what kind of reassurance would be needed to believe that the project still has a good chance of success?". As the project proceeds, new evidence is entered and predictions evolve accordingly.

So, a BBN model, once built, is an extremely powerful tool. It solves a daunting problem in safety analysis, i.e., the complex "propagation" process, from the multifaceted evidence that can be collected to a judgement about the qualities that the assessor must judge. However, this is just the third one of three serious problems in safety assessment: the first problem is *obtaining* evidence that can demonstrate the required qualities with the required confidence. This evidence may not be available, which is not a problem for BBN models: the model will just show that the evidence is insufficient for the positive judgement that is sought. The second, essential problem is correctly describing the relationship between the evidence and the required qualities, i.e., building a correct BBN. This is why we put such emphasis on the validation of BBN models. Assessors need to be clear about how much trust they put in the scientific accuracy of a BBN model. We believe, and this case study gives moderate reassurance in this sense, that the process itself of building and validating BBN models is helpful to this end. Like other formal methods, BBNs help their users to examine their own thinking, and to seek for inconsistencies and factual errors. If this process converges to a BBN that the users trust as "scientifically accurate" — an accurate enough description of their best understanding of the real situation — then the BBN model can be used directly for decision support. Otherwise, the value of BBNs for seeking insight and for producing alternate predictions under different theories may still be enough to justify their use.

In this case study, we have produced a complete first version of the BBN, with complete NPTs. The validation exercise is in progress.

In conclusion, in this case study we have explored issues that arise in building and validating BBNs for safety assessment, and produced useful tools to support these phases. Developing the BBN has been useful for the expert to question and analyze his criteria of judgement. Further experimentation with feedback methods and support tools will help us to develop improved guidelines to assist choices about the topology and complexity of a BBN, so as to facilitate its refinement and its use in communication between experts.

References

[1] N.E. Fenton, B. Littlewood, M. Neil, L. Strigini, D.R. Wright, and P.-J. Courtois. Bayesian belief network model for the safety assessment of nuclear computer-based systems. Technical Report 52, ESPRIT DeVa project 20072, January 1998. Available at http://www.newcastle.research.ec.org/deva/trs/.

[2] B. Littlewood, L. Strigini, D.R. Wright, and P.-J. Courtois. Examination of Bayesian belief network for safety assessment of nuclear computer-based systems. Technical Report 70, ESPRIT DeVa project 20072, December 1998. Available at http://www.newcastle.research.ec.org/deva/trs/.

[3] K.A. Delic, F. Mazzanti, and L. Strigini. Formalising engineering judgement on software dependability via belief networks. *DCCA-6, Sixth IFIP International Working Conference on Dependable Computing for Critical Applications, "Can We Rely on Computers?"*, Garmisch-Partenkirchen, Germany, 1997.

[4] N.E. Fenton and Neil M. A critique of software defect prediction models. *IEEE Transactions on Software Engineering,* 1999.

[5] The serene method manual version 1.0 (d), 1999. EC Project No. 22187 Project Doc Number SERENE/5.3/CSR/3053/R/1. Available from ERA Technology.

[6] A.A. Abdel-Ghaly, P. Y. Chan, and B. Littlewood. Evaluation of competing software reliability predictions. *IEEE Transactions on Software Engineering,* 12, 950–67, 1986.

[7] J. Pearl. *Probabilistic Reasoning in Intelligent Systems: Networks of Plausible Inference.* Mathematics and Its Applications. Morgan Kaufmann, San Mateo, California, 1988. Revised 2nd printing 1991.

[8] B. Littlewood and L. Strigini. Validation of ultra-high dependability for software-based systems. *Comm. Assoc. Computing Machinery,* 36(11), 69–80, Nov 1993.

Vitae

Pierre-Jacques Courtois joined the Philips Research Laboratory in Brussels in 1965 where he became Head of the Computer and Communication Research Department, and stayed until 1991. In October 1991, he joined the AV Nuclear organization, the Belgian authorized inspection agency for nuclear installations, where he is in charge of assessments of safety critical software-based systems. He is Professor at the computer science department of Louvain-la-Neuve University where he lectures on Telecommunications and Computer Distributed Systems. His research interests are in the areas of distributed computer and communication systems engineering, design and assessment of dependable computer systems, and include performance and reliability models applied to these systems. He is currently a consultant of the CEC, the OECD, and the IAEA (International Atomic Energy Agency Vienna) where he is currently contributing to the safety guide on "software important to nuclear safety."

Norman Fenton is Professor of computing science at the Centre for Software Reliability, City University, London and also a Director of Agena Ltd. He is a Chartered Engineer (member of the IEE), a Chartered Mathematician (Fellow of the IMA), and member of the IEEE Computer Society. His research interests include software metrics, empirical software engineering, safety critical systems, and formal development methods. The focus of his current work is on applications of Bayesian nets; these applications include critical system assessment, vehicle reliability prediction and software quality assessment.

Bev Littlewood is Director of the Centre for Software Reliability, which he founded, and professor of software engineering at City University. Dr. Littlewood has worked for many years on problems associated with the modeling and evaluation of software dependability (i.e., reliability, safety and security). He leads several current research projects on the modeling of dependability, involving collaboration with partner institutions throughout Europe. He is a member of IFIP Working Group 10.4 on Dependable Computing and Fault Tolerance, the British Computer Society's Safety-Critical Systems Task Force, the IEEE, and a member of the U.K.'s Nuclear Safety Advisory Committee.

Martin Neil is a Lecturer in computing at the Centre for Software Reliability, City University, London. He holds a first degree in "Mathematics for Business Analysis" from Glasgow Caledonian University and achieved a Ph.D. in "Statistical Analysis of Software Metrics" jointly from South Bank University and Strathclyde University. Before joining the CSR Martin spent three years with Lloyd's Register as a consultant and researcher and a year at South Bank University. He has also worked with JP Morgan as a software quality consultant. His research interests cover software metrics, Bayesian probability and the software process. Martin is a member of the CSR Council, the IEEE Computer Society and the ACM. Martin is also a director of Agena, a consulting company specializing in decision support and risk assessment of safety and business critical systems.

Lorenzo Strigini is Professor of systems engineering at the Centre for Software Reliability, City University, London, which he joined in 1995 after 11 years as a researcher with the National Research Council of Italy. His past research work has addressed issues of fault-tolerant design, high-speed networks and software dependability. He has led several research projects and been a consultant to industry on fault-tolerant design and on software reliability. His current main interests are practical, rigorous methods for assessing the reliability and safety of software and other systems subject to design faults, and for guiding the application of design diversity and testing. He is a member of the IEEE and of IFIP Working Group 10.4 on Dependable Computing and Fault Tolerance.

David Wright is a Research Fellow at CSR and is completing a Ph.D. thesis on software reliability prediction. His research interests include reliability prediction based on failure-count data, the incorporation of "explanatory variables" in reliability predictions, the elicitation and combination of experts' systems-dependability judgements, the application of Bayesian nets to systems dependability assessment, and the question of the extent to which empirical information about achieved reliability levels can be transferred, as a basis for prediction, between systems or execution environments.

Chapter 25

Software Performance Validation Strategies

Giuseppe Iazeolla, Andrea D'Ambrogio and Raffaela Mirandola
University of Roma TorVergata

Abstract   The validation of performance-critical and safety-critical systems requires an extended view of the performance concept, and the improvement of studies on model production methods for the automatic generation of performance models from early-phase software life-cycle artifacts. It also requires a less conventional view of the validation process.

This paper introduces an extensive concept of software performance and of performance validation with the strategies for implementing extended validations.

It discusses the importance of life-cycle validation, and identifies life-cycle validation strategies, methodologies and tools. It also concentrates on the generation of extended performance models from early software artifacts. Only a few references are made to the more well known process of model evaluation.

Keywords: software validation, performance, safety, reliability, model production.

[1]Works partially supported by funds from the University of Roma TorVergata CERTIA Research Center, funds from MURST and from the University of Roma TorVergata research on the Performance Validation of Advanced Systems.

25.1   Introduction

Large efforts have been spent in the study of methods for the "evaluation" of system performance models (analytical methods, numerical, simulation, hybrid methods, etc.), and much lesser in methods for their "production."

The consequence is that only a few methods and tools have been developed to solve the problem that many government agencies are increasingly faced with: the problem of validating and licensing computer-based systems.

Indeed, the validation activity requires knowledge not only of evaluation methods, but also of *model production* methods, i.e., methods for the automatic generation of performance models from early-phase software life-cycle artifacts (the analysis artifact, the preliminary design artifact, etc.), to be used in the validation process.

Moreover, it has been privileged the very limited acceptation of the system "performance" term, interpreted as system "efficiency" (i.e., response time, throughput, and similar), while government agencies are primarily interested in an "extended" acceptation, which includes system efficiency in combination with system reliability and, more specifically, system safety, considered of paramount importance. And, even though performance and reliability have been studied in combination (performability), no study is known of a combination with the safety prerequisite.

Performance research is called both to concentrate on model "production" methods, and to pay particular attention to methods for "extended" models (i.e., that include safety). Also, for the safety case, to recover the lost terrain in the field of safety "evaluation" methods, which have been practically neglected in comparison to the overwhelming literature on efficiency evaluation methods.

This paper deals with the extended concept of software performance, and the generation of extended performance models. It also discusses the concept of performance early validation, and introduces strategies to implement it. It is organized as follows. Section 25.2 introduces the "extended" definitions of software performance, and of software performance validation, with the notions of safety, efficiency and reliability validation. Section 25.3 deals with the strategies for performance validation and Section 25.4 with the methods for model production.

The work is the outcome of concepts developed in the course of the cooperation between the University of Roma "Tor Vergata" (its CERTIA Research Center) and various European organizations, industries and institutions, in a number of studies and projects on modeling approaches and validation strategies for the performance of innovative computer based Air Traffic Management Systems [20, 21, 22, 23, 24, 25].

25.2 Terms Definition

This section introduces the "extended" definitions of software performance, and of software performance validation. It also deals with the notions of safety, efficiency and reliability validation.

25.2.1 Extended Performance Concept

The very limited interpretation of the term "performance" as system "efficiency" (i.e., response time, throughput and similar) has to be extended, in the validation context, to include system safety, considered a prerequisite for any public software application. This leaves the performance analysts to deal with the more general problem of system "quality."

Software quality is a multi-faceted property of software that can be defined by a k-component vector, $q = (c_1, c_2, \ldots, c_k)$ where q denotes quality, and components $c_1, c_2, \ldots, c_k$ denote quality **factors**. Example factors are: software flexibility, usability, performance, adaptability, etc. This paper deals with the performance factor.

Factors can be defined by **attributes**, and each attribute by sub-attributes of various levels.

Table 25.1 illustrates the case for the software **performance** factor. Its first-level attributes are system **efficiency** and system **dependability**. Efficiency is in turn defined in terms of waiting time, response time, queue length, path length, throughput (also called system capacity) and utilization.

Dependability is in turn defined in terms of reliability and safety, as also shown in Table 25.1. There are still other terms often related to dependability, such as system availability, integrity, fault-tolerance and graceful degradation, that are sub-attributes of reliability and not dealt with in this paper.

Table 25.1 Performance Attributes

quality factor	1st level attribute	2nd level attribute
performance	*efficiency*	waiting time
		response time
		queue length
		path length
		capacity
		utilization
	dependability	reliability
		safety

25.2.2 Extended Validation Concept

A well-performing software system is one that yields a system quality rate above a minimum acceptable level. In numbers

$$|q| \geq |q_{min}| \tag{25.1}$$

where quantities in (25.1) are expressed by use of the formula

$$|q| = \sqrt{c_1^2 + c_2^2 + \ldots + c_n^2}\,, \tag{25.2}$$

in other words by the q-vector module (or "length"), which can be computed if software standards [1, 2] are given to express each given factor c_k level by a numerical value.

Figure 25.1 illustrates an example case in which quality q is assumed to be simply dependent upon 3 attributes (c_1 = safety, c_2 = reliability, c_3 = efficiency) of the performance factor.

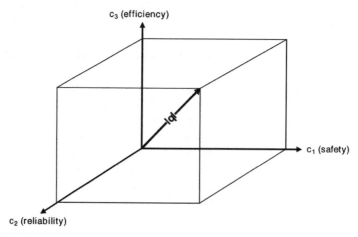

FIGURE 25.1

Software performance view with 3 attributes.

The q-vector "length" (25.2) however, is not a sufficient index to assess quality. It is also necessary to give its angular position. Indeed, one could enhance the value of a given component, say efficiency c_3, to the detriment of safety c_1, and still satisfy inequality (25.1).

A less naive assessment requires that a minimum-value constraint is imposed on each of the vector components in (25.2). In other words relationship (25.1) has to be subject to the set of constraints

$$c_1 \geq c_{1\,min} \qquad c_2 \geq c_{2\,min} \qquad c_3 \geq c_{3\,min} \tag{25.3}$$

to insure that the system is of acceptable performance, and that the level of any component (e.g., *safety*) is not below a given minimum (*safety*$_{min}$) value.

This, however, requires still other considerations, since some attributes can be influenced by some others. In this situation, depending on the linear or non-linear nature of relationships between the attributes, it may happen that the increase in one attribute yields the decrease of the overall system performance.

This is in particular for attributes that are system-wide (the safety is one of these), with respect to attributes that are subsystem-wide (for example, the reliability). A subsystem attribute, indeed, generally affects a system attribute. In this case, increasing the reliability may harm the system safety, as discussed in [4].

To deal with this problem, one may introduce formal or semi-formal expressions that state the relationships between attributes. In formulas:

$$c_1 = f_1(c_2, \ldots, c_n)$$
$$c_2 = f_2(c_1, c_3, \ldots, c_n)$$
$$\ldots$$
$$c_n = f_n(c_1, c_2, \ldots, c_{n-1}) \tag{25.4}$$

where f_1 denotes the relationship that binds attribute c_1 to all remaining ones, f_2 the relationship that binds c_2 to all remaining attributes, and so on.

By use of (25.4) one may perform a careful choice of the attributes to improve and of their level of improvement, in order to satisfy the quality goals (25.1) and (25.3).

So if c_1 is the safety attribute and c_2 the reliability one, it is possible to reasonably modulate the value of reliability c_2, by use of function f_2, as not to abnormally harm safety c_1, while keeping the quality value (25.1) at the desired level.

Software **performance validation** is the process of evaluating its ability to satisfy the user performance goals, synthetically expressed in this paper by (25.1) and (25.3).

Research in safety engineering and performance engineering [4, 5, 7] has emphasized the difference between two approaches (i) and (ii) to system "validation:"

> **(i)** the conventional approach, called *end-cycle* validation (Fig. 25.2), or the process of evaluating (*at the end* of the software product development) the product ability to satisfy the user performance goals (25.1) and (25.3),

and

> **(ii)** the less conventional approach, called *life-cycle* validation (Fig. 25.3), or the process of predicting (at *the early phases* of the development life-cycle) the ability of the to-be product to satisfy (25.1), (25.3), and finally evaluating the ability of the as-is product *at the end*,

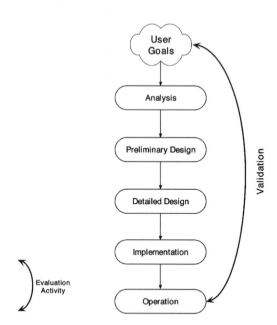

FIGURE 25.2
End-cycle validation approach.

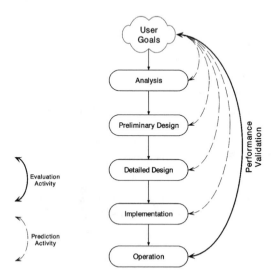

FIGURE 25.3
Life-cycle validation approach.

and has definitely concluded in favor of the latter, on the grounds of two arguments, we call the **build-in** and the **process effectiveness** argument, respectively.

The build-in argument proves that performance, and thus safety, reliability and efficiency are not retrofit or add-on features, but attributes to be "designed into" the system [4, 5, 7]. The process effectiveness argument, instead, proves that the life-cycle validation approach introduces substantial benefits into the software production process, because of the reduction of the *risk*, *time* and *cost* to software development [7, 8, 14, 18]. In this paper the life-cycle approach to validation will then be assumed, as described below.

25.3   Performance Validation Strategy

The performance validation strategy can be defined as the art of devising or employing plans toward the goal of implementing Performance Validation (PV). It can be synthetically described by the so-called PV **Strategy Scheme**, described in Fig. 25.4.

The scheme applies to each phase of the life cycle to determine and optimize performance. It applies to life-cycle artifacts. The term *artifact* is conventionally used to mean either the final software program, or an intermediate version of it. The requirement document, the analysis document, the design documents, etc. are examples of artifacts.

When applied to the ith phase, the scheme assumes that the previously validated $(i - 1)$th phase artifact is received in input. On its basis, a tentative phase (i) artifact is produced, and validated in the PV block by comparing the predicted performance of the *to-be* product with the user performance goals (25.1) and (25.3). In case of unacceptability, if cost effective, a new tentative artifact is produced for better performance. Otherwise (i.e., if it is not cost-effective to produce a new tentative), a feedback loop to the user goals takes place, for goals revision.

The PV block of the Strategy Scheme in Fig. 25.4 consists of 3 main steps, illustrated in Fig. 25.5. According to what was said in Section 25.1, we will mainly deal with Step 1 (PM production). The subsequent Step 2 uses the PM model to provide predictions of the future software performance. To this scope any available evaluation tool can be used for efficiency, reliability or safety evaluation [3, 4, 5, 12]. Step 3 yields the validation results to be used for the subsequent decisions in Fig. 25.4.

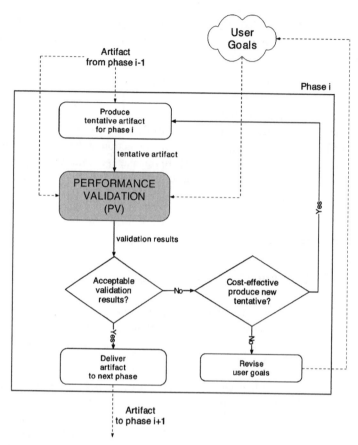

FIGURE 25.4
Performance validation strategy scheme.

25.4   Production of Performance Model

Performance literature offers some methods and tools for the "production" of efficiency-bound models [7, 9, 10, 11, 13, 16, 17], and a few methods for safety-bound model "production" [4, 15, 19]. There is no direct knowledge of works dealing with combined efficiency & dependability model "production," as existing works mainly deal with model "evaluation."

This section gives a synthetic overview of combined efficiency & dependability model "production" methods developed in studies related to the to-be computer-based new European air traffic management system [20, 21, 22, 23, 24, 25].

Step 1.	Performance Model (PM) Production
Step 2.	PM Evaluation
Step 3.	Comparison of evaluation results with user performance goals (25.1) and (25.3).

FIGURE 25.5
Detail of PV block actions.

Depending on the performance attribute to validate, the PV activity of Fig. 25.4 can be distinguished into 2 variants: **dependability validation** and **efficiency validation**.

These are quite similar one to the other, except for the PM production, which can be distinguished into two variants: Dependability Model (DM) production, and Efficiency Model (EM) production, treated further on.

Assume the life-cycle phase (i) in Fig. 25.4 refers to the Preliminary Design phase of the software process. In this case the $(i - 1)$th phase is the Analysis phase. Also assume that the Preliminary Design phase is carried on according to a distributed object oriented approach [6]. In this case one may assume that the following artifacts are available for input to the PV block in Fig. 25.4:

A1) The already validated artifact from the Analysis phase

A2) The just-produced phase (i) tentative artifact.

This is illustrated in more detail in Fig. 25.6, which concentrates on Step 1 (or PM Production, see Fig. 25.5) of the PV block, and shows that the PM production step is divided into "Basic PM" production and "Parametrized PM" production. In such a detailed view, it is also shown that inputs A1 and A2 consist of:

A1 artifacts:

- the Class Diagram (CD)

- a set of Data Flow Diagrams (DFD)

- a set of Interaction Diagrams (ID)

- the user functional profile (FP)

- user workload on software paths (FP1)

- tactical, operational and managerial failure patterns (FP2)

- the platform and software preliminary data (PD)

- equipment capacity data (PD1)

- equipment failure data (PD2)

- software failure preliminary data (PD3)

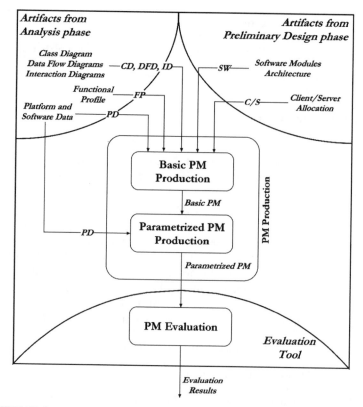

FIGURE 25.6
PM Production at preliminary design phase.

A2 artifacts:

- the partition of the DFD functions into software modules (SW)

- the client/server allocation of such modules (C/S).

Figure 25.6 also illustrates the fact that the PD data are used both for the Basic and for the Parametrized PM, as better detailed in Sections 25.4.1 and 25.4.2. According to Fig. 25.6, the Parametrized PM is finally given in input to any available evaluation tool to perform Step 2 of Fig. 25.5.

Sections 25.4.1 and 25.4.2 will illustrate in more detail the PM production process when applied to dependability validation and to efficiency validation, respectively.

25.4.1 DM Production

This section deals with the Dependability Model production and proves that a DM consists of the pipeline combination of two sub-models: the Reliability Model (RM) and the Safety Model (SM), which will be separately illustrated after a brief review of terminology for the reader less familiar with safety concepts.

25.4.1.1 Terminology

A few terms are to be introduced in order to write about safety. Such terms are failure, accident and hazard.

Failure is the manifestation of a fault (software defect, or equipment, managerial, operational or tactical environment faults) that produces deviation of a service from correct operation. *Failure condition* is the condition or state entered by the system upon occurrence of a failure. *Accident* is an event that results in a specified level of loss (death of men, loss of an aircraft, etc.).

Reliability is the probability (also called reliability level **rl**) that no failure conditions occur in the course of the system lifetime.

Safety is the probability (also called safety level **sl**) that no accident occurs in the course of the system lifetime.

Safety studies deal with the prevention of the series of events that transform a failure condition into an accident. They are concerned with the identification of so-called hazards. An *hazard* is a failure condition that, together with other conditions in the environment of the system, will lead inevitably to an accident. Environment conditions relate to equipment, managerial, operational or tactical environment faults.

According to point (ii) of Section 25.2.2, life-cycle *dependability validation* is the process of predicting (*at the early phases* of the development life-cycle) the ability of the to-be product to satisfy the dependability level (**rl, sl**) the user expects, and finally evaluating such level for the as-is product *at the end*.

In order to perform dependability validation it is necessary to:

1) identify failure conditions

2) classify failure conditions into hazardous and non-hazardous ones

3) identify the event sequences which transform an initiating event into a failure condition

4) identify the event sequences which transform a hazard into an accident

5) perform Step 2 of Fig. 25.5 to predict the to-be, or evaluate the as-is, dependability level.

Operations 1) through 5) are known in literature as "hazard analysis" [4]. Operations 1), 2), 3) and 5) are the basis for reliability validation.

Operations 1) through 5) are instead for safety validation.

The Dependability Model (DM) is the pipeline combination of a Reliability Model (RM) and a Safety Model (SM). RM is the model for operation 3), are SM for operation 4). In other words, the SM takes in input the failure condition formerly identified by the RM and (if hazardous) performs operation 4) to identify if such a condition leads to an accident or not.

Models to perform operations 3) and 4) are known as failure models and accident models, respectively, in literature.

The DM production consists of the production of a failure model in a pipeline with an accident model.

There exist various types of failure models, known as fault-tree (FT) models, continuous-time-Markov-chain (CTMC) models, Petri Net models (PN) etc., [4, 12] with various levels of potentiality, and various types of accident models known as domino (DO) models, chain-of-event (CE) models, system theory (ST) models, Bayesian network (BN) models etc. [4, 15, 19].

Without affecting generality, and for the sake of simplicity, this paper assumes the FT model is used for RM production, and the CE model for SM production. But similar reasonings can be applied if CTMC, PN, DO, ST, BN, etc. models are used instead.

25.4.1.2 RM Production

This section deals with the production of the reliability model RM, which is the model that performs operation 3) of Section 25.4.1.1.

In analogy to the "Basic PM" and "Parametrized PM" definitions of Fig. 25.6, let us define "Basic RM" and "Parametrized RM" as the first and second outcomes of the RM production process, respectively.

The Basic RM can be automatically generated by use of the above mentioned artifacts A1 and A2.

In more detail, a conventional probabilistic Flow Graph (FG) is first derived [26] by use of the CD, DFD, ID, FP, PD, SW and C/S artifacts. In particular:

- the CD, DFD and ID artifacts are used to derive the FG graph, whose nodes are software functions and edges are interactions among functions

- the FP artifact to derive the FG edges branching probabilities

- the SW and the C/S to derive the relative importance of edges.

The FG is now used to identify the software paths that lead to failures, and the failure modes. To each failure an FT is associated, whose top event is the failure itself, and its constituent causes (failures of software functions (FG nodes) or software interactions (FG edges)) are connected by And/Or logic gates, which are then further resolved into sub-constituent causes, and so on until basic events are identified [4].

The PD artifact (PD2 part) is finally used to complete the basic event set with scenarios of possible equipment failures.

From the so-obtained Basic RM, the Parametrized RM is subsequently obtained by associating to each FT event the relating failure rate distribution probabilities, obtained from manufacturer data if related to equipment component failures (from PD2 artifact), and from statistical testing data on emulated or similar software functions if related to software component failures (from PD3 artifact).

Such Parametrized RM can be finally evaluated by conventional evaluation tools such as Sharpe, Save, etc. [5, 12] at Step 2 of Fig. 25.5, to obtain the value of the reliability level **rl**.

25.4.1.3   SM Production

The SM takes in input the failure condition formerly identified by the RM and (if hazardous) performs operation 4) of Section 25.4.1.1, to identify if such a condition leads to an accident or not.

In analogy to the "Basic PM" and "Parametrized PM" definitions of Fig. 25.6, let us define "Basic SM" and "Parametrized SM" as the first and second outcomes of the SM production process, respectively.

The Basic SM can be automatically generated from the above mentioned artifacts A1 and A2. This is obtained by first producing the probabilistic Flow Graph (FG) with the method used in Section 25.4.1.2.

The FG is then used to identify the software paths that lead to accidents, and the accident modes. To each accident a CE is associated, whose top event is the accident itself, and its constituent causes (from FP2 artifact) are connected by And/Or relationships, which are then further resolved into sub-constituent causes [4], and so on until the hazardous events previously identified by the RM are reached.

From the so-obtained Basic SM, the Parametrized SM is subsequently obtained by associating to each CE event the relating failure rate distribution probabilities, obtained from the RM evaluation if related to the hazard input conditions, and from statistical data on equipment (from PD2 artifact), or managerial, operational or tactical environment faults (from FP2 artifact).

Such Parametrized SM can be finally evaluated by conventional evaluation tools [4] at Step 2 of Fig. 25.5, to obtain the value of the safety level **sl**.

25.4.2   EM Production

According to Table 25.1, system efficiency e can be defined in vector form

$$e = (w, r, q, p, c, u) \qquad (25.5)$$

where w denotes the waiting time, r the response time, q the queue length, p the path length, c the capacity and u the utilization.

System efficiency (also called efficiency level **el**) is the probability that values of attributes w through u do not fall below a given minimum in the course of the system life-time (in a simplified acception level **el** can be expressed in terms of average values rather than of probability distribution).

According to point (ii) of Section 25.2.2, life-cycle *efficiency validation* is the process of predicting (*at the early phases* of the development life-cycle) the ability of the to-be product to satisfy the efficiency level (**el**) the user expects, and finally evaluating such level for the as-is product *at the end*.

In order to perform efficiency validation, an EM has to be generated at the considered life-cycle phase.

It is assumed that the produced EM is of a type that can be evaluated, at Step 2 in Fig. 25.5, either by Extended Queuing Network (EQN) Tools [3] or by Layered Queuing Network (LQN) Tools [9, 11].

In analogy to the "Basic PM" and "Parametrized PM" definitions of Fig. 25.6, let us define "Basic EM" and "Parametrized EM" as the first and second outcomes of the EM production process, respectively.

It is proved [26] that the Basic EM can be automatically generated by use of the above mentioned A1 and A2 artifacts.

In more detail, a conventional Execution Graph (EG) [7] is first derived by use of the CD, DFD, ID, FP, PD and SW artifacts. In particular:

- the CD, DFD, and ID artifacts are used to derive the EG graph

- the FP artifact (FP1 part) to derive the EG branching probabilities

- the PD (PD1 part) and SW artifacts to derive the EG demand vectors.

By use of the C/S artifact, the obtained EG is then transformed [26] into a so-called Extended EG (the Basic EM).

From the so obtained Basic EM, a Parametrized EM is subsequently obtained [26] by use of the PD artifact.

Such Parametrized EM is derived either in the form of an EQN, or in the form of an LQN, to be finally evaluated by conventional evaluation tools at Step 2 of Fig. 25.5, to obtain the value of the efficiency level **el**.

25.5 Conclusions

Validation is an important activity in the process of licensing software systems.

It requires extensive knowledge and tools for model production methods, or methods for the automatic generation of performance models from early-phase software life-cycle artifacts.

It also requires an "extended" acceptation of the performance concept, to include system reliability and, more specifically, system safety, considered of paramount importance.

Performance research is called both to concentrate on model "production" methods, and to pay attention to methods for "extended" models that include safety.

This paper has dealt with both such methods, and has discussed the concept of performance early validation, introducing strategies for its implementation.

References

[1] ANSI/IEEE Standard for Software Verification and Validation Plans, ANSI/IEEE Std 1012–1986.

[2] ISO 9001 Model for QA Model for Quality Assurance in design/development, production, installation and servicing.

[3] S.S. Lavenberg, *Computer Performance Modeling Handbook,* Academic Press, New York, 1983.

[4] N. Leveson, *Safeware,* Addison Wesley, 1996.

[5] M.R. Lyu (Editor), *Handbook of Software Reliability Engineering,* McGraw-Hill, 1996.

[6] R.S. Pressman, *Software Engineering: A Practitioners Approach, 4th Edition,* McGraw-Hill, 1997.

[7] C.U. Smith, *Performance Engineering of Software Systems,* Addison Wesley, 1992.

[8] Y.V. Reddy, K. Srinivanas, V. Jagannathan, R. Karinthi, Computer Support for Concurrent Engineering, *IEEE Computer,* vol 26(1), 12–16, January 1993.

[9] J.A. Rolia, K.C. Sevcik, The Method of Layers, *IEEE Transactions on Software Engineering,* 21(8), 689–700, August 1995.

[10] C. Hrischuk, C.M. Woodside, J. Rolia, R. Iversen, Trace-based load characterization for generating software performance models, *IEEE Transaction on Software Engineering,* Volume 25, Number 1, pp. 122–135, January 1999.

[11] G. Franks, A. Hubbard, S. Majumdar, D. Petriu, J. Rolia, C.M. Woodside, A Toolset for Performance Engineering and Software Design of Client-Server Systems, *Special Issue of the Performance Evaluation Journal,* Vol. 24, No. 1–2, pp. 117–135, 1996.

[12] K. Trivedi, G. Ciardo, M. Malhotra, R. Sahnar, Dependability and Performability Analysis, *Performance 93 and Sigmetrics 93 Joint Tutorial Papers,* (L.Donatiello, R.Nelson Eds.), Springer-Verlag, 1993.

[13] C.M. Woodside, A Three-View Model for Performance Engineering of Concurrent Software, *IEEE Transactions on Software Engineering,* vol 21(9), 754–767, September 1995.

[14] J.R. Callahan, T.C. Zhou, R. Wood, Software Risk Management through Independent Verification and Validation, *Proceedings of the 4th International Conference on Software Quality (ICSQ 94),* McLean, VA, October 3–5, 1994.

[15] N.E. Fenton, B. Littlewood, M. Neil, L. Strigini, A. Sutcliffe, D. Wright, Assessing Dependability of Safety Critical Systems using Diverse Evidence, *IEE Proceedings Software Engineering,* 145(1), 35–39, 1998.

[16] U. Herzog, Stochastic Process Algebras Benefits for Performance Evaluation and Challenges, *Concur 98,* pp. 366–372.

[17] U. Herzog, A concept for graph-based process algebras, generally distributed activity times and hierarchical modelling, *Proceedings of the 4-th workshop on Process Algebra and Performance Modelling,* Torino, Italy, July 1996.

[18] G. Iazeolla, A. D'Ambrogio, R. Mirandola, A CSCW Environment to Engineer Quality in Software Products, *Proceedings of the 2nd International Conference on CSCW in Design,* Bangkok, Thailand, Nov. 1997.

[19] M. Neil, B. Littlewood, N. Fenton, Applying Bayesian Belief Networks to Systems Dependability Assessment, *Proceedings of Safety Critical Systems Club Symposium,* Leeds, 6–8, Springer-Verlag, February 1996.

[20] ADAGES, Action Plan Definition on the basis of Architecture Studies from GAAS for EATMS Simulations, Work Package Reports WP1, WP2, WP3, EUROCONTROL, Haren (Belgium), 1995.

[21] DAAS, Dependability Approach to ATM Systems, Work Package Reports WP1, WP2, EUROCONTROL, Haren (Belgium), 1995.

[22] EVAS, EATMS Validation Strategy Document, Edition 1.1, EUROCONTROL, Haren, Belgium, June 1998.

[23] GAAS, Generic Approach to ATM System, Work Package Reports WP2, WP3, WP5, DG XII Commission of the European Community, Aero-

nautics program of the European Economic Community, Bruxelles (Belgium), 1993–1995.

[24] G. Iazeolla, R. Mirandola, Quality-Validation Strategies for ATM Concepts and CNS/ATM Architectures, (Extended Version), Report Certia, CRT.05.97, November 1997.

[25] PAMPAS, Preliminary Approach for Modelling Performance of ATM Systems for EATCHIP Programme, Work Package Reports WP1, WP2, WP3, EUROCONTROL, Haren (Belgium), 1997.

[26] M. Versari, V. Cortellessa, G. Iazeolla, R. Mirandola, Generation Methods of Software Performance Models at Specification and Preliminary Design Time, RI.99.01, Laboratory for Computer Science, University of Roma TorVergata, April 1999.

Vitae

Giuseppe Iazeolla is full professor of Computer Science, Software Engineering Chair, Faculty of Engineering, University of Roma at TorVergata, Italy.

His research is in the areas of software engineering and information system engineering, in relation to system performance and dependability modeling and validation.

Andrea D'Ambrogio received a Laurea degree in Computer Engineering from the University of Roma at TorVergata, Italy, in 1994. He is with the Software Engineering Laboratory at the Department of Computer Science, Systems and Industrial Engineering, University of Rome at TorVergata, Italy. He is a member of IEEE.

His research is in the fields of Distributed Object Computing, Web-based Modeling and Simulation, Computer Supported Cooperative Work and Software Quality Engineering.

Raffaela Mirandola received a Laurea degree in Computer Science from the University of Pisa, Italy, in 1989 and a Ph.D. degree in Computer Science from the University of Rome at TorVergata, Italy, in 1994. At present, she is a researcher at the Department of Computer Science, Systems and Industrial Engineering, University of Rome at TorVergata, Italy.

Her main research interests are in the areas of methodology and tools for the performance and dependability analysis of software systems and of computer and communication systems.

Chapter 26

Performance Validation at Early Stages of Software Development

Connie U. Smith
Performance Engineering Services

Murray Woodside
Carleton University

Abstract   We consider what aspects of software performance can be validated during the early stages of development, before the system is fully implemented, and how this can be approached. There are mature and successful methods available for immediate use, but there are also difficult aspects that need further research. Ease of use and integration of performance engineering with software development are important examples. This paper describes issues in early performance validation, methods, successes and difficulties, and conclusions.

Keywords: software performance, requirements, responsiveness, workload analysis, resource budgets.

26.1   Early Performance Validation

The IEEE defines performance and validation as follows:

Performance: the degree to which a system or component accomplishes its designated functions within given constraints, such as speed, accuracy, or memory usage.

Validation: The process of evaluating a system or component during or at the end of the development process to determine whether it satisfies specified requirements.

This paper focuses on the validation of the responsiveness of systems: response time, throughput, and compliance with resource usage constraints. We consider the particular issues in the early development stages (concept, requirements, and design): in pre-implementation stages complete validation is impossible because measurements of the final system are not yet available. The techniques in pre-implementation stages require construction and evaluation of models of the anticipated performance of the final system.

The result is a *model-based approach.* It is not perfect; the following problems must be addressed:

- In pre-implementation stages factual information is limited: final software plans have not been formulated, actual resource usage can only be estimated, and workload characteristics must be anticipated.

- The large number of uncertainties introduce the risk of model omissions: models only reflect what you know to model, and the omissions may have serious performance consequences.

- Thorough modeling studies may require extensive effort to study the many variations of operational scenarios possible in the final system.

- Models are not universal: different types of system assessments require particular types of models. For example, the models of typical response time are different from models to assess reliability, fault tolerance, performability, or safety.

Thus, the model-based approach is not a perfect solution, but it is effective at risk reduction.

The modeling techniques must be supplemented with a *performance engineering* process (SPE) that includes techniques for mitigating these problems (Smith, [11]). SPE includes the model-based approach to performance validation as well as techniques for gathering data, prediction strategies, management of uncertainties, techniques for model validation, principles for creating responsive systems, and critical success factors.

The goal of the SPE process and the model-based approach is to reduce the risk of performance failures (rather than guarantee that they will not occur). They increase the confidence in the feasibility of achieving performance objectives and in the architecture and design choices made in early life cycle stages. They provide the following information about the new system:

- Refinement and clarification of the performance requirements.

- Predictions of performance with precision matching the software knowledge available in the early development stage and the quality of resource usage estimates available at that time.

- Estimates of the sensitivity of the predictions to the accuracy of the resource usage estimates and workload intensity.

- Understanding of the quantitative impact of design alternatives, that is, the effect of system changes on performance.

- Scalability of the architecture and design: the effect of future growth on performance.

- Identification of critical parts of the design.

- Identification of assumptions that, if violated, could change the assessment.

- Assistance for budgeting resource demands for parts of the design.

- Assistance in designing performance tests.

The remainder of this paper covers the steps in the model-based approach for the quantitative assessment of performance characteristics of an evolving system in early development stages. It addresses the steps in the engineering process, and for each reviews methods used, experience with them, difficulties encountered, and research issues. The final section offers some conclusions on the current state of the art and state of the practice.

26.2 Validation for Responsiveness and Throughput

The general approach to early validation of performance is similar to any other engineering design evaluation. It is based on evaluating a model of the design, and has five steps:

1. Capture performance requirements, and understand the system functions and rates of operation.

2. Understand the structure of the system and develop a model which is a performance abstraction of the system.

3. Capture the resource requirements and insert them as model parameters.

4. Solve the model and compare the results to the requirements.

5. Follow-up: interpret the predictions to suggest changes to aspects that fail to meet performance requirements.

Validation (following the definition above) comes in Step 4 from comparing the evaluation to the requirements. Step 5 creates a loop which is entered if it is necessary to improve a system so it will pass the validation.

Each step has a variety of approaches which pose characteristic problems that have to be solved by the practitioner in each project, and which also may be problems for research. The differences between approaches taken by the present authors and others lie in the state of the design to be evaluated, the methods used to carry out the steps, and the kind of model used.

26.2.1   Methods, Successes, and Difficulties

Each step will be considered in turn, to discuss how it can be carried out and whether there are gaps in the state of the art.

Step 1. Capture Performance Requirements

Sometimes the requirements are clear, as in embedded systems where factors in the outer system determine deadlines for certain types of responses. In systems with human users they are rarely clear, because satisfaction is a moving target. As systems get better, users demand more of them, and hope for faster responses.

In most systems there are several types of response, with different requirements. Users can be asked to describe performance requirements, to identify the types and the acceptable delays and capacity limitations. An experienced analyst must review their responses with the users, because they may be unnecessarily ambitious (and thus potentially costly), or else not testable. This review may have to be repeated as the evaluation proceeds and the potential costs of achieving the goals become clearer.

Experience in obtaining requirements is not well documented, however, it seems clear that they are often not obtained in any depth, or checked for realism, consistency and completeness, and that this is the source of many performance troubles with products. One problem is that users expect the system to modify how it works, so they do not really know precisely how they will use it. Another is that while developers have a good notion of what constitutes well-defined functional requirements they are often naive about performance requirements.

As also for other non-functional requirements, practices for obtaining performance requirements are poorly developed.

Research is needed on questions such as tests for realism, testability, completeness, and consistency of performance requirements; on methodology for capturing them, preferably in the context of a standard software notation such as UML, and on the construction of performance tests from the requirements.

Step 2. Understanding the System and Building a Model

In this step an execution model is created, representing the functions the software must perform, and the design intentions. It traces scenarios through typical execution paths (a path model in the terms of [16]), and it may take different forms.

- The execution graphs of [11] represent the sequence of operations, including precedence, looping, choices, and forking/joining of flows. This is representative of a large family of models such as SP [14], task graphs (widely used in embedded and hard-real-time systems), activity diagrams, etc. This form has been most useful for capturing scenarios which represent different types of response. Automated tools such as SPEED [12] and HIT [2] capture the data and reduce it to formal workload parameters.

- Communicating state machines are captured in software design languages such as UML, SDL, and ROOM, and in many CASE tools, to capture sequence. Some efforts have been made to capture performance data in this way [18, 5] by capturing scenarios out of the operation of the state machines, or [13] by annotating the state machine and simulating the behavior directly.

- Petri nets and stochastic process algebras are closely related to state machines and also represent behavior through global states and transitions. Solutions are by Markov chain analysis in the state space, or by simulation.

- Annotated code represents the behavior by a code skeleton, with abstract elements to represent decisions and operations, and performance annotations to convey parameters. The code may be executed on a real environment, in which case we may call it a performance prototype, or by a simulator (a performance simulation) [1], or it may be reduced to formal workload parameters [8].

- Component-based system assembly models, with components whose internal behavior is well understood, has been used to create simulation models automatically in SES Strategizer (documented at www.ses.com), and to create analytic layered queuing models [10, 17].

A follow-on to each of the above approaches to describing the workload behavior is the creation of a performance evaluation model which is normally different from the behavior model. Demands captured in an execution graph can be converted into parameters of a queuing model or a layered queuing model. State-based models can be converted into a Markov or Semi-Markov Chain, for numerical solution. Any of the models can be converted to a simulation.

Many experiences of applying the above methods have been reported. The methods all seem to work, provided they are applied by experienced analysts. In each case their users are positive about success, but penetration to others has been slow.

There are difficulties at this stage due to time and effort on one hand, and expertise and judgement on the other. Model building is labor intensive and costly. It requires input from valuable people with the central insights into the design problem. The cost of modeling is one of the forces behind the perpetuation of the *fix-it-later* philosophy. Also, the judgements needed to create performance abstractions are difficult for developers to make. Some degree of abstraction is essential, but how much? This is an element of the art of performance modeling, which is not well diffused among software developers. There is no common language for model capture, which makes it difficult to communicate the concerns of the analyst, and the model itself, to others within a project.

Some users are unhappy with constraints on what can be expressed in a given form of model. The abstractions used in a form of model may make it impossible to describe some features of the execution. Designers are creative at finding new behavior patterns with greater flexibility, but higher performance costs (examples might be inheritance, or mobile agents). Some modeling techniques do not capture these patterns easily.

Research problems in model building include a flexible expressive model for capture of behavior, automated capture of behavior from legacy components, and modeling within frameworks familiar to the designer, such as UML.

Step 3. Capture Resource Demands

Within the structure captured at the last step, the actual demand parameters for CPU time, disk operations, network services, and so forth are estimated and inserted at this step. In fact the parameters are often captured at the same time as the structure, but the discussion is separated because the factors governing this step are sometimes different.

There seem to be four different sources of actual values for execution demands:

- measurements on parts of the software which are already implemented, such as basic services, existing components, a design prototype, or an earlier version [15],

- compiler output from existing code,

- demand estimates (CPU, I/O, etc.) based on designer judgement and reviews,

- "budget" figures, estimated from experience and the performance requirements, may be used as demand *goals* for designers to meet (rather than as estimates for the code they will produce) (see the next section for more discussion).

The sources at the top of the list are only useful for parts of the system that are actually running, so early analysis implies at least some of the numbers will be estimated.

There has been considerable experience with estimation using expert designer judgement [11], and it works well provided it has the participation (and encouragement) of a performance expert on the panel. Few designers are comfortable in setting down inexact estimates, and on their own they have a tendency to chase precision, for example by creating prototypes and measuring them. Nonetheless the estimates are useful even if they turn out later to have large errors, since the performance prediction is usually sensitive to only a few of the values.

Cache behavior has important effects on CPU demands, which may differ from one run to another. For embedded and hard-real-time systems, where an exact worst-case value is needed, algorithms have been developed to determine the worst-case impact of caching on execution of code.

Parameter estimation is an important area, yet it is difficult to plan research that will overcome the difficulties. Systems based on re-using existing components offer an opportunity to use demand values found in advance from performance tests of their major functions, and stored in a demand data base. Systems based on patterns offer a similar possibility, but if the pattern is re-implemented it has to be re-measured.

Step 4. Solve the Model

When we consider solving the model, some advantages of one model formalism over another become apparent. Because of uncertainties in parameter values and patterns of usage it may be necessary to solve the model many times, which gives a reward to fast model solvers.

Queuing network models are relatively lightweight and give basic analytic models which solve quickly. They have been widely used [11, 8]. However, the basic forms of queuing network models are limited to systems that use one resource at a time. Extended queuing models, which describe multiple resource use, are more complex to build and take longer to solve. *Layered queuing* is a framework for extended queuing models that can be built relatively easily, and which incorporates many forms of extended queuing systems [10, 17].

Bottleneck or bounds analysis of queuing networks is even faster than a full solution and has been widely used. However, when there are many classes of users or of workloads (which is the case in most complex systems) the bounds are difficult to calculate and interpret.

The difficulty with queuing models is expressiveness; they limit the behavior of the system to tasks providing service to requests in a queue. They cannot express the logic of intertask protocols, for instance.

Petri nets and other state-based models can capture logically convoluted protocol interactions that cannot be expressed at all in queuing models. They can in principle express any behavior whatever. Further, some of them, such as stochastic process algebra, include mechanisms for combining subsystems together to build systems.

Their defect is that they require the storage of probabilities over a state space that may easily have millions of states, growing combinatorially with system size. They do not, and cannot scale up. However, the size of system that can be solved has grown from thousands of states to millions, and interesting small designs can be analyzed this way.

Embedded and hard-real-time systems often use a completely different kind of model, a schedulability model, to verify if a schedule can be found that meets the deadlines. These are considered briefly below.

Simulation is the always-available fallback from any formulation. Some kinds of models are designed specifically for simulation, such as the performance prototype from code. Simulation models are heavyweight in the execution time needed to produce accurate results, and can give meaningless results in the hands of non-experts who do not know how to assess their precision or their accuracy. When models can be solved by both extended queuing techniques and by simulation, the simulation time may easily be three orders of magnitude greater. However, simulation can always express anything that can be coded, so it never limits the modeler in that way.

The unlimited expressiveness of simulation is both a hazard and a benefit. A colleague (Bill Sanders) put it nicely, that "the comfort is in the details," and developers appreciate being able to represent detail whenever they like. However, the temptation is to include excessive detail which can burden and confuse the analysis. It would be useful to have criteria to identify detail that is unnecessary.

Research into modeling technology, including efficient solution techniques, is lively and broadly based. It would be interesting to be able to combine the speed of queuing techniques with state-based techniques to take advantage of the strengths of both, for analytic estimation.

Step 5. Interpret the Model, and Identify Improvements if Performance is Unsatisfactory

If the requirements are not met, the analysis will often point to changes that make it satisfactory. These may be changes to the execution platform, to the software design, or to the requirements. To diagnose changes one must trace the causes of unsatisfactory delays and throughputs, back to delays and bottlenecks inside the system. Sometimes the causes are obvious, for example a single bottleneck which delays all responses and throttles the throughput. Sometimes they are more subtle, such as a network latency that blocks a process, making it busy for long unproductive periods and creating a bottleneck there. Examples are given in [11] and [3]. Woodside describes the process of tracing causality in [16].

Changes to the software design may be to reduce the cost of individual operations, or to reduce the number of repetitions of an operation, as described in [11]. Larger scale changes may be to change the process architecture or the object architecture, to reduce overhead costs, or to simplify the control path. If a single response class, distinct from other processing, is unsatisfactory, then it may be possible to speed it up by using priorities provided it is executed by a separate process.

If the bottleneck is a processing device (processor, network card, I/O channel, disk, or attached device of some kind), then the analysis can be modified to consider more powerful devices. If the cost of adapting the software or the environment is too high, one should finally consider the possibility that the requirements are unrealistic and should be relaxed.

26.2.2 Summary

Practical methods are known to handle all these steps, however, there are difficulties which inhibit their use in many development projects. Two major, broad problems are:

- The high skill level needed to apply them. (Thus, simpler methods or easy-to-use tools should be a goal of research.)

- The separation of performance engineering from development methods. (Thus, ways to integrate the two should be sought.)

Underdeveloped technical areas related to models include performance requirements analysis, resource demand capture for components, and tracing causality of performance shortfalls in complex systems.

26.3 Validation of Resource Budgets

Before a new product is designed there are no figures for resource demands (that is, for the CPU execution demand and the demands for other operations using disks, networks, etc.). Rather than considering the prediction of performance based on demand estimates, it may be better to plan budgets for resource demands for all the operations, and use the validation to check that they will give the required performance. The budgets then become targets to be met by the designers of the subsystems. In this approach the performance requirements are decomposed into budgets for subsystems, and the validation step validates the decomposition.

The methods just described can also be used, without change, to validate budgets. The budgeted resource demands are inserted into the model at Step 3, and the evaluation is carried out. If the validation does not pass, then the adjustments to be considered at Step 5 also include changes to the budgets for some operations.

26.4   Other Aspects of Early Software Validation

Other aspects of software should also be validated at an early stage, however, limitations of space and experience preclude a full discussion here. Examples are:

- Reliability, availability, and performability are approached by techniques very similar in principle to those for responsiveness, using models which include failure and repair mechanisms, and their parameters such as mean-time-to-failure and mean-time-to-repair. The same five steps are applied, but using these different models. An example is given in [4], and other examples may be found in the proceedings of the conference [6]. Many of the same difficulties occur in this area, as in performance validation, and successes are limited to systems of modest size.

- Schedulability is similar to responsiveness, in that it deals with completing responses in time, but it uses different techniques and is concerned with systems that fail if a single response is late. These are sometimes called hard real-time systems. Examples of techniques may be found in the proceedings of the conference [9] or the journal [7]. Excellent techniques exist for single processors, and strong heuristics for more complex systems. However, many aspects of modern computing technology (caching, networks) conspire against deterministic behavior.

26.5   Conclusions

An ideal performance validation methodology would:

- be capable of dealing with multiple alternative deployments of the same software,

- be selectable, so one can apply low-cost, less powerful techniques when performance is not critical, and then step up to more powerful analysis if needed later,

- allow the assessment effort to be incremental, so that additional effort gives additional insight,

- be adaptable so as the design evolves, the original models are extended and the predictions updated,

- be capable of tracking the design as it develops,

- incorporate analysis techniques and process steps to address other aspects of performance: reliability, safety, etc.

Practitioners adapt SPE to address many of these issues in the course of their studies. Unfortunately, the state of the practice is still to apply ad-hoc techniques for each type of system. The SPE process has not yet evolved to prescribe an exhaustive set of procedures based on the type of system. The process is largely practiced by performance specialists. It needs to be better integrated with the software development process with specific SPE deliverable at each stage in the life cycle.

The model-based approach has been successfully applied to validate performance in a variety of systems. The two major difficulties which inhibit its use in many development projects are:

- the high skill level needed to apply them,

- the separation of performance engineering from development methods.

Underdeveloped technical areas related to models include performance requirements analysis, resource demand capture for components, and tracing causality of performance shortfalls in complex systems.

Is it possible to validate performance in early development stages with a model-based approach? Models can identify performance problems but they cannot prove absolutely the absence of problems. It is not possible to completely validate the model until the final system can be measured. Perhaps *verification* is a better concept to apply to performance:

Verification: The process of evaluating a system or component to determine whether the products of a given development phase satisfy the conditions imposed at the start of that phase (IEEE).

If quantitative performance objectives can be set for each stage, it should be possible to measure the product for that stage and determine whether the objective has been met.

Most SPE studies adjust the performance models to match the software as it evolves and new decisions are made. Perhaps a better approach is to "build to the model," that is, if the model predicts that if the system is constructed in this way, with these resource usage requirements, etc., then it will work — then the SPE process should verify that the evolving system matches the specifications of the early models. This strategy is particularly important for safety-critical systems.

References

[1] R.L. Bagrodia, C.-C. Shen, MIDAS: Integrated Design and Simulation of Distributed Systems, *IEEE Trans. on Software Engineering,* 17(10), pp 1042–1058, Oct. 1991.

[2] H. Beilner, J. Mater, N. Weissenberg, Towards a Performance Modeling Environment: News on HIT, *Proc. Int. Conf. on Modeling Tech. and Tools for Comp. Performance Evaluation,* pp 57–75, 1989.

[3] J. Dilley, R. Friedrich, T. Jin, J.A. Rolia, Measurement Tools and Modeling Techniques for Evaluating Web Server Performance, *Proc. 9th Int. Conf. on Modeling Tech. and Tools,* St. Malo, France, June, 1997.

[4] H. Duggal, M. Cukier, W. Sanders, Probabilistic Verification of a Synchronous Round-based Consensus Protocol, *Proc. 16th Symp. on Reliable Distributed Systems,* Durham, NC, October 1997.

[5] H. El-Sayed, D. Cameron, M. Woodside, Automated Performance Modeling from Scenarios and SDL Designs of Telecom Systems, *Proc. of Int. Symposium on Software Engineering for Parallel and Distributed Systems (PDSE98),* Kyoto, April 1998.

[6] IPDS, Proc. IEEE Int. Computer Performance and Dependability Symposium.

[7] Journal of Real-Time Systems, Kluwer, New York.

[8] D.A. Menasce, H. Gomaa, On a Language Based Method for Software Performance Engineering of Client/Server Systems, *Proc. of First International Workshop on Software and Performance (WOSP98),* pp 63–69, Oct. 1998.

[9] Proc. of the Real-Time Systems Symposium, *IEEE Comp. Society,* held annually since 1979.

[10] J.A. Rolia, K.C. Sevcik, The Method of Layers, *IEEE Trans. on Software Eng.,* 21(8), pp 689–700, Aug. 1995.

[11] C.U. Smith, *Performance Engineering of Software Systems,* Addison-Wesley, 1990.

[12] C.U. Smith, L.G. Williams, Performance Engineering Evaluation of CORBA-based Distributed Systems with SPEED, *Proc. 10th Int. Conf. On Modeling Tools and Techniques,* Palma de Mallorca, 1998.

[13] M. Steppler, Performance Analysis of Communication Systems Formally Specified in SDL, *Proc. of First International Workshop on Software and Performance (WOSP98),* pp 49–62, Oct. 1998.

[14] V. Vetland, P. Hughes, A. Solvberg, A Composite Modeling Approach to Software Performance Measurement, *Proc. ACM Sigmetrics Conference on Measurement and Modeling of Computer Systems,* Santa Clara, CA, pp 275–276, May 1993.

[15] V. Vetland, *Measurement-Based Composite Computational Work Modeling of Software,* Ph.D. Thesis, University of Trondheim, Aug 1993.

[16] C.M. Woodside, A Three-View Model for Performance Engineering of Concurrent Software, *IEEE Trans. Software Eng.,* 21(9), pp 754–767, Sept. 1995.

[17] C.M. Woodside, J.E. Neilson, D.C. Petriu, S. Majumdar, The Stochastic Rendezvous Network Model for Performance of Synchronous Client-Server-like Distributed Software, *IEEE Trans. Comp.,* 44(1), pp 20–34, Jan. 1995.

[18] C.M. Woodside, C. Hrischuk, B. Selic, S. Bayarov, A Wideband Approach to Integrating Performance Prediction into a Software Design Environment, *Proc. of First International Workshop on Software and Performance (WOSP98),* pp 31–41, Oct. 1998.

Vitae

Dr. Connie U. Smith is a principal consultant of the Performance Engineering Services Division of L & S Computer Technology, Inc. She specializes in applying performance prediction techniques to software, developing SPE tools, and teaching SPE seminars. She is the author of Performance Engineering of Software Systems, published in 1990 by Addison-Wesley, and numerous scientific papers.

She has over 25 years of experience in computing, more than 20 of which have been in the practice, research, and development of performance prediction techniques. Her other research interests include computer performance modeling and evaluation, object-oriented development, tool interoperability, and tool development.

Dr. Smith received the Computer Measurement Group's AA Michelson Award for technical excellence and professional contributions for her SPE work. She frequently serves on conference and program committees, most recently chairing the First International Workshop on Software and Performance. She served as an officer of ACM SIGMETRICS for 10 years, is a past ACM National Lecturer, and is an active member of the Computer Measurement Group. She received a B.A. degree in mathematics from the University of Colorado and M.A. and Ph.D. degrees in computer science from the University of Texas at Austin.

Murray Woodside received a Ph.D. degree in Control Engineering from Cambridge University, England. He has taught and done research in stochastic control, optimization, queuing theory, and performance modeling of communications and computer systems, with over 100 articles in these subjects. His current interests are software engineering and performance engineering of distributed systems and telecommunications software. He currently holds the OCRI/NSERC Industrial Research Chair in Performance Engineering of Real-Time Software at Carleton University, where he has taught since 1970.

Chapter 27

Impact of Workload Models in Evaluating the Performance of Distributed Web-Server Systems

Valeria Cardellini
University of Rome Tor Vergata

Michele Colajanni
University of Modena

Philip S. Yu
T.J. Watson Research Center

Abstract   Distributed Web-server systems are being proposed to support high request rates to popular Web sites. This architecture is preferable to multiple independent mirrored-servers because it maintains a single interface to the users and can implement some load balancing strategies.

In this paper, we consider two classes of distributed Web architectures that use different dispatching schemes. The former, namely *DNS-dispatcher,* uses the *Domain Name System* server to distribute client requests among the servers through the URL-name to IP-address mapping mechanism. The latter, namely *DNS-dispatcher with server redirection* integrates the DNS with a server redirection request mechanism based on the HTTP protocol.

We compare many alternative schemes under two Web workload models that represent the client activities through exponential and heavy-tail distributions, respectively. The goal is to demonstrate the implication of the workload models on performance of the dispatching algorithms and the choice of the distributed Web architecture. Some schemes that work well under the exponential workload model achieve very poor performance when we consider the more realistic heavy-tail distributions. In most instances, the DNS-dispatcher architecture alone is unable to face the high variance of these latter loads. This motivates the introduction of a further dispatching level. Indeed, a distributed Web-server architecture that combines DNS dispatching and (some) server redirection policies is able to handle highly variable hit rates typical of the WWW environment. In particular, we see that redirection algorithms based on a periodic activation mechanism are preferable to asynchronous policies activated on server demand.

27.1 Introduction

Distributed Web-server systems are commonly adopted to handle Web sites with millions of accesses per day. This architecture guarantees scalability and transparency, but requires some internal mechanism that automatically assigns client requests to the Web server that can offer the best service. The assignment decision can be taken at the *IP level* through some address packet rewriting mechanism [10, 13], or at the local *Domain Name System* (DNS) level through the mapping of the URL-name to the IP-address of one server in the system [1, 6, 14]. Both choices have some drawbacks.

The IP-dispatcher based systems have full control on the incoming requests, but they can be applied only to locally clustered Web servers. (The exception is the Network Dispatcher approach, which can support multiple Network Dispatchers [13].) Moreover, the task of rewriting all packets can cause the IP-dispatcher to become a bottleneck when the system is subject to heavy request load.

The DNS-dispatcher based systems do not present risks of bottleneck, and can easily scale from locally to geographically distributed Web-server systems. The main problem of scheduling through the DNS is due to the IP-address caching mechanism that lets the DNS control only a very small fraction of the user requests. The limited control and the high non-uniformity of the load from different client domains require sophisticated DNS scheduling policies to avoid Web-server overload [6, 7].

In this paper, we consider also an alternative architecture that integrates the DNS dispatching mechanisms with redirection techniques carried out by the Web servers through the redirection protocol provided by HTTP [1, 5]. Such redirection is transparent to the users that at most perceive a small increase in the response time. Unlike the IP-dispatcher based solutions, the HTTP redirection does not require the modification of the IP-address of the packets reaching or leaving the Web-server system.

We propose and evaluate various one-level (*DNS-dispatcher*) and two-level dispatching schemes (*DNS-dispatcher with server redirection*) under two workload models. We demonstrate that an architecture that integrates DNS dispatching with Web-server redirection mechanisms provides excellent load control thus minimizing server overload even when the workload model is characterized by heavy-tail distributions.

The paper is organized as follows. Section 27.2 outlines two distributed Web-server systems. Section 27.3 focuses on the distribution functions that describe the workload reaching a Web system. Section 27.4 presents various dispatching schemes for each distributed Web-server architecture. Section 27.5 presents the performance results achieved through a detailed simulation model of the Web architectures and algorithms. Section 27.6 concludes the paper with final remarks.

27.2 Distributed Web-Server Systems

The users access the WWW services through some client application. Typically, the clients have a (set of) local name server(s) and are connected to the network through local gateways. We will refer to the network sub-domain behind these local gateways as *domain.*

27.2.1 DNS-Dispatcher Systems

The DNS-dispatcher system uses one URL-name to provide a single interface for users. This system consists of homogeneous distributed servers that manage the same set of documents, and a (primary) DNS that translates the URL-name into the IP-address of one of the servers in the Web-server system. Through this mechanism, the DNS can dispatch the client requests among the servers based on some optimization criterion (e.g., load balancing, response time minimization, load sharing). In addition to the DNS base function, the DNS-dispatcher must include a load monitor and a request collector. The load monitor tracks the load index from servers, while the request collector gathers the domain load information from each server and estimates the domain hit rate of each connected domain. In such a way the DNS-dispatcher can assign each address request to one of the Web servers based on some load status.

The entire period of access to the Web site from a single user, namely *client session,* consists of two phases: the *IP-address request* phase, during which the client asks the DNS for a translation of the URL-name of the Web system into the IP-address of one Web server in the system; the *Web page request* phase, in which various pages are requested directly from the selected Web server. Let us focus here on the former phase and postpone a detailed description of the latter phase to Section 27.3. The IP-address request is initially submitted to the local name server of the client domain, because it typically caches the

URL-name to IP-address mapping for a certain period, namely the *time to live* (TTL) interval. If the cache of the local name server has a valid mapping for this URL-name, the page request is sent directly to the Web server without going through the primary DNS. Otherwise, the IP-address request is submitted to subsequent intermediate name servers, and only if the mapping is not cached in any of these name servers, the request reaches the DNS of the Web-server system. The DNS returns the IP-address of one of the servers in the system and the TTL value. Each name server along the path from the DNS to client's domain caches this mapping for the TTL period.

The non-uniform distribution of client requests among the domains is one of the major issues that any dispatching policy has to address. The other problem that obstacles server load sharing through the DNS dispatching mechanism is caused by IP-address caching at local and intermediate name servers that limits the control of the DNS to a small fraction of the requests reaching the Web system. That is to say, during the TTL period bursts of requests can arrive from a domain with a large number of clients to the same server, thereby causing high load skews [10] that are not controllable by the DNS.

27.2.2   DNS-Dispatcher Systems with Redirection

One solution to the problems of one-level DNS-dispatchers is represented by an architecture that integrates the DNS-dispatcher with some redirection techniques carried out by the Web servers through the HTTP protocol. Various alternatives are possible. We analyze those that are fully compatible with existing Web standards and protocols. In particular, the primary DNS and Web servers of the system are the only entities here that collect and exchange load information. Any algorithm or architecture that needs some active cooperation from any other WWW components, such as browsers, name servers and clients, is not considered because this would require some modifications of the WWW environment.

The DNS-dispatcher system with server redirection uses the same one-level dispatcher scheme of the previous architecture and integrates new modules in each Web server of the distributed system. Besides the HTTP daemon server, each Web server requires a redirection module, a load checker and a request counter to implement the redirection algorithms with some status information. The load checker tracks the server utilization and can send this information to the dispatcher and to the local redirection module, according to the selected redirection algorithm. The request counter estimates the number of requests received from each domain and periodically provides the information to the load collector in the DNS system. Finally, the redirection module determines if the client request has to be redirected and, in this case, it determines the target server.

27.3 Model and Parameters

27.3.1 System Model

We assume that clients are partitioned among the domains based on a Zipf's distribution, i.e., a distribution where the probability of selecting the ith domain is proportional to $1/i^{(1-x)}$. (The uniform distribution is obtained by setting $x = 1$, while the pure Zipf's function has parameter $x = 0$.) Indeed, if one ranks the popularity of domains by the frequency of their accesses to the Web server, the distribution on the number of clients in each domain is a function with a short head (corresponding to big providers, organizations and companies, possibly behind firewalls), and a very long tail. For example, a workload analysis on academic and commercial Web sites shows that in average 75% of the client requests come from only 10% of the domains [18].

Since the focus here is on Web-server system performance, we are not interested in the Internet traffic models [8]. However, we consider major network components that impact the performance of the Web-server system. This includes the model of the *primary DNS* that dispatches some client requests through the URL-name to IP-address mapping, the *local* and *intermediate name servers* that through their IP-address caching mechanisms limit the control of the DNS dispatcher to few percentage units of all requests reaching the Web system, and all the details concerning a *client session* that consists of an *IP-address request* phase followed by a *Web page request* phase. We have already described in Section 27.2 the IP-address request phase that returns to the client the IP-address of a Web server. Here, we focus on the Web page request phase during which various pages are requested to the Web system, initially to the selected Web server, and then to the same server or other servers if some redirection mechanism is activated in the two-level dispatching architecture.

A summary of the system parameters that we used in our simulation experiments is reported in Table 27.1.

Table 27.1 Parameters of the System Model

Category	Parameter	Value (default)
Web system	Number of servers	7
	Average system utilization	0.6667
Domain	Connected	50
	Client distribution among domains	Zipf ($x = 0.0$)
	Time-to-live (TTL)	300 seconds
Client	Number	2500

27.3.2 Workload Model

We consider two workload models. The *exponential model* was commonly used in most performance studies on distributed systems. The *heavy-tail model* incorporates all most recent results on the characteristics of realistic WWW load.

Let us first describe the main features of this latter workload model. The high variability and self-similar nature of Web accesses are modeled through heavy-tailed distributions, that is, functions where $P[X > x] \sim x^{-\alpha}$ as $x \to \infty$, for $0 < \alpha < 2$. This means that a random variable following a heavy-tailed distribution can take an extremely large value with non-negligible probability. Typical long-tail functions proposed for modeling Web workloads are the Pareto, lognormal and Weibull distributions [2, 3, 4, 8, 9].

The number of *page requests* per client session, that is, the number of consecutive Web pages a user will request from the Web-server system, is modeled according to the inverse Gaussian distribution [12]. This distribution does not have a closed form, while its probability density function is given by $f(x) = \sqrt{\frac{\lambda}{2\pi x^3}} e^{\frac{-\lambda(x-\mu)^2}{2\mu^2 x}}$, where $\mu = 3.86$ and $\lambda = 9.46$.

The time between the retrieval of two successive Web pages from the same client, namely the *user think time,* is modeled through a Pareto distribution $F(x) = P[X \le x] = 1 - (k/x)^\alpha$ [4, 9], which has probability density function equal to $f(x) = \alpha k^\alpha x^{-\alpha-1}$, where $\alpha = 1.4$, $k = 2$ and $x \ge k$. Crovella and Bestavros explain the self-similarity of Web traffic requests with the super-impositions of heavy-tailed ON-OFF periods [8]. Indeed, each user behavior is modeled as a bursty ON-OFF process, where ON periods correspond to the transfer of Web files, and OFF periods correspond to the silent intervals between transmissions.

The number of *embedded references* per page, that is, the number of hits that make up a Web page including the base HTML page and its referred files, is also obtained from a Pareto distribution [4, 16] with parameters $\alpha = 1.33$, $k = 2$.

The *inter-arrival time of hit requests* to the servers, that is, the processing and displaying time spent by the browser parsing a document component and preparing the new TCP connection, is modeled by a heavy-tailed function distributed as a Weibull [15], $F(x) = P[X \le x] = 1 - e^{-(x/b)^a}$, which has the following density function $f(x) = \frac{ax^{a-1}}{b^a} e^{-(x/b)^a}$, where $a = 0.382, b = 0.146$ and $x > 0$ [3].

The function that models the *hit size distribution*, that is, the distribution of the file sizes *requested* to a Web server (note that this measure differs from the distribution of the file sizes *stored* in the server's file system), is obtained from a hybrid distribution, where the body is modeled according to a lognormal distribution, while the tail is given by a heavy-tailed Pareto distribution [2]. The lognormal distribution does not have a closed form, while its probability density function is given by $f(x) = \frac{1}{x\sqrt{2\pi\sigma^2}}e^{\frac{-(lnx-\mu)^2}{2\sigma^2}}$, where $\sigma = 1.705$ and $\mu = 7.640$. The Pareto distribution has parameter values $\alpha = 1.383$ and $k = 2924$, respectively.

This hit size distribution is also taken as a model for the Web server capacity, which is denoted as served bytes per second.

Let us now consider a less skewed workload model where all heavy-tailed distribution functions are replaced by exponential and Poissonian distributions. Note that the exponential model, although less realistic for a WWW environment, is commonly used in most important studies on distributed systems [17]. Taking into account an alternative Web model is important because we will see that it will lead to quite different conclusions about the performance and relative rank of the proposed dispatching schemes and redirection policies.

The number of page requests per session (with a mean of 12 pages/session) and the time between two page requests from the same client are assumed to be exponentially distributed [18]. The number of embedded hits per HTML page are obtained from a uniform distribution in the discrete interval (5–15). The hit service time and the inter-arrival time of hit requests to the servers are assumed to be exponentially distributed. A summary of the parameters of the two workload models is in Table 27.2.

Table 27.2 Parameters of the Workload Models

Parameter	Exponential model	Heavy-tail model
Web page requests per session	Exp. (mean 12)	Inverse Gaussian $(\mu = 3.86, \lambda = 9.46)$
User think time	Exp. (mean 15)	Pareto $(\alpha = 1.4, k = 2)$
Embedded references per Web page	Uniform in [5–15]	Pareto $(\alpha = 1.33, k = 2)$
Inter-arrival time of hits	Exp. (mean 0.25)	Weibull $(a = 0.382, b = 0.146)$
Hit size request	Exp.	Lognormal $(\mu = 7.640, \sigma = 1.705)$ Pareto $(\alpha = 1.383, k = 2924)$

Although quite different parameters are used for each workload model, the comparison is fair because in all experiments the system utilization is in average kept to 66% of the capacity of the entire Web system. This value is obtained as a ratio between the *system* (or *offered*) *load*, that is, the average number of bytes per second requested to the Web-server system, and the *system capacity,* that is, the sum of the capacities of all Web servers in the system. The offered load is generated by an average number of 2500 clients, which are assumed to be partitioned among the domains based on a pure Zipf's distribution. Other experiments based on Zipf's distributions with different parameters also support the conclusions of this paper. Similarly, considering a much larger number of connected domains to emulate a more realistic scenario does not affect the main results of this paper. Indeed, these additional domains would just make longer the Zipf distribution tail that represents a very low source of offered load for the Web system.

27.4   Dispatching Schemes

27.4.1   DNS-Dispatcher Algorithms

Web sites that use a DNS dispatcher for load balancing generally take the round-robin (RR) algorithm to map different client requests to the servers [14]. However, as a result of address caching, a large number of the subsequent client requests from a particular domain are mapped to the same server during the TTL period. This can lead to load imbalance among the servers, as quantified in [10]. In [6], it was found that RR works well only under the unrealistic hypothesis that all domains have the same client request rate.

The first goal is to estimate the *domain hit rate* in order to evaluate the average number of client requests from each domain during a TTL interval. This value, referred to as the hidden load weight, denotes the average number of requests issued from each domain to a server after an address mapping decided by the DNS. Various scheduling algorithms that take into account the hidden load weight and source domain address of requests have been proposed and evaluated in [6] for a homogeneous distributed server environment, e.g., *minimum dynamically accumulated load* (DAL), *minimum residual load* (MRL), *two-tier Round-Robin* (RR2). In this paper, we focus on RR2 policy that generally gives satisfactory results in homogeneous systems. It is based on the following simple concept. Since the clients are unevenly distributed among the domains the hidden load weight of each domain is typically very different. Therefore, this policy assumes a partition of the domains into two classes: *normal* domains and *hot* domains. A *class threshold* χ is introduced such that each domain with a relative hidden load weight greater than χ is included in the hot class. For each address request, RR2 first determines the class of the source domain and then selects the next server in round-robin order following the server scheduled for the last request in that class. The objective is to reduce the probability that requests from the hot domains are assigned too frequently to the same server.

An alternative class of DNS dispatching disciplines uses an *adaptive TTL* (AdpTTL) combined with the basic RR algorithm or its RR2 variant [7]. The basic idea here is to assign to each address request a different TTL value by taking into account not only the data request rate of the source domain originating the request, but also the capacity of the server chosen by the DNS. The motivation for this approach comes from the observation that the number of data requests following an address request, independent of its origin, increases with the TTL value. By properly selecting the TTL value for each address request, we can reduce the load skews that are the main cause of overloading. The objective of the proposed approach is to even out the impact of the subsequent requests during the TTL interval on each server. More specifically, we want the subsequent requests from each domain to consume a similar amount of server utilization or percentage of server capacity.

27.4.2 Web-Server Redirection Algorithms

Various redirection algorithms have been recently proposed [5]. We classify the different redirection approaches based on the activation trigger mechanism (synchronous vs. asynchronous) and activation decision process (centralized vs. distributed). Moreover, we consider the entities that are redirected which can be individual clients within a domain or entire domains and some clients.

Here we assume that the activation decision is assigned to either the DNS in the centralized decision case or the Web servers in the distributed case. Once a redirection decision has been made, the redirection process is carried out always by the Web servers. Moreover, the synchronous (or periodic) activation is always combined with a centralized decision by the DNS, while an asynchronous (or on-demand) activation comes always together with a distributed decision by any of the Web servers. Hence, we can group the alternative approaches into two main classes. In *centralized synchronous redirection* (in brief, synchronous redirection), the decision about redirection is taken periodically at the DNS. Neither trigger from clients nor servers is considered. In *distributed asynchronous redirection* (in brief, asynchronous redirection), the redirection decision process can be activated by any Web server that is becoming overloaded.

Both these classes of alternatives are fully compatible with existing WWW standards and do not require any code modification in the protocols, browsers and domain gateways. As the HTTP redirection mechanism works on an individual basis, *domain redirection* means that all clients of the same domain are subject to the same redirection decision. Redirection is done by indicating, on the header of a response from a server, the IP-address of the new server and the code 301 (i.e., Server Moved Permanently) [11]. The IP-address cache of the client that receives this response is automatically modified, hence, all subsequent requests of the session from this client will go to the newly assigned server. On the other hand, the other clients of the same domain are not affected by this redirection reply, because the IP-address cache of the domain gateway has not been modified. Hence, when an entire domain is redirected, the HTTP redirection mechanism would need to redirect every client from that domain.

27.4.2.1   Synchronous Redirection Algorithms

The common features of the synchronous redirection algorithms regard the load information exchange.

- The decision is centralized at the DNS. Every t seconds (e.g., $t = 60, 120, 240, 300$) each Web server sends some status information (server load index and domain hit rate) to the DNS. On the basis of the domain hit rates, the DNS orders the domains from the most to the least popular. Through the server load index, the DNS orders the servers from the least to the most loaded.

- In the second step, the DNS builds the so called *Assignment Table*, where it specifies for each active domain the Web server to serve it. The server bin is updated based on the domain load after each assignment. In the first phase, the most popular domain is assigned to the least loaded server and so on until each server gets one domain. The other domains are assigned by selecting each time the server with the lowest bin level.

- The DNS serves the address resolution requests by using the Assignment Table.

The entities redirected by the synchronous policies can be individual clients (SynC) or entire domains and some clients (SynDC).

In SynC policy the Assignment Table is used only in the first level assignment carried out by the DNS when it receives an address resolution request. The redirection or second level assignment carried out by the Web servers is instead based on the so called *Server Percentage List* to indicate the percentage of client requests that need to be redirected. This is built by the DNS in the following way. The DNS first estimates the average bin level across all servers. The servers with bin level less than a certain range above the average (where the value of this range is a parameter of the algorithm) have a server percentage (in the Server Percentage List) set to 0%. For the other servers, the DNS evaluates the percentage of additional load exceeding the average as its server percentage to be reassigned. For example, let us suppose that the server WS_2 has a bin level which is 30% higher than the average. WS_2 is assigned with a server percentage equal to 30% in the Server Percentage List.

Once the Server Percentage List is obtained, the DNS broadcasts it to each server. This list is used for implementing the following probabilistic redirection mechanism based on individual clients. The Web servers that have a server percentage equal to 0% do not reassign any request. On the other hand, a Web server with a server percentage higher than 0% at each page request generates a random number p uniformly distributed between 0 and 1. If it comes higher than its server percentage (considering as example WS_2, if $p > 0.3$), the server will return the required information. Otherwise, it redirects the requests coming from that client in a cyclic way to all servers with percentage equal to 0% in the Server Percentage List.

An alternative to client redirection is to combine redirection of individual clients with redirection of entire domains, namely SynDC policy. This mechanism requires both the Assignment Table and Server Percentage List at each server. Now the Assignment Table is used not only by the DNS for the first level assignment but also by the Web servers for the second level (re)assignment. For this reason, the DNS has to periodically broadcast both of them to the Web servers.

At the arrival of a client request, each Web server checks the current Assignment Table to verify if it has to serve the requests coming from that domain. If not, the server redirects the requests according to the Assignment Table. Otherwise it checks the Server Percentage List. If its percentage is equal to 0%, the server serves the request and returns the required information. Otherwise, it implements the probabilistic redirection mechanism.

27.4.2.2 Asynchronous Redirection Algorithms

Any of the previous synchronous algorithms can be combined with a feedback alarm mechanism. When a server finds that its load is exceeding a threshold parameter, it sends an alarm message to the DNS. The DNS excludes this server from further assignments in the Assignment Table until it receives another message from the same server that signals the return to a normal load status. However, the feedback alarm mechanism can be used to activate the redirection process itself. This leads to a new class of distributed reassignment schemes that are asynchronously activated on a Web-server demand, namely AsynC.

No Assignment Table needs to be generated now. The Web system remains a typical DNS-dispatcher based system where the DNS carries out the first level assignment through an RR or RR2 scheme [6] or more sophisticated algorithms [7]. This DNS assignment process is integrated with a second level (re)assignment mechanism triggered by any overloaded server. Threshold-based load balancing policies are popular in distributed computer systems. They have been shown to be useful especially when jobs are independent and consist of single threads of control (common features for Web requests).

The DNS, acting as a centralized collector, maintains the so called *Available Server List,* which is the list of servers that are not overloaded at that moment. This list is transmitted in reply to a server alarm message that the server sends to the DNS when its utilization has exceeded a given load threshold.

As regards the selection policy, each overloaded server may redirect its client requests to any server in the Available Server List through the same HTTP-based protocol used by the synchronous algorithms. The selection of a server from the Available Server List is done through a simple algorithm such as round-robin because this choice does not have a large impact on performance.

27.5   Experimental Results

27.5.1   Performance Metrics

The main goal of this study is to investigate the impact of the redirection algorithms on load sharing, that is, avoiding that some Web server in the system becomes overloaded. Since the load balance of the overall system is only an indirect goal, popular metrics such as the standard deviation of server utilizations are not useful for our purposes. Therefore, we define the *system maximum utilization* at a given instant as the highest server utilization at that instant among all Web servers in the system. Specifically, the major performance criterion is the *cumulative frequency* of the system maximum utilization, i.e., the probability (or fraction of time) that the system maximum utilization is below a certain value. By focusing on the highest utilization among all Web servers, we can deduce whether the Web system is overloaded or not. Hence, the performance of the various redirection schemes is evaluated by tracking at periodic intervals the system maximum utilizations observed during the simulation runs. The server with the maximum utilization changes over time. However, if the system maximum utilization at an instant is low, it means that no server is overloaded at that time. By tracking the period of time the system maximum utilization is above or below a certain threshold, we can get an indication of how well a dispatching scheme works.

In some figures showing sensitivity to other system parameters, we use the probability that no server of the Web system is overloaded as the performance metric. This typically is the 95 percentile of the system maximum utilization (or not exceeding 95% maximum utilization).

The simulators, based on the Independent Replication Method, were implemented using the CSIM package. Each value is the result of five or more simulation runs with different seeds, where each run is for six hours of the Web-server system activity. For all simulation results, confidence intervals were estimated and the 95% confidence interval was estimated to be within 5% of the mean.

The goal of the experiments is twofold: 1) to estimate the impact of the workload model on the dispatching algorithms and distributed architectures; 2) to measure how effectively the redirection schemes can improve the limited control of the DNS on the address resolution requests so as to maximize load sharing in a distributed Web-server system. The underscore after the name of the algorithm denotes if we are considering the exponential (exp) or the heavy-tail (ht) workload model.

27.5.2 Performance of DNS-Dispatcher Algorithms

We first consider the DNS-dispatcher architecture. In Figs. 27.1 and 27.2 we show the results for the constant and adaptive TTL algorithms.

The RR performances are poor for both the exponential and the heavy-tail model. The result for the RR2 policy is much more interesting. We can see in Fig. 27.1 that the RR2 policy that achieves rather good performance for an exponential model, is unacceptable if we consider the heavy-tail model (the probability that no server is overloaded drops from 0.8 to 0.3).

Analogous even if less serious result is achieved by the adaptive TTL policy in Fig. 27.2. This policy guarantees that no server is overloaded for the exponential workload model, while for the more realistic workload, the probability that some server is overloaded is about 0.2.

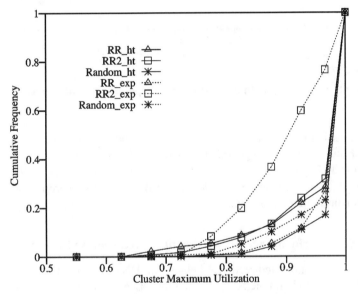

FIGURE 27.1
Constant TTL algorithms for the DNS-dispatcher architecture.

The results in Figs. 27.1 and 27.2 were part of the main motivation that led us to search for a different distributed Web system with a two-level dispatching mechanism (at the DNS and server level). Indeed, the redirection activated by heavily loaded servers can overcome the so called TTL constraint. With IP-address caching at name servers, DNS-dispatcher loses direct control of the subsequent client requests to the assigned server for the TTL period following the name-to-IP assignment. So it takes longer for the overloaded server to recover because the DNS-dispatcher policies can only stop the new DNS assignments to the overloaded server. There is no means to remove the already

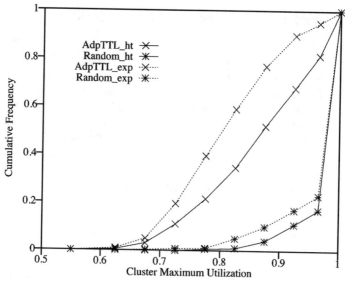

FIGURE 27.2

Adaptive TTL algorithms for the DNS-dispatcher architecture.

made assignments until the TTL expires. On the other hand, with redirection the over-utilized server can get rid of a fraction of the previously assigned requests before TTL expires.

In the next sections we consider the performance of synchronous and asynchronous redirection schemes.

27.5.3   Performance of Synchronous Redirection Schemes

In synchronous redirection schemes, the DNS has to collect some status information to build the Assignment Table. Every t seconds each Web server communicates server and domain load information to the DNS. This interval t is referred to as the *Assignment Table update* interval.

We first consider the issue of redirection granularity. The load control granularity obtainable by the redirection of entire domains is too coarse. The risk is to reassign continuously the largest domain to a different server that becomes overloaded in few seconds. A finer grain redirection is achieved by client redirection schemes (SynC) and domain and client redirection schemes (SynDC), which reassign individual clients and both entire domains and individual clients, respectively.

In Fig. 27.3 we show the performance of SynC and SynDC schemes. This figure shows that client redirection combined with domain redirection improves substantially the performance of the client redirection only scheme. The probability that no server is overloaded is almost guaranteed (that is, higher than 0.97) even when we consider the heavy-tail model. On the other hand, the client redirection policy is much more sensitive to the workload model. The optimum performance for the exponential workload model drops considerably for the more realistic workload model.

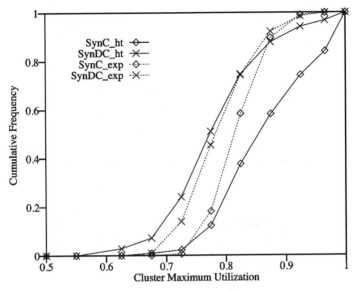

FIGURE 27.3
SynC and SynDC redirection schemes.

Once observed that the synchronous redirection policies are able to share the load in a distributed Web-server system, the next step aims at tuning at best these algorithms. In particular, we consider the issue on how to minimize the communication overheads and reduce request reassignments. Indeed, if the period of activation is short, the periodic centralized activation of the synchronous redirection algorithms can cause high computation and communication overheads due to gathering status information, building the Assignment Table and broadcasting it to the servers. Hence, one important goal is to reduce the frequency of updating the Assignment Table.

In Figs. 27.4 and 27.5 we analyze the sensitivity to the Assignment Table update interval using the probability that no server of the system is as overloaded (exceeding 95% utilization) as the performance metric. We consider SynDC schemes for the exponential (27.4) and heavy-tail (27.5) models.

In experiments not shown we observed that the performance of the SynC policy becomes very poor as the update interval of the Assignment Table increases. On the other hand, the SynDC scheme is insensitive to the update interval for both workload models. This stability is very important because larger update

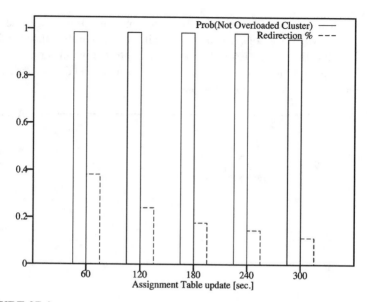

FIGURE 27.4

Sensitivity of performance and redirection percentage of the SynDC scheme to the frequency of the Assignment Table updating (*exponential model*).

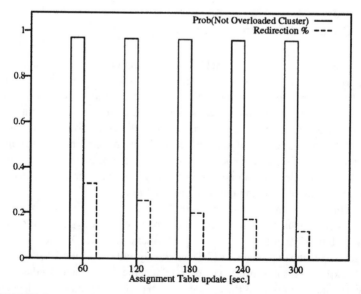

FIGURE 27.5

Sensitivity of performance and redirection percentage of the SynDC scheme to the frequency of the Assignment Table updating (*heavy-tail model*).

intervals diminish not only the computation/communication overhead but also the number of reassigned requests. So we can limit the percentage of users that perceive an increase in the response time without affecting the performance for the SynDC scheme. Figure 27.5 shows that increasing the update interval from 60 to 300 seconds causes a substantial reduction of reassigned requests (from 0.35 to 0.12) with no performance degradation of the SynDC policy.

27.5.4 Performance of Asynchronous Redirection Schemes

In asynchronous redirection schemes the DNS has to collect alarm messages from heavily loaded servers. The utilization threshold that triggers the alarm message is set to 0.75. (Similar results were observed for different alarm thresholds such as 0.7 and 0.8.) In the shown results, each server evaluates if its utilization has exceeded the alarm threshold every 16 seconds, referred to as the *check-load interval.*

In Fig. 27.6 we compare the performance of the asynchronous scheme with that of RR and RR2 where the DNS first level assignment is not integrated with a second level server reassignment. The improvement in favor of the asynchronous algorithm is considerable for the exponential model, while it is less consistent for the heavy-tail model. The client redirection can overcome the drawbacks caused by the IP-address caching mechanisms. Even stateless schemes such as RR, which was shown to perform very poorly under skewed workload on client distributions, when combined with a client redirection mechanism have performed better than stateful schemes at the DNS (e.g., RR2 with alarm feedback [6]) and close to that of more sophisticated algorithms (e.g., adaptive TTL [7]).

On the other hand, Fig. 27.7 shows that the asynchronous redirection schemes are very sensitive to the length of the *check-load interval.* The performance results of the asynchronous policies deteriorate from more than 0.9 to 0.6 as the check-load interval increases, while the percentage of redirected requests remains constant. Nevertheless, it is reasonable to use short periods such as 8 or 16 seconds because the server load evaluation does not necessary imply an activation of the redirection mechanism. Furthermore, the communication overhead is just a packet-size message sent from the Web servers to the DNS. This is in contrast to shortening the Assignment Table update interval in the synchronous redirection instance, which causes much higher communication and computation overheads.

The performance comparison among synchronous and asynchronous redirection policies is carried out as a function of some critical system parameters, such as the client distribution among the domains. Figure 27.8 compares the performance of the redirection policies in a system where the distribution of the clients among the domains varies from the pure Zipf ($x = 0$) to the uniform distribution ($x = 1$).

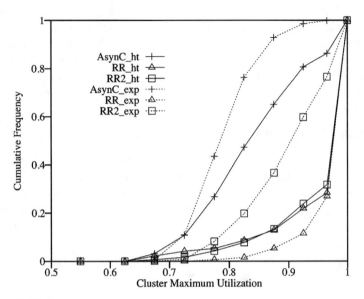

FIGURE 27.6
Asynchronous redirection schemes and DNS-dispatching algorithms.

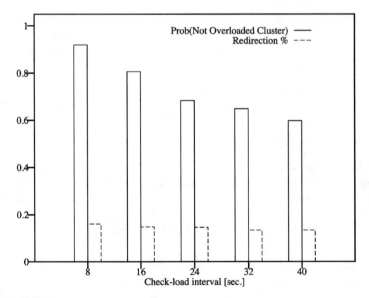

FIGURE 27.7
Sensitivity of performance of asynchronous algorithms to the frequency of the check-load interval (*heavy-tail model*).

The interesting result is that SynDC algorithm achieves better results than the asynchronous approach for both the heavy-tail and the exponential workload model. The robustness with respect to the client distribution is important because in the real WWW environment the client scenarios tend to change frequently.

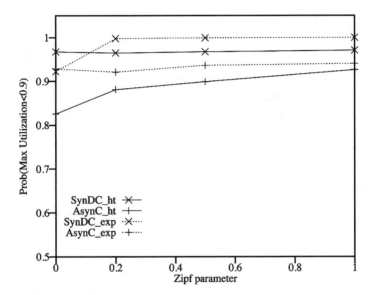

FIGURE 27.8
Sensitivity to client distribution among domains.

27.6 Summary

In this paper, we have studied Web-system architectures based on the DNS-dispatcher (which can be integrated or not with some redirection mechanism) under two workload models for various dispatching algorithms. Besides the expected improvement of all the policies under a less skewed workload model, we observe the following main results.

Redirection is a very useful mechanism to avoid overloading Web servers. Even stateless algorithms, such as RR that has been shown to perform very poorly in DNS-dispatcher under skewed request load, when combined with a client redirection mechanism, can have performance better than that of more sophisticated algorithms such as adaptive TTL [7].

The centralized synchronous algorithm gives the best results for a wide set of system parameters. However, the performance difference with distributed asynchronous approaches is not appreciable unless we consider realistic heavy-tailed workload model. Moreover, although in principle the communication overhead of synchronous algorithms is typically higher than that introduced by asynchronous policies, these latter have to augment much the frequency of intra-cluster communications to achieve results analogous to those of synchronous algorithms.

For a heavy-tail workload model, SynDC appears clearly the best algorithm. Although the SynC policy does not give good performance for a heavy-tail workload model, its results change completely when we consider an exponential workload model. The best synchronous algorithm is still the one that combines domain and client redirection, but the differences between the two policies can be appreciated only for a heavy-tailed workload model.

References

[1] D. Andresen, T. Yang, V. Holmedahl, O.H. Ibarra, SWEB: Toward a scalable World Wide Web server on multicomputers, *Proc. of IPPS'96,* Honolulu, pp. 850–856, April 1996.

[2] P. Barford, A. Bestavros, A. Bradley, M. Crovella, Changes in Web client access patterns: Characteristics and caching implications, to appear in *World Wide Web Journal,* 1999.

[3] P. Barford, M. Crovella, Generating representative Web workloads for network and server performance evaluation, *Proc. of ACM Sigmetrics '98,* Madison, Wisconsin, June 1998.

[4] P. Barford, M. Crovella, A performance evaluation of Hyper Text Transfer Protocols, *Proc. of ACM Sigmetrics '99,* Atlanta, Georgia, May 1999.

[5] V. Cardellini, M. Colajanni, P.S. Yu, Redirection algorithms for load sharing in distributed Web-server systems, *Proc. of IEEE ICDCS'99,* Austin, Texas, June 1999.

[6] M. Colajanni, P.S. Yu, D.M. Dias, Analysis of task assignment policies in scalable distributed Web-server systems, *IEEE Trans. on Parallel and Distributed Systems,* 9(6), pp. 295–302, June 1998.

[7] M. Colajanni, P.S. Yu, V. Cardellini, Dynamic load balancing in geographically distributed heterogeneous Web-servers, *Proc. of IEEE ICDCS'98,* Amsterdam, pp. 295–302, May 1998.

[8] M. Crovella, A. Bestavros, Self-similarity in World Wide Web traffic: Evidence and possible causes, *IEEE/ACM Trans. on Networking,* 5(6), pp. 835–846, Dec. 1997.

[9] S. Deng, Empirical model of WWW document arrivals at access link, *Proc. of IEEE Int. Conf. on Communication,* (ICC'96), Dallas, Texas, pp. 1797–1802, June 1996.

[10] D.M. Dias, W. Kish, R. Mukherjee, R. Tewari, A scalable and highly available Web server, *Proc. of 41st IEEE Computer Society Intl. Conf.* (COMPCON 1996), pp. 85–92, Feb. 1996.

[11] R. Fielding, J. Gettys, J. Mogul, H. Frystyk, T. Berners-Lee, Hypertext Transfer Protocol — HTTP/1.1, RFC 2068, Jan. 1997.

[12] B. Huberman, P. Pirolli, J. Pitkow, R. Lukose, Strong regularities in World Wide Web surfing, *Science,* no. 280, pp. 95–97, 1998.

[13] G.D.H. Hunt, G.S. Goldszmidt, R.P. King, R. Mukherjee, Network Dispatcher: A connection router for scalable Internet services, *Proc. of WWW7,* Brisbane, Australia, Apr. 1998.

[14] T.T. Kwan, R.E. McGrath, D.A. Reed, NCSA's World Wide Web server: Design and performance, *IEEE Computer,* vol. 28, pp. 68–74, Nov. 1995.

[15] A.M. Law, W.D. Kelton, *Simulation Modeling and Analysis,* Mc-Graw Hill, 1991.

[16] B.A. Mah, An empirical model of HTTP network traffic, *Proc. of IEEE Int. Conf. on Computer Communication,* (INFOCOM'97), Kobe, Japan, April 1997.

[17] Y.T. Wang, R.J.T. Morris, Load sharing in distributed systems, *IEEE Trans. on Computers,* C-34(3), pp. 204–217, Mar. 1985.

[18] C.L. Williamson, M.F. Arlitt, Internet Web server: Workload characterization and performance implications, *IEEE/ACM Trans. on Networking,* 5(5), pp. 631–645, Oct. 1997.

Chapter 28

Validation in the European Air Traffic Management Program (EATMP)

Dr. Ulrich Borkenhagen, Dr. Helmut Schröter, and Hans Wagemans

EUROCONTROL

Abstract   This paper provides on overview of the validation approach for the short-, medium-, and long-term development of European Air Traffic Management (ATM) systems. A performance-driven management process is adopted. The performance attributes considered in this paper are capacity and safety. A method to break down overall capacity targets into more detailed target values at the local level is explained. Capacity is currently related to air traffic controller workload and the need to increase controller productivity is expressed. A large-scale validation demonstration related to the increase of controller productivity is also outlined. Finally, initial results of a systematic approach to analytically model the collision risk of aircraft in relation to the separation of air-routes in the early concept development phase is outlined.

Keywords: validation, performance, capacity, safety, workload.

28.1   Introduction

The amount of air traffic (not only) in Europe has shown a continuous growth in the past, and a further increase is anticipated (see Fig. 28.1).

This permanent growth has some implications, and an important one concerning the effect on delays is depicted in Fig. 28.2.

The data have been assembled from 1995 to 1997. The increase of delay vs. traffic indicates that the system is saturated and that the situation will worsen

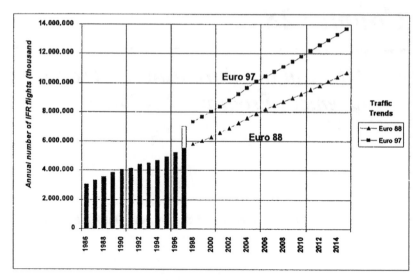

FIGURE 28.1
Traffic statistics and forecast for the ECAC area[1] [2].

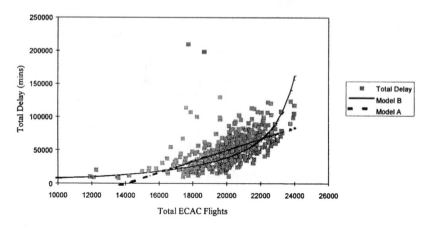

FIGURE 28.2
Total delay vs. total ECAC flights — weekdays [8].

if no effective counter measures were taken. (Figure 28.2 also depicts "fits"

---

[1]Source: STATFOR, DED4 EUROCONTROL Doc.No: 98.70.14 dated June 1998. Continuous historical traffic data prior to 1997 is available only for the Euro 88 area (Austria, Belgium/Luxembourg, France, Germany, Ireland, Netherlands, Portugal — inc the Azores, Spain — inc Canary Islands, Switzerland and the UK). Data for the Euro 97 area (the Euro 88 area plus Cyprus, Czech Republic, Denmark, Greece, Hungary, Italy, Malta, Turkey, Norway, Slovakia,

of the growth of delay. However, the theoretical modeling is difficult as there are permanent system optimizations and enhancements. A progressive growth according to model B appears to be more realistic as the inherent complexity of the traffic, and the potential interaction of flights, also grows progressively.)

In the late 1980s the number of delayed flights and overall delays had already reached a level that raised serious public complaints. The European Ministers of Transport, as organized in the *European Civil Aviation Conference (ECAC)*, approved the ECAC Strategy for the 1990s [4] and tasked the EUROCONTROL Agency with the management of the *European Air Traffic Control Harmonization and Integration Program (EATCHIP)* to implement the strategy. Despite the continual growth in traffic demand, EATCHIP managed to reduce delays to some extent. However, the improvement potential of the initial EATCHIP activities appeared to be exhausted, and 1998 was again perceived as a bad year. As this development was anticipated, the EUROCONTROL Agency, together with its stakeholders, developed the ATM 2000+ Strategy [2] which is expected to be approved by the ECAC Ministers of Transport in early 2000. The EURO-CONTROL Agency is then expected to be tasked to manage its implementation through the *European Air Traffic Management Program (EATMP)*.

The ATM 2000+ Strategy prescribes a new approach to solve the problems of the present European ATM by integrating and improving the ATM-related resources and activities of all stakeholders in an improved, *performance-driven management process.*

The major performance or quality attributes relevant for this paper are:

- *Capacity:* To provide sufficient capacity to accommodate the demand in typical busy hour periods without imposing significant operational, economic, or environmental penalties under normal circumstances. To enable airports to make the best use of possible capacity, as determined by infrastructure in place (both landside and airside), political/environmental restrictions, and the economic handling of the traffic demand.

- *Safety:* To improve safety levels by ensuring that the number of Air Traffic Management (ATM)-induced fatal accidents and serious or risk bearing incidents do not increase, and where possible, decrease.

Further major objectives of the ATM 2000+ Strategy are Economics, Environment, National Security and Defence Requirements, Uniformity, Quality, and Human Involvement and Commitment.

Slovenia and Sweden) is available for 1997 only at present, and both Euro 88 and Euro 97 projected traffic growth figures are shown in the diagram.

28.2   Validation

The European ATM Program (EATMP) is aimed at implementing the ATM 2000+ Strategy measures. The following levels may be identified (Fig. 28.3 — the transitions will be continuous):

Level	Timeframe	Capacity-Gain	Measure
1	Until 2005	+ 60 % from the year 1995	Optimization, Adaptation
2	2005 – 2010	+ 20 – 40 % from Step 1	Integration of systems
3	2010 – 2015	+ 20 – 40 % from Step 2	Redistribution of tasks

FIGURE 28.3
Implementation of the ATM 2000+ strategy.

The optimization of flight trajectories (more direct routes,[2] optimal flight profiles, reduction of holdings) is also expected to a reduce the fuel consumption per flight.

The change associated to most of the measures of level 1 is not radical, is more evolutionary, and is managed on a year to year basis in a trouble shooting approach. The enhancements can mostly be implemented by a limited number of EATMP organizational units and states. By the year 2005 the capacity gain potential of those measures will have been exhausted and more substantial changes compared to today's systems will become necessary. This has been referred to as the *"capacity wall."* However, these changes involve risk and more research and development will require lead times of several years. Many EATMP organizational units, programs, and states will need to be involved. Timely and stable decisions and proper planning are important.

Validation is the process through which a desired level of confidence in the ability of a proposed system enhancement to operate in a real-life environment may be demonstrated against a pre-defined level of functionality, operability and performance. The role of validation is to provide the relevant decision-making body in the EUROCONTROL Organization with appropriate information on which development and implementation decisions can be made. Accordingly the flavor of validation is different for the three levels. There is a rolling transition between them.

---

[2]Direct routes follow the great circle between two points. The current flight routes tend to be longer, due to approach procedures around the airports and non-direct air-routes.

28.2.1 Validation in ATM 2000+ Strategy Level 1

In this level the system enhancements/optimizations are aimed at the short-term. That is, problems experienced in one summer season should be fixed by the next one. It should also be possible to react to short-term demand evolutions. The process has some similarity to day to day management as indicated in the management cycle in Fig. 28.4.

FIGURE 28.4

Management cycle. The phase *"Measure effective?"* corresponds to validation.

This cycle crucially depends on the timely availability of detailed and accurate data. To collect and analyze detailed flight data at the overall European level or even the state or ATM unit level and to make those data available is obviously a non-trivial problem. Some infrastructure would be required which is not yet everywhere available. On the European level the EUROCONTROL *Central Flow Management Unit (CFMU)* is a proper data source. Some states have developed systems to provide them with near real-time situation awareness and statistical evaluations as shown in Fig. 28.5. These systems are designed as management information systems to drill down to detailed information — even down to specific flights [1]. Based on those near real-time management information systems at least the capacity impacts of system enhancements can be validated immediately.

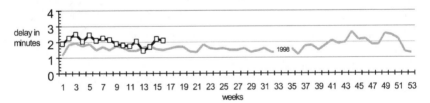

FIGURE 28.5

Delay of controlled flights in the airspace of the Federal Republic of Germany.

28.2.2 Validation in ATM 2000+ Strategy Level 2

This validation aims toward the period of time 5 to 10 years ahead. This corresponds roughly to the development and deployment time of new systems or components. A mandatory change for aircraft, for example the mandatory carriage of upgraded or new radio or navigation equipment, needs a time of 7 years from the official publication. Every concerned aircraft has to be given the opportunity to upgrade, which is usually done during a planned major maintenance.

The focus of validation is to build up the necessary confidence of the decision-makers in the effectiveness of the envisaged measure, and to get their approval and support. Normally major decisions are taken by agreement after an intensive preparation and consultation process that involves representatives of all stakeholders. The costs for Europe-wide system upgrades tend to be high. Under the existing rules, these costs will be recovered from the airspace users through route charges. But the airspace users also have to carry the additional cost for the complementary aircraft equipment. As frequently different classes of users (airlines, charter, general aviation, military) are differently affected by the costs and the benefits, the decision making is difficult. Validation can facilitate this process by neutrally providing the relevant data.

With regard to the medium term implications, the decisions also have to provide a significant level of detail and need to be stable (e.g., correct and complete specifications on the appropriate level).

The implementation decisions in this level 2 originate typically from level 3.

28.2.3   Validation in ATM 2000+ Strategy Level 3

Validation with regard to level 3 is concerned with the options for the decisions to be taken for level 2. Those options may involve a redistribution of responsibilities in ATM. It might be better to leave the decision as to which flights have to be delayed to the concerned airlines. Also the work-sharing of tasks between controllers and pilots has to be investigated. The exchange of data will change from analog voice to digital data ("Data Link"). Data Link is the prerequisite to integrate air, namely the *Flight Management System (FMS)* and ground ATM systems. This air-ground integration is itself a prerequisite of many options for the future operation of ATM. Obviously it is necessary to investigate the necessary equipment, procedures, and acceptable traffic densities.

Another example is the change to satellite navigation as the sole means of navigation or to use augmented satellite navigation as precision landing systems under all weather conditions, also for taxiing at the airport. A further issue is the *Automatic Dependent Surveillance (ADS)*. With ADS the aircraft reports its own position to the controller, providing high accuracy and making the radar obsolete.

Safety is a critical issue; long term quality and overall availability of satellite signals is not yet fully proven. ADS would add a common point of error to navigation and surveillance systems. The need to build redundant and safety critical systems with substantially increased complexity may be beyond the industry's capabilities, at least at high risk or prohibitive cost.

Transition from a baseline system to the envisaged system is also a very important issue.

Obviously there is a rolling transition between the levels. Validation has to be seen as a continuous process with varying objectives, methods, and techniques.

The rest of this paper focuses on capacity and touches upon safety validation at the levels 2 and 3.

28.3 Capacity Target Setting

The traffic demand for the ECAC areas is depicted in Fig. 28.1 as one total figure per year. However, this traffic is not homogeneously distributed, neither geographically (as shown in Fig. 28.6 [5]), nor in time.

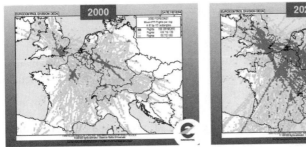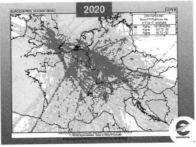

FIGURE 28.6
Expected traffic distribution in Europe in the years 2000 and 2020.

Therefore, the actual capacity needed varies from location to location. Also the locally available capacity varies due to differences of traffic complexity and infrastructure. This results in a delay situation as depicted in Fig. 28.7 [3].

The units here are *Area Control Centers (ACCs),* operational centers housing the controller working positions. They are equipped with ATM systems with a different level of sophistication across Europe. It is highly remarkable that only 15 % of the ACCs produced 90% of the delay! It appears to be attractive to focus just on those. Unfortunately those ACCs tend to be the most complex and already fully optimized ones. The removal of a bottleneck might also simply open up other bottlenecks which until then have been "protected." Other very important bottlenecks are airports (not depicted in Fig. 28.7).

The dependence of the overall capacity on local effects and traffic flows is illustrated by the simplistic model in Fig. 28.8 [8].

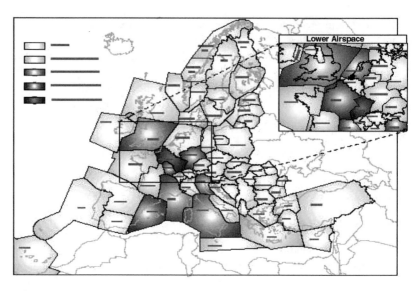

FIGURE 28.7
ACC ATFM delay in 1996 (21/06/99).[3]

Therefore, the capacity planning is based on a modeling/simulation method-ology. Three simulation levels are identified (see Fig. 28.9, for a more detailed explanation please refer to [10]):

- Macroscopic analysis of the overall ECAC area based on the operational flow management algorithms.

- Airspace classification based on complexity and equipment.

- Microscopic analysis of representative airspace types with respect to workload and capacity by evaluating ATM actions and their impact on workload and capacity.

This is a relative straightforward approach for short-term planning as the modeling can be based on existing airspace structure and procedures. For the medium and long-term it is much more difficult as many assumptions for the future airspace structures and working procedures are necessary. The capacity target values are determined in an iterative process based on the simulations as described above.

---

[3]We apologize that the texts in the figure is not readable due to problems during the production of the paper. The message, however, should be clear.

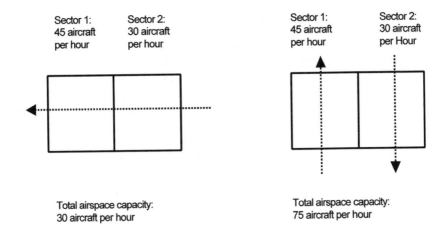

FIGURE 28.8
Simplistic capacity model.

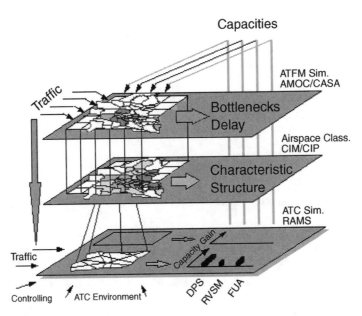

FIGURE 28.9
Capacity planning simulation methodology.

28.4   Capacity Increase

It is generally accepted that the main constraints for the increase of capacity are air traffic controller workload/productivity and safety. Of course controller workload and safety are also closely related. For smaller evolutionary changes, the acceptance of the workability by the controllers is a good indication for safety. However, for more substantial changes different approaches to safety are necessary, as discussed at the end of this paper. First the need and an approach to increase the controller productivity will be described.

A straightforward approach to reduce the workload per controller is simply to subdivide control sectors. One would expect an increase of capacity proportional to the number of sectors in one region or ACC. To an extent this is true, as depicted in Fig. 28.10.

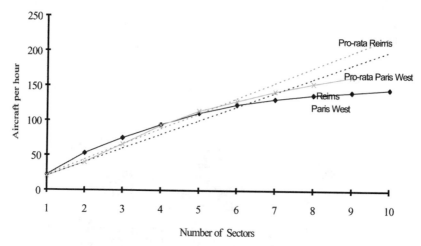

FIGURE 28.10

Examples for capacity increases with the number sectors in one ACC [7].

It can also be seen that from a certain number of sectors in the evaluated ACC the increase of capacity flattens and finally nearly levels off. The *rule of diminishing results* is due to the fact that there is a standard amount of work, e.g., associated with sector-to-sector co-ordination, that is not reduced but increases with the number of sectors.

The increase of the number of sectors reduces their extension and consequently the *Sector Transition Time (STT)*. (It would be possible to reduce the vertical range of a sector and therefore keep the STT, but this is another issue.) Under the assumption that the needed capacity would be only generated by increasing the number of sectors and not increasing the productivity, the number of sectors in Europe with unreasonably short STT would increase to an unacceptable level. Another negative side-effect of the short STTs is that a controller has only a very short time to take corrective action, and hence that action would become more and more abrupt and invasive.

As depicted in Fig. 28.11, from a certain point in time it is necessary to increase the controller productivity. This requires new ATM approaches and working procedures based on more comfortable or automated tools. The objective of the *Program for Harmonized ATM Research in EUROCONTROL (PHARE)* is to organize, co-ordinate, and conduct studies and experiments aimed at proving and demonstrating the feasibility and merits of future air-ground integrated air traffic management system in all phases of flight. The results of the program should help to refine the description of the future air traffic systems concepts needed to satisfy demand, and provide information on the transition from current to the new system.

PHARE started in 1989 and was completed in 1999. Since 1994 PHARE was managed by one of the authors. Ten European ATM R&D organizations participated in PHARE with close liaison to the U.S. Federal Aviation Administration (FAA).

Tools like an Experimental Flight Management System that supports 4D[4] flight management, air and ground human interfaces, machine, advanced controller tools, and validation tools have been developed and integrated into a Common Modular Simulation Environment. They are now available to the European R&D community and are incorporated in several other experimental set-ups.

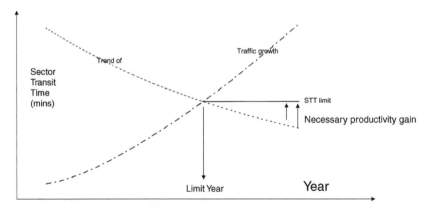

FIGURE 28.11
Determination of productivity requirements [8].

---

[4]The flight management system navigates the aircraft the according to a predefined trajectory in the 4 dimensions.

PHARE [9] carried out three *PHARE Demonstrations (PD/1, PD/2, and PD/3)* with different experimental set-ups. PD/1 aimed at the en-route, PD/2 at the approach phase of flights. PD/3 combined these phases into one set-up. Some of these set ups were iterated to test some modifications (indicated by an appended "+:" PD/1+, PD/1++). Experimental aircraft took part in the demonstration in a simulated air traffic scenario. So not only the procedural part was covered but also its technical feasibility.

In the PHARE Demonstration PD/1++ [9] direct routes and larger sectors were simulated. Computer assistance tools and Reduced Vertical Separation Minima (RVSM) were included and it was assumed that 70% (parameter in the experimental set-up) of aircraft had a 4D FMS and datalink capability. Direct routes and larger sectors were simulated:

- In the direct route organizations only aircraft with a 4D FMS and datalink flew above Flight Level FL300, where they followed direct routes. 4D FMS equipped aircraft departing from airports within the UK FIR flew along the structured routes system until they reached FL300, when they then flew a direct route towards their destination. The converse was true for 4D FMS equipped aircraft landing in the UK FIR. Aircraft which were not equipped with 4D FMS were restricted to flying the current structured route system below FL300;

- A larger sector was created by removing the boundary between sectors S10 and S11.

Four airspace organizations (ORG0 – ORG3, see Fig. 28.12) were set up and the corresponding controller workloads measured and compared.

Figure 28.13 depicts the resulting number of aircraft in the corresponding sector that were perceived by the radar controller as the highest amount of traffic. A self-assessment method was used.

In the context of this paper, the principal conclusions are as follows:

- Within the scenarios investigated, the PD/1++ operational concept enabled the controllers to handle the increased traffic that resulted from the introduction of larger sectors and direct routes;

- The increase in traffic from the introduction of larger sectors and direct routes resulted in an increase in workload that was acceptable to the controllers.

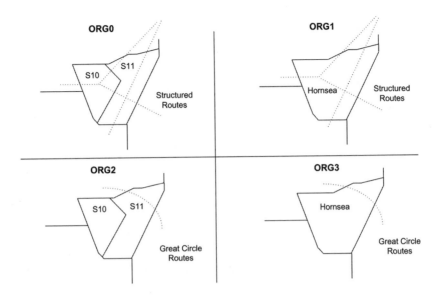

FIGURE 28.12
The PD/1++ organizations.

28.5 Safety

ATM embraces a complex interaction between distributed technical systems, procedures, and human operators. It is the complex interaction between the various elements which determines safety. Hence, it is not sufficient to make sure that each of the individual elements works properly. The corresponding interactions and also the non-nominal situations have to be considered. A common approach to study safety issues is to carry out real-time simulations. The results are then based on the assessments of the participating air traffic controllers. However safety assessment should also be incorporated into early analytical studies. Analytical studies appear also to be the only appropriate approach to assess the probability of very rare events, as sketched in Fig. 28.14 [6].

The right-hand side denotes frequency of occurrence of events per flight hour; frequent events are at the foot of the berg, rare events are at the top. The left-hand side denotes different assessment approaches. It appears that real-time human-in-the-loop based evaluations can be used to assess frequent events only. A catastrophic event in air traffic however is typically a tragic combination of very rare and non-nominal events. A modeling approach [6] is based on hazard analysis. Those hazards and their dependencies are modeled in a colored Petri Net, taking into account the associated transition probability

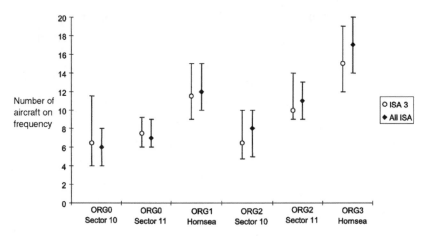

FIGURE 28.13
Number of aircraft instantaneously in sector for each sector in each ORG, radar controller.

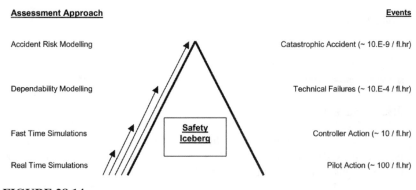

FIGURE 28.14
ATM safety iceberg.

distributions. Procedures and human behavior can also be incorporated into the model.

It would be straightforward to evaluate the model in a Monte Carlo simulation. Due to the very low probabilities the necessary simulation time would be prohibitive. Hence, the colored Petri Net has to be evaluated in a more analytical approach.

In the study, the accident risk of opposite traffic along parallel one-way airroutes as a function of the route separation was studied for a given Required Navigation Performance (RNP).

Stochastic models like this can certainly provide useful insights into the safety mechanics of highly complex distributed systems and procedures. It is particularly important that different procedures and human behavior can also be modeled. In how far those methods can provide substantial data with sufficient accuracy remains to be validated.

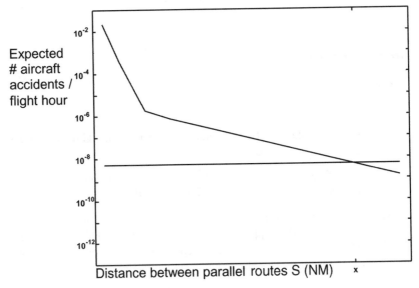

FIGURE 28.15

Expected number of aircraft accidents per flight hour, as function of spacing between parallel routes. Horizontal line is maximally allowed level of risk.

28.6 Concluding Remark

In the past, ATM validation has frequently been performed in an ad hoc manner. A lot can be gained by a performance-driven management of the development process. Validation is an ongoing and integrated part of the development process from long-term oriented R&D to short-term system optimizations. This is now well recognized and improvements of the validation management are under way.

A specific challenge is the management of European ATM because it consists of a big variety of systems and co-operating organizations. It is crucial to find the relevant macroscopic performance criteria which can be understood by the user community, can be quantified, and be suitable to further manage the development process at the more detailed levels. The most critical issues are controller workload and overall safety issues. The traditional way to cope with those issues is by real-time simulations and demonstrations. But there is now progress in the introduction of analytic models before directly going to the much more expensive simulations and demonstrations.

References

[1] Air Traffic Statistic from Deutsche Flugsicherung GmbH, see also www.dfs.de/lize/index.htm.

[2] ATM 2000+ Strategy, Volume 1 and 2, currently available at www.eurocontrol.be/projects/eatchip/atmstrat/.

[3] M. Dalichampt, G. Flynn, R. Hickling, S. Mahlich, A. Tibichte, Future ATM Profile Capacity Shortfalls in Europe (1996-2006), *EURO-CONTROL Experimental Center Report,* 324, Brétigny, 1998, see also www.eurocontrol.fr/public/reports/eecreports/1998/324.htm.

[4] ECAC Strategy for the 1990s, Paris 1990, published by *European Civil Aviation Conference (ECAC),* 3 bis Villa Emile Bergerat, 92522 Neuilly-sur-Seine, France.

[5] EUROCONTROL Agency, Brussels, Airspace Management and Navigation Unit.

[6] M.H.C. Everdij, H.A.P. Blom, Testing Operational Scenarios for Concepts in ATM, TOSCA-II, Work Package 4, Nationaal Lucht- en Ruimtevaartlaboratoriom (NLR), Amsterdam, in preparation.

[7] Dr. S. Mandal, V. Overend, National Air Traffic Services LTD (NATS), London, May 1996, R&D Report 9614, Assessment of Capacity Shortfall in the ECAC Airspace through 2000–1015.

[8] S. Mandal, D. Timlin, P. Donovan, C. Bushell, National Air Traffic Services LTD (NATS), London, May 1998, R&D Report 9832, Capacity Shortfall in the ECAC Airspace, Phase 2 Assessment.

[9] NATS Trial Team, PD/1++ Trial Report, PHARE/NATS/PD1++–2.10, EUROCONTROL, in preparation. See also www.eurocontrol.fr/public/partners/phare/public/qds.cgi.

[10] J.M. Pomeret, S. Mahlich, Piloting ATM through Performance, *Proc. of the 1st USA Europe Air Traffic Management R&D Semi-*

nar, Saclay France, June 17–20, 1997, see also http://atm-seminar-97.eurocontrol.fr/pomeret.htm.

Vitae

Dr. Helmut Schröter is Head of the Strategy, Concept, and System (SCS) Unit of EUROCONTROL Agency. Since 1994 he has also been the PHARE program manager.

Dr. Ulrich Borkenhagen and Hans Wagemans are experts for Validation Management in the SCS Unit.

Index